Leadership Theory and Research

Leadership Theory and Research

Perspectives and Directions

Edited by

Martin M. Chemers
Department of Psychology
Claremont McKenna College

Roya Ayman
Department of Psychology
Illinois Institute of Technology

Academic Press
San Diego New York Boston
London Sydney Tokyo Toronto

This book is printed on acid-free paper. ♾

Academic Press, Inc.
A Division of Harcourt Brace & Company
525 B Street, Suite 1900, San Diego, California 92101-4495

United Kingdom Edition published by
Academic Press Limited
24–28 Oval Road, London NW1 7DX

Library of Congress Cataloging-in-Publication Data

Leadership theory and research : perspectives and directions / edited by Martin M. Chemers, Roya Ayman.
p. cm.
Includes index.
ISBN 0-12-170609-5
1. Leadership–Research. I. Chemers, Martin M. II. Ayman, Roya.
HD57.7.F88 1992
303.3'4–dc20 92-11014
CIP

PRINTED IN THE UNITED STATES OF AMERICA
96 97 BC 9 8 7 6 5 4 3 2

Dedicated to Fred Fiedler for 40 years of distinguished scholarship in the field of leadership

Contents

5 *Leadership, Values, and Accountability*

Terence R. Mitchell

6 *Leadership Perception: The Role of Gender and Culture*

Roya Ayman

7 *The Contingency Model in Cross-Cultural Perspective*

Harry C. Triandis

Contributors

Numbers in parentheses indicate the pages on which the authors' contributions begin.

Bruce J. Avolio (49), Center for Leadership Studies, State University of New York at Binghamton, Binghamton, New York 13902.

Roya Ayman (137, 321), Department of Psychology, Illinois Institute of Technology, Chicago, Illinois 60616.

Bernard M. Bass (49), Center for Leadership Studies, State University of New York at Binghamton, Binghamton, New York 13902.

Lee Roy Beach (271), Department of Management and Policy, University of Arizona, Tucson, Arizona 85721.

Martin M. Chemers (293, 321), Department of Psychology, Claremont McKenna College, Claremont, California 91711.

Fred E. Fiedler (1), Department of Psychology, University of Washington, Seattle, Washington 98195.

Deborah H Gruenfeld (217), Department of Psychology, University of Illinois at Urbana-Champaign, Champaign, Illinois 61820.

Edwin P. Hollander (29), City University of New York Doctoral Subprogram in Industrial/Organizational Psychology, Baruch College and University Graduate Center, New York, New York 10010.

John R. Hollenbeck (245), Department of Management, Michigan State University, East Lansing, Michigan 48824-1117.

Robert J. House (81), Department of Management, The Wharton School of the University of Pennsylvania, Philadelphia, Pennsylvania 19104.

Daniel R. Ilgen (245), Departments of Psychology and Management, Michigan State University, East Lansing, Michigan 48824-1117.

Renate R. Mai-Dalton (189), School of Business, University of Kansas, Lawrence, Kansas 66049.

Debra A. Major (245), Department of Psychology, Michigan State University, East Lansing, Michigan 48824-1117.

Joseph E. McGrath (217), Department of Psychology, University of Illinois at Urbana-Champaign, Champaign, Illinois 61820.

Terence R. Mitchell (109), Department of Management and Organization, University of Washington, Seattle, Washington 98195.

Douglas J. Sego (245), Department of Management, Michigan State University, East Lansing, Michigan 48824-1117.

Boas Shamir (81), Department of Sociology and Anthropology, The Hebrew University of Jerusalem, Jerusalem 91905, Israel.

Harry C. Triandis (167), Department of Psychology, University of Illinois at Urbana-Champaign, Champaign, Illinois 61820.

Preface

This volume was conceived as a tribute to Fred Fiedler in honor of his fortieth year of research and scholarship in the study of leadership and organizational effectiveness. Fiedler's contributions to this field have been of such magnitude that the term *paradigm shift* does not seem out of place in describing them. As Harry Triandis points out in his chapter in this book, the study of leadership can be fairly divided into before and after Fiedler's introduction of contingency theories. The realization that leadership effectiveness depends on the interaction of qualities of the leader with demands of the situation in which the leader functions made the simplistic "one best way" approaches of earlier eras obsolete. The implications of contingency notions spread like sonic waves throughout the field of organizational studies.

A second inspirational facet of Fiedler's career has been his consistent orientation toward the future, a dedication to bring new perspectives and fresh ideas to his work. An emphasis on the future need not mean an abandonment of the past; in order to push further into the scientific unknown, Fiedler has always tried to build on the foundation of what is known.

Time and again, Fiedler has introduced novel ideas or approaches in an attempt to extend our understanding of complex leadership processes. Whether the focus was on integrating leadership training and experience effects into the contingency model or on his more recent work with Garcia creating a new model to explain the effects of leader intelligence, Fiedler was drawn to extending his work in new directions. Fittingly, Fiedler's contribution to the current volume breaks new ground with a novel approach to explaining dramatic shifts in leader behavior.

It was this sense of the researcher moving forward, leaning into the wind, that we wanted to be a major aspect of this book. The contributors were asked to direct the thrust of their analyses toward the future, to define what they saw as the important and productive areas of future research in leadership and related topics. Poised on the advent of a new century, the authors have tried to show where their work is and where it is going.

A final characteristic of Fiedler's work that informs this research collection is the emphasis on theory-driven empiricism. To Fiedler, as many of his students have discovered to our embarrassment, theory without data was conjecture, and data without theory were meaningless. The authors included in this book share that dedication.

The contributors were chosen from scholars in leadership, group, and organizational research who have had a close association with Fred Fiedler over the course of his career. Represented in that group are former students, colleagues, collaborators, and long-time associates. Some of the contributors fit into several of those categories. More important, they were chosen because they have valuable things to say, rooted in empirical research and illuminated by carefully conceived theory, about the future of our field. We have brought together an eminent group of scholars and asked them to tell us about their current research and the directions they see their own work and the field of leadership taking.

While we are dependent for specific points on the insights of the individual contributors, as editors we came to this endeavor with some broad ideas about the contemporary problems and theoretical issues that might frame the discussions. We saw a few themes, current both within academic circles and the larger community, that seemed ripe for discussion. We encouraged the inclusion of those topics in this book.

In society at large, there appears to be a growing recognition of the importance of teamwork for productive and satisfying relations in groups and organizations. The harnessing of collective energies in groups and teams is a challenge and an opportunity. Comparisons of American companies with foreign organizations (especially, but not only, the Japanese) have revealed that there is much we can learn about teamwork. We feel that the study of teamwork will be a major aspect of organizational research in this decade and beyond, and we have included several chapters that focus on group and interpersonal processes.

Another issue that has been growing in prominence recently and looms large on the horizon is the role of cultural and subcultural diversity in organizational dynamics. The globalization of the world economy has sent modern organizations scrambling to learn more about cultural differences and how those differences affect the way their organizations must operate. That trend will continue, and the need for sound empirical research on the role of culture in leadership and organizational processes will be even more manifest.

Closer to home, diversity is a compelling aspect of the workforce of the future. Nontraditional employees, including women, ethnic minorities, and immigrants, will be filling positions at all levels. The successful integration of these people and the effective utilization of their talents and energies demand greater understanding of the processes affected by diversity.

Finally, one would have to be the proverbial Martian visitor to be unaware of the public call for an examination of ethical considerations in leadership. One residue of the eighties that will affect the discussions of the nineties concerns the appropriate functions of leadership. Organizational theorists have tended to ignore the value-laden issues embedded in ethical questions. That is beginning to change, and the future will bring greater change in this area. We have sought to bring questions of teamwork, culture and diversity, and ethics to the fore in this book.

Theoretical issues also influenced our choice of topics. One of these issues is the need to address the role of subjective versus objective aspects of leadership. Positivist views of leadership that regard the descriptions of leader behavior and the effects of group effort as real and tangible have been challenged recently. Many theorists argue that leadership, like other social phenomena, is more constructed perception than reality. While it is not our goal to resolve this controversy, it is our intention to reflect the importance of the question.

In another domain, the hegemony of particularistic conceptions of leadership, such as contingency theories stressing the unique effects of situation or culture, have been challenged by the revival of universalistic theories that reassert the existence of an overriding "best" leadership style. Many of the chapters in this book concern themselves with this question.

Theorists are beginning to recognize that the role of time in interpersonal and organizational dynamics cannot be ignored. While leadership researchers have not been totally blind to temporal issues, we have seen them as a research agenda that we can deal with later, partly because our data gathering, analytic tools, and paradigms have not been well suited to the study of longitudinal effects. It appears that currently developing theories will no longer tolerate that oversight.

Finally, now as in the past, our research must place greater emphasis on elucidating the cognitive, affective, and interpersonal *processes* in leadership. It is not so much that we have ignored process. We have made gains in this area; but our theories will be more satisfying to us, as scientists, and to our practitioner clients, to the extent that the processes of leadership are better explained. The chapters in this book, more than most recent collections on leadership research, address these issues of subjectivism, universality, temporality, and process. Chapters have been solicited to reflect the latest work of a group of outstanding scholars in the areas of leadership, group, and organizational effectiveness. The chapters point toward the topics that may represent the dominant research questions in the next period of inquiry and reflect the important issues facing our national and global society.

Fiedler's opening chapter addresses the effect of stressful situations on the behavioral repertoire of leaders. Drawing on his own research, as well as on studies in social, clinical, and learning psychology, he offers the premise that under trying circumstances, people revert to earlier, more primitive or more ingrained patterns of behavior for coping with situational demands. The effects of situational variables in many contingency-oriented theories, including the contingency model and cognitive resource theory, may be explained by this behavioral regression. Fiedler's theorizing may open the door to the integration of contingency or interactive theories of leadership with similar theories in other areas of study.

Chapter 2, by Edwin P. Hollander, draws its breadth and depth from its roots in a long and voluminous research program. Hollander explores the critical importance of the role that followers play in the legitimation of a leader's authority and prerogatives. He relates the legitimation process to current and promising trends in the leadership literature, including leader–follower exchanges, perceptions of charismatic influence, and aspects of group decisionmaking.

The next two chapters turn our attention to leadership processes that underlie the intense follower reactions observed in so-called charismatic or visionary leadership. Chapter 3, by Bernard M. Bass and Bruce J. Avolio, offers a comprehensive description of the development and validation of transformational leadership theory. In response to criticisms of the conceptualization, measurement, and evidential bases of the theory, the authors bring together the results of an impressively extensive program of research. They identify what they consider to be both the strengths of their approach as well as the areas needing further development. Finally, they offer a future agenda for research and training.

In Chapter 4, Robert J. House and Boas Shamir present an integration of a number of contemporary leadership theories labeled charismatic, transformational, or visionary. They argue that it is the leader's ability to tie a follower's self-concept, and ultimately self-esteem, to the actualization of the leader's goals that comprises the essence of charismatic leadership effects. House and Shamir show how integrating aspects of self-theory with traditional models of motivation provides a basis for understanding the powerful effects that some leaders have on followers.

Taking a somewhat different tack from most of the literature on powerful leadership, Terence R. Mitchell in Chapter 5 focuses on the potential dangers posed by strong leaders. Mitchell argues that trustworthy leadership involves reliable stewardship and social responsibility. Many of the failures of contemporary organizations, from insider trading to destruction of the environment, may be rooted in the capability of leaders to avoid scrutiny of their actions. Mitchell reports on recent research that investigates the processes and effects of administrative accountability.

Chapters 6, 7, and 8 are heavily influenced by considerations of culture and diversity. In Chapter 6, Roya Ayman focuses on the central role of perception in the leadership process and on the complexities that arise when key players (e.g., leaders, followers, and superiors) hold divergent templates for appropriate leadership traits and behaviors. Drawing on the literature in social cognition, gender studies, and cross-cultural psychology, Ayman directs our attention to the theoretical and practical significance of leadership prototypes and their relation to cultural and subcultural stereotypes.

In Chapter 7, Harry C. Triandis presents a case for viewing cultural differences in values as the ultimate moderator variable in leadership theory. Using Fiedler's contingency model as a starting point, Triandis shows how a society's expectations about the appropriate roles of power and authority, individual versus collective responsibility, and the predictability and control of the environment determine the interpretation of situational parameters and the leader's behavior. Triandis offers suggestions for a research agenda that might spawn a new generation of culturally integrative contingency theories.

Addressing the pragmatic importance of diversity, Renate R. Mai-Dalton devotes Chapter 8 to a call for organizations to pay attention to the implications of a vastly changing American working population. Mai-Dalton alerts us to the fact that the workforce in the year 2000 will be compositionally quite different from that of earlier generations. The successful integration of women, minorities, and immigrants as psychologically healthy and productive members of our organizations will require new ways of managing. She addresses issues at the individual, group, and organizational levels of analysis that must be considered and offers a theoretical model and some empirical examples to guide corporate strategies.

Chapters 9, 10, and 11 examine phenomena of group dynamics relevant to effective organizational functioning. Joseph E. McGrath and Deborah H Gruenfeld, in Chapter 9, show us the potential richness in the study of group processes when research strategy is broadened to include the true complexity of group activity. The study of multiple and simultaneous group processes must be examined. The relationship of those activities to temporal factors of flow, rhythm, and continuity requires research designs that go beyond static, slice-in-time experiments. McGrath and Gruenfeld describe and integrate six research programs that consider temporal variables from a variety of theoretical and methodological orientations.

Starting from a theoretical approach that is compatible with McGrath's and Gruenfeld's, but with a more pragmatic agenda, Daniel R. Ilgen,

Debra A. Major, John R. Hollenbeck, and Douglas J. Sego discuss team research in Chapter 10. Reviewing the literature on groups and teams over the last 40 to 50 years, they argue that we must change our approach to team research if we want to reap the potential benefits of teamwork. Showing how and why research has been concentrated in areas that have not yielded the information needed by "real world" organizations, they direct our attention to more productive possibilities.

In Chapter 11, Lee Roy Beach offers a very future-oriented view of research on managerial decisionmaking. He describes the revolutionary changes taking place in the study of decisionmaking and examines the assumptions that underlie recent research. He directs our attention to the next major shift in approach that is on the horizon. Beach argues that, after moving away from economic models that assume highly rational processes of human information processing, the field of decision sciences is moving toward a more psychologically oriented view that stresses the kinds of cognitive processes that are involved in actual decisionmaking.

In Chapter 12, Martin M. Chemers attempts to integrate the dominant themes in contemporary leadership theory to suggest where we have been and where we might be going. He argues that we must adopt a functional approach to leadership, in which we analyze leader and follower actions and interactions in terms of their functional significance for the individuals and groups involved. His integrative model addresses theoretical and empirical commonalities that unite seemingly divergent approaches. Like the analyses in earlier chapters, Chemers gives prominence to perceptual processes and cultural expectations.

In the final chapter, we offer some conclusions about the nature of future leadership research that we have gleaned from the ideas in this volume. Several areas that seem promising are discussed.

Finally, we would like to express our appreciation to individuals and institutions that made this volume possible. Financial support was provided by Claremont McKenna College (CMC), The Claremont Graduate School, generous individual donations to the CMC Leadership Program by Henry Kravis and Lorinda DeRoulet, and by special funds from President Jack Stark of CMC. Life-saving logistical support was provided by Pamela Hawkes, Jane Grey, Kenneth Perlman, and all the students in the Leadership Seminar at CMC; by the Marian Miner Cook Athenaeum and its staff, including director Jill Stark, manager David Edwards, and Bonnie Snortum; and by the CMC psychology department, including Marjorie Charlop, Mark Costanzo, Bill Hunt, and Harvey Wichman. Lastly, the editors would like to extend a special thanks to Stuart Oskamp for his participation in bringing the contributors together.

For comments on earlier drafts of various parts of this book, we thank Mark Costanzo, Barbara Goza, and Harvey Wichman.

1

The Leadership Situation and the Black Box in Contingency Theories

Fred E. Fiedler
Department of Psychology
University of Washington

Leadership Theory and Research: Perspectives and Directions

INTRODUCTION

Contingency theories are based on the premise that the performance of a group or organization depends not only on the leader but also on the situation. While there is very little question today that the leadership situation plays an important part in affecting the group process, its underlying meaning and function is unclear. Precisely what do we mean by "leadership situation," and why and how does it affect the behavior and performance of the leader and the group?

In an attempt to address these questions, I want to make two prefatory points. First, it is meaningless to talk about leadership outside the situational context. Without a group task or a shared objective there can be no group, and without a group there can be no leader. Second, while there are many operational definitions of the leadership situation and its components, I shall argue that the "active ingredient" in the situation is the degree to which the situation causes uncertainty and stress, and therefore anxiety. When a certain threshold level of anxiety is reached the leader falls back on previously overlearned behavior, or on simpler or perhaps less mature ways of coping with the problems that the task presents.

PSYCHOLOGICAL MEANING OF THE LEADERSHIP SITUATION

The term *leadership situation* has been applied to a wide variety of conditions: physical locale (Sells, 1976), group member motivation (House, 1971), organizational structure (Burns and Stalker, 1961), task difficulty and complexity (Vroom and Yetton, 1973), interpersonal relations, or the stressfulness of the task (Fiedler and Garcia, 1987).

The main question here is how the leadership situation affects the leader and the group. I suggest that it is the degree to which the environment is structured and predictable and therefore gives the leader a feeling of control over the outcome of the task and over the group process. A lack of structure and predictability causes stress, uncertainty, and a feeling of being powerless.

People differ in how they cope with uncertainty and stress (Appley and Trumbull, 1967, p. 10). Many try to avoid stress altogether and find even a moderate risk highly aversive and anxiety arousing. Others crave stress and the concomitant risk and excitement. They work best with tight deadlines; like difficult jobs, games of chance, physically dangerous sports, and intellectual challenges; and they tend to become uneasy and anxious when things are going too well. Thus, personality and situational factors interact in generating feelings of uncertainty and anxiety. I propose that this interaction is at the heart of contingency theories. To develop this point, this chapter briefly summarizes the contingency model and cognitive resource theory, and the main interactions between personal attributes and situational factors. The chapter then proposes an interpretation of these interactions and their relevance for understanding contingency theories.

THE CONTINGENCY MODEL OF LEADERSHIP EFFECTIVENESS

This theory has been described extensively elsewhere (e.g., Fiedler, 1964, 1967; Fiedler and Garcia, 1987). For those not familiar with it, the theory postulates that leadership effectiveness depends on two factors. One is the degree to which the leadership situation gives the leader control and influence over the group process and group performance. The second factor reflects an attribute of the person, an aspect of the leader's goal or focus of concern, specifically, whether the leader's primary goal, and the consequent primary concern, is with task performance or with interpersonal relations.

Situational Control

The contingency model defines "situational control" on the basis of three dimensions: (1) the leader's relationship with the group; (2) the degree to which the group task is structured, that is, whether it is clearly described, and there is a proven method for doing the job; and (3) the organization's backing of the leader in the form of rules, and the rewards and sanctions that are at the leader's disposal. The three dimensions are combined by giving leader–member relations a weight of 4, task structure a weight of 2, and position power a weight of 1. An empirical study by Nebeker (1975) supported this procedure of scaling situational control.

Borden (1980) identified uncertainty as being related to situational control, and also showed that we need to take into consideration "boss stress," meaning that the leader sees the relationship with his or her immediate superior or boss as tense, stressful, and threatening (see also Potter and Fiedler, 1981). If there is high boss stress, the leader will experience a high degree of uncertainty about the boss's support and evaluation of the leader's performance. Although situational control and stress tend to have similar effects on leader behavior and performance (e.g., Fiedler et al., 1969), control and stress are not highly correlated. Stressful relations with subordinates by definition imply relatively poor leader–member relations, but boss stress may, of course, exist in groups in which the leader has good relations with subordinates.

The Least Preferred Coworker (LPC) Score

We cannot fully understand the role of situational factors without also understanding the personal attributes with which situational factors interact in determining the leader's behavior and performance. In the contingency model, the personality variable measures the tendency to give priority to task accomplishment or to good interpersonal relations (task-motivated and relationship-motivated) (Fiedler, 1972; Fiedler and Garcia, 1987, pp. 59–79).

LPC is measured by asking leaders first to think of all the people with whom they have ever worked, and then to "describe the one person with whom you have had the most difficulty in getting the job done." The description of this "least preferred coworker," or LPC, is usually made on 18 bipolar scales that list personality attributes, for example,

Friendly ___ : ___ : ___ : ___ : ___ : ___ : ___ : ___ Unfriendly
8 7 6 5 4 3 2 1

Since descriptions of others are notoriously inaccurate (Kelly and Fiske, 1951), the LPC score can be interpreted much like a projective test. The score tells us the degree to which the leader attributes negative personality characteristics to someone merely because that person is a poor coworker—it is a negative halo effect.

Let us assume, for the moment, that you are highly task-motivated (called a low-LPC person), but that Joe, your assistant, is careless, unreliable, and incompetent. Because it is extremely important to you to get the task done, there is a good chance that you will be upset with Joe because he prevents you from accomplishing your goal. You will then tend to see Joe in a very unfavorable light. In other words, you feel so strongly about getting the job done that you reject Joe as a person because he is a poor coworker, because he thwarts your efforts to accomplish the task. For this reason we interpret an unfavorable description of the least preferred coworker (low LPC) as indicative of a "task-motivated" person.

If you are a high-LPC person, you may say in effect that Joe may well be someone with whom you certainly don't want to work, but, after all, "work isn't everything, and Joe may have other redeeming virtues. He may be incompetent but he is pleasant; he may not be very bright but he is honest." This attitude implies that Joe is seen not just as a means for getting a job done but also as a complex individual who, apart from the work situation, might even be likable and worth knowing. Given this concern with others, the high-LPC person also tends to be more tactful and socially adroit, and tries to avoid conflict.

Interaction between LPC and Situational Control

The contingency model tells us that task-motivated (low-LPC) leaders perform best in situations in which they have either very high control, or in situations in which they have relatively low control. Relationship-motivated (high-LPC) leaders perform best in situations in which they have moderate control. A schematic presentation of the model is shown in Figure 1.1, in which situational control is indicated on the horizontal axis (abscissa) and performance on the vertical axis (ordinate).

The solid line shows the performance of high-LPC leaders; the broken line, of low-LPC leaders. The figure shows that a shift in situational control changes performance, and that these changes are in opposite directions for high- and low-LPC leaders. The graph thus indicates that leadership performance will decrease as the task-motivated leader moves from a high- to a moderate-control situation, and improves again as the leader moves from a moderate- to a high-control situation. The performance of relationship-motivated leader improves with a shift from low to moderate control, and decreases from moderate to high control.

Although the contingency model has been subjected to considerable criticism, its validity is now well established. Most studies support its predictions (e.g., Fiedler, 1971), and two separate meta-analyses demonstrate

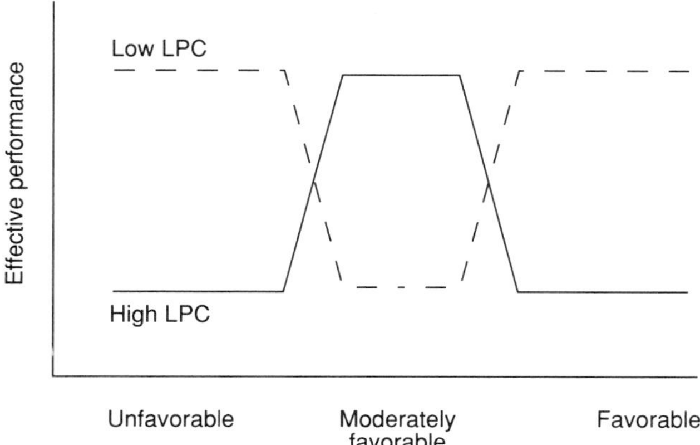

Figure 1.1. Predicted relationship between LPC, situational favorableness, and performance.

that the model's predicted effects are extremely reliable across studies (Strube and Garcia, 1981; Peters et al., 1985).

The contingency model does have its problems. One concerns the LPC score. While we know that LPC is an internally consistent and stable measure (Rice, 1978a,b), we do not know what causes a person to become relationship-motivated or task-motivated. One study by Chemers (1970) shows that low-LPC persons are somewhat more likely to be first-born than are later-born children, and Hardy et al. (1973) obtained significant LPC effects in a study of elementary-school children. Thus, insofar as one can generalize from these data, the focus reflected by LPC is developed early in life.

Another major problem with LPC is that the score does not correlate with the usual psychometric tests or behavior observation scales, and that it is not face-valid. The interpretation of the score has, therefore, been a subject of considerable controversy and premature obituaries (e.g., Rice, 1978a, 1978b; Schriesheim and Kerr, 1977). One problem that has disturbed the critics is the failure of LPC to predict such leader behaviors as, for instance, consideration and structuring. As it turns out, the score does predict these and similar behaviors, but only in conjunction with situational control or stress (Fiedler, 1972; Fiedler and Garcia, 1987). And this, as we shall see shortly, is critical for understanding the contingency model. The interpretation that seems to fit the idea best is that the score measures a motivational hierarchy. The goal of task accomplishment is given priority over good relations by low-LPC persons, and the goal of having good interpersonal relations is given priority over task accomplishment by high-LPC persons (Fiedler, 1972).

THE EFFECT OF SITUATIONAL CONTROL ON BEHAVIOR CHANGES

The most important flaw in the contingency model is that the model has remained a "black box" even after 25 years of intensive research. While the meta-analyses (Strube and Garcia, 1981) indicate that the theory is strongly supported, the link between LPC and situational control to effective performance has remained unclear. We need to understand the interaction between these two variables and to specify how this leads to specific changes in leader behavior. This chapter suggests this linkage.

Studies of LPC show that leaders who report stress, or have moderate or low control, behave just as indicated by the labels: Task-motivated (low-LPC) leaders show concern with getting the job done. They tell people what to do, are punitive, and are not too concerned about others' feelings.

Relationship-motivated (high-LPC) leaders are considerate, provide rewards, are nondirective, and invite subordinate participation (e.g., Bons and Fiedler, 1976).

These behaviors are almost exactly reversed when leaders have a high degree of situational control. Now that the completion of the task is virtually assured, the task-motivated leaders can focus on relationships and become nondirective and considerate; relationship-motivated leaders who have good relations with their subordinates can focus on the task and become more bossy and less considerate (Fiedler, 1967; Fiedler and Garcia, 1987).

The profoundly different effects of increased situational control on the behavior of the two kinds of leaders were dramatically shown in a study by Chemers (1969). Leaders were trained so that they would have better leader–member relations with subordinates who came from a different culture, thus giving the leaders greater situational control. The results showed that relationship-motivated leaders with training were *less considerate* and less esteemed by the group than were relationship-motivated leaders without this training, and who, therefore, had a lower degree of situational control. In contrast, task-motivated leaders with training (high situational control) were more considerate and more highly esteemed by their group members than were untrained (low-situational-control) task-motivated leaders. Similar effects have been found in a number of studies (see, e.g., Bons and Fiedler, 1976; Chemers, 1969; Fiedler, 1967, pp. 181–196; 1972; Fiedler and Garcia, 1987, pp. 175–185; Green et al., 1976). This is critical for understanding the contingency model, and two studies are briefly summarized here to illustrate this point.

Engineering Managers

Larson and Rowland (1973) conducted a workshop for a group of male engineers in managerial positions of a highway department. The training included an experiment in which half the managers were given an "in-basket" exercise under relaxed conditions; the other half worked on the exercise under stressful conditions. The manager was given a stack of 31 letters, memos, directives, and messages to which he had to respond. His replies were categorized into responses showing concern with the task and those concerned with interpersonal relationships.

In the high-stress condition, the task-motivated (low-LPC) managers showed more task concern; that is, they were more directive and less considerate than relationship-motivated managers. In the low-stress condition they were more concerned with interpersonal relations, that is, less directive and more considerate. The relationship-motivated (high-LPC)

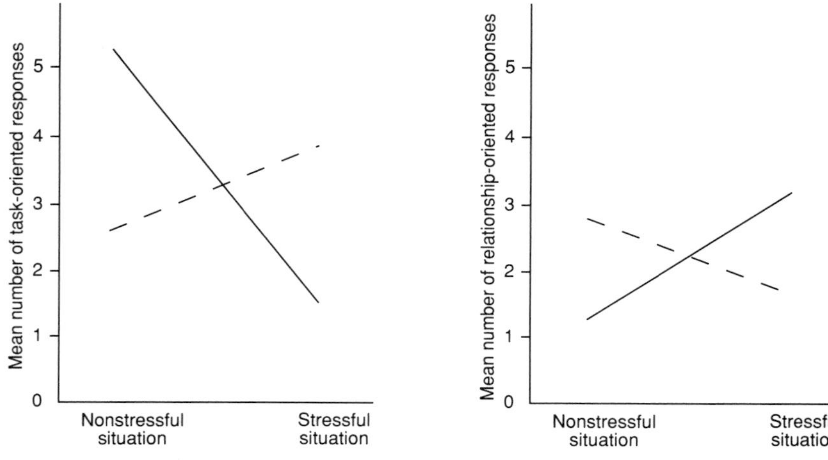

Figure 1.2. Comparison of high-LPC (*solid lines*) and low-LPC (*dashed lines*) engineering managers on task- and relationship-oriented responses to in-basket items in stressful and nonstressful situations (Larson and Rowland, 1973).

leaders acted in exactly the opposite way: in the high-stress condition they were nondirective and considerate; in the low-stress condition they were rated as inconsiderate and directive (Fig. 1.2).

The "Rat Learning" Experiment

Sample and Wilson (1965) also showed that leaders reversed their behavior as the structure of the task changed. They divided a large psychology class into small four-person groups, each with an appointed leader and an observer. Each group was given a white rat and told to perform a learning study.

The task, carried out over the duration of the course, consisted of planning the study, running it, and writing the report. In each of the three task phases, the observer evaluated the leader's comments using Bales's (1950) "interaction process analysis" method, noting the frequency of socioemotional and task-oriented responses.

As Shirakashi (personal communication) has pointed out, planning an experiment is the least structured part of the task, and thus gives relatively low situational control. Running the experiment is highly structured, and thus gives the leader relatively high control. Writing the report falls in between. Figure 1.3 shows the proportion of task-relevant and socioemotional leader comments in each of these three phases. As can be seen, the proportion of task-relevant comments and socioemotional comments are practically mirror images of the high- and low-situational-control conditions.

While running the experiment according to a predetermined protocol, the task-motivated leaders were more considerate and less concerned with the task. In the planning phase, when they had relatively low control, they were concerned with the task and less considerate. The relationship-motivated leaders behaved in exactly the opposite manner. In other words, as the leadership situation gave the leader more control or less control, a radical change occurred not only in leader performance but also

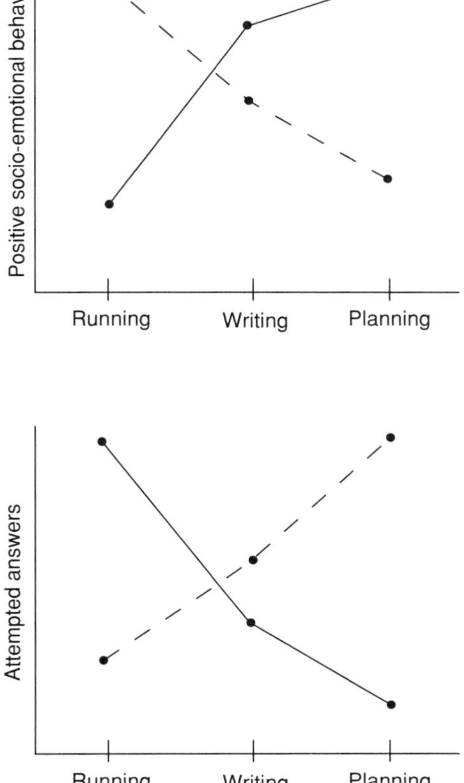

Figure 1.3. Comparison of behaviors by relationship-motivated (high-LPC, *solid lines)* and by task-motivated (low-LPC, *dashed lines)* leaders in three phases of an experimental task involving a class project of running a rat maze study (Sample and Wilson, 1965).

in leader behavior. It is worth noting that our personality theories do not account well for these shifts in behavior.

Interactions of somewhat similar nature are seen in research on cognitive resource theory (CRT), and these studies provide some important clues for interpreting the function of situational factors. We shall, therefore, discuss CRT before suggesting a further interpretation of the interaction between LPC and situational control.

COGNITIVE RESOURCE THEORY

The roles played by intelligence and experience in determining leadership performance have been highly puzzling. Correlations between leader intelligence and leader performance, as well as group and organizational productivity, have been consistently low, as shown by our own research (Fiedler, 1970; Fiedler and Garcia, 1987, p. 34) as well as research by others (e.g., Ghiselli, 1963; Mann, 1959; Stogdill, 1948). These findings are counterintuitive because leadership involves such intellectual functions as recognizing and solving problems, planning, and making decisions. For this reason alone we would expect fairly high correlations between leader intelligence and performance. Likewise, job-related experience and performance do not correlate highly, notwithstanding the fact that practically every employment procedure asks about, and uses, previous work history as a major consideration in hiring and promotion decisions. During the past 20 years the present author and his colleagues have attempted to explain these low correlations, partly in the hope that this line of research would also help to explain the contingency model.

Before going further, it is important to define intelligence and experience as these terms are used in this paper. Sternberg and Detterman (1986) list no fewer than 21 different definitions of intelligence. We shall follow here the definition advanced by Berry (1986) that intelligence is "the end-product of individual development in the cognitive-psychological domain." Berry specifically excludes abilities related to motor, emotional, and social functioning.

We shall use *Webster's Dictionary* (McKechnie, 1966, p. 645) definition of work experience "as time spent in a job or an organization." Experience is thus operationalized as time in the organization or in a leadership job. This is also the definition in common usage in organizations, as indicated by such questions as "How long have you worked for the XYZ Corporation?" or "How long have you managed the Accounting Department?" Neither of these time-based definitions (nor, for that matter, any other definitions) captures all of the important elements of what one might mean by experience. Other aspects might include, for instance, the richness of the experience, its relevance (e.g., Bettin and Kennedy, 1990), diversity, or what actually has been learned. We have used time-based measures in our research because they are easily obtained and highly reliable, and especially suited for exploratory research on leaders whose careers follow similar patterns.

Despite the fact that the correlations between performance and leader intelligence and experience are generally low and insignificant, our research shows that intellectual abilities as well as experience do correlate highly with performance under certain conditions. For example, leader intelligence correlates with group performance if leaders are directive and have the group's support. As we shall see below, stress, especially with superiors, plays a major role as a moderator in determining the contribution of leader intelligence and experience to performance.

Job Stress and Stress with Boss

There can be little doubt that stress has a major effect on cognitive resources. However, most leadership research on this topic has focused primarily on the effect of job stress and performance, that is, the effects of time pressure, task complexity, role ambiguity, or noxious working conditions (e.g., Schuler, 1980; Beehr, 1985; Harrison, 1985).

Aside from concerns with role conflict and job ambiguity, which may be in part ascribed to inadequacies of the boss, the effect of stress with the boss or key subordinates has largely been ignored (Beehr, 1985; Buck, 1972). Stress related to one's boss's evaluation is particularly important since the superior plays such an important role in how we view ourselves and our future in the organization. One bad performance evaluation or an unfavorable job recommendation can destroy an entire career. The anxiety about how the boss will evaluate the subordinate's work is, therefore, potentially strong and quite realistic.

A relationship with a superior who is seen as hostile and threatening is especially likely to create severe stress, anxiety, and apprehension about how this superior will evaluate the subordinate. This has important consequences for the way in which the subordinate can function intellectually. Those who feel that the relationship with their boss is stressful and evaluative tend to ruminate about their own inadequacies, the possible consequences of failing, of getting a new job, or having an unpleasant encounter with the boss (Sarason, 1984; Spielberger and Katzenmeyer, 1959). These ruminations divert the leader's attention from the task and thus prevent the effective use of his or her intellectual resources for accomplishing the job. As a result, leaders who have a stressful relationship with their boss are then likely to revert to skills and behaviors that have worked in the past. One of the major findings of cognitive resource theory has been that leaders use their intelligence but not their experience when stress with the boss is low; they use their experience but not their intelligence when stress with the boss is high (e.g., Fiedler et al., 1979; Fiedler and Garcia, 1987; Potter and Fiedler, 1981). Even more interesting, as we shall discuss below, is a totally unexpected finding: When stress is low, performance correlates *negatively* with leader experience; when stress is high, it correlates *negatively* with intelligence. Thus, leaders use their intelligence but "misuse" their experience when stress with the boss is low; they use their experience but misuse their intelligence when job or boss stress is high. This finding is illustrated below.

Combat Infantry Division Leaders

Borden (1980) conducted a study of 160 combat infantry division officers and 167 noncommissioned officers (NCOs). Performance evaluations were obtained from two to five superiors, using a scale developed for military leaders by Bons and Fiedler (1976). This scale asked superiors to rate the degree to which the subordinate's performance exceeded, met, or failed to meet performance standards on such items as "how well he carries out administrative actions," "how well he organizes his group," and "how well he handles his job when the demands are extra heavy." Stress was measured by asking leaders to rate the extent to which their relationship with the boss or the job was "not stressful at all" or "very stressful."

The subjects above and below the median on intelligence scores and on experience (time in service) within each job category were divided into thirds on the job-stress and boss-stress scales. Figure 1.4 shows the average standardized performance scores for relatively more intelligent and experienced leaders and less intelligent and experienced leaders who reported varying levels of boss stress. As can be seen, the more intelligent leaders performed substantially better under low stress, but substantially less well under high stress. The opposite was the case for experience: the more experienced leaders performed best in the stressful condition but relatively poorly in the low-stress condition.

Coast Guard Personnel

Similar findings emerged in a study of 130 Coast Guard officers and petty officers assigned to a large headquarters organization (Potter and Fiedler, 1981). All subjects took the Wonderlic (1977) personnel test and filled out questionnaires indicating how long they had been in the Coast Guard and

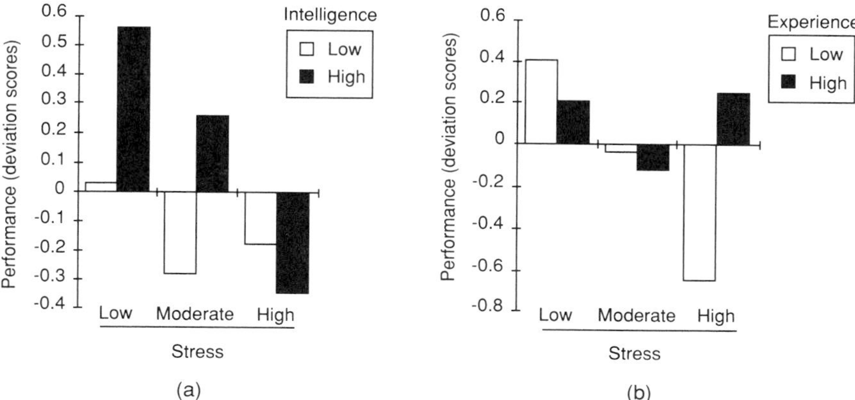

Figure 1.4. Average performance of leaders with relatively high and low intelligence scores (a) and experience (b) who reported relatively low or high stress with their superiors. (Borden data, weighted average across five samples.)

the degree of perceived job and boss stress.

Again, when stress was low, neither intelligence nor experience correlated significantly with performance. However, stress with boss moderated the relations between cognitive resources and overall performance; when stress with the boss was high, the correlation between the leader's intelligence and performance was significantly negative ($-.27$, $n = 51$, $p < .05$) while the correlation between experience and performance was significantly positive ($.48$, $n = 48$, $p < .01$). These results were substantially stronger when we limited the analysis to those officers and petty officers whose jobs were intellectually demanding, that is, jobs that require decisionmaking, advising on policy issues, and "administrative support" (filling in for someone else on a temporary basis). These are situations in which it is difficult to satisfy a hostile boss. In these jobs, the highly intelligent person who does his or her own thinking and uses his or her own judgment is more likely to run afoul of the hostile boss than is a person who is not too bright, quietly adheres to the routine, and follows orders (see Table 1.1).

It is important to note that in all jobs, experience improved performance when boss stress was high. This was most notable in jobs that require tact and ability to deal with difficult interpersonal relations. Examples of this type are jobs that call for evaluating a field unit commanded by a higher-ranking officer, advising the commanding officer on policy matters, or representing the Coast Guard in confrontations with the press.

Experience was also valuable under stressful conditions in unchalleng-

Table 1.1
Correlations between Intelligence and Experience with Performance in Decision and Supervisory Functions of Coast Guard Personnel

	Intelligence and performance		Experience and performance	
	Low	High	Low	High
	Boss stress			
Decisionmaking				
Making decisions	.11 (21)	−.47 (13)	.01 (23)	.47 (14)
Policy advising	.27 (30)	−.46[a] (22)	.06 (35)	.43[a] (22)
Communicating orders				
Supervising subordinates	.07 (29)	.04 (18)	−.06 (31)	.41 (19)
Training	.11 (26)	−.17 (21)	−.09 (31)	.42[b] (23)
Administration				
Paperwork	−.01 (25)	−.25 (21)	−.28 (27)	.44[a] (22)
	Job stress			
Decisionmaking				
Making decisions	.15 (25)	−.53[a] (14)	−.00 (32)	.31 (16)
Policy advising	.06 (29)	−.24 (23)	−.06 (30)	.44[a] (29)
Communicating orders				
Supervising subordinates	.15 (23)	−.01 (24)	.08 (23)	.10 (27)
Training	.03 (16)	−.12 (24)	−.26 (24)	.38[a] (30)
Administration				
Paper work	−.03 (25)	−.16 (21)	−.06 (27)	.01 (22)

[a]$p < .05$.

ing and repetitive jobs, that is, handling routine paper work and training field units. However, also note that the correlations between experience and performance on these functions were often negative when boss stress was low. Thus, in a situation in which the boss was friendly and tolerant, more experienced leaders were likely to perform worse than their less experienced colleagues.

Fire Service Officers

The effect of experience on performance under low and high stress is further illustrated by a study of fire department companies. The usual level of stress is notoriously high in these work units, and a nonstressful component of the job will, therefore, stand out all the more. Fire fighting is one of the most stressful and physically dangerous civilian occupations. Therefore, experience should play a major role in determining leadership performance in these jobs. Frost (1980) collected data on 76 lieutenants and 45 captains, each of whom headed a company of three to five fire fighters. The officers reported the degree to which the job and the relationship with their immediate superior seemed stressful. Battalion chiefs rated how their subordinate officers performed at the scene of the fire and also in administrative tasks. Two measures of experience are shown: time in the fire service and time in rank. Neither predicted performance for the entire sample.

Table 1.2 shows, first of all, that the correlations between experience and fire combat are negative under low stress and positive under high stress. Administrative tasks are obviously less stressful than fire combat, and we find that the correlations between administrative performance and experience are even higher in the negative direction than they are for fire combat. Moreover, three of the four negative correlations between experience and performance under low stress were significant. An explanation for these unexpected results is offered later in this chapter.

WHAT'S INSIDE THE BLACK BOX?

This chapter briefly described the main features of the contingency model and cognitive resource theory. In both of these two models of leadership (1) the prediction of behavior and performance from leader attributes is strongly moderated by situational factors, (2) situational factors are related to uncertainty and stress, and (3) the situational factors are associated not only with major changes in, but also reversals of, leader behavior and performance.

Table 1.2

Correlations between Various Types of Fire Department Experience and Performance in Fire Combat and Administrative Duties for Officers with High and Low Perceived Boss and Job Stress

	Boss stress		Job stress	
	Low	High	Low	High
Fire combat	(22)	(23)	(25)	(20)
Time in service	−.24	.23	−.34	.41
Time as officer	−.23	.25	$-.40^{b}$	$.68^{c}$
Administration				
Time in service	−.31	−.19	$-.41^{b}$	−.06
Time as officer	$-.40^{a}$	−.24	$-.58^{a}$	.10

$^{a}p < .10$; $^{b}p < .05$; $^{c}p < .01$

The two models differ in the type of leader behavior that they predict. In the contingency model, the behaviors of interest seem to reflect affective responses: situational control or stress changes the behavior of the high-LPC leader from being directive to nondirective and from considerate to inconsiderate, while the low-LPC person's behavior changes in the opposite way. In CRT, the changes are in cognitive approaches to the problem. High stress and low situational control change the leader's reliance in decisionmaking and problem solving from one based on logical, analytical thinking to reactions based on past experience. The present formulation that is offered here attempts to integrate these two theories, although this integration should also have implications for understanding such other contingency theories of leadership as path–goal theory (House, 1971) and Vroom and Yetton's normative decision model (1973). The essential argument is as follows:

1. The basis for contingent relations in leadership theories lies in the nature of the situational factors, namely, uncertainty and stress, which arouse leader anxiety.
2. Anxiety-arousing conditions cause the leader to fall back on previous successful reinforced behavior patterns. On a cognitive level these behaviors reflect what was learned from experience. On the affective level these behaviors reflect an earlier mode of coping with interpersonal problems, and these modes of coping differ from one type of personality to another.
3. The effectiveness of the leader's behavior and the resulting group and organizational performance depend on the degree to which the evoked leader reactions match the demands of the situation.

THE EFFECT OF STRESS, UNCERTAINTY, AND ANXIETY ON BEHAVIOR

If uncertainty, stress, and anxiety are, indeed, the "active ingredients" of situational factors in leadership, how do they affect the leader's behavior and performance? Some stress and uncertainty are, of course, a normal and ubiquitous part of organizational life with which the leader must cope. The question is how relatively high levels of anxiety stress and uncertainty affect the leader's behavior and performance.

One important method of coping is to seek safety by falling back on behavior that has proved successful in the past. This mode of coping often evokes behavior from an earlier phase of the individual's development and tends to reflect a less mature and less differentiated and integrative mode of thinking. For example, a study by Barker et al. (1941) investigated children's play behavior before and after a mildly stressful experience. The study showed that the children's behavior became markedly simpler and less mature after the frustrating experience.

Suedfeld and his associates (e.g., Porter and Suedfeld, 1981; Wallace and Suedfeld, 1988) developed an index of integrative complexity. This measure indicates the individual's ability to identify and simultaneously react to different elements in the environment. A still higher cognitive level is defined by "integration," the ability to see relationships among seemingly different or unrelated elements of the environment, such as identifying hail, rain, and snow as different forms of precipitation.

Suedfeld and his coworkers found dramatic decreases in integrative complexity during a period of stress in an individual's life. This is seen in speeches, letters, and written documents of statesmen during a political crisis. Likewise, letters and manuscripts of writers who were in poor health showed a marked decline in cognitive complexity during the 5 years preceding their deaths.

A decrease in cognitive complexity in stressful conditions was also reported by Streufert (1970). His research shows that individuals who are attempting to deal with such stresses as conflict, overload, or failure show simpler, less integrated thought processes than do those operating under less stressful conditions. Stress thus induces simpler, less integrated, and less complex types of thought and behavior, and at least in some instances, a regression to less mature behavior.

EFFECTS OF STRESS AND UNCERTAINTY ON THE USE OF EXPERIENCE

Experience represents problem solving that is based on intuition and hunches derived from past impressions, and what has been learned informally from the past, rather than on the basis of logical and analytical thinking. In stressful conditions, experience-based actions are guided by overlearned and reflexive actions that often cannot be verbalized or addressed by logical and analytic thinking.

If a situation is so stressful and anxiety arousing that "it is difficult to think straight," the individual typically reacts with reflexive, automatic behavior that has worked well on previous occasions. This automatic reaction undoubtedly had evolutionary survival value; when threatened by a saber-tooth tiger, it was considerably healthier to run than to stop and weigh the merits of all other options. In general, the fallback to earlier or simpler behavior enhances performance if the task itself is simple and overlearned or can be done by rote. It is detrimental if the task is new, complex, or requires the development of ideas, plans, and action strategies (e.g., Zajonc, 1965).

Experience as a Product of an Earlier Developmental and Previously Learned Behavior

What is the evidence that experience predates logical and analytic thinking? Cognitive psychologists are not unanimous on this or other related points. However, Suedfeld's as well as Streufert's studies imply that integrative complexity is developed at a later stage in life than is simple, nonintegrative thinking and behavior.

More direct support for this hypothesis also comes from Luria's (1976) research on illiterate and semi-illiterate peasants in Uzbekistan and Kirghizia who were otherwise comparable in intellectual abilities. These villagers were given logical and practical problems to solve. In contrast to villagers who had at least one or two years of schooling, the typical illiterate villager was unable to solve simple abstract problems (p. 130) . . . [because] "their thought processes [still] operate on the level of graphic and functional practical experience" (p. 132). As Luria further points out,

> The very young child perceiving an unfamiliar object does not name it; he uses different mental processes from an adolescent who has mastered language and thus analyzes incoming information with the aid of verbal meanings. A child who develops habits by drawing conclusions from immediate personal experience uses different mental devices from an adolescent who mediates each behavioral act through norms established by social experience. The direct impressions that dominate the young child give way in the adolescent to the omnipresent abstractions and generalizations of external and internal speech. (p. 11)

There is reason then to believe that stress and uncertainty cause leaders to fall back to a mode of thinking that is based on practical knowledge, skills, and behaviors when the situation is stressful. In stress-free situations, leaders tend to shift to problem solving based on logical and analytic thought processes.

THE EFFECT OF STRESS AND UNCERTAINTY IN THE CONTINGENCY MODEL

A parallel explanation might serve to clarify the role of situational factors in the contingency model. The explanation requires evidence that (1) high stress and changes in situational control cause anxiety; (2) anxiety changes leader behavior; and (3) the behavior was learned at an earlier time, or is simpler and/or less mature.

1. *Stress and uncertainty cause anxiety.* There is little doubt that stress and uncertainty cause anxiety (e.g., McGrath, 1976; Beehr, 1985, pp. 74–78; Fiedler, 1967), and this point needs no further elaboration. It is considerably more difficult to see, however, why an increase in situational control should cause anxiety. Nevertheless, this is the case. The most compelling support for this counterintuitive finding comes from an investigation by Chemers et al. (1985), who defined LPC and situational control as being "in match" when the leader's LPC and situational control are likely to result in good leadership performance. LPC and situational control were defined as not "in-match" when low-LPC leaders are in moderate-control situations and high-LPC leaders are in either high- or low-control conditions. Chemers et al. (1985) obtained measures of LPC and situational control as well as data on personal adjustment, psychosomatic disorders, and anxiety from 59 university administrators. Their study showed that administrators whose LPC scores were mismatched with their situational control reported not only significantly more job stress but also more anxiety, health problems, and absenteeism than those who were "in match." Almost identical results were obtained in a subsequent study by Shirakashi (1988) on Japanese managers, using anxiety as the dependent variable. Similar findings emerged in reanalyses of our own data on army squad leaders and infantry officers (S. Holste, personal communication, 1991). Together, these studies leave little doubt that a change in the interaction between LPC and situational control from one of being "in-match" to one of being not "in-match" causes the leader stress and anxiety, stemming most likely from a perceived inability to deal with situations of this nature.

2. *Anxiety is associated with changes in leader behavior and performance.* That these behavior changes occur has already been discussed in this chapter, as well as amply documented elsewhere, and should require no further amplification (e.g., Bons and Fiedler, 1976; Chemers, 1969; Fiedler et al., 1969; Fiedler et al. 1989; Gibson et al., 1990; Potter and Fiedler, 1981; Larson and Rowland, 1973; Sample and Wilson, 1965).

3. *Anxiety induces behavior that is simpler or represents a regression to an earlier stage in the leader's personality development.* This hypothesis, as it applies to CRT, seems supported to a reasonable degree. The more difficult problem is to determine whether, and how well, it also applies to the contingency model. The hypothesis was originally advanced about 25 years ago in an attempt to explain the nature of the LPC score. As already mentioned, it proposed that LPC reflects a hierarchy of goals or motivations. The high-LPC leader's basic goal is to have close and supportive relations with

coworkers, while task accomplishment is important but secondary. The low-LPC leader's primary and basic goal is task accomplishment, while good work relations are desirable but secondary, that is, "business before pleasure." The question is how and why situational factors change the leader's goals and behaviors (Fiedler, 1967).

We must recall here that the primary motivation to focus either on task achievement or on good interpersonal relations is presumably acquired early in the individual's development. It becomes dominant under stressful or anxiety-arousing conditions when the overlearned and more basic motivations and concomitant behaviors become dominant over secondary goals (Fiedler, 1967, pp. 45–46; Fiedler, 1972). A test to show that the hypothesis is tenable for explaining LPC, therefore, requires evidence that (1) one displays a more basic aspect of one's personality under stressful than under nonstressful conditions and/or (2) that the behavior that becomes dominant under stress is characteristic of an earlier phase in one's development.

The hypothesis that individuals reveal their basic personality under stress also accounts for the widely held but yet untested belief that crises and emergencies reveal the "real person." That is, we assume that a person's behavior under stress is likely to be more impulsive, less concerned with consequences, less controlled, and hence, less "mature."[1] It is the rationale for stress interviews, cross-examinations, and such spectacles as debates between presidential candidates.

That stress makes the leader's verbal behavior appear less well developed and less controlled is illustrated by a recent study (Gibson et al., 1990) that compared typescripts of group discussions under relatively stressful and stress-free conditions. The study showed that the language of leaders assigned to the high-stress situation was less controlled and less relevant. The leaders' language was rated as less understandable, and it contained more voice hesitations, breaks and automatic phrases, and fewer task-relevant comments than did the language in the low-stress condition. In terms of their verbal ability, the leaders in the stressful condition thus operated in a manner reminiscent of an earlier stage of their language development.

That thought processes tend to be less controlled and appropriate, and presumably less mature, in stressful than nonstressful conditions is also shown in a recent study of 121 male cadets at the U.S. Coast Guard Academy (Fiedler et al., manuscript in progress). The cadets completed

[1]While this hypothesis sounds eminently reasonable, I have not been able to find any studies that either support or refute the hypothesis, nor have cross-country telephone calls to authorities in this area revealed any past or ongoing research.

several tests and questionnaires, and rated various stressful conditions that they experienced, including stress with their military superiors and the academic staff.

One questionnaire asked how cadets deal with stressful situations in the barracks. Some of the questionnaire items focused on the cadet's academic and military duties, and others on interpersonal relations (e.g., "As far as my course work goes, I feel pretty much in control of how well I do," "Sometimes I worry about how to fit in all the things I have to do." "If your classmates don't like you, it is difficult for you to graduate").

An 11-item questionnaire asked the cadet about thoughts "you might have . . . *while doing the task on which you are working*. Indicate how often each occurred." This questionnaire yielded one factor based on task-relevant thoughts and included items about the importance of doing well, feeling competent, and concern with passing examinations. A second factor contained items about thoughts that are irrelevant to the task, such as "I thought about members of my family, friends, and something that happened in the past." Thoughts about the comforting relations with family and old friends, and reveries about the distant past or fantasies about the future, are obviously dysfunctional to performing an important task, but they constitute an immature method for coping with an unpleasant or stressful situation.

The study showed that these irrelevant thoughts and reveries about the past occur more frequently in stressful than stress-free situations. Thus, cadets who reported high stress related to their academic work also recalled a significantly greater number of irrelevant thoughts than those reporting low stress (F 7.423, $n = 51, p < .01$), while there was no difference between stress conditions in the frequency of task-relevant thoughts.

Even more important for our understanding of contingency theories is the preliminary support for the hypothesis that stress has a different effect on the thought processes of high- and low-LPC leaders. Preliminary analyses show, for example, that cadets with high and middle LPC scores tended to escape into task-irrelevant ruminations when they experienced a high degree of stress. Task-related thoughts are seemingly more frequent for high LPCs in the moderately stressful condition, and for low LPCs in the low- and high-stress conditions. Future studies need to determine whether different levels of situational control have similar effects on leaders' thought processes.

We have hypothesized that stress results in thoughts and behaviors that are characteristic of an earlier stage of development, or of previously overlearned behaviors. This implies that increased stress and anxiety change in the leader's motivation, thought processes, and behaviors from a more mature, or more recently acquired mode to one that is less mature or stems from an earlier phase of the individual's development. The data lend support to this hypothesis insofar as task-irrelevant thoughts and fantasies about family, friends, and past and future events on the job can be seen as indicative of a relatively immature method of coping with stress in the work environment.

In sum, there is good evidence that situational factors affect leader behavior by increasing or decreasing the level of uncertainty, stress, and anxiety. Research on CRT shows that stress evokes simpler, overlearned, or less mature thought processes and behavior. The evidence that similar processes operate in the contingency model is as yet weaker and requires further research.

On the basis of what we know now, I am proposing here an admittedly oversimplified and speculative model to account for the contingent relationships in contingency theories:

1. The critical importance of situational factors lies in their ability to create anxiety stress and uncertainty for the leader.
2. Anxiety, stress, and uncertainty cause leaders to fall back on behavior and ideation that was previously learned, or that stems from an earlier phase of the individual's development.
3. Under conditions of anxiety, stress and uncertainty, the leader's thought processes and behaviors that become dominant are based on previously learned knowledge and reactions. This is represented in the cognitive domain by experience rather than logical and analytical thinking, and in the affective domain by goals and motivation that reflect the more basic aspect of the leader's personality.

The recent findings have been highly encouraging, but they are preliminary. We need to determine in future studies how much of the perceived stress is attributable to the environment and how much to the individual's predilection to be anxious. We also need to know more about the effects of different types of stress, and how they affect the thinking and behavior of leaders. This brings forth the obligatory plea for more research.

ANCILLARY ISSUES

Negative Correlations of Performance with Intellectual Abilities and Experience

Two additional sets of findings require comment, although they are not central to the main argument of this chapter. First, how can we explain the substantial negative correlations between leader intelligence and performance found under high stress, and the negative correlations between leader experience and performance under conditions of low stress? This question has been fully discussed in detail in two recent papers (Fiedler, 1992; Fiedler, in press) and is presented here only in outline.

In brief, the argument is that one cannot simultaneously solve problems intellectually while reacting on the basis of experience that under stress evokes essentially automatic and unthinking behavior. Intellectual effort and experience thus interfere with one another. The probable reason for the negative correlations is that highly intelligent individuals rely on intellectual problem solving for which they have been rewarded since childhood, and they distrust hunch and intuition in making decisions. Experienced people "know what has worked before" without necessarily taking into consideration changing conditions or different circumstances. In relying on what they have learned over time, they tend to be impatient or distrustful of "still another study" when they feel that they have covered the same ground again and again.

Thus, in emergencies or stressful situations, when quick action is required, the leader with relatively high intellectual abilities will be inclined to engage in a careful review of alternative methods of dealing with the problem. Conversely, in situations that are relatively stress-free and call for thoughtful consideration of all options, the more experienced leaders will be impatient and seek quick solutions rather than tolerating lengthy consideration of a problem. Hence, under stressful conditions, intellectual abilities and effort interfere with hunch and automatic behavior based on experience, and therefore correlate negatively with performance. In stress-free situations, where logical and analytical problem solving may be required, experience interferes with appropriate intellectual effort and therefore correlates negatively with performance.

Sudden Changes in Behavior and Performance

The changes in behavior and performance, which are caused by an increase or decrease in the level of stress or situational control, appear to be precipitous rather than gradual. Moreover, the changes in leader behavior that do occur as a result of changes in situational factors involve a broad spectrum of individual actions as well as performance.

Thus, a study by Bons and Fiedler (1976) showed that an increase in situational control strongly affected such leader behaviors as being rewarding, punitive, strict or lenient with disciplinary offenders, and considerate and structuring. In other words, a leader who was considerate, nondirective, and nonpunitive at one point suddenly switched to be inconsiderate, punitive and directive, and vice versa (see also Fiedler, 1976; Fiedler, 1967; Shiflett and Nealey, 1972). These findings strongly suggest that one entire pattern of complex behavior is substituted for another when situational factors change.

Sudden behavior changes occur rather frequently in everyday life. We may work hard on a particular project until it suddenly seems no longer worth the effort and is dropped. Or we may try to be considerate and conciliating in dealing with a hostile or obstreperous group of subordinates. If that strategy fails, we may suddenly become punitive and autocratic, such as "No more Mr. Nice Guy! From now on you do it my way, or else!"

The radical changes in behavior and performance obtained in contingency theories suggest that we develop at least two alternative patterns of behavior or scripts: one designed for coping with "normal conditions" and a different set of behaviors designed for coping with emergencies—a crash-plan for conditions that are out of control. This hypothesis is, of course, highly speculative, but deserves serious consideration in light of our findings and those of other contingency theorists. Most psychological research is based on linear models. As psychologists we are taught to believe in monotonic relations: the more a student knows, the better is the school performance; the higher the anxiety level, the higher is the galvanic skin response (GSR). However, many important events in real life do not follow monotonic laws.

It is important to recognize that the unidimensional models of behavior and performance are inadequate to account for many important real-life phenomena. Much of our life is built on contingent rather than monotonic dimensions, and we shall have to work harder to understand the complex pretzel-shaped interactions and contingencies which now bedevil our research.

While it is to be hoped that the relationship between the contingency model and cognitive resource theory has become more understandable, we still have a long way to go. I also hope that hypotheses that I have advanced in this chapter will stimulate further research on this fascinating problem.

Acknowledgments

This paper was presented at the Fourth Annual Claremont McKenna College Leadership Conference, entitled "The Future of Leadership Research: A Tribute to Fred Fiedler" (February 22–23, 1991). The conference was organized by Martin M. Chemers, Henry Kravis Professor of Leadership, Claremont McKenna College, and Roya Ayman, Associate Professor of Psychology, Illinois Institute of Psychology, Chicago.

I want to express my appreciation to Mr. Henry Kravis, whose generous support made this conference possible. I would also like to express my deep appreciation to my colleagues who gave me the benefit of their helpful suggestions and criticisms. I am especially indebted to Lee R. Beach, Roya Ayman, Martin M. Chemers, Judith Fiedler, Dennis Hrebec, and Thomas Link.

The research reported in this paper was funded mainly by contracts MDA 903-86-S-0300 and MDA 903-89-K-0193 with the U.S. Army Institute for Research in the Behavioral and Social Sciences (Fred E. Fiedler, principal investigator). The opinions and conclusions expressed in this paper do not necessarily reflect those of the sponsoring agency or the Department of Defense.

References

Appley, M. H., and Trumbull, R. (1967). *Psychological Stress.* New York: Meredith.

Bales, R. F. (1950). *Interaction process analysis.* Reading, MA: Addison-Wesley.

Barker, R., Dembo, T., and Lewin, K. (1941). Frustration and regression: An experiment with young children. *University of Iowa Studies: Studies in Child Welfare. 18*(1), 1–62. Iowa City: University of Iowa Press.

Beehr, T. A. (1985). Organizational stress and employee effectiveness. In T. A. Beehr and A. Bhagat (Eds.), *Human stress and cognition in organizations.* New York: Wiley Interscience.

Berry, J. W. (1986). A cross-cultural view of intelligence. In R. J. Sternberg and D. K. Detterman (Eds.), *What is intelligence?: Contemporary viewpoints on its nature and definition.* Norwood, NJ: Ablex.

Bettin, P. J., and Kennedy, J. K., Jr. (1990). Leadership experience and leader performance: Some empirical support at last. *Leadership Quarterly, 1*(4), 219–228.

Bons, P. M., and Fiedler, F. E. (1976). Changes in organizational leadership and the behavior of relationship- and task-motivated leaders. *Administrative Science Quarterly, 21,* 453–473.

Borden, D. F. (1980). *Leader-boss stress, personality, job satisfaction and performance: Another look at the interrelationship of some old constructs in the modern large bureaucracy.* Unpublished doctoral dissertation, University of Washington, Seattle.

Buck, V. E. (1972). *Working under pressure.* New York: Crane.

Burns, T., and Stalker, G. M. (1961). *The management of organizations.* Chicago: Quadrangle Books.

Chemers, M. M. (1969). Cross-cultural training as a means for improving situational favorableness. *Human Relations, 22,* 531–546.

Chemers, M. M. (1970). The relationship between birth order and leadership style. *Journal of Social Psychology, 80,* 243–244.

Chemers, M. M., Hays, R. B., Rhodewalt, F., and Wysocki, J. (1985). A person environment of job stress: A contingency model explanation. *Journal of Personality and Social Psychology, 3,* 628–635.

Fiedler, F. E. (1964). A contingency model of leadership effectiveness. In L. Berkowitz (Ed.), *Advances in Experimental Social Psychology* (Vol. I, pp. 149–190). New York: Academic Press.

Fiedler, F. E. (1967). *A theory of leadership effectiveness.* New York: McGraw-Hill.

Fiedler, F. E. (1970). Leadership experience and leader performance—another hypothesis shot to hell. *Organizational Behavior and Human Performance, 5,* 1–14.

Fiedler, F. E. (1971). Validation and extension of the contingency model of leadership effectiveness: A review of empirical findings. *Psychological Bulletin, 76,* 128–148.

Fiedler, F. E. (1972). Personality, motivation systems, and behavior of high and low LPC persons. *Human Relations, 25,* 391–412.

Fiedler, F. E. (1992). Time-based measure of leadership experience and organizational performance: A review of research and a preliminary model. *Leadership Quarterly, 3*(1), 5–23.

Fiedler, F. E. (in press b). The role and meaning of leadership experience. In K. E. Clark, M. B. Clark, and D. P. Campbell (Eds.), *Impact of leadership.* Greensboro, NC: Center for Creative Leadership.

Fiedler, F. E., and Garcia, J. E. (1987). *Improving leadership effectiveness: Cognitive resources and organizational performance.* New York: Wiley.

Fiedler, F. E., McGuire, M. A., and Richardson, M. (1989). The role of intelligence and experience in successful group performance. *Journal of Applied Sport Psychology, 1*(2), 132–139.

Fiedler, F. E., O'Brien, G. E., and Ilgen, D. R. (1969). The effect of leadership style upon the performance and adjustment of volunteer teams operating in a stressful foreign environment. *Human Relations, 22,* 503–514.

Fiedler, F. E., Potter, E. H., III, Zais, M. M., and Knowlton, W., Jr. (1979). Organizational stress and the use and misuse of managerial intelligence and experience. *Journal of Applied Psychology, 64*(6), 635–647.

Frost, D. C. (1980). *The mediating effects of interpersonal stress on managerial intelligence and experience utilization.* Unpublished master's thesis, University of Washington, Seattle.

Ghiselli, E. E. (1963). Intelligence and managerial success. *Psychological Reports, 12,* 898.

Gibson, F. W., Fiedler, F. E., and Daniels, K. (1990). *Stress, babble, and utilization of leader intellectual abilities* (Technical Report No. 90-1). Seattle: University of Washington, Organizational Research Group.

Green, S. C., Nebeker, D. M., and Boni, M. A. (1976). Personality and situational effects on leader behavior. *Academy of Management Journal, 19,* 184–194.

Hardy, R. C., Sack, S., and Harpine, F. (1973). An experimental test of the contingency model on small classroom groups. *Journal of Psychology, 86,* 3–16.

Harrison, R. V. (1985). The person-environment fit model and the study of job stress. In T. A. Beehr and R. S. Bhagat (Eds.), *Human stress and cognitions in organizations.* New York: Wiley Interscience.

House, R. J. (1971). A path-goal theory of leadership effectiveness. *Administrative Science Quarterly, 16,* 59–78.

Kelly, E. L., and Fiske, D. W. (1951). *The prediction of performance in clinical psychology.* Ann Arbor: University of Michigan Press.

Larson, L. L., and Rowland, K. M. (1973). Leadership style, stress and behavior in task performance. *Organizational Behavior and Human Performance, 9,* 407–420.

Luria, A. R. (1976). *Cognitive development: Its cultural and social foundations* (pp. 117–133). Cambridge, MA: Harvard University Press.

Mann, R. D. (1959). A review of the relationship between performance in small groups. *Psychological Bulletin, 56,* 241–270.

McGrath, J. E. (1976). Stress and behavior in organizations. In M. D. Dunnette (Ed.), *Handbook of industrial and organizational psychology.* Chicago: Rand McNally.

McKechnie, J. L. (1966). *Webster's new 20th century dictionary of the english language.* Cleveland: World Publishing.

Nebeker, D. M. (1975). Situational favorability and perceived environmental uncertainty: An integrative approach. *Administration Science Quarterly, 20,* 281–294.

Peters, L. H., Hartke, D. D., and Pohlmann, J. T. (1985). Fiedler's contingency theory of leadership: An application of the meta-analysis procedure of Schmidt and Hunter. *Psychological Bulletin, 97,* 274–285.

Porter, C. A., and Suedfeld, P. (1981). Integrative complexity in the correspondence of literary figures: Effects of personal and societal stress. *Journal of Personality and Social Psychology, 40,* 321–330.

Potter, E. H., III, and Fiedler, F. E. (1981). The utilization of staff member intelligence and experience under high and low stress. *Academy of Management Journal, 24*(2), 361–376.

Rice, R. W. (1978a). Psychometric properties of the esteem for least preferred coworker (LPC scale). *Academy of Management Review, 3,* 106–118.

Rice, R. W. (1978b). Construct validity of the least preferred coworker. *Psychological Bulletin, 85,* 1199–1237.

Sample, J. A., and Wilson, T. R. (1965). Leader behavior, group productivity and ratings of the least preferred co-worker. *Journal of Abnormal and Social Psychology, 1,* 266–270.

Sarason, I. (1984). Stress, anxiety and cognitive interference: Reactions to tests. *Journal of Personality and Social Psychology, 46,* 929–938.

Schriesheim, C. A., and Kerr, S. (1977). R. I. P. LPC: A response to Fiedler. In J. G. Hunt and L. L. Larson (Eds.), *Leadership: The cutting edge.* Carbondale: Southern Illinois University Press.

Schuler, R. S. (1980). Definition and conceptualization of stress in organizations. *Organizational Behavior and Human Performance, 25,* 184–215.

Sells, S. B. (1976). Organizational climate as a mediator of organizational performance. Science Technology and The Modern Navy, Department of Navy, ONR, Arlington, VA.

Shiflett, S., and Nealey, S. M. (1972). The effects of changing leader power: A test of "situational engineering." *Organizational Behavior and Human Performance, 7,* 371–382.

Shirakashi, S. (1988). Job stress of Japanese managers: A contingency model analysis. Paper presented at the 24th International Congress of Psychology, Sydney, Australia.

Spielberger, C. D., and Katzenmeyer, W. G. (1959). Manifest anxiety, intelligence, and college grades. *Journal of Consulting Psychology, 22,* 278.

Sternberg, R. J., and Detterman, D. K. (Eds.) (1986). *What is intelligence?: Contemporary viewpoints on its nature and definition.* Norwood, NJ: Ablex.

Stogdill, R. M. (1948). Personal factors associated with leadership: A survey of the literature. *Journal of Psychology, 25,* 35–71.

Streufert, S. (1970). Complexity and complex decision making: Convergences between differentiation and integration approaches to the production of task performance. *Journal of Experimental Psychology, 6*(4), 494–509.

Strube, M. J., and Garcia, J. E. (1981). A meta-analytical investigation of Fiedler's contingency model of leadership effectiveness. *Psychological Bulletin, 90,* 307–321.

Vroom, V. H., and Yetton, P. W. (1973). *Leadership and decision-making.* Pittsburgh, PA: University of Pittsburgh Press.

Wallace, M. D., and Suedfeld, F. (1988). Leadership performance in crisis: Longevity-complexity link. *International Studies Quarterly, 32,* 451.

Wonderlic, E. F. (1977). *Wonderlic personnel test.* Northfield, IL: Wonderlic.

Zajonc, R. R. (1965). Social facilitation. *Science, 149,* 269–274.

2

Legitimacy, Power, and Influence: A Perspective on Relational Features of Leadership

Edwin P. Hollander
City University of New York Doctoral Subprogram in Industrial/Organizational Psychology
Baruch College and University Graduate Center

INTRODUCTION

Leadership is not something a leader possesses so much as a process involving followership. Without followers, there plainly are no leaders or leadership. Yet, far less attention has been given to followers, who accord or withdraw support to leaders. Much of the literature on the study of leadership, while ostensibly focused on the effects of the leader, neglects to acknowledge or even recognize the important role of followers in defining and shaping the latitudes of a leader's action.

By their role in legitimating leadership, followers affect the strength of a leader's influence, the style of a leader's behavior, and the performance of the group, through processes of perception, attribution, and judgment. In short, influence and power flow from legitimacy, which is in several ways determined or affected by followers, and their response to leaders. Although leader legitimacy has to do initially with how a leader attains that status, Read (1974) observed that it goes on to involve a complex interac-

Leadership Theory and Research: Perspectives and Directions

tion of attitudes toward the leader and source of authority, with a leader's behavior contributing substantially to influence and continuing legitimacy (p. 203).

As Stewart (1982) has noted, leadership operates within the constraints and opportunities presented by followers. The constraints include the expectations and perceptions of followers which can influence leaders (Hollander, 1985, 1986; Lord and Maher, 1990). Also noteworthy is how follower expectations about leader qualities can affect who is seen to be appropriate for the role (see Lord et al., 1986).

An early proponent of the general view that followers are crucial to any leadership event, and deserve more attention, was Fillmore Sanford (1950). Sanford said, "There is some justification for . . . arguing that research directed at the follower will eventually yield a handsome pay-off. Not only is it the follower who accepts or rejects leadership, but it is the follower who perceives both the leader and the situation and reacts in terms of what he perceives" (p. 4). Mary Parker Follett expressed a related point, tied to her concept of "power with," in a paper delivered at the University of London in the early 1930s (Follett, 1949). She asserted that it is the dynamic between the leader and the follower that is critical in team success, and not the ability of the leader to dominate his or her followers (see also Hollander, 1992b).

Another reason for attending to followers is that they are most likely to know the actuality of the leader's approach to leadership, as lived out in daily events. Useful to understanding this process, therefore, is a serious study of the followers' perspective on it. The importance of this departure has become increasingly evident in recent work on leadership, especially as it affects successful or unsuccessful outcomes (see Hollander and Offermann, 1990; Kelley, 1988).

This chapter examines the leader–follower relationship both historically and conceptually, and brings into focus its role in contemporary developments in leadership study. As already indicated, legitimacy plays a pivotal part in this relationship because it affects how followers perceive and respond to the leader. Among its manifestations, legitimacy implicates such qualities as credibility, trust, loyalty, and the leader's ability to be effective in exercising power and influence.

THE RELATIONSHIP BETWEEN LEADERSHIP AND FOLLOWERSHIP

Although leadership and followership have traditionally been seen in highly differentiated terms, they represent interdependent, reciprocal systems.

Fundamental to them is a process of exchange "in which the leader both gives something and gets something. The leader provides a *resource* in terms of adequate role behavior directed toward the group's goal attainment, and in return receives greater influence associated with status, recognition, and esteem [contributing to] 'legitimacy' in making influence assertions and in having them accepted" (Hollander and Julian, 1969, p. 388). In a fundamental way, a leader's legitimacy depends on his or her standing with followers.

Leadership and followership also can both be active roles, considering the reality that hierarchical organizations require both functions at every level. The usual expectation of the follower role as essentially passive is misleading when considering followership as an accompaniment to leadership. Leaders do command greater attention and influence, but there now is an increasing realization that followers can affect leaders actively in more than trivial ways, if only because followers are usually the leader's most attentive strategic audience (Hollander, 1992a).

The role of follower therefore can be seen to hold within it the potential of leadership, and behaviors found to represent effective leadership in fact include attributes of good followership (see Hollander and Webb, 1955; Kouzes and Posner, 1987) such as dependability, competence, and honesty. Even with an imbalance of power, influence can be exerted in both roles, as part of a social exchange (Homans, 1961). Effective leadership is more likely to be achieved by a process in which there is reciprocity and the potential for two-way influence and power sharing, rather than a sole reliance on power over others.

Power and influence are not the same, although they are at times used as virtual synonyms. Classically, power is considered to be the ability to exert some degree of control over other persons, things, and events. In institutional terms, it is associated with authority relationships, and actual or implied coercion. By contrast, influence involves more persuasion, with the recipient having latitude for a free choice, rather than be subject to imposed authority. Regarding these distinctions, I noted further elsewhere:

> While power and influence constitute different processes, they are intertwined insofar as leaders may use both depending upon the circumstances and the particular followers involved. Even appointed leaders, "put in charge" within an organization, must rely on influence, in the sense of persuasion, as much as or more than on power. The unfettered use of power can be highly dysfunctional in creating numerous points of resistance and lingering negative feelings. Therefore both elected and appointed leaders are called upon to use persuasion in many instances, instead of the full power supposedly at their disposal. (Hollander, 1985, p. 489)

Information can legitimate power over others when its possessors provide a definition of reality, even when it is not based on fact. Although this may have the appearance of persuasion, it is more indicative of dependence, which is associated with leaders as "meaning makers," in Conger's (1991) usage. In a still larger sense, leaders define situations for followers. Yet followers must be willing to "buy" that definition, which in the broadest sense means accepting a "vision," with associated values. At its pinnacle, this involves strong identification with the leader.

Within an organizational context, such definitions would include dealing with the task at hand, interpreting pertinent history, resource allocation, competition versus cooperation, as well as fostering other psychological states. Important among the latter, for instance, is how conflict is viewed, approached, and resolved. On the international level, the implications of this process have been recognized by behaviorally oriented political scientists. Richard Snyder and his colleagues (1962), among others, stated what seems increasingly plain—that "the key to the explanation of why the state behaves as it does lies in the way its decisionmakers define their situation" (p. 51), not just for themselves but for their populace as well (see also Jervis, 1976).

In a line of work on "groupthink" phenomena extending back almost two decades, Janis (1972) examined the process by which decisions may be flawed by a too loyal acceptance of a particular reality, or set of options, from a leader. In his later work, *Crucial Decisions,* Janis (1989) elaborated on this analysis to scrutinize the leader's *selective* information seeking and other *uncorrected* processes of reaching decisions in a crisis. He found that such bad outcomes can be traced to excessive reliance on the leader's judgment, as with the intense identification said to be present in charismatic leadership.

TRANSACTIONAL MODELS OF LEADERSHIP

Process-oriented "transactional" models of leadership developed largely from a social exchange perspective, emphasizing the implicit relational qualities of the transaction that exists between leader and followers, which yields effectiveness (see Hollander, 1964, 1978; Hollander and Julian, 1968, 1969; Homans, 1961). The transactional view considers that a leader gives benefits to followers, such as direction, vision, recognition, and other esteem needs that are reciprocated by followers in heightened responsiveness to that leader. Hence, the transactional approach accords a more active role to followers, who rather than simply being coerced and complying, have the potential for perceiving and influencing a leader in a two-way influence relationship.

As another approach within social exchange/transactional models, Graen (1975) developed the leader–member exchange (LMX) model of leader–follower relations, emphasizing rolemaking between a leader and particular followers (see Dienesch and Liden, 1986; Graen and Scandura, 1987). In brief, the LMX model distinguishes between the relationships a leader has with followers who are close to the leader and those who are more distant. The first have a better quality relationship with the leader, but also have higher expectations for their loyalty and performance; the others receive fewer personal demands from the leader, but also fewer rewards. Liden and Graen (1980), for instance, found that subordinates reporting a high-quality relationship with their supervisors assumed more job responsibility, contributed more, and were rated as higher performers than those with low-quality relationships.

Generally, transactional models center on the followers' perceptions of and expectations about the leader's actions and motives, in accordance with attributional analysis. Heider's (1958) earlier work on the attribution of intentions through interpersonal perception exemplifies this analysis in the distinction between "can" and "will." If a leader is perceived to be able to achieve a favorable outcome, but doesn't because of an apparent failure of will, this causes a greater loss of following than the reverse, that is, an inability to achieve something desirable but with an evident try, nonetheless. Conveying a positive intention is redeeming to a degree, in instances where legitimacy may be threatened.

IDIOSYNCRASY CREDIT

Another social exchange concept, the "idiosyncrasy credit" model of innovative leadership (Hollander, 1958, 1964), deals with legitimacy functionally as the latitude followers provide a leader to bring about change. The model describes a dynamic process of interpersonal evaluation, and is nonnormative since it does *not* take a position on *how* things *ought* to be but reflects more how they seem to be in relatively noncoercive, less power-oriented situations.

The essential formulation in the model is that credits are earned over time in the perceptions of others by *competence* in helping to achieve the group's task goals, and *conformity* to the group's norms, as a sign of loyalty. Credits may then be drawn on to take innovative actions in line with expectations associated with the leader's role. This yields the prospect that *early signs of competence and conformity will permit later nonconformity, in the form of innovations, to be better tolerated.* This formulation was first verified in an experiment with groups of male engineering students in a group-decision task (Hollander, 1960), and has subsequently been supported elsewhere (e.g., Hollander, 1961), with some qualifications to be noted.

The idea of credit is embedded in our everyday language in such general terms as "receiving credit," "taking credit," and "being discredited." In its refinement, the idiosyncrasy credit (IC) model illustrates how credits accumulate and have operational significance in permitting innovations that would be perceived to be "deviations" if introduced by another person with less credit. Seniority can contribute to the accumulation of credits, but without uniform impact. A person may also benefit by having "derivative credit," as in a favorable reputation from another group, or from the society at large, as in high socioeconomic status. Most usually, however, a new member of a group is in a poor position to assert influence, especially in the direction of change, unless that person has a unique qualification. An example would be an idea that helps deal with a major group problem, or a badly needed skill. In these circumstances the new member's credit is gained by maximizing on the competence factor. But credit may not accrue as readily to those who are perceived to be different, as in the case of a woman in an otherwise male group (see Wahrman and Pugh, 1974).

Unless stigmatized, therefore, credit may result from calling attention to oneself in a positive way. This has been found to be associated with initial quantity of participation, which is perceived positively as a sign of a group member's motivation. In their experiment on this process, Sorrentino and Boutillier (1975) found that only later contributions were more likely to be evaluated for quality. In this vein, Ridgeway (1981) has contended that nonconformity may be a greater initial source of influence and has presented experimental evidence that appears contradictory to the IC model. Certainly it is true that within a brief time one may call attention to oneself by manifest nonconformity to prevailing norms. However, this will be evaluated in due course by the standard of the task contribution made, and a point of dysfunctionality may be reached where rejection may result.

Unused credits can be lost by failing to fulfill follower expectations for the leader role, including inaction in the face of need. Also, the leader's self-serving and other negatively viewed behaviors can drain credits, as can perceptions of weak motivation, incompetence, and the responsibility for failure (see Alvarez, 1968).

Underlying the IC model is a recognition that a process of making attributions is significant to accepting influence. The same behavior seen to be nonconforming if shown by one group member may not be so perceived when displayed by another. In short, nonconformity is defined within a group context, and the particular actor perceived within it, especially regarding that person's status (see Hollander 1958, 1961). In addition, nonconformity can be viewed with regard to the common expectancies applied generally as a norm for group members, and the particular expectancies applied to a high-status member. Accordingly, leaders may initiate change, perhaps in seemingly nonconforming ways, but be fulfilling an accepted innovative role. While there may be greater tolerance of nonconformity for the high-status member in some ways, there are restrictions imposed regarding particular expectancies, which can be thought of as role behaviors.

At least two reasons explain why these restrictions may be imposed: first, because status is usually perceived to carry with it greater self-determination, those of higher status are assumed to be more responsible for their actions; second, having greater status means having more potential for influencing important outcomes for the members of a group (Hollander, 1964, Chap. 20). More generally, Nemeth and Wachtler (1983) have found that influence is more likely to be determined by who holds a particular position rather than by its accuracy. For example, Torrance (1955) earlier found in three-man aircrews that if the correct answer to a problem was held by the lowest status group member (the gunner), it was least likely to be accepted by the others (the pilot and navigator). Here again, attributions of legitimacy play a determinant role in authority and the acceptance of influence.

FEATURES AND EFFECTS OF LEADER LEGITIMACY

Crucial to legitimacy is how followers perceive the leader's source of authority, and then respond to that leader. The evidence indicates that a major difference exists in the realm of appointment or election as sources of a leader's authority. In both cases, the possibility of being perceived to be a leader, and acting as one, depends to some degree on validation by those who are to be followers.

In an early experiment varying the basis of legitimacy, Goldman and Fraas (1965) had leaders in male groups selected by three methods: election by a group vote, appointment after selection with a measure of ability, or appointment randomly, plus a control condition without a leader. The task used was the game "Twenty Questions," and the dependent measures were time required, and number of questions needed, to reach a solution. Groups with leaders appointed for their competence performed best, with those having elected leaders performing a close second. Groups with randomly appointed leaders and no leaders showed poorer performance, which was attributed to the weak basis of their legitimacy (Hollander, 1986).

The election case is, of course, an obvious instance of emergence, which more closely approximates the IC model. Moreover, election usually creates a heightened psychological identification between followers and the leader, with followers having a greater sense of responsibility for and investment in the leader. One explanation is to view this as a social exchange in which the group gives the leader a "reward" in advance, by electing that individual, and then group members feel a claim on that person to "pay back" by producing favorable outcomes (Jacobs, 1970).

Correspondingly, it is also true that the support of followers exacts a higher demand on the leader. Elected leaders who fail to perform well have been found to be more vulnerable to criticism than appointed leaders, particularly if they are seen to be competent in the first place (Hollander and Julian, 1970, 1978). Although election and appointment may create different psychological climates between leaders and followers, this does not negate the very real possibility that organizational leaders may attain a "following" by doing more than exercising authority. As Katz and Kahn (1978) have observed, organizational leadership is "the influential increment over and above mechanical compliance with . . . routine directives" (p. 528).

An experiment on source of authority by Hollander et al. (1969) studied the effects on appointed or elected leaders of disagreements with their followers. Cast within the IC model, the intent was to determine the leader's willingness to deviate from group decisions about the ranking of programs to alleviate typical urban problems in a city called "Collosus." A "strong" or "not strong" support treatment cut across the condition of leader election or appointment. Figure 2.1 shows that elected leaders who had been told they had strong group support were significantly more likely to make total reversals of their group's decision—indeed, for about half the critical trials—than were those in the other conditions. In addition, elected leaders with strong support showed lower conciliation in their responses to group judgments, based on a content analysis of their messages to the group. Evidently, the elected leader in this condition felt freer to expend their credits by challenging group judgments.

A subsequent series of experiments in our laboratory pursued this line of research on source of authority. In one of these (Hollander et al., 1977), four-member college student groups were studied whose leaders were appointed or elected and whose members were told either that they had done well ("success") or had not done well ("failure") right after their first phase of activity. The task used was the same "Collosus" urban problems one in the experiment just discussed.

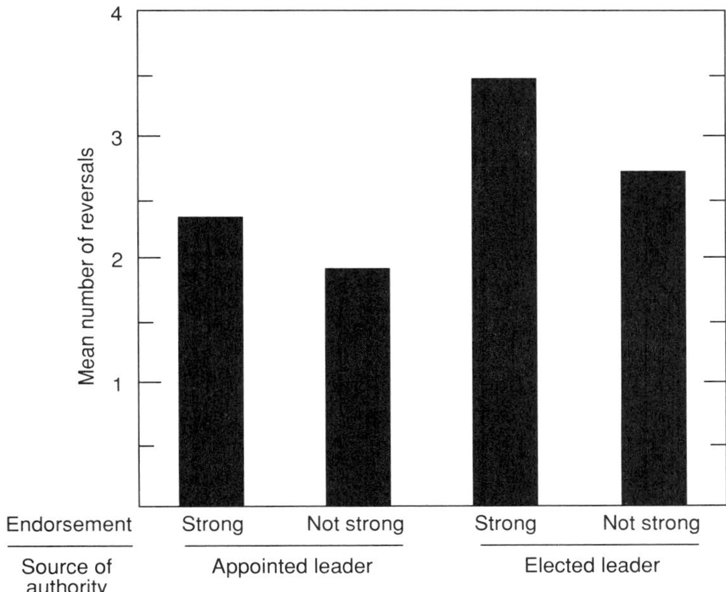

Figure 2.1 Mean number of seven critical trials on which leaders reversed team's first rank choice ($N = 10$ subjects for each treatment). From Hollander and Julian (1970, p. 143).

In general, it was found that elected leaders had more influence on the group rankings than did appointed ones. Furthermore, the influence of elected but not appointed leaders increased after the initial failure feedback and decreased after success feedback. This effect was interpreted via Hamblin's (1958) concept that a "crisis," in this case created through an apparent failure, produces the effect of "rallying around" the elected leader, at least initially. In the success condition, with no crisis, group members acted out of a greater security in their own judgments, and the leader did not gain that benefit. When the groups were studied for still another phase, however, the elected leader in the failure condition showed a distinct loss of status, with credits depleted and followers willing to depose him. Interestingly, before the group learned how they were performing, a group member could be identified who was gaining influence as the likely successor to the elected leader. That member emerged as the group's choice when another election was held after the failure had persisted (Hollander, 1986, p. 47).

Also relevant are the processes occurring within a group or organization by appointment or election, and the leader's psychological connection to followers. To study these, another experiment (Ben-Yoav et al., 1983) was done, again using the same urban-problems task. Primary attention was on interaction processes in four-member college groups with appointed or elected leaders. They were directly studied by having two observers independently rate the groups, at 90° from one another, behind one-way vision mirrors. Postinteraction measures were also obtained. Elected leaders were found to be significantly more likely to contribute to group discussion. They also received higher ratings from followers on responsiveness to their needs, interest in the group task, and competence. This finding accords with the IC model regarding effects from the leader's source of authority, although suitable attention is needed to the setting, task, and particulars of the group's composition.

To look again at the way leaders react to followers under appointment of election conditions, Elgie et al. (1988) did an experiment on leader evaluations of followers displaying each of four types of behavior. These were the combinations of either positive or negative subordinate feedback with either high or low task activity. In that study, 46 subjects, 20 female and 26 male, were randomly placed in the appointed or elected conditions of leader legitimacy and told they were leading four same-sex followers in a group problem-solving task. The dependent measure was a composite score made up of 10 semantic differential ratings of each follower.

Because they are likely to have a greater sense of commitment and indebtedness to their groups, it was expected that elected leaders would react more favorably to high- than to low-performing followers, with less marked differences for appointed leaders. On the basis of Fiedler's (1972, 1978) proposal that leader motives are most clearly revealed under stressful conditions that pose a serious threat to leader goals, it was predicted that high-activity followers who gave negative feedback would represent the greatest condition of stress. Therefore, we expected that the lowest evaluations of followers would be for the combination of high activity and negative feedback, especially with appointed leaders. This outcome was predicted because of the heightened threat to their status, and the likely consequence of then giving such followers lower evaluations than elected leaders would give.

As shown in Figure 2.2, a three-way interaction supported the prediction that elected and appointed leaders would respond differently to high- and low-activity followers, especially under the negative-feedback condition. In general, a main effect showed that elected leaders were more positive than appointed leaders in judgments of their followers, in the manner predicted.

Taken as a whole, the main thread running through these results is the

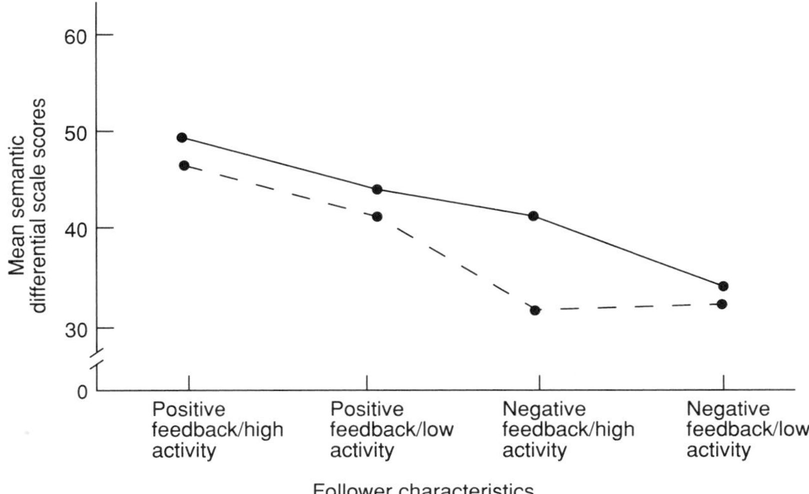

Figure 2.2 Mean semantic differential scores assigned by two types of leaders [$N = 23$ each, appointed (*dashed line*) or elected (*solid line*)] to four types of followers. From Elgie et al. (1988, p. 1367).

difference in support and involvement that was manifest in the two kinds of leader legitimacy conditions. While both may involve a social exchange process, it may be more evident in leader–follower relations when the leader is elected. But it also is present with appointed leaders, as seen in the work of Graen and others (see Graen, 1975; Dienesch and Liden, 1986).

ATTRIBUTIONS ABOUT LEADER QUALITIES AND PERFORMANCE

A modern-day framework for the credit-building process is evident in attribution theory, which speaks to follower attributions about a leader that incline them to respond affirmatively or otherwise to that leader. This framework of study is part of the great attention being given to cognitive elements in leader–follower relations, represented by follower "implicit leadership theories" (ILTs), among other concepts (see Calder, 1977; Lord et al., 1986; Rush et al., 1977). Lord and Maher (1990) say that perceptions of a leader are checked against prototypes followers hold of leader attributes, such as intelligence, and expectations of how leaders should perform.

Calder (1977), Pfeffer (1977), and Meindl and Ehrlich (1987) are among the proponents of a perceptual–attributional perspective that says that leaders are credited or blamed for outcomes with which they had little to do, such as the economy picking up with oil prices down under Reagan or faltering when they had been raised by OPEC (Organization of Petroleum-Exporting Countries) under Carter. This is seen to be a perceptual pattern that reflects the "romance of leadership," as Meindl and Ehrlich (1987) term it. They found that in perceiving group and organizational performance, positive or negative outcomes are more likely to be attributed to the leader than to other factors. Because leaders are symbols, Pfeffer (1977) says that if something goes wrong, the whole staff or entire team cannot be fired, but firing the manager can convey a sense of rooting out the basis for the problem. Obviously, it is less simple to dismiss an office-holder, especially in midterm after formal election or appointment, even though it occurs.

One consequence of the attributional approach is to make more explicit the significance of followers' and others' perceptions of the leader, not least regarding expectations about leader competence and motivation. Realistically, imagery and self-presentation may still obscure the truth about the leader's intentions and dealings, yet there remains the basic question of the degree to which followers are able to evaluate the leader.

The usefulness of the follower's perspective, as an avenue to understanding leadership, is illustrated by the work on "derailment" by McCall et al. (1988). They studied 400 promising managers, who were seen to be on a fast track. Those failing to reach their expected potential were mainly found to show various kinds of inconsiderate behavior toward others, but rarely to lack technical skills. With a sample of 2600 top-level managers, Kouzes and Posner (1987) looked at qualities these managers admired in their leaders. Among the most frequently chosen qualities were being honest and providing inspiration, in addition to being competent and forward-looking. Here again the interpersonal or relational realm was viewed as playing a significant role.

In a study using critical incidents and rating scales with an initial sample of 81 organizational respondents, since augmented to a total of 240, Hollander and Kelly (1990, 1992) found that relational qualities were emphasized in the rewards distinguishing good from bad leadership. Four relational qualities that consistently differentiated the two were scales of perceptiveness, involvement, trustworthiness, and rewardingness. Positive rewards of sensitivity to followers, support, and praise dominated good but were absent or opposite in bad leadership.

CHARISMA AND TRANSFORMATIONAL LEADERSHIP

In recent decades there has been a revitalization of interest in the older concept of the "charismatic leader." Max Weber (1921), the eminent sociologist of bureaucracy, coined it from the Greek word "charisma" for divine gift. Such a leader has considerable emotional appeal to followers and great power over them, especially in a time of crisis when there are strong needs for direction. This can be seen as a reflection of a vast amount of idiosyncrasy credit at the leader's disposal. Indeed, charisma is a quality that can be considered to be invested by followers and accorded or withdrawn by them (see Hollander, 1992a, p. 73).

In an update by House (1977) in line with his path–goal theory, the leader–follower bond is seen to be less based on an emotional appeal than on the leader's program of action that grips followers, that is, a goal and the path to achieve it. From his political science perspective, Burns (1978) developed a related concept of the "transformational leader" as one who changes the outlook and behavior of followers.

Burn's idea of the leader as a transforming agent has been applied to organizational leadership by Bass (1985) and Bennis and Nanus (1985), especially regarding how exceptional performance occurs. The essential point is that the leader strives to go beyond the usual norm, to redirect and bring about a change in follower thinking and action (see Fiedler and House, 1988). This formulation is highly resonant with the IC model.

Indeed, rather than be a dichotomy, transformational leadership can be seen as an extension of transactional leadership, with greater leader intensity and follower arousal (see Ehrlich et al., 1990). In fact, the Bass (1985) and Yammarino and Bass (1990) measure of transformational leadership involves two highly limited transactional factors, in addition to charisma, intellectual stimulation, and individual attention to followers. All of these can be seen as transactional rewards of an intangible nature, recognizing that charisma can be directed to the leader's self-serving ends, rather than to a larger good, as Burns (1978) indicated.

Post (1986) observed that the potential for damage from a leader with charismatic appeal is often due to narcissistic needs for continual approval from others. Coupled with personalized power needs, the outcome of a charismatic appeal can be destructive, as Hogan et al. (1990) have shown in their work on "the dark side of charisma." In addition to narcissists, they identify two other flawed leader types, such as the "high-likability floater" and the "resentful person," all of whom appear to have good social skills, rise readily in organizations, and take a financial and human toll in reduced productivity, poor morale, and excessive turnover (see also, e.g., Conger, 1990; Byrne et al., 1991).

In short, charismatic appeals based on emotional arousal provide ample opportunities for abuse. While all charismatic–transformational leaders do not occasion problems in these ways, their potential for affecting individuals and institutions adversely requires attention, if only to rectify an overbalance in the other direction. The essential value question of "leadership toward what ends" continually needs to be raised (Hollander, 1985, p. 526).

SOME IMPLICATIONS AND CONCLUSIONS

Granting the importance of leaders, a major implication of the presentation here is that their legitimacy is based on their relationship with followers. Specifically, the involvement of followers has to be recognized as a key component of effective leadership. The long-standing emphasis on the extent of leader ascendance, whether through assertions of influence or power, is not sufficient to address these broader concerns. Otherwise, the study of leadership becomes captive again of its leader-centered origins. That consideration makes relational skills such as responsiveness to followers an important requisite to these leadership roles. In its place, however, imagery and other devices may be employed manipulatively, as when intense emotions are aroused.

Whatever power is imputed to an organizational role, actualizing it depends on its perception by followers. Power becomes real when others perceive it to be so, and respond accordingly. But an emphasis on power over others tends to give it greater salience, at the expense of empowerment and resistance to unwanted power assertions, which we have called "power to" and "power from" (Hollander and Offermann, 1990). In that paper, we reviewed and assessed research on organizational leadership and power. Among other things we considered are the benefits of, and sources of resistance to, delegation and empowerment of followers. On balance, we found that by sharing power and allowing followers to influence them, leaders foster leadership skills in others, as well as achieve other gains through their greater participation and involvement. But a major question posed is how a return to leader-centered approaches can be reconciled with this trend toward greater follower empowerment and influence.

In sum, the main implication here is to accord a more active role for those who are followers. Every benefit need not be seen to depend on the leader. Initiatives need not be expected to come only from the leader, although the leader can be a facilitator of them. Indeed, being a leader and being a follower need not be viewed as sharply exclusive categories. Understanding the relational nature of leadership and followership opens up richer forms of involvement and rewards in groups, organizations, and society at large (see Hollander, 1992a).

Acknowledgment

The helpful assistance of Tracye D. Julien and Dennis R. Kelly in the preparation of this chapter is gratefully acknowledged.

References

Alvarez, R. (1968). Informal reactions to deviance in simulated work organizations: A laboratory experiment. *American Sociological Review, 33,* 895–912.

Bass, B. M. (1985). *Leadership and performance beyond expectations.* New York: Free Press.

Bennis, W. G., and Nanus, B. (1985). *Leaders.* New York: Harper & Row.

Ben-Yoav, O., Hollander, E. P., and Carnevale, P. J. D. (1983). Leader legitimacy, leader-follower interaction, and followers' ratings of the leader. *Journal of Social Psychology, 121,* 111–115.

Boyatzis, R. E. (1982). *The competent manager.* New York: Wiley-Interscience.

Burns, J. M. (1978). *Leadership.* New York: Harper & Row.

Byrne, J. A., Symonds, W. C., and Siler, J. F. (1991). CEO Disease. *Business Week,* April 1, 52–60.

Calder, B. J. (1977). An attribution theory of leadership. In B. M. Staw and G. R. Salancik (Eds.), *New directions in organizational behavior.* Chicago: St. Clair Press.

Conger, J. A. (1990). The dark side of leadership. *Organizational Dynamics, 19*(2), 44–55.

Conger, J. A. (1991). Inspiring others: The language of leadership. *Academy of Management Executive, 5*(1), 31–45.

Dienesch, R. M., and Liden, R. C. (1986). Leader-member exchange model of leadership: A critique and further development. *Academy of Management Review, 11,* 618–634.

Ehrlich, S. B., Meindl, J. R., and Viellieu, B. (1990). The charismatic appeal of a transformational leader: An empirical case study of a small, high technology contractor. *The Leadership Quarterly, 1*(4), 229–247.

Elgie, D. M., Hollander, E. P., and Rice, R. W. (1988). Appointed and elected leader responses to favorableness of feedback and level of task activity from followers. *Journal of Applied Social Psychology, 16,* 1361–1370.

Evans, M. G. (1970). The effects of supervisory behavior on the path-goal relationships. *Organizational Behavior and Human Performance, 5,* 277–298.

Evans, M. G. (1974). Extensions of a path-goal theory of motivation. *Journal of Applied Psychology, 59,* 172–178.

Fiedler, F. E. (1961). Leadership and leadership effectiveness traits. In L. Petrullo and B. M. Bass (Eds.), *Leadership and interpersonal behavior* (pp. 179–186). New York: Holt.

Fiedler, F. E. (1964). A contingency model of leadership effectiveness. In L. Berkowitz (Ed.), *Advances in experimental social psychology* (Vol. 1, pp. 149–190). New York: Academic Press.

Fiedler, F. E. (1967). *A theory of leadership effectiveness.* New York: McGraw-Hill.

Fiedler, F. E. (1972). Personality, motivational system, and the behavior of high and low LPC persons. *Human Relations, 25,* 391–412.

Fiedler, F. E. (1978). Recent developments in research on the contingency model. In L. Berkowitz (Ed.), *Group processes* (pp. 209–225). New York: Academic Press.

Fiedler, F. E., and Garcia, J. E. (1987). *New approaches to effective leadership.* New York: Wiley.

Fiedler, F. E., and House, R. J. (1988). Leadership theory and research: A report of progress. In C. L. Cooper and I. Robertson (Eds.), *International review of industrial and organizational psychology* (pp. 73–92). London: Wiley.

Follett, M. P. (1949). The essentials of leadership. In L. Urwick (Ed.), *Freedom and coordination.* London: Management Publication Trust, pp. 47–60.

Gleason, J. M., Seaman, F. J., and Hollander, E. P. (1978). Emergent leadership processes as a function of task structure and Machiavellianism. *Social Behavior and Personality, 6,* 33–36.

Goldman, M., and Fraas, L. A. (1965). The effects of leader selection on group performance. *Sociometry, 28,* 82–88.

Graen, G. (1975). Role-making processes within complex organizations. In M. D. Dunnette (Ed.), *Handbook of industrial and organizational psychology* (pp. 1201–1245). Chicago: Rand McNally.

Graen, G. B., and Scandura, T. A. (1987). Toward a psychology of dyadic organizing. In B. Staw and L. L. Cummings (Eds.), *Research in organizational behavior* (Vol. 9, pp. 175–208). Greenwich, CT: JAI Press.

Green, S. G., and Mitchell, T. R. (1979). Attributional processes of leaders in leader-member interactions. *Organizational Behavior and Human Performance, 23,* 429–458.

Hamblin, R. L. (1958). Leadership and crises. *Sociometry, 21,* 322–335.

Heider, F. (1958). *The psychology of interpersonal relations.* New York: Wiley.

Hogan, R., Raskin, R., and Fazzini, D. (1990). The dark side of charisma. In K. E. Clark and M. B. Clark (Eds.), *Measures of leadership* (pp. 343–354). West Orange, NJ: Leadership Library of America.

Hollander, E. P. (1958). Conformity, status, and idiosyncrasy credit. *Psychological Review, 65,* 117–127.

Hollander, E. P. (1960). Competence and conformity in the acceptance of influence. *Journal of Abnormal & Social Psychology, 61,* 361–365.

Hollander, E. P. (1961). Some effects of perceived status on responses to innovative behavior. *Journal of Abnormal & Social Psychology, 63,* 247–250.

Hollander, E. P. (1964). *Leaders, groups, and influence.* New York: Oxford University Press.

Hollander, E. P. (1978). *Leadership dynamics: A practical guide to effective relationships.* New York: Free Press/Macmillan.

Hollander, E. P. (1983). Women and leadership. In H. H. Blumberg, A. P. Hare, V. Kent, and M. Davies (Eds.), *Small groups and social interaction* (Vol 1). London & New York: Wiley.

Hollander, E. P. (1985). Leadership and power. In G. Lindzey and E. Aronson (Eds.), *The handbook of social psychology,* 3rd ed. (Vol. II, pp. 485–537). New York: Random House.

Hollander, E. P. (1986). On the central role of leadership processes. *International Review of Applied Psychology, 35,* 39–52.

Hollander, E. P. (1992a). The essential interdependence of leadership and followership. *Current Directions in Psychological Science, 1*(2), pp. 71–75.

Hollander, E. P. (1992b). Leadership, followership, self, and others. *The Leadership Quarterly, 3*(2), pp. 41–53.

Hollander, E. P., and Julian, J. W. (1968). Leadership. In E. F. Borgatta and W. W. Lambert (Eds.), *Handbook of personality theory and research* (pp. 890–899). Chicago: Rand McNally.

Hollander, E. P., and Julian, J. W. (1969). Contemporary trends in the analysis of leadership processes. *Psychological Bulletin, 71,* 387–397.

Hollander, E. P., and Julian, J. W. (1970). Studies in leader legitimacy, influence, and innovation. In L. L. Berkowitz (Ed.), *Advances in experimental social psychology* (Vol. 5, pp. 33–69). New York: Academic Press.

Hollander, E. P., and Julian, J. W. (1978). A further look at leader legitimacy, influence, and innovation. In L. Berkowitz (Ed.), *Group processes* (pp. 153–165). New York: Academic Press.

Hollander, E. P., and Kelly, D. R. (1990). Rewards from leaders as perceived by followers. Paper presented at the Eastern Psychological Association, Philadelphia, PA (March 30).

Hollander, E. P., and Kelly, D. R. (1992). Appraising relational qualities of leadership and followership. Paper presented at the 25th International Congress of Psychology, Brussels, Belgium (July 24).

Hollander, E. P., and Offermann, L. (1990). Power and leadership in organizations: Relationships in transition. *American Psychologist, 45,* 179–189.

Hollander, E. P., and Webb, W. B. (1955). Leadership, followership, and friendship: An analysis of peer nominations. *Journal of Abnormal and Social Psychology, 50,* 163–167.

Hollander, E. P., Fallon, B. J., and Edwards, M. T. (1977). Some aspects of influence and acceptability for appointed and elected group leaders. *Journal of Psychology, 95,* 289–296.

Hollander, E. P., Julian, J. W., and Sorrentino, R. M. (1969). *The leader's sense of constructive deviation.* ONR Technical Report No. 12. Buffalo: State University of New York Psychology Department. Reported in Hollander and Julian (1970), above.

Homans, G. C. (1961). *Social behavior: Its elementary forms.* New York: Harcourt, Brace and World.

House, R. J. (1971). A path-goal theory of leader effectiveness. *Administrative Science Quarterly, 16,* 321–338.

House, R. J. (1977). A 1976 theory of charismatic leadership. In J. G. Hunt and L. L. Larson (Eds.), *Leadership: The cutting edge*. Carbondale: Southern Illinois University Press.

House, R. J., and Mitchell, T. R. (1974). Path-goal theory of leadership. *Journal of Contemporary Business, 3*(4), 81–97.

Howard, A., and Bray, D. (1988). *Managerial lives in transition: Advancing age and changing times*. New York: Dorsey.

Jacobs, T. O. (1970). *Leadership and exchange in formal organizations*. Alexandria, VA: Human Resources Research Organization.

Jacobs, T. O., and Jaques, E. (1987). Leadership in complex systems. In J. Zeidner (Ed.), *Human productivity enhancement* (pp. 7–65). New York: Praeger.

Janis, I. (1972). *Victims of groupthink: A psychological study of foreign policy decisions and fiascos*. Boston: Houghton Mifflin.

Janis, I. (1989). *Crucial decisions: Leadership in policymaking and crisis management*. New York: Free Press.

Jervis, R. (1976). *Perception and misperception in international politics*. Princeton: Princeton University Press.

Katz, D., and Kahn, R. L. (1978). *The social psychology of organizations*, 2nd ed. New York: Wiley.

Kelley, R. E. (1988). In praise of followers. *Harvard Business Review* (Nov.–Dec.), *88*(6), 142–148.

Kouzes, J. M., and Posner, B. Z. (1987). *The leadership challenge: How to get extraordinary things done in organizations*. San Francisco: Jossey-Bass.

Kraut, A. I., Pedigo, P. R., McKenna, D. D., and Dunnette, M. D. (1989). The role of the manager: What's really important in different management jobs? *Academy of Management Executive, 3*(4), 286–293.

Levinson, H., and Rosenthal, S. (1984). *CEO: Corporate leadership in action*. New York: Basic Books.

Liden, R. C., and Graen, G. (1980). Generalizability of the vertical dyad linkage model of leadership. *Academy of Management Journal, 23*, 451–465.

Lord, R. G., and Maher, K. J. (1990). Leadership perceptions and leadership performance: Two distinct but interdependent processes. In J. Carroll (Ed.), *Advances in applied social psychology: Business settings* (Vol. 4, pp. 129–154). Hillsdale, NJ: Erlbaum.

Lord, R. G., DeVader, C. L., and Alliger, G. M. (1986). A meta-analysis of the relation between personality traits and leadership perceptions: An application of validity generalization procedures. *Journal of Applied Psychology, 71*, 402–409.

McCall, M. W., and Lombardo, M. M., and Morrison, A. M. (1988). *The lessons of experience*. Lexington, MA: Lexington Books.

Mitchell, T. R., Green, S. G., and Wood, R. E. (1981). An attributional model of leadership and the poor-performing subordinate: Development and validation. In B. Shaw and L. Cummings (Eds.), *Research in organizational behavior* (Vol. 3, pp. 197–234). Greenwich, CT: JAI Press.

Meindl, J. R., and Ehrlich, S. B. (1987). The romance of leadership and the evaluation of organizational performance. *Academy of Management Journal, 30,* 90–109.

Nemeth, C., and Wachtler, J. (1983). Creative problem solving as a result of majority vs. minority influence. *European Journal of Social Psychology, 13,* 45–55.

Pfeffer, J. (1977). The ambiguity of leadership. In M. W. McCall, Jr., and M. M. Lombardo (Eds.), *Leadership: Where else can we go?* Durham, NC: Duke University Press.

Post, J. M. (1986). Narcissism and the charismatic leader-follower relationship. *Political Psychology, 7,* 675–688.

Read, P. B. (1974). Source of authority and the legitimation of leadership in small groups. *Sociometry, 37,* 189–204.

Ridgeway, C. L. (1981). Nonconformity, competence, and influence in groups: A test of two theories. *American Sociological Review, 46,* 333–347.

Rush, M. C., Thomas, J. C., and Lord, R. G. (1977). Implicit leadership theory: A potential threat to the internal validity of leader behavior questionnaires. *Organizational Behavior and Human Performance, 20,* 93–110.

Sanford, F. (1950). *Authoritarianism and leadership.* Philadelphia: Institute for Research in Human Relations.

Snyder, R. C., Bruck, H. W., and Sapin, B. (1962). *Foreign policy decision-making: An approach to the study of international politics.* New York: Free Press.

Sorrentino, R. M., and Boutillier, R. G. (1975). The effect of quantity and quality of verbal interaction on ratings of leadership ability. *Journal of Experimental Social Psychology, 11,* 403–411.

Stewart, R. (1982). *Choices for the manager.* Englewood Cliffs, NJ: Prentice-Hall.

Torrance, E. P. (1955). Some consequences of power differences in permanent and temporary three-man groups. In P. Hare, E. F. Borgatta, and R. F. Bales (Eds.), *Small groups* (pp. 482–492). New York: Knopf.

Wahrman, R., and Pugh, M. D. (1974). Sex, nonconformity and influence. *Sociometry, 37,* 137–147.

Weber, M. (1921). The sociology of charismatic authority. Republished in translation (1946) in H. H. Gerth and C. W. Mills (Transl., Eds.), *From Max Weber: Essays in sociology* (pp. 245–252). New York: Oxford University Press.

Yammarino, R., and Bass, B. M. (1990). Long term forecasting of transformational leadership and its effects among Naval Officers: Some preliminary findings. In K. E. Clark and M. B. Clark (Eds.), *Measures of leadership.* West Orange, NJ: Leadership Library of America, pp. 151–169.

3

Transformational Leadership: A Response to Critiques

Bernard M. Bass and Bruce J. Avolio
Center for Leadership Studies
State University of New York at Binghamton

INTRODUCTION

For 40 years Fred Fiedler (1983) has had to battle the critics with rebuttals, arguments, and copious empirical studies. The least preferred coworker (LPC) score has survived and been revised and improved, "bloody but unbowed." As a consequence of these ongoing debates, a great deal has been learned about the impact of situational factors on the leadership influence process. Through criticism and rebuttal, alternative models and emphases have emerged, including Fred Fiedler's own work on cognitive resource theory (Fiedler, 1986).

In the 1990s, a new frontier for debate is emerging, to which we hope to offer some direction in this chapter. This new frontier deals with the development of transformational leadership theory and its measurement.

It is a little over a decade since Burns's (1978) seminal book on leadership and only six years since the appearance of *Leadership and performance beyond expectations* (Bass, 1985), which presented preliminary measurement scales and quantitative analyses of a factor analytic model of transformational and transactional leadership. The first published journal article using an early version of the multifactor leadership questionnaire (MLQ) previewed in Bass (1985), also appeared in 1985 (Singer, 1985).

Our intention here is to try to emulate Fiedler by pointing to the strawmen that have accompanied the legitimate criticisms of transformational and transactional leadership theory, as well as indicate the facts that have been gathered that may dispel at least some of the misconceptions regarding this new model of leadership, and its measurement. At the same time, we will point to criticisms that we think are valid and, where feasible, are sources of needed research. We are confident that at the end of this discussion, the doors to a new way of thinking regarding leadership will remain open to further inquiry and important discoveries.

EMERGENCE OF THE CONCEPT AND THEORY OF TRANSFORMATIONAL LEADERSHIP

The conceptualization of transformational leadership by Downton (1973) and Burns (1978) stimulated interest in understanding leadership influence processes that went beyond transactions based on consideration and initiation of structure (Avolio and Bass, 1988; Bass and Avolio, 1990a). Initiation and consideration were not sufficient to explain the full range of leadership behaviors commonly associated with the best and also the worst leaders (Seltzer and Bass, 1990).

In the 9 years between the publication of the second and third editions of the *Bass & Stogdill's Handbook of Leadership* in 1981 and 1990 (Bass, 1990a), interest and research in transformational leadership boomed. In 1981, Bass presented some commentary and two pages of needed research on transformational leadership. In 1990, well over a hundred pages of research results were reviewed on the subject. Current work on operationalizing and measuring the higher-order construct of transformational leadership[1] and predicting a wide range of criteria from absenteeism rates of prison inmates (Crookall, 1989) to performance in the military (Yammarino and Bass, 1990a), or industry (Hater and Bass, 1988), has produced a rather long list of findings in a relatively short period of time (e.g., Bass and Avolio, 1990a, pp. 26–28).

[1]The term "higher-order construct" is used here to represent a general construct or factor of transformational leadership that is composed of individual factors that are conceptually distinct, such as intellectual stimulation and individualized consideration, but nevertheless, may be intercorrelated.

A MODEL OF TRANSFORMATIONAL AND TRANSACTIONAL LEADERSHIP

A range of seven factors appears in most of our work, including factors of laissez-faire through to charismatic leadership. But, as noted below, there may also be two additional factors that have been uncovered since the original conceptualization of the model back in 1985. These two factors represent a finer distinction concerning behaviors associated with management-by-exception and contingent reward leadership.

Looking back to 1985, based on a higher-order factor analysis of an earlier version of the MLQ, seven factors representing laissez-faire and transactional and transformational leadership were categorized into a higher-order factor representing *active* and *passive* leadership. However, partitioning these leadership factors into active and passive categories should not negate the theoretical relevance or significance of any of the seven factors constituting the model; rather, it simply defines more precisely these respective constructs. Moreover, basing this range of leadership on these factors, does not represent a new two-factor theory of leadership, or an old one dressed in new form; rather, it helps to define the range of leadership behaviors commonly observed by followers, namely, very active through very inactive leaders.

A common problem with leadership research is that one new theory often is substituted for an "older" theory that has fallen into disfavor. Rather than build on earlier theories, there is a tendency to discount them for the sake of introducing a "new way of thinking." We disagree with this strategy and in fact, the model that we have tested over the last 8 years incorporates essential constructs from exchange theories of leadership, which have dominated leadership research for the last 40 years. The model also includes constructs that we associate with transformational leadership, including charisma and inspirational motivation. The seven primary factors of this model of leadership are described below.

Transformational Leadership Factors

Factor 1: Charisma (idealized influence) Generally defined with respect to follower reactions to the leader as well as to the leader's behavior. Followers identify with and emulate these leaders, who are trusted and seen as having an attainable mission and vision. Such leaders are thoroughly respected, have much referent power, hold high standards, and set challenging goals for their followers. Sample item: "Has my trust in his or her ability to overcome any obstacle."

Factor 2: Inspirational motivation May or may not overlap with charismatic leadership, depending on the extent to which followers seek to identify with the leader. Provides symbols and simplified emotional appeals to increase awareness and understanding of mutually desired goals. Sample item: "Uses symbols and images to focus our efforts."

Factor 3: Intellectual stimulation Encourages followers to question their own way of doing things or to break with the past. Followers are supported for questioning their own values, beliefs, and expectations, as well as those of the leader and organization. Followers are also supported for thinking on their own, addressing challenges, and considering creative ways to develop themselves. Sample item: "Enables me to think about old problems in new ways."

Factor 4: Individualized consideration Followers are treated differently but equitably on a one-to-one basis. Not only are the maturity of their needs raised, but their means for more effectively addressing goals and challenges are dealt with. With individualized consideration, assignments are delegated to followers to provide learning opportunities. Sample item: "Coaches me if I need it."

Transactional Leadership Factors

Factor 5: Contingent reward Involves a positively reinforcing interaction between leader and follower that emphasizes an exchange (e.g., the leader provides appropriate rewards when followers meet agreed on objectives). Emphasis is on facilitating the achievement of objectives agreed to by followers. Their needs are identified, and then linked both to what the leader expects to accomplish and to rewards for the followers if objectives are met. Sample item: "Makes sure there is close agreement between what he or she expects me to do and what I can get from him or her for my effort."

Factor 6: Management-by-exception Only when things go wrong will the leader intervene to make some correction. Leaders may remain passive until problems emerge that need correcting, or they may arrange to more actively monitor the performance of followers so as to intervene when followers make mistakes. Generally, the modes of reinforcement are correction criticism, negative feedback, and negative contingent reinforcement, rather than the positive reinforcement used with contingent reward leadership. Punishment and discipline are likely to be evidence of management-by-exception. Sample item: "Takes action only when a mistake has occurred."

The Nonleadership Factor

Factor 7: Laissez-faire Leadership is absent. Intervention by the nominal leader is avoided. With laissez-faire (avoiding) leadership, there are generally neither transactions nor agreements with followers. Decisions are often delayed; feedback, rewards, and involvement are absent; and there is no attempt to motivate followers or to recognize and satisfy their needs. Sample item: "Doesn't tell me where he or she stands on issues."

A key concept of this model of leadership involves what Bass (1985) referred to as the "augmentation effect." The augmentation effect predicts that by measuring transformational leadership behaviors we can achieve a higher level of precision in predicting extra levels of effort and other relevant criteria, than if we simply rely on previous models of transactional leadership. In the same vein, transformational leadership theory can be viewed as building on earlier theories of leadership in a constructive and integrative manner to explain more fully the range of behaviors and outcomes impacted by various styles of leadership.

Our research has indicated that a more optimal profile of leadership is represented by a higher frequency of occurrence of behaviors associated with active transactional leadership (contingent reward) and transformational leadership—labeled the four *I*s: *i*dealized influence or charisma, *i*nspirational motivation, *i*ntellectual stimulation, and *i*ndividualized consideration. Thus leaders who display these behaviors more frequently are also generally viewed as more effective based on ratings collected from the same source, as well as in situations where effectiveness data were collected from an independent source (e.g., Howell and Avolio, 1991).

In contrast, individual leaders who are inactive and laissez-faire or who focus on correcting followers predominantly after the fact, tend to produce less than desirable results, lower follower motivation, and are seen by followers as ineffective leaders. Emphasizing the more positive qualities associated with contingent reward leadership, produces higher levels of effectiveness with even higher performance achieved when leaders are also transformational (i.e., augmented by transformational leadership). In a more "optimal" leadership profile, proactive and active leadership behaviors are more frequently observed; reactive and passive behaviors are less frequent. So in the optimal profile, the leader takes corrective action when needed and may maintain a "hands-off" approach to certain problems and/or situations, but such leader behavior is less frequent than in the suboptimal profile.

The factors represented in the model of transactional and transformational leadership described above, have been generalized across a wide variety of organizations (Hicks, 1990), cultures (e.g., Bass and Yokochi, 1991), and levels within organizations (e.g., Yammarino and Bass, 1990b). Transactional and transformational leadership has been observed in varying degrees at all organizational levels of management (Bass, 1990a; Yammarino and Bass, 1990b), in organizations involved in health (Bryant, 1990; Gottlieb, 1990), industry (Ruggiero, 1989; Hater and Bass, 1988), education (Cowen, 1990; Koh, 1990), government (Crookall, 1989), religious institutions (Onnen, 1987), and the military (Boyd, 1988; O'Keefe, 1989; Curphy, 1992; Salter, 1989; Yammarino and Bass, 1990a).

Although much that has been written about transformational leadership (Burns, 1978; Bennis and Nanus, 1985; Tichy and Devanna, 1985), has concentrated on leaders at the top of organizations and movements, we have been able to observe and measure transformational leadership at all levels, even at the lowest organizational levels of supervision and among nonsupervisory project leaders, as well as among student leaders. However, even though transformational leadership behavior has been observed at lower organizational levels, it is likely to occur more frequently at the highest organizational levels.

In the following section, and for the remainder of this chapter, we will address what we consider to be 10 important points of contention regarding transformational leadership theory. Undoubtedly, there are other arguments that could be added to this list; nevertheless, we see these 10 as among the most significant concerns.

THE 10 ARGUMENTS

The 10 arguments are presented below to help clarify where matters stand at present. These arguments concern the conceptualization of transformational and transactional leadership, the measurement of their respective factors, how the factors should and do relate to various measures of performance, how this framework of leadership builds on and differs from earlier models of leadership, and whether transformational leadership is trainable. Since much research is currently in progress, and much more is needed, what we discuss here may be appropriately subject to change as new findings and revelations emerge. We begin with criticisms and our responses concerning methods, and then consider arguments about content. The arguments are stated in the affirmative in support of where we stand on each issue and either point to supportive evidence, or indicate where such evidence awaits further research.

1. Questionnaires/Surveys Are Being Used Appropriately[2]

When does one judge that a line of investigation is ready for the use of survey questionnaires? What alternative methods of investigation are more appropriate at the early stages of developing a theoretical model? Should it not rather be asked whether the items and scales of the questionnaire have content, predictive, and construct validity? Should not it be asked whether there is a theory and model underlying the scale construction or whether appropriate means have been employed to create the questionnaires? While we admit that there is much more to be done, we've attempted to systematically answer some of the critical questions regarding the primary instrument we have used to measure the leadership factors described above (see Bass and Avolio, 1989, 1990a). Furthermore, and contrary to some critics' position, we've done considerably more in our line of investigation than depend exclusively on survey questionnaires to measure the various factors comprising the model. However, much of this evidence has appeared so far only in test and training manuals (Avolio and Bass, 1991a) and unpublished technical reports (e.g., Bass and Avolio, 1991).

To begin at the beginning, our very first collection was of qualitative data in 1980. We asked 70 South African senior executives informally, and in open-ended fashion, if anyone had ever behaved toward them like a transformational leader, as generally described by Burns (1978). Specifically, they were asked if there had been individuals in their past who had raised their awareness to broader and more important goals; moved them toward higher-level motives [on Maslow's (1954) scale]; or aroused them to transcend their own self-interests for the good of their group, organization, or society. If so, what did this influential person do to effect such changes? The reactions of these executives and a follow-up independent questionnaire sample of U.S. Army colonels describing their superiors were a preliminary source of our initial questionnaire items (Bass, 1985). Moreover, one executive's comment that a transformational leader had moved him to go far beyond his initial expectations of what he could accomplish sparked our thinking regarding the need for a model of leadership that went beyond a simple exchange paradigm of rewards for effort provided to one that emphasized the greater impact of transformational leadership.

In addition to our earlier work, we have systematically collected critical incidents and behaviors illustrative of each factor in the model from a variety of organizations using individual and group interviews with sam-

[2]See Hunt (1991), Smith and Peterson (1988), and Yukl (1989) for the substantive criticism on this issue.

ples of senior and junior executives. In one setting, we asked senior managers to identify factors they associated with leadership. Similarly, other managers have been asked to generate behaviors and incidents representing either effective or ineffective leaders. Then, these same managers, as well as independent samples, produced behaviors and incidents representing each of the factors that emerged earlier. In other settings, we have provided the factors and have asked managers to identify specific behaviors that would represent each factor, partitioning those behaviors into effective and ineffective leadership. In still other settings, we have provided brief definitions of transformational and transactional leadership asking managers whether they have met such leaders and if so, to list the behaviors those leaders exhibited. Over time, and in a number of independent samples, we have generated a reliable list of behaviors cor-

Table 3.1

Behavioral Indicators of Transformational Leadership[a]

Individualized consideration	
Recognizes individual strengths and weaknesses	Enlarges individual discretion commensurate with ability and needs
Shows interest in the well-being of others	Encourages a two-way exchange of views
Assigns projects based on individual ability and needs	Promotes self-development
Inspirational motivation	
Convinces followers that they have the ability to achieve levels of performance beyond what they felt was possible	Raises expectations by clarifying the challenges
Sets an example for others to strive for	Thinks ahead to take advantage of unforeseen opportunities
Presents an optimistic and attainable view of the future	Provides meaning for actions
Intellectual stimulation	
Encourages followers to reexamine their assumptions	Creates a "readiness" for changes in thinking
Takes past examples and applies to current problems	Creates a "holistic" picture that incorporates different views of a problem
Encourages followers to revisit problems	Puts forth or listens to seemingly foolish ideas
Idealized influence	
Transmits a sense of joint mission and ownership	Addresses crises "head on"
Expresses dedication to followers	Eases group tension in critical times
Appeals to the hopes and desires of followers	Sacrifices self-gain for the gain or others

[a]Collected by interviews with managers in a large European multinational firm.

responding to the factors in the model specified above, which have been included in various forms of the MLQ. As an example, Table 3.1 presents a list of such reported intellectually stimulating, inspirational, and individually considerate behaviors generated by senior managers who were asked to identify behaviors associated with transformational leadership.

Bass and Yokochi (1991) reported on data collected from 2-hour interviews with chief executive officers from 17 of the largest firms in Japan. Transformational and charismatic leadership behaviors were observed in these CEOs, although there were some cultural differences in the specific qualifications needed by leaders in Japanese firms, which places a high premium on modesty. Nevertheless, in-depth interviews with samples of the CEOs, coupled with ratings produced by followers using the MLQ, unearthed the primary leadership factors that constitute the MLQ and that have been found elsewhere. More or most successful and effective leadership was associated both qualitatively and quantitatively with transformational and active transactional leadership behavior.

2. Some Attributions and Effects on Followers Are Being Measured, but Much Is Description of Leadership Behavior

The standard MLQ survey (Form 5R) measures seven leadership factors. In six of the scales, most of the items are behaviors, according to a consensus of six expert judges trained in organizational behavior. In the scale that assesses charismatic leadership (or idealized influence), most of the items are attributions since this factor represents, in part, how frequently followers identify with their leader. Nevertheless, the correlation between charismatic attribution items, "Makes me proud to be associated with that person" and charismatic behavioral items, such as "communicates a sense of mission" are as high as the items' reliabilities (Howell and Avolio, 1991). Furthermore, an experimental MLQ Form 10 has been developed, which according to eight independent expert judges trained in organizational behavior, contains only behavioral items for each of the constructs including charisma, such as "transmits a sense of mission" rather than "makes me feel proud to be associated with him or her." The MLQ Form 10 factor structure was tested by Howell and Avolio (1991) using partial least-squares analysis, a rigorous analytic strategy, in two independent samples of approximately 250 managers. The factor structure that was reported by Bass (1985), Hater and Bass (1988), and now in several other investigations, emerged as before with discriminately valid dimensions. Results regarding the factor structure paralleled those found previously with MLQ Form 5R, which includes items in the charisma scale that represent attributions, or impact of leadership.

Similar to earlier work reported by Hater and Bass (1988) and Waldman et al. (1990), who used part or all of MLQ Form 5R, Avolio and Howell (1992) also found using Form 10 that transformational leadership (measured exclusively in terms of behaviors) augmented transactional leadership in predicting business unit performance over a one-year time interval. Corroborating earlier factor analytic results, the primary factors of transformational and transactional leadership emerged from the partial least-squares (PLS) analysis. Difficulty however, arises in establishing discriminant validity for each of the four transformational factors. These four factors have been typically correlated with each other in the .5–.8 range. A similar problem emerged in the Howell and Avolio investigation, although using PLS, three discriminately valid scales were produced: charisma, intellectual stimulation, and individualized consideration. Furthermore, the factors and scales are conceptually distinguishable from each other. More will be said about this problem later on in this chapter.

Charisma is undoubtedly both a behavior and an attribution for it requires particular follower emotional reactions to the leader to be identified as such. We have no quarrel with this operational definition of charisma. Nor do we necessarily disagree with the work of Lord and his associates regarding the effects of implicit leadership theories, and their impact on survey ratings (see Lord et al., 1984). Again, to be considered charismatic, certain behavior may have to be observed and certain attributions about other behaviors which may not have been observed may be involved, perhaps partly because of the implicit theories of leadership. Where we do disagree is with those authors who insist that charismatic leadership can only be assessed by measuring behaviors, rather than considering attributions and impact. We agree with House et al. (1991) that there is a need to differentiate "attributed" from "behavioral" charisma.

It should suffice to say that future research must work toward disentangling the contribution of behaviors, attributions, and implicit theories to the perception individuals have of effective leadership. Also, we would include the work of Meindl and his colleagues, and Binning and Lord (1980), as we argue that we also need to tease out the effects of performance and its impact on individual perceptions of leadership. If all there is to leadership is being liked or disliked and then attributing behaviors all of which fall under a single rubric of effective and ineffective leadership, then why do we find the convergent and divergent validities among the varieties of behaviors that are conceptually distinct from each other? Popularity does correlate with various factors of leadership but so does a host of other variables that increase or decrease their frequencies of occurrence.

From the above discussion, we can conclude that transformational leadership is an observable phenomenon with distinctive and salient features. More importantly, one managerial group after another has identified transformational leadership and leaders as being highly desirable figures and role models. The positive halo associated with such leaders may, in part, contribute to the difficulty in separating out each of the respective factors comprising transformational leadership. What has not been surprising is that followers' ideal conceptions of leaders correspond markedly to transformational leadership, and correlate highly with the composite list of traits that Lord et al. (1984) referred to as those of the prototypical superordinate leader. In other words, when people are asked to describe their "ideal" leader, they tend to describe persons who exhibit a lot of transformational leadership behaviors. Of course, we agree that there is some degree of error associated with such general categorizations. Yet, we have conducted routinely a training exercise in which trainees present their "ideal" leader—someone who has had a profound impact on them in their respective careers or life-span development. Their ideal leader is commonly ascribed by the hundreds of trainees who have completed this exercise the attributes and behaviors we associate with transformational and constructive transactional leadership and in some instances, corrective transactional leadership but never laissez-faire leadership.

It seems premature to immediately discount these results as attributional error. At this point, we may want to ask why the prototypical leader has many attributes and behaviors that have been linked to transformational leadership. To address this issue future research should focus on such questions such as what sort of developmental experiences, critical life events, early role models, and children's stories contributed to this prototype. Understanding how leadership prototypes emerge, and whether they generalize across cohorts seems much more interesting and worthwhile than simply attributing the high intercorrelation among the transformational leadership factors to measurement error.

3. The Factor Structure Underlying the MLQ Is Empirically Supportable

The original factor analyses of the MLQ were completed using two samples of a total of 196 U.S. Army colonels, based on their responses to 73 items about their superiors. A higher-order factor analysis disclosed two clusters of factors. An active higher-order dimension included charisma, inspirational motivation, individualized consideration, intellectual stimulation, and contingent reward. Management-by-exception (MBE) and laissez-faire leadership were identified by means of a passive dimension of leadership (Bass, 1985). Hater and Bass (1988) collected data on items representing five of the seven factors, producing support for the same factor structure, except Hater and Bass differentiated on active and passive forms of MBE.

Adding to this, a similar factor structure emerged (Waldman et al., 1987) from a large sample of industrial and military leaders described by their subordinates. Also generally supportive of the factor structure were analyses by Hoover (1987) and more recently by Koh (1990). However, a single transformational factor instead of four emerged in an unpublished U.S. Air Force officer study, in an unpublished analysis for U.S. Naval officers, and in the study by Koh (1990) with Singaporean principals.

As noted earlier, the multicollinearity which emerged among the transformational scales led Howell and Avolio (1991) to use a PLS analysis instead of the traditional principal components factor analysis. Their analysis for approximately 250 Canadian managers used Forms 10A and 10B versions of the MLQ, which contain about half the items of MLQ Form 5R plus additional behavioral items generated from research and training activities conducted since 1986.

In general, the PLS analyses confirmed much of the factor structure that has been employed to date. Charisma, individualized consideration, and intellectual stimulation were statistically distinguishable factors of transformational leadership. Consistent with Yammarino and Bass's (1990a) study of naval officers, contingent reward split into two factors: negotiates exchanges (or promises) and rewards. With contingent negotiations or rewards, the leader provides recognition for a job well done. Contingent recognition represents a higher-level transaction in that follower needs are considered by the leader. With a lower-level exchange, the leader takes no particular notice of the needs of each individual follower. The leader either simply clarifies what needs to be done and who will do it, or points out the desired behavior and provides rewards for doing it. In this instance, the leader exhibits what Bass (1960) referred to as control but not power to influence. Here, the leader may promise or provide rewards which are of no interest to the follower.

The two-level distinction regarding contingent reward leadership is useful in that contingent recognition is closer to what we consider individualized consideration: recognition of the individual accomplishments of followers. However, we can also view contingent reward as a lower-order transaction, where the only consideration is on what needs to be done, rather than on the individual who is being asked to do the work. The conceptual differences between contingent recognition and individualized consideration is that transformational leaders not only recognize the needs of their followers but also work to elevate those needs. In all, contingent reward comes close to being transformational and highly effective when it involves growth needs of followers and they acknowledge interest in such needs. Contingent rewards can fall to zero correlation with the transformational scales and effectiveness, and fail as an attempted transaction when the leader cannot deliver on his or her promises and has no control of what followers see as rewarding to them.

Hoover (1987) and Yammarino and Bass (1990a) also found that management-by-exception can be split into an active and a passive factor. The active manager arranges to monitor and correct deviations; the passive manager waits for them to occur before taking corrective action. We have found passive MBE to be negatively correlated with various measures of effectiveness, while active MBE has a near zero, and sometimes low but positive significant relationship with effectiveness.

An unpublished oblique factor analytic solution of Navy officer data collected by Yammarino and Bass supported the independence of contingent reward, active and passive MBE, and laissez-faire leadership, but similar to analyses with some industrial samples, only a single transformational factor emerged of items representing charisma, inspirational motivation, intellectual stimulation and individualized consideration.

Elsewhere, Bass (1974) proposed that the rigorousness of measurement in its relation to theory depends on where one is in the time-line of investigation. Rigor and precision are demanded late in the time-line; early on, it makes sense to "hang loose." Given the recency of its conception and empirical data gathering about it, the theoretical factor structure of transformational leadership theory cannot be fully confirmed with complete confidence from the empirical work done so far. This neither negates the theory nor the way it is modeled and measured. Theory is generally more definite, depending mainly on the adequacy of its assumptions and logic, than the measures available to test the theory. Atoms, X rays, and quarks were discussed and conceptualized long before they could be observed and accurately measured. Theories can evolve and be further refined to better fit the data even if measures lag behind, which they often do. But it is in its eventual evolvement that theories lead to the advancement of our understanding and better ways to find confirmatory reliable and valid measurements.

In sum, we conclude that the original factor structure presented by Bass (1985) does still represent conceptually and in many instances empirically, the factors of transformational, transactional, and laissez-faire leadership. But already we see that the structure is more complex than originally proposed. Further refinements are in the offing.

4. Charisma and Transformational Leadership Are Not Synonymous

Paralleling the surge of interest in transformational leadership, there has been a growing amount of attention directed to modeling and measuring charismatic leadership beginning with House's (1977) theoretical formulation of charisma. As Bass (1985) reported, the factor analysis of the original

MLQ data sets indicated that the construct of charisma accounted for the largest amount of variance in ratings associated with transformational leadership. The three other transformational factors tend to correlate more highly with charisma than each other as if it were a more general factor. However, the three additional transformational factors, although intercorrelated with charisma, are conceptually distinct from charisma. The intellectually stimulating leader might or might not be charismatic but could still question followers' assumptions and encourage followers to consider old problems in new ways. The inspirational leader can provide meaning, and a sense of mission and excitement without being the target of identification like the charismatic leader. In a similar vein, the individually considerate leader could be transformational without being charismatic by attending to the differential developmental needs of his or her followers.

One could use a strict definition of a transformational leader, and require that each factor be represented in the behaviors exhibited by the leader. In most cases, leaders who do exhibit transformational leadership behaviors on one factor, do so for all four factors in varying degrees. Yet, there are instances where a leader has been intellectually stimulating, but not transformational in terms of the remaining factors. For instance, Lyndon Johnson emphasized his "just plain folks" background and ability, yet managed to propose and succeed with much more legislative and administrative actions than did John F. Kennedy. Kennedy surrounded himself with the "best and the brightest," and was generally perceived as much more highly gifted as a person, and with whom the American public formed a strong, deep, emotional attachment. The depression that gripped the country when Kennedy was assassinated illustrated the tendency of followers to emotionally identify with this charismatic leader. Such emotional attraction and identification were absent in the case of Lyndon Johnson. Johnson could and did inspire by setting out clear goals and making them meaningful through his Great Society agenda. He simplified ideologies and used colorful language and heavy doses of transactional contingent reinforcement. Both Kennedy and Johnson were in their own ways transformational, yet Kennedy has been seen as far more charismatic than Johnson. Both were highly transactional as well. It should suffice to say that each factor, particularly charisma, is worth studying in its own right; moreover, given the impact of implicit theories (Lord et al., 1984) and attributions, much more work is required in refining each respective construct and how they are measured. Measuring all facets of charisma as a most powerful, explanatory variable will challenge us for years to come (Bass, 1988a).

To date, most research examining transformational leadership has examined charisma. Some studies, however, have focused exclusively on the construct of charisma, testing basic propositions delineated in House's (1977) theory of charisma. The samples of leaders included in this body of research have covered a broad range such as CEOs (Conger, 1989), U.S. presidents (House et al., 1991), trained actors (Howell and Frost, 1988), leaders of social movements (Trice and Beyer, 1986), educators (Roberts, 1986), and third world leaders (Willner, 1968).

From both practical and theoretical perspectives, the differentiation of charisma along continua such as intentions, values, and motives (Howell, 1988) has helped to advance our overall understanding and measurement of this construct, and its link with transformational leadership. Still much remains to be done regarding how to measure charisma with greater accuracy, and how such charismatic leaders develop (Avolio and Gibbons, 1988; Gardner and Avolio, 1991; Kuhnert and Lewis, 1987). The same is true for transformational leadership in which some communalities and some differences are likely to emerge as we gather more data.

Although the accomplishments over the last decade have been significant with respect to broadening the boundaries of leadership research, all of this work has not been without appropriate criticism, nor have all the answers to key questions been satisfactorily resolved (Hunt, 1991; Smith and Peterson, 1988; Yukl, 1989). Criticism and debate about their operational definitions and how they are measured are essential to the growth and understanding of these complex concepts. Our position is that we must be willing to question old assumptions and procedures to determine whether they still meet assessment, development, and research needs as we expand our notions of what constitutes leadership.

5. Individualized Consideration Is Not a Reincarnation of the Consideration Scale of the Leader Behavior Description Questionnaire (LBDQ)

Although some critics jumped to conclude that consideration and individualized consideration were synonymous (Hunt, 1991), individualized consideration conceptually builds on two aspects of behavior, individualization among followers (e.g., "gives personal attention to those who seem neglected") and development of followers (e.g., "gets me to look at problems as learning opportunities"). The LBDQ consideration scale was concerned with being a good guy or gal (e.g., "He is friendly and approachable"). Perhaps, use of the term "consideration," in individualized consideration, may have resulted in some of the confusion regarding this factor. And the two variables are correlated as noted in a study by Seltzer and Bass (1990), who found a correlation of .69 between LBDQ consideration and MLQ individualized consideration. Empirically there is overlap between the two measures, some of which may be due to measurement error, halo effect, and single-source variance. As we have just noted, conceptually there is an important distinction to be made between these two respective factors. The distinction becomes particularly important in management training and development, where one is attempting to convince trainees that simply being a "nice guy or gal," or more participative, is *not* necessarily displaying individualized consideration. The individualized aspects of consideration are knowing your followers' needs and raising them to more mature levels. Not at all included in LBDQ consideration, individualized consideration emphasizes the use of delegation to provide opportunities for each follower to self-actualize and to attain higher standards of moral development. Some leaders can be quite directive rather than participative in such actions.

The empirical distinction between LBDQ consideration and individualized consideration is increased by higher-level transactions associated with contingent reward leadership. Specifically, items which deal with giving recognition for work well done, often load highly on individualized consideration and the transactional factor of contingent reward. Our dilemma is that if, to increase factorial precision, we remove items in which the leader provides recognition for quality performance, we eliminate important leadership behavior. So far we have chosen to live with the overlap between individualized consideration and contingent reward leadership caused by items dealing with providing recognition to followers for work done.

6. Initiation of Structure and Consideration Cannot Conceptually and Empirically Account for Transformational and Transactional Leadership

In early attempts to publish our results we were challenged by referees with the question, "What is different about transformational leadership? Doesn't initiation of structure and consideration account for the same leadership behaviors?"

Howell and Frost's (1988) experiment with three styles of leadership—charisma, initiation of structure, and consideration—clearly pointed to the need to go beyond initiation of structure and consideration in leadership research. Howell and Frost found that while initiation of structure could maintain high worker productivity when work group norms supported such productivity, only charismatic leadership could maintain high productivity in the face of conflicting low-productivity norms.

Aside from the conceptual distinctions already addressed, Seltzer and Bass (1990) empirically demonstrated that while initiation of structure and consideration might substitute for transactional leadership, much additional variance in effectiveness was accounted for by transformational leadership. Again, qualitative interview data as well as questionnaire survey data revealed highly reliable differences among the conceptions of managers, project supervisors, CEOs, military officers, principals, and other administrators in the distinctions between transactional leadership, transformational leadership, consideration, and initiation of structure. There is clearly some overlap between these various constructs (e.g., all are active and constructive forms of leadership).

7. Transformational Leadership Can Be Either Directive or Participative, as Well as Democratic or Authoritarian, Elitist or Leveling

Critics have perceived transformational leadership to be elitist and antidemocratic. Indeed, particularly when dealing with charisma, Weber (1924/1947) and his successors (e.g., Trice and Beyer, 1986) emphasized the extent that the leader directed his or her dependent followers out of crises with radical solutions to deal with their problems. Again, inspirational leaders were seen to be highly directive in their means and methods. The intellectually stimulating leader challenged his or her followers, and the individually considerate leader could rise above the demands for equality from his or her followers to treat them differently according to their different needs for growth.

At the same time, such transformational leaders could share the building of visions and ideas that could be a democratic and collective enterprise. They could encourage follower participation in the change processes involved. In the same way, transactional leadership can be either directive or participative.

Table 3.2 illustrates formulaic statements illustrating that transformational and transactional leadership can be either directive or participative, democratic or authoritarian. We have found this theorization, not only useful, but essential to convincing trainees that transformational leadership is not a veiled attempt at resurrecting participative leadership. It can be participative, as well as more directive, in orientation (Avolio and Bass, 1991b) depending on situational and personal considerations.

8. Transformational Leadership Is Not Necessarily Synonymous with Effective Leadership; nor Is Transactional Leadership (Especially MBE) Synonymous with Ineffective Leadership

When both the effectiveness of performance/satisfaction with the leader and transactional/transformational leadership ratings are obtained from a single source, such as the leader's subordinates, a clear hierarchy of correlations results. The correlations with effectiveness and satisfaction typically range from .6 to .8 for transformational leadership (*usually highest for charisma*), .4 to .6 for contingent reward (*depending on whether it is promises or rewards*), −.3 to +.3 for MBE (*depending on whether it is passive or active*),

Table 3.2
Formulaic Illustrations of Participative and Directive Leadership That Are Transactional and Transformational

	Participative	Directive
Laissez-faire	"Whatever you think is the correct choice is OK with me."	"If my followers need answers to questions, let them find the answers themselves."
Transactional		
Management-by-exception (MBE)	"Let's develop the rules together that we will use to identify mistakes."	"These are the rules and this is how you have violated them."
Contingent reward	"Let's agree on what has to be done and how you will be rewarded if you achieve the objectives."	"If you achieve the objectives I've set, I will recognize your accomplishment with the following reward."
Transformational		
Individualized consideration	"What can we do as a group to give each other the necessary support to develop our capabilities."	"I will provide the support you need in your efforts to develop yourself in the job."
Intellectual stimulation	"Can we try to look at our assumptions as a group without being critical of each other's ideas until all assumptions have been listed?"	"You must reexamine the assumption that a cold fusion engine is a physical impossibility. Revisit this problem and question your assumption."
Inspirational motivation	"Let's work together to merge our aspirations and goals for the good of our group."	"You need to say to yourself that every day you are getting better. You must look at your progress and continue to build upon it over time."
Idealized influence (charisma)	"We can be a winning team because of our faith in each other. I need your support to achieve our mission."	"*Alea icta est*" (i.e., "I've made the decision to cross the Rubicon, so there's no going back.") "You must trust me and my direction to achieve what we have set out to do."

and −.3 to −.6 for laissez-faire leadership. Table 3.3 lists results obtained for a diverse group of target leaders, rated by immediate subordinates on the leadership and outcome measures.

In the many instances where ratings of leadership and effectiveness were obtained from a single source, the positive relationship between the four transformational leadership factors and rated effectiveness was shown to

Table 3.3

Correlations of MLQ Scores Related to the Effectiveness of the Organizations Led by the Described Leaders (Form 5 Supervisees)

	Leadership score							
	Transformational					Transaction		
Sample	*N*	CH	IL	IS	IC	CR	MBE	LF
U.S. Army officers	104	.85	NA	.47	.70	.41	.23	NA
New Zealand professionals and managers	45	.56	NA	.52	.62	.43	−.03	NA
World-class leaders, student raters	67	.58	NA	.34	.40	.21	−.17	NA
New Zealand educational administrators	23	.76	NA	.66	.63	.39	−.48	NA
Division heads, Fortune 500 high-tech firm	49	.72	NA	.44	.47	.15	.06	−.49
Indian professionals and managers	58	.59	.56	.54	.46	.35	.15	−.39
Project leaders, Fortune 500 high-tech firm	75	.66	.44	.55	.55	.48	.16	−.34
Religious ministers, parishioners	28	.61	NA	.52	.54	.17	.06	−.29
Vice presidents, Fortune 500 high-tech firm	9	.71	NA	.59	.53	.34	.07	−.45
Middle managers, Fortune 500 high-tech firm	38	.75	NA	.60	.66	.41	.07	−.41
Middle-level managers at Federal Express	26	.88	.79	.79	.79	.43	NA	NA
U.S. Junior Navy officers[a]	186	.87	.73	.74	.73	.48 (.66)[b]	.50 (.11)[c]	−.60
U.S. Senior Navy officers[a]	318	.83	NA	.72	.73	.48 (.60)[b]	.17 (.04)[c]	−.57
U.S. Army officers (NATO)	341	.72	NA	.61	.56	.25	.20	NA
Canadian field-grade Army officers	226	.53	NA	.38	.53	.09	.04	NA
German field-grade Army officers	167	.40	NA	.41	.38	.19	.25	NA
Japanese middle-level managers	132	.62	NA	.50	.51	.33	−.02	−.21

Note: All samples were collected independently from separate organizations.
[a]A parallel form for the MLQ was developed for use with the naval officer samples.
[b]Contingent reward was divided into two scales: promises and rewards (in parentheses).
[c]Management-by-exception was divided into two scales: active and passive (in parentheses).
Source: Bass, B. M., and Avolio, B. J. (1990). *Transformational leadership development: Manual for the multifactor leadership questionnaire.* Palo Alto, CA: Consulting Psychologist Press.

be inflated by single-source variance. Nevertheless, corrections for this inflation indicated that the hierarchical relationships although lowered, were still positive and significant. Thus, even after correcting for some of the presumed effects attributable to single-source bias or effects, the relationship of transformational and transactional leadership to effectiveness has been consistent with earlier predictions and the hierarchy of relationships noted earlier (Avolio et al., 1991).

A considerable number of investigations using objective criteria of performance and outcome measures have found the same pattern of leadership–outcome correlations reported with subjective measures of performance. Onnen (1987) reported that when Methodist ministers were more transformational versus transactional, church attendance and new church memberships were higher. Longshore (1988) found that with more transformational and less transactional leadership, groups led by U.S. Marine officers were more productive. Avolio et al. (1988) found that the more presidents of 27 simulated business firms were evaluated as transformational, the higher was the financial performance of their firms. Waldman and his associates have obtained parallel findings with survey and financial data collected from Fortune 500 firms (Waldman, personal communication). Bryant (1990) reported that nursing supervisors who were rated by their followers as being more transformational ran units with lower turnover rates.

Curphy (1992) similarly found, with a large sample of cadets from the Air Force Academy, that both transformational and transactional leadership had positive and strong relationships with performance indices that represented the need for interdependent effort among cadets. The relationship between leadership and performance was higher as the criterion data matured for cadet squadrons over a one-year interval. Curphy's results indicate that it may take some time for the leadership behaviors of squadron leaders to take effect on team performance.

Atwater et al. (1991) provided additional support for Curphy's results in a sample of cadets from a second military academy. Transformational leadership ratings were highly correlated ($r = .59, p < .01$) with camp performance grades collected 3 months after the collection of leadership measures. Yammarino and Bass (1990b) reported results indicating that junior officers seen by their followers as transformational were also evaluated independently by their superiors, as having higher cumulative fitness reports, and were more often given recommendations for early promotion. Clover (1989) reported that 40 U.S. Air Force officers, who were rated highly on transformational leadership were chosen by cadets significantly more often as role models than their nontransformational counterparts.

Nevertheless, some contradictory evidence has also surfaced in military settings complicating these interpretations. Atwater and Yammarino (1989) found that leaders rated by peers as transformational among midshipmen at Annapolis did not receive better performance appraisals from their superiors. For U.S., Canadian, and German Army officers in NATO, there was no increase, as would have been expected, in the mean transformational scores of junior on up to senior officers (Boyd, 1988). Yammarino and Bass (1990a) reached the same conclusion with naval officers.

Our findings regarding current patterns of leadership in the military may suggest that many top-level officers might have been promoted on the basis of their transactional abilities to work within the system. However, the military is undergoing some fundamental changes, which may result in a different type of leader emerging at the top. We may see more Norman Schwartzkopfs who display all of the transformational factors and less of those generals who only know how to "work the system" transactionally.

Even when predictions regarding objective performance outcomes support the model, we are still faced with plausible alternative cause-and-effect relationships. For instance, a possible explanation for Bryant's results with nursing units is that employees may have been more committed to units run by transformational leaders, as well more satisfied. In this vein, Avolio and Howell (1990) found that followers of transformational leaders were more committed to the goals of the unit and the leader than were followers of transactional leaders. An alternative explanation is that nursing units with lower turnover rates in Bryant's study may have had more resources or were less stressful places to work than other units. It will be important to separate out other potential mediating variables that might explain the pattern of results observed in this and other concurrent investigations.

Augmentation Effect. One of the fundamental propositions in Bass's (1985) model of transformational and transactional leadership is that transformational leadership will augment transactional in predicting individual and group effort and effectiveness of performance. The "augmentation hypothesis" has been tested in part by Hater and Bass (1988), Waldman et al. (1990), and most recently by Avolio and Howell (1992). In these three investigations, different subjective and objective performance criteria were used. Some depended on variables such as effectiveness as rated by followers who also provided the leadership ratings. Other analyses employed independently collected supervisory appraisals or business unit performance. In all three studies, using independent samples, the augmentation hypothesis was tested by first entering the transactional measures in a stepwise hierarchical regression analysis, followed by the transformational factors. In each case, transformational leadership added significantly to the prediction of performance, thus augmenting transactional leadership behaviors. Seltzer and Bass (1990) went one step further, substituting the LBDQ initiation and consideration scales for the MLQ transactional scales and achieved the same augmentation effect of transformational leadership.

The augmentation effect was tested only using the charisma scale by Waldman et al. (1990), while in the Hater and Bass (1988) investigation the test was completed indirectly, with three of the four transformational factors. However, in the Avolio and Howell (1992) study, all four transformational factors were included and perhaps most significantly, the performance data were collected approximately one year after the collection of leadership ratings. Hence, in their study the augmentation hypothesis was tested and validated over time, rather than concurrently as in the two earlier investigations.

Some New Avenues for Criterion-Based Research. Collectively, findings from the respective investigations reviewed in this section confirm that transformational leadership adds unique variance to transactional leadership in predicting criteria such as rated effectiveness, extra effort, satisfaction, supervisory appraisals, and unit performance. Although still limited to a rather small subset of criterion variables, the evidence to date indicates that viewing transformational leadership as an extension to transactionally based models of leadership is clearly warranted.

Results from previous work also suggest that we appear to be assessing features of leadership that can have a direct and/or indirect impact on the amount of potential tapped in followers above and beyond the potential tapped by transactional forms of leadership. What has not been tested directly, however, is the link between transformational leadership and the "untapped reserve potential" of individual followers, as well as the untapped potential within organizational systems. Moreover, the effects of transformational leadership on persistence toward completing a task, on the performance of individuals over extended periods of time, and at multiple levels in organizations including a broader range of performance criteria, under varying levels of stress, still remains to be examined [although Seltzer et al. (1989) provided preliminary evidence showing that followers experience less stress and burnout under highly transformational leaders than do highly transactional leaders].

Generalizing the augmentation effect to nonprofit organizations and volunteer agencies would also significantly contribute to our understanding of the construct validity of transformational and transactional leadership. Interviews and discussions conducted by the authors with approximately 70 community leaders, many of whom work in volunteer and nonprofit agencies, has indicated that how we interpret transactional leadership may differ between the profit and nonprofit sectors. These differences could affect our results when testing the augmentation hypothesis across these diverse organizational settings.

Some Alternative Interpretations of Performance-Based Effects. Other factors that may affect our interpretation of the above results include the possibility that the augmentation effect seen in earlier research may be due in part to attribution error and/or the effects of reciprocal causation (Avolio et al., 1988; Binning et al., 1986). Specifically, follower knowledge regarding the prior performance of their leader may impact on subsequent leadership ratings given to their leaders. Ratings may be a function of the behaviors observed by followers and their awareness of the leader's previous accomplishments. To test this assumption, one would have to collect leadership survey data at time 1 and performance data at times 2, 3, 4, and so forth to test whether leadership predicts performance, controlling for the follower's judgment of the leader's past performance, including in this analysis, some examination of whether the follower's evaluation of the leader's performance is accurate. Although feasible, this type of analysis has not yet been undertaken; therefore, this alternative explanation for the results cannot be ignored.

Waldman et al. (1990), using retrospective criteria, had shown that the augmentation hypothesis is not reversible when retrospective criteria of effectiveness were used. Transactional leadership does not augment transformational leadership as transformational leadership augmented transactional leadership in the stepwise hierarchical regression analyses that were employed.

Avolio and Howell (1992) suggested there may be some utility in examining the augmentation effect from such a reverse perspective. They argue that when examined over time, there is reason to believe that transactional leadership may act as a moderator of transformational leadership and its impact on performance. Let's take an extreme example to help clarify this position. A leader who exhibits only transformational leadership behaviors may run into problems as necessary structures' follower tasks and role requirements fail to be provided. Everybody is highly motivated, but all is in chaos. The transformational leader who also is seen demonstrating transactional leadership or contingent reward behaviors should produce higher levels of performance. Tests for this reverse augmentation effect are currently under way.

Building on the above discussion of moderator effects, when criterion outcomes are collected a year after leadership data, Howell and Avolio

(1991) have shown that the organization's culture can significantly moderate the impact of transactional and transformational leadership in predicting individual/group effort and business unit performance. For example, the level of support for innovation within units led by leaders in their sample significantly moderated the effects of transformational leadership on performance.

Additional moderators that should be considered in the formulation of the augmentation hypothesis are likely to include the conflict, goal clarity, and level of resource munificence in the units led by the leader. Also, we suspect that some transformational leaders first change the culture of their units or organizations, and then direct their sights toward affecting performance. The attention to the culture and its alteration may operate as a mediating variable in explaining subsequent levels of effort and performance at the follower, leader, and/or unit level.

Finally, the overall patterns of results reported above have been generalized across national boundaries with leaders in countries such as Japan (Bass and Yokochi, 1991), Singapore (Koh, 1990), Italy (Bass and Avolio, 1990c), Canada (Avolio and Howell, 1992), and Spain (Bass, 1988b). Although some aspects of transformational and transactional leadership vary across national boundaries, there appears to be a general understanding of the basic characteristics associated with each of these respective leadership constructs.

9. The Best of Leaders Are Both Transformational and Transactional; the Worst Are Neither; the Worst Avoid Displaying Leadership

We have already addressed this argument in detail in our discussions of the augmentation hypothesis and the hierarchy of correlations of transformational, transactional, and laissez-faire leadership. Uniformly, we find a negative correlation between being described as a laissez-faire leader and levels of effectiveness, satisfaction, and individual/organizational performance. Instances can be cited of the utility of a "wait and see" attitude by a leader, but the laissez-faire leader is seen as both procrastinating and uncaring, leading to low levels of innovation and performance, as well as potential conflict, where followers are more likely to take control of the situation. Perhaps the most consistent finding in our research has been that laissez-faire leadership is seen uniformly as being ineffective, highly dissatisfying for followers, and one of the more undesirable forms of leadership. These findings have appeared in every organization and every country in which we have collected data (see Bass and Avolio, 1990b).

10. Leaders Can Be Taught and Motivated to Be More Transformational with Consequential Effects on the Organization's Programs and Policies for Improving Itself

The developmental models of leadership presented by Kuhnert and Lewis (1987) and Avolio and Gibbons (1988) argue that certain life events and experiences help shape individuals to be more transformational. For example, Gibbons (1986) found that leaders who were rated by their immediate followers as highly transformational, reported in retrospective interviews that their parents provided them with difficult challenges but also supported the nascent leaders' efforts whether they resulted in success or failure. As long as you tried your best, mistakes were considered part of the learning process. Similarly, Yammarino and Bass (1990a) found that those naval officers who were rated as more transformational tended to be more involved in high-school sports activities, particularly team sports. We have followed up on this preliminary work by attempting to design a life-history inventory, which assesses life events that may promote the emergence of transformational leadership behavior. We are currently collecting data using this inventory with a large sample of community leaders.

Consequently, development and training of transformational leadership includes in vivo development, such as described above, and in vitro training where focal leaders are involved in structured training interventions. Training efforts should actually be viewed as "retraining" since they involve building on, reshaping, or in some cases, altering the effects of earlier life-span experiences on leadership development.

Preliminary data on training transformational leadership supports the basic premise that individuals to a varying degree, and depending on the individuals' point of development. Pile (personal communication) reported that providing feedback to senior managers using the MLQ profile (see Bass and Avolio, 1990a, 1990b) coupled with approximately 3 hours of contact time between an OD consultant and the leader, resulted in a significant increase in transformational leadership ratings by subordinates from the first to the second administration 6 months later, of the MLQ survey. Pile reported no significant changes in MLQ ratings for a lagged control group that had not yet received feedback.

Crookall (1989) reported that a 3-day training intervention that focused on improving transformational leadership resulted in a significant improvement in transformational leadership ratings, performance, and absenteeism rates, as compared to a comparison group that received situational leadership training.

We routinely collect self-reports and incidents to assess the impact of continuing, extensive, and comprehensive training programs on transformational leadership effectiveness. These 6-day programs have already been completed by approximately 180 senior executives in profit and 200 administrative leaders in nonprofit organizations and are described by Bass and Avolio (1990c). Each report or incident is an illustration of the impact on the leader's subsequent performance back on the job, as well as how that individual is seen by followers and clients. Such reports usually deal with ways the trainees were all individually considerate and delegative, intellectually stimulating, and responsive as well as less managing-by-exception.

A 3-year effort using surveys, interviews, and objective criterion measures is under way to systematically examine the impact of transformational leadership training on 400 community leaders from both profit and nonprofit organizations. Once this effort is completed, we will be able to determine the impact of the training effort at the individual, group, organizational, and—with some measures—community levels. Similar and less extensive efforts are continuing in a large multinational organization based in Europe. In the European setting, preliminary data have been collected 3 months following the first phase of the workshop. The data indicate that leaders are able to develop behaviors associated with transactional and transformational leadership and that those behaviors have an impact on follower effort and performance. What still remains unanswered is whether training interventions can affect the attitude and value structure of the leader, particularly their moral development. These remain important tests with regards to assessing the impact of training transformational leadership.

CONCLUSION

By relaxing the criteria set forth by Weber (1929/1947) for what is to be considered charismatic (Bass, 1985), by operationalizing and measuring it, and then including it as one of four dimensions of transformational leadership, we have seen that a great deal can be learned about transformational leadership and charisma. Perhaps most significant is that we have been able to develop a much better understanding of the behaviors exhibited by such leaders, key personality characteristics underlying those behaviors, and their impact on how leaders develop.

The data can be gathered using the same instruments, constructs, and model across all levels of leadership (Yammarino and Bass, 1991): microleadership (leadership of the small group), macroleadership (leadership of the large organization), and metaleadership (leadership of movements and societies) (Nicholls, 1987). Thus, we see applications at the micro level (Hater and Bass, 1988), at the macro level (Bass and Yokochi, 1991) and at the meta level (Bass et al., 1987) of the same model of transformational leadership. It also generalizes across nationalities and language (e.g., Francois, 1990).

Beyond the typical differences found between self and subordinate ratings, an important point to emphasize here is that we have measured each of our model's leadership factors using multiple sources and multiple procedures and across a diverse range of settings. In this vein, we intend to continue to collect data using a variety of sources and procedures to develop a better understanding regarding how these various leadership factors manifest themselves across different situations. These future projects will include collecting data over multiple time periods to examine how transformational leadership evolves, as well as examining observations of transformational leaders, that is, close up by immediate subordinates, peers, and superiors and by subordinates at an organizational distance from the leader (two or more hierarchical echelons below, as well as by external customers and clients).

Over the last 10 years, a number of new key leadership concepts associated with transformational leadership have emerged and have been refined in terms of their construct validity. Measures of these constructs have now gone through a number of iterations using an extremely broad sample of leaders with extensive replication. In addition to our measurement instruments, many of our colleagues have concentrated on measuring the behaviors that are associated with transformational leadership with some degree of success. At this point in time, we remain confident in the basic premise that transformational leadership behaviors add value to a leader's portfolio of behaviors in terms of energizing followers to higher levels of performance.

It is also important to note that not all of the behaviors and characteristics that could be associated with transformational leadership have been identified, or accurately measured if they have been identified. Much more work remains in the operationalization of this high-order construct; the linkage to other constructs such as personality, values, and moral development; and in terms of how it generalizes across organizational–societal cultures. Moreover, we have only scratched the surface in terms of connecting the model of transformational leadership to other models such as vertical dyad linkage theory (Graen and Cashman 1975) and the Dansereau et al. (1984) levels-of-analysis framework. These remain important linkages to be made not only in terms of refining the model but also in terms of its measurement and with respect to developing such leaders.

Particularly scarce so far are controlled experimental studies of changes in the specific perceptions and behavior in leaders as well as followers connected with the leader's display of a designated pattern of transformational and transactional leadership. Because the subject reaches across micro (dyadic and small group leadership), macro (organizational leaderships), and meta (leaders of movements, nations, and societies) leadership levels, efforts to throw a theoretical bridge across those areas of leadership can be undertaken. At the micro level much experimental work is needed; at the macro level, there is much room for quantitative efforts and case analysis; and at the meta level much awaits to be done with documentary and historical endeavors.

In sum, much more work remains to be done regarding the conceptualization and measurement of our constructs. In this regard, we invite critics and supporters alike to join in the effort to shape a theory and model of leadership that captures a broader array of leadership behaviors and attributes than previously studied. This broader array makes it possible to initiate an examination of its implications for many aspects of management (Bass, 1990b), organizational and societal development (Bass and Avolio, 1990b) as well as its diffusion into quality improvement, organizational decisionmaking, innovation in research and development, multifunctional team processes, rightsizing, and other personnel programs.

References

Atwater, L., Lau, A., and Avolio, B. J. (1991). *A retrospective/prospective view of leadership development, emergence, and performance.* Unpublished manuscript.

Atwater, L., and Yammarino, F. J. (1989). *Predictors of military leadership. A study of midshipmen leaders at USNA* (ONR Technical Report No. 7). Binghamton: State University of New York, Center for Leadership Studies.

Avolio, B. J., and Bass, B. M. (1988). Transformational leadership, charisma and beyond. In J. G. Hunt, H. R. Baliga, H. P. Dachler, and C. A. Schriesheim (Eds.), *Emerging leadership vistas.* Lexington, MA: Heath.

Avolio, B. J., and Bass, B. M. (1991a). *Transformational leadership development: Manuals.* Binghamton, NY: Bass, Avolio & Assoc.

Avolio, B. J., and Bass, B. M. (1991b). *Transformational leadership and innovation in organizational improvement and human resources management in organizational settings.* Turin, Italy: ISVOR-FIAT.

Avolio, B. J., Yammarino, F. J., and Bass, B. M. (1991). Identifying common methods variance with data collected from a single source: An unresolved sticky issue. *Journal of Management, 173,* 571–587.

Avolio, B. J., and Gibbons, T. C. (1988). Developing transformational leaders: A life span approach. In J. Conger and R. Kanungo (Eds.), *Charismatic leadership: The elusive factor in organizational effectiveness* (pp. 276–308). San Francisco: Jossey-Bass.

Avolio, B. J., and Howell, J. M. (1990). The effects of leader-follower personality congruence: Predicting follower satisfaction and business unit performance.

Paper presented at the 1990 International Association of Applied Psychology, Kyoto, Japan.

Avolio, B. J., and Howell, J. M. (1992). The impact of leader behavior and leader-follower personality match on satisfaction and unit performance. In K. E. Clark, M. B. Clark, and D. R. Campbell (Eds.), *Impact of leadership*. Greensboro, NC: The Center for Creative Leadership.

Avolio, B. J., Waldman, D. A., and Einstein, W. O. (1988). Transformational leadership in a management simulation: Impacting the bottom line. *Group and Organization Studies, 13,* 59–80.

Bass, B. M. (1960). *Leadership, psychology and organizational behavior.* New York: Harper.

Bass, B. M. (1974). The substance and the shadow. *American Psychologist, 39,* 870–886.

Bass, B. M. (1985). *Leadership and performance beyond expectations.* New York: Free Press.

Bass, B. M. (1988a). Evolving perspectives on charismatic leadership. In J. Conger and R. N. Kanungo (Eds.), *Charismatic leadership: The elusive factor in organizational effectiveness.* San Francisco: Jossey-Bass.

Bass, B. M. (1988b). El impacto de los directores transformacionales en la vida escolar. In R. Pascual (Ed.), *La gestation education ante la innovacion y elcambio.* Narcio: Bilbao.

Bass, B. M. (1990a). *Bass and Stogdill's handbook of leadership,* 3rd ed. New York: Free Press.

Bass, B. M. (1990b). From transactional to transformational leadership: Learning to share the vision. *Organizational Dynamics, 18*(3), 19–36.

Bass, B. M., and Avolio, B. J. (1989). Potential biases in leadership measures: How prototypes, leniency, and general satisfaction relate to ratings and rankings of transformational and transactional leadership constructs. *Educational and Psychological Measurement, 49,* 509–527.

Bass, B. M., and Avolio, B. J. (1990a). *Manual for the multifactor leadership questionnaire.* Palo Alto, CA: Consulting Psychologist Press.

Bass, B. M., and Avolio, B. J. (1990b). The implications of transactional and transformational leadership for individual, team and organizational development. In R. W. Woodman and W. A. Passmore (Eds.), *Research in organizational change and development.* Greenwich, CT: JAI Press.

Bass, B. M., and Avolio, B. J. (1990c). Training and development of transformational leadership: Looking to 1992 and beyond. *European Journal of Industrial Training, 14,* 21–27.

Bass, B. M., and Avolio, B. J. (1991). The transformational and transactional leadership behavior of women and men as described by the men and women who directly report to them. *CLS Report No. 91-3,* Center for Leadership Studies, State University of New York at Binghamton, Binghamton, NY.

Bass, B. M., Avolio, B. J., and Goodheim, L. (1987). Biography and the assessment of transformational leadership at the world-class level. *Journal of Management, 13,* 7–19.

Bass, B. M., and Yokochi, N. (1991). Charisma among senior executives and the special case of Japanese CEO's. *Consulting Psychology Bulletin, Winter/Spring, 1,* 31–38.

Bennis, W. G., and Nanus, B. (1985). *Leaders: The strategies for taking charge.* New York: Harper & Row.

Binning, J. F., and Lord, R. G. (1980). Boundary conditions for performance effects on group process ratings: Familiarity versus type of feedback. *Organizational Behavior and Human Performance, 26,* 115–130.

Binning, J. F., Zaba, A. J., and Whattam, J. C. (1986). Explaining the biasing effects of performance cues in terms of cognitive categorization. *Academy of Management Journal, 29,* 521–535.

Boyd, J. T. (1988). *Leadership extraordinary: A cross national military perspective on transactional versus transformational leadership.* Doctoral dissertation, Nova University, Fort Lauderdale, FL.

Bryant, M. A. (1990). *Relationship between nurse managers' perceived transformational versus transactional leadership styles and staff nurse turnover.* Master's thesis, University of Akron, Akron, OH.

Burns, J. M. (1978). *Leadership.* New York: Harper & Row.

Clover, W. H. (1989). Transformational leaders: Team performance, leadership ratings and first hand impressions. In K. E. Clark and M. B. Clark (Eds.), *Measures of leadership.* West Orange, NJ: Leadership Library of America.

Conger, J. (1989). *The charismatic leader: Beyond the mystique of exceptional leadership.* San Francisco: Jossey-Bass.

Cowen, S. S. (1990). *A study of the relationships between perceived leadership behaviors of presidents at public four-year institutions of higher education in the U.S. and the changes in FTE enrollment, perceptions of effectiveness, subordinate satisfaction, and other factors of the presidency.* Doctoral dissertation, Gonzaga University, Washington State.

Crookall, P. (1989). *Leadership in the prison industry.* Doctoral dissertation, The University of Western Ontario, Ontario, Canada.

Curphy, G. J. (1992). An empirical investigation of the effects of transformational and transactional leadership on organizational climate, attrition and performance. In K. E. Clark, M. B. Clark, and D. R. Campbell (Eds.). *Impact of leadership.* Greensboro, NC: The Center for Creative Leadership.

Dansereau, F., Alutto, J. A., and Yammarino, F. J. (1984). *Theory testing in organizational behavior: The varient approach.* Englewood Cliffs, NJ: Prentice-Hall.

Downton, J. V. (1973). *Rebel leadership: Commitment and charisma in a revolutionary process.* New York: Free Press.

Fiedler, F. E. (1983). The contingency model—a reply to Ashour. *Organizational Behavior and Human Performance, 9,* 356–368.

Fiedler, F. E. (1986). The contribution of cognitive resources and leader behavior to organizational performance. *Journal of Applied Social Psychology, 16,* 532–548.

Francois, P. H. (1990). Être un leader, avoir du charisme. (To be a leader, have some charisma.) *Journal de Psychologues, 81,* 54–60.

Gardner, W. L., and Avolio, B. J. (1991). *Charismatic leadership: The role of impression management.* Unpublished manuscript.

Gibbons, T. C. (1986). *Revisiting the question of born vs. made: Toward a theory of development of transformational leaders.* Doctoral dissertation, The Fielding Institute.

Gottlieb, T. W. (1990). *Transactional and transformational leadership styles of chief and associate chief nurses in Department of Veterans' Affairs Medical Centers: A descriptive study.* Doctoral dissertation, Columbia University, New York.

Graen, G., and Cashman, J. F. (1975). A role-making model of leadership in formal organizations: A developmental approach. In J. G. Hunt and L. L. Larson (Eds.), *Leadership frontiers.* Kent, OH: Kent State University Press.

Hater, J. J., and Bass, B. M. (1988). Superiors' evaluations and subordinates' perceptions of transformational and transactional leadership. *Journal of Applied Psychology, 73,* 695–702.

Hicks, R. S. (1990). *Effectiveness of transactional and transformational leadership in turbulent and stable conditions.* Doctoral dissertation, Claremont University, Claremont, CA.

Hoover, N. R. (1987). *Transformational and transactional leadership: A test of the model.* Doctoral dissertation, University of Louisville, Louisville, KY.

House, R. J. (1977). A 1976 theory of charismatic leadership. In J. G. Hunt and L. L. Larson (Eds.), *Leadership: The cutting edge.* Carbondale: Southern Illinois University Press.

House, R. J., Spangler, W. D., and Woycke, J. (1991). Personality and charisma in the U.S. presidency: A psychological theory of leadership effectiveness. *Administration Science Quarterly, 36,* 364–396.

Howell, J. M. (1988). Two faces of charisma: Socialized and personalized leadership in organizations. In J. Conger and R. Kanungo (Eds.), *Charismatic leadership: The elusive factor in organizational effectiveness.* San Francisco: Jossey-Bass.

Howell, J. M., and Avolio, B. J. (1991). *Predicting consolidated unit performance: Leadership ratings, locus of control and support for innovation.* Paper presented at the 51st Annual Meeting of the Academy of Management, Miami, FL.

Howell, J. M., and Frost, P. J. (1988). A laboratory study of charismatic leadership. *Organizational Behavior and Human Decision Processes, 43,* 243–269.

Hunt, J. B. (1991). *Leadership: A new synthesis.* London: Sage Publications.

Koh, W. L. (1990). *An empirical validation of the theory of transformational leadership in secondary schools in Singapore.* Doctoral dissertation, University of Oregon.

Kuhnert, K. W., and Lewis, P. (1987). Transactional and transformational leadership: A constructive/developmental analysis. *Academy of Management Review, 12,* 648–657.

Longshore, J. M. (1988). *The associative relationship between transformational and transactional leadership styles and group productivity.* Doctoral dissertation, Nova University, Fort Lauderdale, FL.

Lord, R. G., Foti, F. J., and Devader, C. L. (1984). A test of leadership categorization theory. Internal structure, information processing, and leadership perceptions. *Organizational Behavior and Human Performance, 34,* 343–378.

Maslow, A. H. (1954). *Motivation and personality.* New York: Harper.

Nicholls, J. (1987). Leadership in organizations: Meta, macro, and micro. *European Management Journal, 6,* 16–25.

O'Keeffe, M. J. (1989). *The effects of leadership style on the perceived effectiveness and satisfaction of selected army officers.* Doctoral dissertation, Temple University, Philadelphia, PA.

Onnen, M. K. (1987). *The relationship of clergy and leadership characteristics to growing or declining churches.* Doctoral dissertation, University of Louisville, Louisville, KY.

Roberts, N. C. (1986). Organizational power styles: Collective and competitive power under varying organizational conditions. *Journal of Applied Behavioral Science, 22,* 443–458.

Ruggiero, M. B. (1989). *A comparative analysis: Leader behavior of military and industrial project managers as related to organizational authority.* Doctoral dissertation, Temple University, Philadelphia, PA.

Salter, D. J. (1989). *Leadership styles in United States Marine Corps transport helicopter squadrons.* Master's Thesis, Naval Postgraduate School, Monterey, CA.

Seltzer, J., and Bass, B. M. (1990). Transformational leadership: Beyond initiation and consideration. *Journal of Management, 16,* 693–703.

Seltzer, J., Numerof, R. E., and Bass, B. M. (1989). Transformational leadership: Is it a source of more burnout and stress? *Journal of Health and Human Resources Administration, 12,* 174–185.

Singer, M. S. (1985). Transformational vs. transactional leadership: A study of New Zealand company managers. *Psychological Reports, 57,* 143–146.

Smith, P. B., and Peterson, M. F. (1988). *Leadership, organizations and culture.* New York: Sage.

Tichy, N., and Devanna, M. (1985). *Transformational leadership.* New York: Wiley.

Trice, H. M., and Beyer, J. M. (1986). Charisma and its routinization in two social movement organizations. *Research in Organizational Behavior, 8,* 113–164.

Waldman, D. A., Bass, B. M., and Einstein, W. O. (1987). Leadership and outcomes of the performance appraisal process. *Journal of Occupational Psychology, 60,* 177–186.

Waldman, D. A., Bass, B. M., and Yammarino, F. J. (1990). Adding to contingent reward behavior: The augmenting effect of charismatic leadership. *Group & Organization Studies, 15,* 381–394.

Weber, M. (1924/1947). *The theory of social and economic organizations* (T. Parsons, Transl.). New York: Free Press.

Willner, A. R. (1968). *Charismatic political leadership: A theory.* Princeton, NJ: Center for International Studies.

Yammarino, F. J., and Bass, B. M. (1990a). Long-term forecasting of transformational leadership and its effects among Naval officers: Some preliminary findings. In K. E. Clark and M. B. Clark (Eds.), *Measures of leadership.* Greensboro, NC: Center for Creative Leadership.

Yammarino, F. J., and Bass, B. M. (1990b). Transformational leadership and multiple levels of analysis. *Human Relations, 43,* 975–995.

Yammarino, F. J., and Bass, B. M. (1991). Person and situation views of leadership: Multiple levels of analysis approach. *Leadership Quarterly, 2,* 121–139.

Yukl, G. A. (1989). *Leadership in organizations.* Englewood Cliffs, NJ: Prentice-Hall.

4

Toward the Integration of Transformational, Charismatic, and Visionary Theories

Robert J. House
Department of Management
The Wharton School of the University of Pennsylvania

Boas Shamir
Department of Sociology and Anthropology
The Hebrew University of Jerusalem

BACKGROUND

Shamir et al. (1992) recently presented a self-concept-based theory of motivation to explain the effects of charismatic leaders on followers' motivation, commitment, and performance. These authors noted that

> in the mid 1970's, a major paradigm shift in leadership research took place. Attention was shifted from an emphasis on the relationship of leader behavior to follower cognitions and reinforcement and leader–follower relationships to an emphasis on exceptional leaders who have extraordinary effects on their followers and eventually on social systems. Such leadership—alternatively called "charismatic," "visionary," or "transformational"—is claimed to affect followers in ways that are quantitatively greater and qualitatively different than the effects specified in past theories. (p. 1)

We refer to this new genre of theories as charismatic because charisma is a central concept in all of them, either explicitly or implicitly.

According to this new genre of leadership theory (House, 1977; Burns, 1978; Bass, 1985; Bennis and Nanus, 1985; Tichy and Devanna, 1986; Conger and Kanungo, 1987; Sashkin, 1988), such leaders transform the needs, values, preferences, and aspirations of followers from self-interests to collective interests. Further, they cause followers to become highly committed to the leader's mission, to make significant personal sacrifices in the interest of the mission, and to perform above and beyond the call of duty.

Shamir et al. (1992) argued that charismatic leaders engage follower self-concepts and cause followers to link valued aspects of their self-concepts to their involvement in the leader's vision and mission. Bennis and Nanus (1985) and Tichy and Devanna (1986) argue that such leaders also have a transforming effect on the organizations that they lead, as well as on their followers. In the present paper we argue that charismatic leaders also arouse followers' nonconscious motives that are relevant to mission attainment.

As observed by Shamir et al. (1992), in contrast to earlier theories, charismatic theories take as their dependent variables emotional attachment to the leader on the part of the followers; emotional and motivational arousal of the followers as a consequence of the leader's behaviors, and thus enhancement of follower valences with respect to the mission articulated by the leader; follower self-esteem, trust, and confidence in the leader; values that are of major importance to followers; and follower intrinsic motivation.

The leader behavior specified by charismatic theories is also different. The earlier theories describe leader behavior in terms of leader–follower exchange relationships (Hollander, 1964; Graen and Cashman, 1975), providing direction and support (Evans, 1970; House, 1971; Wofford and Shrinivasan, 1983), and reinforcement behaviors (Ashour, 1982; Podsakoff et al., 1982). In contrast, the new leadership paradigm emphasizes symbolic leader behavior, visionary and inspirational ability, nonverbal communication, appeal to ideological values, intellectual stimulation of followers by the leader, high leader expectations for follower performance, high leader confidence in followers, and leader concern with her or his image in the eyes of followers and other important constituents.

Further, charismatic leaders theoretically transform organizations by infusing into them ideological values and moral purpose, thus inducing strong commitment rather than by affecting the cognitions or the task environment of followers, or by offering material incentives and the threat of punishment.

EMPIRICAL EVIDENCE

Numerous studies have demonstrated support for the theoretical relationships between leader behavior and follower response. As pointed out by Shamir et al. (1992), these studies were conducted across a wide variety of samples, including students and managers who served as laboratory subjects (Howell and Frost, 1989; Puffer, 1990), military combat and noncombat leaders (Yukl and Van Fleet, 1982; Curphy, 1990), numerous middle- and lower-level managers (Smith, 1982; Waldman et al., 1987; Bass and Yammarino, 1988; Avolio and Bass, 1987; Hater and Bass, 1988; Podsakoff et al., 1990), U.S. educational leaders (Roberts, 1985; Roberts and Bradley, 1988; Sashkin, 1988), world class national leaders (Bass et al., 1987a), reputed charismatic political leaders (Willner, 1984), top-level corporate leaders (Bennis and Nanus, 1985), U.S. presidents (House et al., 1991), Presidents of Alcoholic Rehabilitation Organizations (Trice and Beyer, 1986), and emergent informal project champions (Howell and Higgins, 1990a,b), middle managers in India (Pereria, 1988) and secondary-school principals in Singapore (Koh et al., 1991).

Further, the studies supporting this new genre of leadership theory have relied on a wide variety of methods such as two case studies (Roberts, 1985; Roberts and Bradley, 1988), two longitudinal observational studies (Trice and Beyer, 1986), numerous field surveys (e.g., see Avolio and Bass, 1987; Hater and Bass, 1988; Smith, 1982; Yukl and Van Fleet, 1982; Podsakoff et al., 1990), analysis of behavior in a management game (Avolio et al., 1988), two rigorous laboratory experiments (Howell and Frost, 1989; Puffer, 1990), an interpretative analysis of interviews (Bennis and Nanus, 1985), a rigorous content analysis of interviews (Howell and Higgins, 1990b), a rigorous analysis of historical archival information (House et al., 1991), and a rigorous longitudinal analysis of the effects of leader behavior on U.S. Air Force Academy cadets (Curphy, 1990).

On the basis of a review of the above studies, Shamir et al. (1992) assert that "it can be safely concluded that there is a strong convergence of the findings from studies concerned with charismatic leadership and those concerned with transformational and visionary leadership" (p. 8). All of these studies demonstrate the importance of the leader behaviors identified in earlier theorizing by House (1977) and Burns (1978) and are consistent with later theorizing by Bass (1985), Bennis and nanus (1985), Tichy and Devanna (1986), Conger and Kanungo (1987), Kuhnert and Lewis (1987), Sashkin (1988), and Trice and Beyer (1988).

Collectively, these findings indicate that leaders who engage in the theoretical charismatic behaviors produce the theoretical charismatic effects, receive higher performance ratings, have more satisfied and more highly motivated followers, and are viewed as more effective leaders by their superiors and followers than others in positions of leadership. Further, the effect size of charismatic leader behavior on follower satisfaction and performance is consistently higher than prior field study findings concerning other leader behavior, generally ranging well below .01 probability of error due to chance, with correlations frequently ranging in the neighborhood of .50 or better. Finally, such effect size remains high and significant after controlling for common source and common-method bias (Curphy, 1990; Podsakoff et al., 1990; Koh et al., 1991).

THE PROBLEM

A major problem concerning this new genre of theory is that there are various versions of charismatic theory in the current literature (Weber, 1947; House, 1977; Burns, 1978; Bass, 1985; Trice and Beyer, 1988; Bennis and Nanus, 1985; Conger and Kanungo, 1987; Kuhnert and Lewis, 1987; Sashkin, 1988). Table 4.1 presents the leader behaviors specified by the theories that have some claim to empirical validity. While these theories are complementary, they each specify somewhat different leader behaviors to account for the charismatic leadership phenomena. To date, there is no coherent framework into which these theories and the supporting empirical evidence can be integrated. In this paper, we advance a speculative theoretical explanation that provides some integration of current charismatic theories.

In the following sections of this paper, we first clarify our terms. Next, we take one cognitive leadership theory—the original path–goal theory (House, 1971)—as our point of departure, and add to this theory the self-concept theory advanced by Shamir et al. (1992). We also add propositions concerning how leaders arouse nonconscious motives of followers.

Table 4.1

Behaviors Specified in Charismatic, Transformational, and Visionary Theories of Leadership

	Weber, 1947	House, 1977	Burns, 1978	Bass, 1985	Bennis and Nanus, 1985	Conger and Kanungo, 1987	Sashkin, 1988	Shamir et al., 1991
Visionary	X	X	X	X	X	X	X	X
Frame alignment								X
Empowering								
Showing confidence in and respect for followers		X	X	X	X	X	X	X
Setting challenging expectations	X							X
Role modeling								
Setting personal example	X	X		X		X	X	X
Showing self-confidence	X	X		X			X	X
Image building								
Establishing trustworthiness		X				X	X	X
Displaying competence	X	X				X	X	X
Behaving exceptionally	X				X	X	X	X
Taking risks	X					X	X	X
Supporting								
Showing consideration and/or concern				X			X	
Adapting								
Showing versatility							X	
Environmentally sensitive						X	X	
Intellectually stimulating				X				X

We then specify some leader behaviors that affect follower self-concepts and arouse follower motives. We apply the expanded theory to show how it can be used to explain leadership effects that cannot be explained by current behavioral, exchange, expectancy or goal-setting views of motivation and leadership. We offer a new set of propositions that are testable and can be used to guide future research. Finally, we show how the proposed theory integrates the leader behaviors specified in prior theories.

CLARIFICATION OF TERMS

Following Shamir et al. (1992), we use the term "charismatic leadership" because it is a central construct in all the theories of the new leadership paradigm described above. We use the term "transformational" to refer to certain hypothesized effects of charismatic leaders.

Charismatic leadership can be distinguished from other types of leadership on the basis of four factors: a set of behaviors, a set of personality traits, specific perceptions and attributions by the followers, and specific effects on the followers. Any of these factors can serve as the basis for defining charismatic leadership.

For purposes of this essay we define charismatic leadership in terms of the effects of charismatic leaders on followers. Specifically, we define charismatic leadership as an interaction between leaders and their followers that results in (1) making followers' self-esteem contingent on their involvement in the vision and the mission articulated by the leader, (2) strong internalization of the leaders' values and goals by the followers, (3) strong personal or moral (as opposed to calculative) commitment to these values and goals, and (4) a willingness on the part of followers to transcend their own self-interests for the sake of the collective (team or organization). We shall refer to these consequences as "the transformational effects of charismatic leadership."

A POINT OF DEPARTURE: PATH–GOAL THEORY

In order to compare and contrast the motivational mechanisms that produce transformational effects with those that do not, we shall use as our point of departure the dependent variables of the path–goal theory of leadership (House, 1971). The major dependent variables of path–goal theory are presented in the following figure:

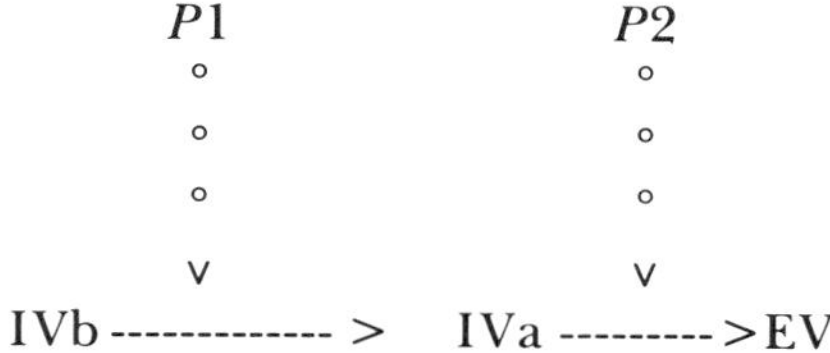

The basic formulation of path–goal theory contains five categories of variables. These are the deendent variables of the theory and represent five possible "levers" that leaders can use to influence the motivation of their followers. According to this formulation, motivation is a function of

IVb The intrinsic valence of the relevant behavior or effort.
***P*1** The estimated probability that this behavior or effort will lead to goal attainment.
IVa The intrinsic valence of goal attainment or task accomplishment.
***P*2** The estimated probabilities that goal attainment will lead to desired extrinsic outcomes.
EV The valences of the extrinsic outcomes.

According to the path–goal theory, "the motivational functions of the leader consist of increasing the number and kinds of personal payoffs to subordinates for work-goal attainment and making paths to these payoffs easier to travel by clarifying the paths, reducing road blocks and pitfalls, and increasing the opportunities for personal satisfaction en route" (House, 1971, p. 85).

The importance of the five variables mentioned above is that they all have motivational consequences. We add to these variables a further set of dependent variables, referred to as "self-concept variables" and "motive arousal." We argue that a leader has significant motivational effects on followers to the extent that the leader has an impact of any of these variables. Table 4.1 specifies the primary ways by which charismatic and noncharismatic leaders influence these variables. Figure 4.1 provides an overview of the charismatic leadership process. Figure 4.2 explicates the process with respect to the effects of charismatic leaders on follower self-concept. We recognize that leaders can have motivational effects by influencing other variables as well. However, we assume that the major motivational impact of charismatic leaders on followers is through the

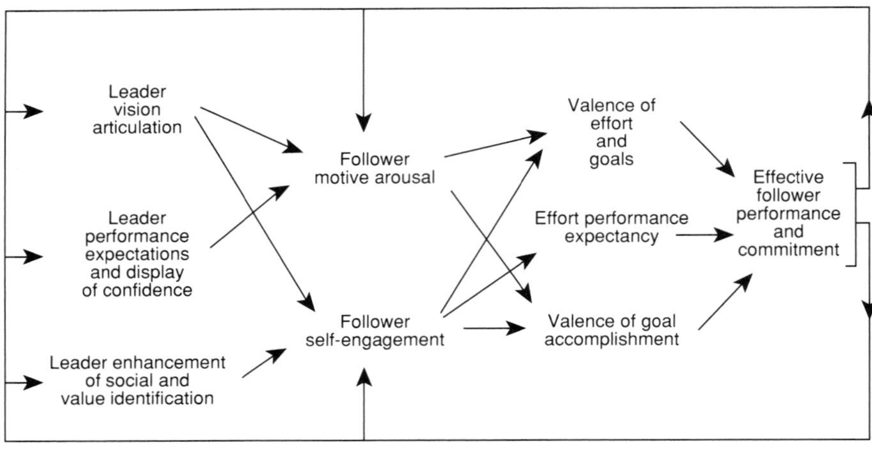

Figure 4.1 A model of the charismatic leadership process.

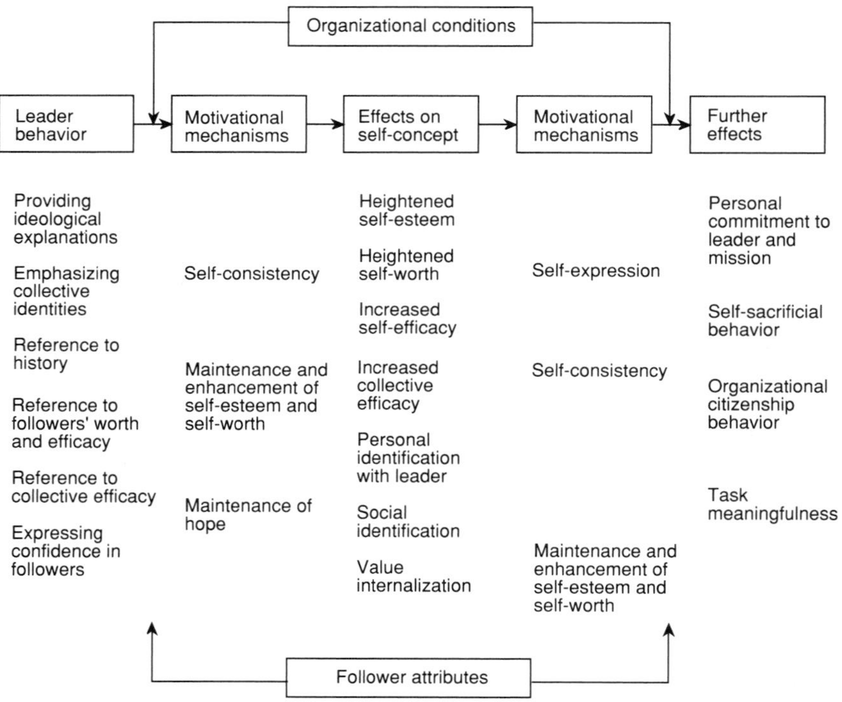

Figure 4.2 Leader behaviors and follower self-effects.

leaders' effect on the variables specified above; follower self-concepts and follower motive arousal. We now turn to a discussion of self-concepts.

THE SELF-CONCEPT THEORY AS AN EXTENSION OF THE PATH–GOAL THEORY

While the path–goal theory of leadership specifies intrinsic valence of effort and goal attainment, the major thrust of the empirical research relevant to this theory has been concerned with the effects of leaders on the expectations of followers. In contrast, the motivational theory advanced by Shamir et al. (1992) asserts that charismatic leaders achieve transformational effects, to a major extent, by implicating the self-concept of followers as well.

The self-concept theory rests on a number of assumptions. For the sake of brevity, we shall summarize these assumptions very briefly here. For a more complete discussion of these assumptions, the reader is referred to the original text by Shamir et al. (1992).

Assumptions

1. *Human beings are not only pragmatic and goal oriented—they are also self-expressive of feelings, aesthetic values, and self-perceptions.* This expressiveness accounts for self-sacrificial behavior that cannot be accounted for by instrumental, rational, hedonic, purposive theories that assume that individuals are always motivated by self-interest.

2. *People are motivated to maintain and enhance their self-esteem.* Self esteem has two components: self-worth and self-efficacy. Feelings of self-worth are derived from a sense of virtue and morality and are grounded in social norms and cultural values concerning conduct. Self-efficacy concerns feelings about one's ability to control one's own destiny and to master the tasks necessary for effective performance.

3. *People are motivated to maintain and enhance their sense of self-consistency.* Consistency refers to correspondence among components of the self-concept at a given time, to continuity of the self-concept over time (Turner, 1968), and to correspondence between the self-concept and behavior.

4. *The self-concept is composed, in part, of identities, which are organized in the self-concept in a salience hierarchy.* These identities allow one to locate the self (or selves) into socially recognizable categories such as family member, occupational member, member of a particular organization, or member of a social movement (McCall and Simons, 1978; Tajfel and Turner, 1985). The identity hierarchy determines the relative importance of each identity

and is relatively stable, but is subject to social influence by others whom one views positively and as important in one's life.

5. *Humans are motivated by faith as well as rational calculation of expected success or failure.* Being hopeful in the sense of having faith in a better future is an intrinsically satisfying and motivating condition. The opposite, being in a state of despair, is a debilitating and demotivating condition.

Charismatic Behavior and the Transformational Effects of Charismatic Leaders

The self-concept theory asserts that some of the most important effects of charismatic leaders are that they increase the intrinsic value of effort and goal accomplishment, as well as followers' level of self-worth and self-efficacy, expectancies of goal or mission accomplishment, faith in a better future, and commitment to the values of the leader's vision and consequently to the goals of the mission set forth by the leader.

More specifically, such leaders increase the intrinsic valence of efforts and goals by linking them to valued aspects of the follower's self-concept, thus harnessing the motivational forces of self-expression, self-consistency, self-esteem, and self-worth. Further, charismatic leaders change the salience hierarchy of values and identities within the followers' self-concept, thus increasing the probability that these values and identities will be implicated in action.

Since values and identities are socially based, their control of behavior is likely to represent a shift from the instrumental to the moral and from concern with individual gains to concern with contributions to a collective. Finally, the theory asserts that charismatic leaders increase self-efficacy and collective efficacy through positive evaluations and higher performance expectations, and by emphasizing the individual's ties to the collective. These effects on followers' sense of efficacy result in the instantation of faith in a better future.

The theory also asserts that when leaders engage in the behaviors specified in the 1976 Theory of Charismatic Leadership articulation of an ideological vision, behaviorally role modeling the values implied in the vision by personal example, expressing high-performance expectations of followers, and expressing a high degree of confidence in followers' ability to meet such expectations, followers' self-concepts will become strongly engaged (House, 1977). The first proposition of the extended theory is

Proposition 1. In comparison with followers of noncharismatic leaders, followers of charismatic leaders will experience a unique set of psychological states. Specifically, followers of charismatic leaders are hypothesized to experience

1. A higher salience of the collective identity in their self-concept.
2. A higher sense of consistency between their self-concept and their actions on behalf of the leader and the collective.
3. A higher level of self-esteem and a greater sense of self-worth.
4. A higher similarity between their self-concept and their perception of the leader.
5. A higher sense of collective efficacy.
6. A higher sense of "meaningfulness" in their work and lives.

In addition to engaging follower self-concepts, we argue that charismatic leaders also arouse nonconscious motives of followers. We now turn to a discussion of the effects of leaders on such follower motives.

LEADER MOTIVE AROUSAL AS A FURTHER EXTENSION

In this section, we argue that charismatic leaders selectively arouse powerful motivations of followers and that such motive arousal results in important effects: further engagement of follower self-concepts, strong enhancement of intrinsic valence of goal accomplishment, follower intrinsic satisfaction from participation in the charismatic mission, and finally, increased commitment to the vision and the mission articulated by the leader. We now turn to a discussion of each of these issues.

Selective Arousal of Relevant Follower Motives

We argue here that leaders selectively arouse follower nonconscious achievement, affiliation and power motives (and possibly other motives as well). These are nonconscious stable motives that have strong and enduring behavioral consequences. We further argue that motive arousal results in increased engagement of the self, self-monitoring, and self-evaluation. Such arousal engages the self-worth component of motivation and increases motivation on the part of followers.

We stated that leaders *selectively* arouse follower motives because the performance consequences of motive arousal are contingent on the requirements of the mission. More specifically, when task demands of subordinates require the assumption of calculated risks, achievement-oriented initiative, the assumption of personal responsibility, and persistence toward challenging goals, the arousal of the achievement motive is hypothesized to enhance intrinsic satisfaction and motivation and will facilitate effective performance and goal attainment.

When the task demands of subordinates require them to be persuasive, assert influence or exercise control over others, or be highly competitive or combative, it is hypothesized that the arousal of the power motive will enhance intrinsic motivation and satisfaction and facilitate performance.

When task demands require affiliative behavior, as in the case of tasks requiring cohesiveness, teamwork, and peer support, the arousal of the affiliative motive is hypothesized to be highly relevant to intrinsic motivation, satisfaction, and performance. Thus, we assert that one of the major effects that charismatic leaders have on their followers is the arousal of motives that are especially relevant to the mission envisioned by the leader.

Further Engagement of Follower Self-Concepts

Under conditions of motive arousal, individuals engage in what Bandura (1986) refers to as "self-regulatory behavior." Under such conditions, individuals increasingly focus their attention on their own behavior in pursuit of motive satisfaction. They focus attention on the goals pursued, sharpen their cognitive representations of goal attainment, and anticipate and vicariously experience the feelings they will have as a consequence of goal attainment and as a consequence of failure. They consider the barriers to goal attainment, form strategies to overcome barriers, anticipate the support they will receive from others, calculate their own strengths and weaknesses with respect to goal attainment, monitor and reflect on their progress, use available information for assessing progress toward their goals, seek out and create additional sources of feedback, and adjust their behavior to correct mistakes and dysfunctional strategies. [See McClelland (1985) for a discussion of the effects of motive arousal.]

Motive arousal results in these behaviors spontaneously and for the most part nonconsciously; that is, individuals are not likely to be able to explain their behavior in response to motive-arousal stimuli. Individuals may or may not even be aware of the specific stimuli that arouse their motives or the specific behaviors that are mobilized by such stimuli.

As a consequence of motive arousal, individuals become further self-engaged, and their feelings of self-worth and self-efficacy become contingent on satisfying the aroused motives.

Enhancement of Follower Intrinsic Valence of Goal Accomplishment

This is perhaps the most important consequence of charismatic leadership. As stated above, self-engagement enhances the intrinsic valence of goal accomplishment. Further, aroused motives lead to increased intrinsic satisfaction resulting from goal accomplishment because the goals become more valent when motives are aroused than when they are not. This is a well-established empirical generalization that has been demonstrated repeatedly in experimental studies (McClelland, 1985).

Enhancement of Follower Intrinsic Satisfaction from Participation in the Mission

Since motive arousal makes goals more valent, the behavior involved in pursuit of the goals also becomes more positively or negatively valent, depending on whether the individual experiences progress or failure in pursuit of the goal. Satisfaction results from progress. Feelings of frustration and sometimes even depression result from failure to experience progress.

Increased Commitment to the Mission

Since motive arousal results in increased self-engagement, and since the experience of self-worth and self-efficacy are contingent on goal attainment, it becomes highly dissonant for the individual to resist commitment to the vision and mission of the leader. Thus, motive arousal stimulated by the leader will result in enhanced and rather internalized commitment to the leader's goals and values.

It should be noted, however, that commitment is a double-edged sword; to the extent that the leaders' goals and values are in conflict with those of the organization, such as when leaders represent a challenge to the status quo, charismatic leadership is likely to induce negative attitudes toward the organization and resistance to directives from management by organizational members. Thus, charismatic leadership represents a strong force for or against member commitment to organizational goals.

LEADER BEHAVIORS

The effects of leaders on followers discussed above suggests additional leader behaviors that have charismatic effects. In this section, we will discuss these leader behaviors in more detail.

Motive-Arousal Behaviors

In the prior section, we asserted that the arousal of motives activates self-regulation and thus engage the self-worth component of followers' self-concept. Such motive arousal is achieved differentially for each of the three motives. McClelland and his associates (1985) have shown these motives to have substantial effects on individual short-term behavior and long-term (as long as 20 years) orientation.

There is also a substantial amount of evidence that these motives can be aroused from experimental inductions. For example, the achievement motive has been aroused by suggesting to subjects that the experimental task is a measure of personal competence, or that the task is a standard against which one can measure one's general level of ability.

The affiliative motive has been aroused by having fraternity members rate one another, while all were present, on a sociometric friendship index, while at the same time requiring each person to be rated by the other members of the fraternity on a list of trait adjectives (Shipley and Veroff, 1952).

The power motive has been aroused experimentally by (1) evoking the image of, or reminding one of, an enemy; (2) having subjects observe the exercise of power by one person over another; or (3) allowing subjects to exercise power over another (Winter, 1978).

Motives can be aroused, easily within a few minutes, by use of the appropriate experimental treatments by psychologists. Thus, it seems obvious that leaders can also arouse motives. Because charismatic leaders are viewed as credible, trusted, admired, and respected, they should be able to have rather profound motive arousal effects on followers.

For example, Gandhi's exhortations of love and acceptance of one's fellow humans likely aroused the need for affiliation, a need especially relevant to the goal of uniting Hindus, Moslems, and Christians.

Military leaders often employ symbols of authoritarianism and evoke the image of the enemy, thus arousing the power motive, a motive especially relevant to effective combat performance. For example, Patton, when addressing infantry recruits, would do so against the background of a large American flag, dressed with medals of his accomplishments, carrying a cropping whip, and wearing a shiny helmet displaying four stars indicating the status of general. In his biography of General George Patton, Martin Blumenson (1985) states that Patton said to him: "As in all my talks, I stressed fighting and killing" (p. 222). He would rather dramatically point out the threat of the Huns. To the troops he said, "An army is a team, lives, sleeps, fights, and eats as a team. . . . I can assure you that the Third United States Army will be the greatest army in American history. We shall be in Berlin ahead of everyone. . . . We are going to kill German bastards—I would prefer to skin them alive—but, gentlemen, I fear some of our people at home would accuse me of being too rough . . ." (pp. 222–223).

There is evidence that formally appointed leaders in a laboratory situation are capable of arousing subordinates' achievement motive (Litwin and Stringer, 1968). Industrial leaders and leaders of scientists frequently stress challenge and excellence of performance as a measure of one's worth, thus arousing the achievement motive. This motive is especially relevant to the assumption of personal responsibility, persistence, and pride in high-quality work performance. McClelland (1985) has shown that the achievement motive level in societies predicts their economic development and that the achievement motive is predictive of entrepreneurial behavior and success.

The behavior of John Gardner illustrates how a leader might arouse the achievement motive in followers. John Gardner, on assuming the office of Secretary of Health, Education and Welfare under Lyndon B. Johnson, addressed the top 500 or so administrators in that agency. He stated that the problems of the world are sickness, ignorance, and poverty, and that we are in the business of solving these problems—the business of health, education, and welfare! Our time has come. Under this administration our mission is given highest priority. We can and we will make a difference in the world! (Gardner, 1965).

These considerations suggest the following proposition:

Proposition 2. Leaders who have charismatic effects are more likely to engage in behaviors that arouse motives relevant to the accomplishment of the mission than are those who do not have charismatic effects.

Note that in all of the above examples, the leader couples motive arousal behavior with appeal to the collective, thus making role identities salient and enhancing follower identification with the mission and the collective. Thus

Proposition 3. Leaders who have charismatic effects are more likely to arouse motives in the context of references to the mission and the collective than are those who do not have charismatic effects.

Role Modeling

Shamir et al. (1992) state that vicarious learning occurs when the relevant messages are inferred by followers from observation of leaders' behavior, lifestyle, emotional reactions, values, aspirations, preferences, and the like. The leader becomes a "representative character" (Bellah et al., 1985)—a symbol that brings together in one concentrated image the way people in a given social environment organize and give meaning and direction to their lives. He or she becomes an image that helps define for the followers just what kinds of traits, values, beliefs, and behaviors it is good and legitimate to develop. Observation of achievement, affiliative or power-oriented behavior by the leader is likely to arouse the achievement, affiliative, or power motives of followers.

This line of reasoning explains one of the processes by which leaders effect followers. Thus

Proposition 4. Leaders who have charismatic effects are more likely to behave in a manner that provides a personal and vivid example of the values of the mission than are leaders who do not.

The discussion thus far sets the stage for integrating the various versions of charismatic theory.

TOWARD THE INTEGRATION OF CHARISMATIC, VISIONARY, AND TRANSFORMATIONAL THEORIES

The behaviors specified by charismatic, visionary, and transformational leadership theories are listed in Table 4.1. The effects of most of these leader behaviors can be explained by the motivational theory of the transformational effects of charismatic leadership presented above (see Table 4.2). We now turn to a discussion of how the effects of these behaviors can be explained by the theory presented above.

Table 4.2
Summary of the Motivational Effects of Traditional and Charismatic Leadership Processes

Motivational component	Traditional leadership processes	Charismatic leadership processes
Intrinsic value of behavior	Marking the task more interesting, varied, enjoyable, challenging, as in job enrichment	Linking behavior to followers' self-concepts, internalized values and cherished identities
Behavior-accomplishment expectancy	Coaching, training, providing material and emotional support, clarifying goals, providing instrumental support, e.g., coordination, expertise, cooperation from others	Increasing general self-efficacy (through increasing self-worth and communication of confidence and high expectations); emphasizing collective efficacy
Intrinsic value goal accomplishment	Goal setting, increasing task identity, providing feedback	Linking goals to the past and the present and to values in a framework of a "mission," which serves as a basis for identification; motive arousal
Accomplishment reward expectancies	Establishing clear performance evaluation and tying rewards to performance	Generating faith by connecting behaviors and goals to a "dream" or a utopian ideal vision of a better future
Valence of extrinsic rewards	Taken into consideration in rewarding performance	Not addressed

Visionary Behavior

According to all of the theories, charismatic leaders are visionary. More specifically such leaders articulate an ideological goal that describes a better future for followers. This goal is ideological in the sense that the leader asserts that it is the moral right of followers to realize the goal. As Burns (1978) states, such leaders emphasize fundamental values such as beauty, order, honesty, dignity, and human rights.

House describes such goals as transcendent in the sense that they are ideological rather than pragmatic, and are laden with moral overtones. In fact, articulation of an ideological goal as a vision for a better future, for which followers have a moral claim, is the sine quo non of all charismatic, visionary theories. Since the vision of the leader is ideological, it is stated in terms of values. If the values are congruent with those of the followers the vision strongly engages the followers' self-concepts and follower motives become aroused, as described above. Further, since the leader asserts that it is the moral right of followers to realize the vision, articulation of the vision enhances followers' sense of self-worth. Having complete faith in the moral correctness of one's conviction gives one the strength and confidence to behave accordingly.

Image Building

That leaders consciously engage in building a positive image in the eyes of followers, and an image of a lifestyle that is consistent with the values of the vision, appears to be a reasonable inference, on the basis of anecdotal observation of such outstanding leaders.

Gandhi dressed in swaddling clothes and lived a life of forebearance and poverty that was consistent with the condition of his followers and his exhortations that Indians would have to make significant sacrifices in the interest of his vision of a free India. Gandhi stated that when India was set free of British domination. Indian leaders and high-level public servants would clean their own toilets.

Churchill and Hitler were known to spend long hours practicing their speeches before mirrors in order to create dramatic effects on followers. Patton and Montgomery displayed their insignia of rank, their medals of honor and braids, signifying powerful leadership. These military generals fashioned their attire and demeanor to appeal to machismoism, authoritarianism, and patriotism in the interest of arousing soldiers to a state of fervor and readiness to do battle.

Leader image building contributes to followers' perception of the leader as competent, credible, nurturing, trustworthy, and motivated to serve the rightful and morale interests of the mission and the collective (House, 1977). Thus, leader image building sets the stage for effective role modeling, since followers identify with the values of role models, who are highly admired, and perceived as credible and competent. Leader image building is likely to be a necessary, but not sufficient, condition for leaders to have charismatic effects. However, leader image building alone is not likely to differentiate charismatic from noncharismatic leaders or to produce charismatic effects.

Empowering Behaviors

House, Burns, Bass, Bennis and Nanus, Conger and Kanungo, and Sashkin all assert that charismatic leaders in some manner, demonstrate determination, optimism, self-confidence, and confidence in themselves and the collective ability to accomplish the mission and realize the vision. Such behavior is claimed to be empowering for followers in the sense that it inspires confidence and thus self-efficacy, and provides a role model of confidence, optimism, and determination. Empowering behaviors of this kind engage the self of followers by enhancing follower efficacy and self-worth.

A second behavior implicated in charismatic leadership is display of confidence in followers willingness to make self-sacrifice and their ability to accomplish exceptional goals. As demonstrated in a substantial number of studies (Rosenthal and Jacobson, 1968; Korman, 1970, 1971; Eden, 1990), followers' behavior rise to the expectations of leaders who are respected and show confidence in followers, and sink to the despair of leaders who show that they anticipated poor performance from followers. This generalization has been established with respect to students (Rosenthal and Jacobson, 1968), managers (Korman, 1970, 1971; Eden, 1990), and Israeli soldiers (Eden, 1990). Accordingly, the combination of high performance expectations and display of confidence in followers, by both word and deed, enhances follower generalized self-confidence (Smith, 1982) as well as specific task relevant efficacy expectations (Eden, 1990; Bandura, 1986). Such leader behavior is a powerful motivational force. The expression of confidence in followers is implicit in all of the charismatic theories discussed in this paper. Further, the assertion that these behaviors differentiate charismatic from noncharismatic leaders is illustrated by slogans used by famous leaders such as those of Martin Luther King, "I have a dream" and John Fitzgerald Kennedy, "Ask not what your country can do for you but what you can do for your country."

Risk Taking and Self-Sacrificial Behavior

By taking risks, making personal sacrifices (Sashkin, 1988), and engaging in unconventional behavior (Conger and Kanungo, 1987), charismatic leaders demonstrate their own courage and conviction in the mission and thus earn both credibility and acceptance as a role model of the values of the vision and the mission. In a recent unpublished study House and Woycke identified 10 charismatic and 10 noncharismatic leaders of underdeveloped nations. These leaders are matched by continent, size of nation, and time of reign (see Table 4.3). It is noteworthy that 7 of the 10 charismatic leaders spent time in prison, while only 2 of the noncharismatic leaders did so. This is evidence of the charismatic leaders' willingness to take risks and make self-sacrifices in the interest of their vision and their collectives. Thus we view these behaviors as charismatic and expect these behaviors to differentiate charismatic from noncharismatic leaders.

Table 4.3
Third World Leaders

Leader	Nation
Charismatic	
Castro	Cuba
Peron	Argentina
Mkurman	Ghana
Ken Yatta	Kenya
Myere	Tanzania
Nassar	Egypt
Ataturk	Turkey
Nehru	India
Mao	China
Sukarno	Indonesia
Noncharismatic	
Trujillo	Dominican Republic
Betancourt	Venezuela
Vargas	Brazil
Tubman	Liberia
Gbote	Uganda
Mobuto	Zaire
Nurial-Said	Iraq
Reza Shak Pahlavi	Iran
Synagman Rhee	Korea
Phipum	Thailand

Intellectual Stimulation

According to Bass (1985), transformational leaders intellectually stimulate their followers. Intellectual stimulation involves more than merely verbally encouraging followers to use their intelligence or experience. It involves challenging followers' assumptions, asking them to see the world from a different perspective, encouraging them not to defend stereotypes and generalizations that they have accepted in the past, and even encouraging people to think independently of the leader.

Intellectually stimulating messages of the leader are likely to be dissonant with some of the followers' beliefs. Thus, such messages most likely fall within the follower's normal zone of rejection (Sherif et al., 1965). That is, such messages are likely to be so far removed from the attitudes and beliefs of followers that they would ordinarily be dismissed out of hand by a person with whom the followers do not have a charismatic relationship. However, because the followers view the leader as credible, respected, and admired; attribute trustworthiness to the leader; share important values with the leader; and identify with the leader; they are more likely to accept and internalize the leader's message. Thus, the intellectual stimulation dimension of Bass's theory of transformational leadership and its effects on followers can be explained on the basis of the self-implication theory presented here. Specifically, messages from the leader that would ordinarily be unacceptable to followers will be accepted because, since followers self-concepts are engaged in the charismatic relationships, it would be very dissonant not to accept such messages. The choice to reject the message implies a choice to reject the leader and the mission. Thus

Proposition 5. Leaders who have charismatic effects are more likely to challenge the assumptions, stereotypes, generalizations, and worldviews (weltanschauung) of followers than are leaders who do not have such effects.

Proposition 6. Followers who are in a charismatic relationships with their leaders are more likely to be intellectually stimulated by their leader's challenges to their assumptions stereotypes, generalizations, and worldviews, than are followers who are not in such a relationship.

Supportive Leader Behavior

Contrary to Bass (1985) and Sashkin (1988), we do not see supportive person-oriented behaviors as uniquely charismatic. Bass argues that individualized consideration is a transformational leader behavior, while Sashkin (1988) believes that personal communication, developing credibility and trustworthiness, and displaying respect toward followers are characteristics of visionary leaders. We see these and other supportive person- and group-oriented behaviors as necessary, but not sufficient in themselves, to distinguish charismatic from noncharismatic leaders. Further, we believe that individuals can engage in these behaviors to a great extent and still not be charismatic. Clearly, the studies by Bass and his associates, based on follower perceptions of leaders, demonstrates consistently that charismatic leaders are also perceived as high on individualized consideration. The self-concept theory presented here suggests that individualized consideration is seen by subordinates as a result of shared values and the belief that the leader has the interests of the collectivity strongly in mind. Scores on the individualized consideration scale most likely reflect not only the behaviors described in Bass's (1985) individualized consideration scale,[1] but also the positive attributions by followers associated with the charismatic relationship.

Adaptive Behavior

Conger and Kanungo's (1987) theory of charismatic leadership and Sashkin's (1988) theory of visionary leadership, assert that charismatic leaders are more sensitive to the environment and monitor the environment more than noncharismatic leaders. We do not believe these behaviors distinguish between the two types of leaders. We believe environmental sensitivity, environmental monitoring, and adaptiveness are attributes of effective leaders in open systems in uncertain and changing environments. While these behaviors have pragmatic value in such circumstances, we see no self-implicating or motive-arousing effects on followers of these behaviors. Thus we do not believe these attributes to be unique to charismatic leaders.

We believe there are limits to the adaptability of charismatic as well as other leaders. Specifically, with respect to charismatic leaders, we believe that individuals who are charismatic in a given situation are likely to be charismatic in similar situations but not in other situations that are dissimilar. By "similar situations" we mean situations that involve essentially the same ideological base and involve followers who have similar value systems. Historically, most charismatic leaders have been charismatic with respect to one movement or one kind of movement only. This observation is illustrated by the experience of Vince Lombardi, a reputed charismatic

[1]The precise factorial structure hypothesized in Bass's (1985) theory of transformational leadership has not been supported in an extensive study of 12,000 Air Force cadets (Curphy, 1990). However, the charismatic leader behaviors specified in Bass's theory have consistently been strongly related to the theoretical dependent variables described above.

and great football coach. Lombardi took over the head coaching responsibility for the Green Bay Packers when they were at the bottom of the league. He soon brought them to the top of the league and lead them to many championships. He was then "promoted" to the position of general manager, which he found unchallenging, uninteresting, frustrating, and dissatisfying. No one heard of him as a great general manager, and his charisma was not apparent. As a result of disenchantment, he moved to become head coach of the Washington Redskins, who were at the bottom of their league. Again he repeated the performance of bringing the team to the top of the league and winning many championships.

While Lombardi was clearly a charismatic professional football coach, it is conceivable that he could be a charismatic combat leader since football coaching and combat leadership are similar with respect to both ideology and values of the followers. Lombardi's style was based on the ideology of winning. "Winning isn't everything, it's the only thing." He stressed "giving one hundred percent" and physical conditioning, "fatigue makes coward of us all." Combat requires a similar ideology of winning, extra physical effort, and physical conditioning.

However, it is doubtful that Lombardi could lead an organization in which the dominant values are the acquisition of knowledge, scientific advancement, pacifism, and nonviolent disobedience or passive resistance.

Ghandi was a charismatic leader in the interest of nonviolent resistance to the British and, as stated above, unification of the diverse religious sects of India. It is doubtful that Ghandi could have been a charismatic leader of combat troops or football players, even if he had the necessary knowledge.

Since charismatic leaders must have a passion for the ideological goal that they set forth, it is most likely that they are rather nonadaptable with respect to changes in the vision or the values underlying it. In fact, there is evidence that individuals who are extremely high or low with respect to values and attitudes or more inflexible than those who are closer to the neutral point (Sherif et al., 1965).

This argument does not imply that charismatic leaders are strategically or tactically rigid. Rather, we believe that such leaders are able to change strategy and tactics in the interest of the vision but are likely to be unable to compromise the major thrust of the mission, or its underlying values and ideology.

Thus we see charismatic leader adaptability to be limited to incremental, tactical, and strategic change and not be generalizable from situation to situation when such situations are fundamentally different with respect to ideology and with respect to the values of the followers involved.

In summary, we see most of the behaviors theoretically specified as charismatic, transformational, or visionary by other authors, to be explainable within the theory of motivation presented here. Figure 4.1 presents a model of this theory. According to this model, leader behaviors activate motivational mechanisms that, in turn, affect self-concepts and further motivational mechanisms. These intervening variables and processes, in turn, have a strong positive impact on the behaviors and psychological states specified in Figure 4.1. Heightened follower commitment, self-sacrifice, motivation, and performance, in turn, feed back on and sustain follower motivation and reinforce follower self-concepts. When observed by the leader, these follower responses further reinforce and therefore sustain the charismatic behaviors at a level appropriate for the mission.

CONCLUSION

In this paper, we have argued that certain effects on followers are unique to charismatic leaders. We have argued that these effects are produced by leadership actions that arouse follower motivations and implicate the self-concept of the followers. Such effects engage the related motivations for self-expression, self-esteem, self-worth, and self-consistency. We have advanced a set of propositions that links leader behavior and followers through follower motives and self-concepts.

Collectively, these propositions form a speculative theoretical integration of current theories of charismatic and transformational leadership with respect to the behaviors of charismatic leaders (House, 1977; Bass, 1985; Bennis and Nanus, 1985; Conger and Kanungo, 1987; Sashkin, 1988). Hopefully, our explanation helps to provide greater insights concerning the charismatic phenomena. We recognize that the theory is speculative. However, we believe such speculation is warranted because it permits a coherent and parsimonious integration of current charismatic, transformational and visionary theories of leadership. Further, the propositions of the theory are testable. Shamir et al. (1991) previously noted that

> Some scholars have voiced skepticism concerning whether or not leaders can make a difference in organizational performance (Salancik and Pfeffer, 1977; Pfeffer, 1977; Meindl et al. 1985). This skepticism reflects the argument that people are biased toward overattributing to leaders influence on events which are complex and difficult to understand. As a result, leadership in general, and charismatic leadership in particular, could be dismissed as an exaggerated perception on the part of the followers which does not have strong substantial effects on organizational outcomes, and is therefore not worthy of much attention by students of organizations.

We disagree with such skepticism. We believe that the evidence in support of the various versions of charismatic theory is too strong to be dismissed. We have offered a theoretical explanation for the effects of charismatic leadership found in a large number of empirical investigations. Our theoretical speculations suggest the existence of previously unspecified motivational mechanisms without which the transformational effects of charismatic leadership cannot be explained.

We have presented our arguments in the form of testable propositions and have reviewed relevant supporting evidence. Our propositions are, for the most part, not in contradiction to existing theories. Rather, they are complementary in the sense that they explain the motivational processes by which leader behavior described in charismatic, visionary, or transformational theories produce the transformational effects of leaders on followers.

We have labeled this paper "*Toward* the Integration of Transformational, Charismatic, and Visionary Theories" because we offer an integration of only one of the major aspects of the theories considered here, namely, charismatic behaviors. Much remains to be integrated. Some of the theories specify personality characteristics of charismatic leaders (Weber, 1947; House, 1977; Sashkin, 1988). Others suggest attribution processes by which leaders gain and maintain the status of charisma (Weber, 1947; Conger and Kanungo, 1987). Some theories also specify environmental conditions that facilitate the emergence and performance of charismatic leaders (Weber, 1947; House, 1977; Shamir et al., 1992).

Hopefully, future research and theorizing will lead to a parsimonious explanation that accounts for and integrates the personality characteristics and environmental conditions that are implicated in the charismatic phenomenon. Further, we hope that the theoretical framework presented here will be pruned, modified, and extended as a result of future theorizing and empirical testing.

References

Ashour, A. S. (1982). A framework for a cognitive behavioral theory of leader influence and effectiveness. *Organizational Behavior and Human Performance, 30,* 407–430.

Avolio, B. J., and Bass, B. M. (1987). Charisma and beyond. In J. G. Hunt, B. R. Baliga, H. P. Dachler, and C. A. Schriesheim (Eds.), *Emerging Leadership Vistas.* Lexington: MA: Heath.

Avolio, B. J., Waldman, D. A., and Einstein, W. O. (1988). Transformational leadership in management game simulation. *Group and Organization Studies, 13*(1), 59–80.

Bandura, A. (1986). *Social foundations of thought and action: A social cognitive theory.* Englewood Cliffs, NJ: Prentice-Hall.

Bass, B. M. (1985). *Leadership and performance beyond expectations.* New York: Free Press.

Bass, B. M., Avolio, B. J., and Goodheim, L. (1987a). Biographical assessment of transformational leadership at the world-class level. *Journal of Management, 13,* 7–19.

Bass, B. M., and Yammarino, F. J. (1988). *Long term forecasting of transformational leadership and its effects among naval officers: Some preliminary findings* (Technical Report No. ONR-TR-2). Arlington, VA: Office of Naval Research.

Bellah, R. N., Madsen, R., Sullivan, W. M., Swidler, A., and Tipton, S. M. (1985). *Habits of the heart: Individualism and commitment in American life.* New York: Harper & Row.

Bennis, W., and Nanus, B. (1985). *Leaders: The strategies for taking charge.* New York: Harper & Row.

Blumenson, M. (1985). *Patton: The man behind the legend 1885–1945.* New York: William Morrow.

Burns, J. M. (1978). *Leadership,* New York: Harper & Row.

Collins, L., and LaPierre, D. (1973). *Freedom at midnight.* New York: Simon and Schuster.

Conger, J. A., and Kanungo, R. A. (1987). Towards a behavioral theory of charismatic leadership in organizational settings. *Academy of Management Review, 12,* 637–647.

Curphy, G. J. (1990). An empirical study of Bass (1985). *Theory of transformational and transactional leadership.* Unpublished doctoral dissertation, The University of Minnesota.

Eden, D. O. V. (1990). *Pygmilian in management.* Lexington, MA: Heath.

Evans, G. (1970). The effects of supervisory behavior on the path-goal relationship. *Organizational and Human Performance, 5,* 277–298.

Gardner, J. (1965). Inaugural address to the executives of the Department of Health, Education and Welfare.

Graen, G., and Cashman, J. F. (1975). A role-making model of leadership in formal organizations: A developmental approach. In J. G. Hunt and L. L. Larson (Eds.), *Leadership Frontiers* (pp. 143–165). Kent, OH: Kent State University Press.

Hater, J. J., and Bass, B. M. (1988). Supervisor's evaluations and subordinates' perceptions of transformational leadership. *Journal of Applied Psychology, 73,* 695–702.

Hollander, E. P. (1964). *Leaders, groups, and influence.* New York: Oxford University Press.

House, R. J. (1971). A path goal theory of leader effectiveness. *Administrative Science Quarterly, 16*(3), 321–338.

House. R. J. (1977). A 1976 theory of charismatic leadership. In J. G. Hunt and L. Larson (Eds.), *Leadership: The Cutting Edge,* (pp 189–204). Carbondale, IL: Southern Illinois University Press.

House, R. J., Spangles, W. D., and Woycke, J. (1991). Personality and charisma in the U.S. presidency: A psychological theory of leadership effectiveness. *Administrative Science Quarterly,* (in press).

Howell, J. M., and Frost, P. J. (1989). A laboratory study of charismatic leadership. *Organizational Behavior and Human Decision Processes, 43*(2), 243–269.

Howell, J. M., and Higgins, C. (1990a). Champions of technological innovation. *Administrative Science Quarterly, 35,* 317–341.

Howell, J. M., and Higgins, C. A. (1990b). Leadership behaviors, influence tactics, and career experiences of champions of technological innovation. *Leadership Quarterly, 1*(4), 249–264.

Koh, W. L., Terborg, J. R., and Steers, R. M. (1991). The impact of transformational leadership on organizational commitment: Organizational citizenship behavior teacher satisfaction and student performance in Singapore. Paper presented at the Academy of Management, Fontenbleu, FL.

Korman, A. K. (1970). Toward an hypothesis of work behavior. *Journal of Applied Psychology, 54,* 31–41.

Korman, A. K. (1971). Expectancies as determinants of performance. *Journal of Applied Psychology, 55,* 218–222.

Kuhnert, K. W., and Lewis, P. (1987). Transactional and transformational leadership: A constructive/developmental analysis. *Academy of Management Review, 12,* 648–657.

Litwin, G. H., and Stringer, R. A., Jr. (1968). *Motivation and organizational climate.* Boston: Harvard Business School Press.

McCall, G. H., and Simmons, J. T. (1978). *Identities and interaction,* rev. New York: Free Press.

McClelland, D. (1985). *Human motivation.* Chicago: Scott, Foresman.

Meindl, J. R., Ehrlich, S. B., and Dukerlch, J. M. (1985). The romance of leadership. *Administrative Science Quarterly, 30,* 78–102.

Pereira, D. F. (1988). Factors associated with transformational leadership in an Indian engineering firm. Paper presented at the annual meeting of Administrative Science Association of Canada.

Pfeffer, J. (1977). The ambiguity of leadership. *Academy of Management Review, 2,* 104–112.

Podsakoff, P. M., Mackenzie, S. B., Morrman, R. H., and Fetter, R. (1990). Transformational leader behaviors and their effects on followers' trust in leader, satisfaction, and organizational citizenship behaviors. *Leadership Quarterly, 1*(2), 107–142.

Podsakoff, P. M., Todor, W. D., and Scov, R. (1982). Effects of leader performance contingent and non-contingent reward and punishment behaviors on subordinate performance and satisfaction. *Academy of Management Journal, 25,* 812–821.

Puffer, S. M. (1990). Attributions of charismatic leadership: The impact of decision style, outcome, and observer characteristics. *Leadership Quarterly, 1*(3), 177–192.

Roberts, N. (1985). Transforming leadership: A process of collective action. *Human Relations, 38,* 1023–1046.

Roberts, N. C., and Bradley, R. T. (1988). The limits of charisma. In J. A. Conger and R. N. Kanungo (Eds.), *Charismatic leadership: The elusive factor in organizational effectiveness.* San Francisco: Jossey-Bass.

Rosenthal, R., and Jacobson, L. (1968). *Pygmalion in the classroom: Teacher expectation and pupils' intellectual development.* New York: Holt, Rinehart and Winston.

Salancik, G. R., and Pfeffer, J. (1977). Constraints on administrators discretion: The limited influence of mayors on city budgets. *Urban Affairs Quarterly* (June).

Sashkin, M. (1988). The visionary leaders. In J. A. Conger and R. A. Kanungo (Eds.), *Charismatic leadership: The elusive factor in organizational effectiveness,* (pp. 122–160). San Francisco: Jossey-Bass.

Shamir, B., House, R. J., and Arthur, M. B. (1992). The motivational effects of charismatic leadership: A self-concept-based theory. *Organizational Science,* (in press).

Sherif, C. W., Sherif, M., and Nabergall, R. E. (1965). *Attitudes and attitude change,* Philadelphia: Saunders.

Shipley, T. E., and Veroff, J. (1952). Projective measure of need for affiliation. *Journal of Experimental Psychology, 43,* 349–356.

Smith, B. J. (1982). *An initial test of a theory of charismatic leadership based on the responses of subordinates.* Unpublished doctoral dissertation, University of Toronto, Canada.

Tajfel, H., and Turner, J. C. (1985). The social identity theory of intergroup behavior. In S. Worchel and W. G. Austin (Eds.), *Psychology of intergroup relations,* 2nd ed. (pp. 7–24). Chicago: Nelson-Hall.

Tichy, N. M., and Devanna, M. A. (1986). *The transformational leader.* New York: Wiley.

Trice, H. M., and Beyer, J. M. (1986). Charisma and its routinization in two social movement organizations. In B. M. Staw and L. L. Cummings (Eds.), *Research in organizational behavior* (pp. 113–164). Greenwich, CT: JAI Press.

Waldman, D. A., Bass, B. M., and Einstein, W. O. (1987). Leadership and outcomes of performance appraisal processes. *Journal of Occupational Psychology, 60,* 177–186.

Weber, M. (1947). *The theory of social and economic organization.* (A. M. Henderson and T. Parsons, Transls.; T. Parsons, Ed.). New York: Free Press. (Originally published in 1924.)

Willner, A. R. (1984). *The spellbinders: Charismatic political leadership.* New Haven, CT: Yale University Press.

Winter, D. G. (1978). *Navy leadership and management competencies: Convergence among tests, interviews, and performance ratings.* Boston: McBer.

Wofford, J. C., and Srinivasan, T. N. (1983). An experimental test of leader-environment-follower interaction theory of leadership. *Organizational Behavior and Human Performance, 32,* 35–54.

Yukl, G. A., and Van Fleet, D. D. (1982). Cross situational, multimethod research on military leader effectiveness. *Organizational Behavior and Human Performance, 30,* 87–108.

5

Leadership, Values, and Accountability

Terence R. Mitchell
Department of Management and Organization
University of Washington

INTRODUCTION

In the last few years I have written with my colleague Bill Scott a number of critical essays on the status of America's leaders (e.g., Mitchell and Scott,

Leadership Theory and Research: Perspectives and Directions

1987, 1990). These papers have taken the position that we have serious problems in this country and that some of the causes of these problems can be attributed to the values of our leaders. The first part of this paper focuses on some of these problems and is based on these earlier papers. Next we focus on the issue of values—what values seem to be related to these problems and how the problems can be confronted. One conclusion that we have drawn from this analysis is that more accountability is needed to curb managerial abuses and provide legitimacy for managerial actions.

We then spend a major portion of the paper discussing some research on accountability. We describe in detail one completed study, one study in progress, and two that are being planned. Finally, we end the paper with a discussion of what we think needs to be done in the way of reforms.

AMERICA'S PROBLEMS

While many problems face our society, one of our earlier papers focused on some of the major issues that could be partly traced to the behavior of administrators and to some extent reflected their values (Mitchell and Scott, 1990). The problems are environmental decay, a growing underclass, and ethical abuses, which reflect actions that can in the long run undermine the physical, social, and moral foundations of the republic.

Environmental Decay

The physical deterioration of our environment is apparent everywhere. Red tides of algae consume large quantities of oxygen in the water, resulting in the death of numerous aquatic life forms (*New York Times,* May 3, 1988). Industrial discharges, sewage, fertilizer runoff, and pollutants in the air contribute to the problem. Acid rain is a major concern as a cause of loss of marine life, damage to forests and lakes, and even the erosion of buildings. We have far more toxic waste than we can effectively handle (*Washington Post,* Aug. 11, 1989). The Great Lakes are threatened by industrial effluent and municipal sewage (*New York Times,* July 13, 1988). Alaska's oil development has caused substantial environmental damage (*New York Times,* May 11, 1989). The dreaded "greenhouse effect" is predicted to cause wild swings in temperature, increased cancer rates, the globe covered with clouds, and many present coastlines completely obliterated by water (*Seattle Post Intelligencer,* 1988). Also, great holes in the ozone layer have been created by burning fossil fuels, cutting down our forests, releasing large amounts of nitrous oxide from fertilizers and car emissions, and the use of chlorofluorocarbons in marketing and industrial processes (*New York Times,* May 4, 1989).

Beyond this, we continue to use up the earth's natural resources at an alarming rate—far outstripping our ability to replace them. Environmental pillage is partly due to the behavior and decisions of American business and government leaders.

The Underclass

Another major problem is that there is an increasing number of people who are simply disconnected from our society. They are America's "invisible" people, whose existence provides a sharp contrast between the advantaged and disadvantaged in our society. The gap between rich and poor is widening (*New York Times,* Nov. 16, 1987).

According to the 1990 census, there are now more than 34 million people living below the poverty level (*New York Times,* Dec. 20, 1987). These people are defined as the "underclass"—generally uneducated, unemployed, poor, and more likely to use drugs or engage in criminal activity than the rest of the population. There is a greater percentage of minorities in this group than in the population as a whole, and they tend to live in the core of most major cities in the United States. The types of jobs available for the underclass are being reduced, the quality of their education is getting worse, and the use of drugs is increasing as is its associated violence (*New York Times,* March 23, 1987).

The most disturbing fact about the situation is that these people seem to have permanently dropped out of American society. Government welfare does not seem to help and is viewed by some as institutionalizing dependency. In short we are faced with a potentially catastrophic situation of human degradation. Many of our inner cities are unsafe and dirty and filled with grief. The invisible people are moved and more isolated from mainstream America, and their numbers are growing larger.

Leader Corruptness

We believe the most serious threat to our society is the failure of stewardship of American leaders. The management abuses of the public and private trust are everywhere, and some say the lack of moral leadership is America's number one problem. Over the last few years we have had major stock scandals, connections between organized crime and banks, "golden parachutes," greenmail operations, and the proliferation of junk bonds that threaten the stability of the banking system. We witnessed the E. F. Hutton check-kiting practices, General Electric's contract frauds, and insider trading scandals. More recently there was the WedTech contract favoritism issue; stock manipulation by GAF Corporation; allegations of influence peddling at HUD (Department of Housing and Urban Development); racketeering and fraud indictments at Drexel, Burnham, Lambert; and, of course, Irangate and the Defense Department procurement probe, which has uncovered indications of rampant bribery. In an issue focusing on ethical violations in both the private and public sectors, *Time Magazine* (May 25, 1987) stated "White collar scams abound, insider trading, money laundering, greenmail, greed combined with technology has made stealing more tempting than ever. Result: What began as the decade of the entrepreneur is becoming the age of the pinstriped outlaw" (p. 20). In the same issue, discussing the public sector, *Time* said "a relentless procession of forlorn faces assaults the nations moral equanimity, characters linked in the public mind not by any connection between their diverse dubious deeds but by the fact that each in his or her own way has somehow seemed to betray the public trust" (p. 14).

Whether corruption is now more, the same as, or less than it has been in the past is impossible to say and pointless to argue about. Corruption is wrong regardless of how extensive it is. But the coverage given to miscreant managers by the media has heightened America's awareness of wrongdoing by those in power, leaving us with an alienated distrusting populace.

THE ETHIC OF PERSONAL ADVANTAGE

The data for the problems cited above are fairly easy to acquire as well as interpret. People may differ on the degree to which they consider these problems to be serious, but there is little doubt about the problems themselves. The evidence is massive that we, as a society, are degrading our physical environment, have a significant portion of our population that is alienated from the rest of society, and have engaged in widely reported amounts of fraud, crime, and unethical behavior.

An investigation of the literature on values also presents a fairly clear picture (Mitchell and Scott, 1990). Our conclusion after this review was that three major sets of opposing values are central themes in the literature: (1) a present versus a future orientation, (2) an instrumental as opposed to a substantive focus, and (3) an emphasis on individualism contrasted with community. Each value in the three sets is in constant tension with the one to which it is paired. However, the emphasis on these values in our society is not equal. The data (Mitchell and Scott, 1990) suggest that American values now reflect a present, instrumental, individualistic orientation and that this orientation is associated with the problems discussed above (*Seattle Times,* Jan. 15, 1989; *Washington Post,* April 5, 1988). That is, these values are reflected in behavior that maximizes personal advantage in the short run and discounts the long-run costs of disregarding ethics, the underclass, and the environment (*Seattle Post Intelligencer,* May 7, 1989). We call this combination of values the ethic of personal advantage, and we believe the problems in America have the ethic of personal advantage as their common denominator. It is our leaders who have gained legitimacy and subscribe to these values that have exacerbated rather than reduced these problems.

LEADER LEGITIMACY

One can trace the concepts of legitimacy from the early works of Weber and Barnard, through the works of French and Raven, March, and Dahl to the current works of Mintzberg, House, and Pfeffer. While different labels are used by these authors to describe legitimacy, a recent review of the academic literature and popular press suggests that three main criteria are involved: expertise, entrepreneurship, and stewardship. Legitimacy resides in people's beliefs that their leaders are competent (experts), are personally compelling and dynamic (entrepreneurial), and are stewards (trustworthy). However, the evidence for legitimacy based on expertise or entrepreneurship is questionable for a number of reasons (Mitchell and Scott, 1987).

First, there appears to be little consensus about what constitutes individual expertise or what constitutes effectiveness and how they are related. "Expertise" refers to administration's economic function of allocating resources so that they will be more productive of the material values that an organization and its clients seek. But beyond this is an ideology, according to MacIntyre, which holds that the administrative class possesses, with the virtual exclusion of anyone else, a systematic expertise "in controlling a certain (economic) aspect of social reality" (MacIntyre, 1981, p. 71).

The practical skills associated with this expertise are knowledge based and rely heavily on value-neutral generalizations of the social sciences. By access through formal education, administrative training, and organization socialization, administrators are believed to possess an arcane learning which allows them to be expert in their tasks (Barnard, 1938).

But neither expertise nor effectiveness is defined very well. The literature on leadership suggests that there is simply no consensus about what attributes make an administrator an expert or effective. In fact, most of the current research in this area presents either contingency-type models (some traits in some settings are effective on some dimensions), situational theories (the situation determines the leader's behavior), or what is called "substitutes for leadership"—settings where leadership expertise makes no difference at all or theories where leadership is all in the eye of the beholder (Meindl, 1990).

The same problem occurs with effectiveness. Most objective criteria are really just subjective criteria once removed such that it is often seen as an "abstraction." Brief et al. (1981) stated that "what frequently happens is that the definition of effectiveness remains vague and is not explicitly stated. Rather, the standards habitually used are assumed to be related to effectiveness." Recent views by Cameron and Whetton (1983) and Lewin and Minton (1986) agreed with these assessments, with Cameron going so far as to indicate that there are built-in paradoxes in the notion of organizational effectiveness and that "consensus regarding the best, or sufficient, set of indicators of effectiveness is impossible to obtain" (p. 528). Again, factors such as the internal organizational design, the external economic and competitive environment, and other chance events often are as important as anything that is done by the organization or its leaders.

Similar problems occur when one tries to define entrepreneurship and demonstrate its relationship to effectiveness. "Entrepreneurship" originally referred to the well-known economic function of business startups, where innovative and visionary individuals exploited an invention or niche in the market to produce a new commodity or service (Schumpeter, 1947). However, the economists' notion of entrepreneurial expertise was overlaid with a mantle of social symbolism that attributed wondersomeness to certain individuals. Entrepreneurship became an administrative concept that identified certain administrators as the source of innovation and progress (Sloan, 1963). It is de rigueur to read in the popular business press and in the house organs of public agencies about a vice president or a deputy agency director urging their subordinates to be entrepreneurial.

This modern version of entrepreneurship has become a necessary legitimizing concept for administrators. It strengthens the argument that the administrators of large organizations are the present-day counterparts of the entrepreneurs of the past. The legitimizing potential of this argument when wedded to expertise is enormous. It suggests that only a few have the skill and vision to lead and that these few dwell, as administrators, in interdependent public and private organizations. More importantly, administrators have the right to draw great economic benefits from their organizations without suspicion of economic exploitation. They are receiving their just desserts for doing a job few could do. Thus, entrepreneurship and expertise are joined in a doctrine of legitimacy that, on one hand, sidesteps the pejorative implications of economic exploitation and, on the other hand, incorporates flattering symbols of an administrative elite inspiring progress within large organizations.

This web of social and economic theory is not represented in today's organizations. Entrepreneurship is a highly personalized concept of progress that is most often applied to situations where the individual can function with considerable autonomy and freedom. These conditions do not exist in most large organizations, and in the public sector they may run counter to normative and legal constraints. Consequently, in entrepreneurship, vast contradictions are found between its individualistic symbols and the collective reality of modern organizations.

Empirical work on entrepreneurship is in utter disarray. There is simply no empirical support for the idea that certain traits (such as vision or risk taking) lead to either innovation or successes. Gasse's (1980) thorough literature review led him to conclude that "no clear link has yet been established between the personality characteristics of entrepreneurs and the success of their business ventures," and Kent et al. (1980) conclude that being in the right line of business at the right place and time is probably the most important single determinant of success. In the public sector Doig (1983) points out that many program agencies need leaders with initiative and vision and that these people are called "policy entrepreneurs"; yet later he points out that these same agencies are infrequently held accountable and that these entrepreneurs are often guilty of both corruption and simple incompetence.

Thus, just as for expertise, entrepreneurship is hard to define, and those definitions that do exist do not seem to be very helpful in predicting success. The factors that make an administrator appear expert and visionary seem to be as much determined by the situation and its circumstances as by the characteristics of the administrator. As theoretical and factual sources of legitimate authority, expertise and entrepreneurship are unproven guides.

The above considerations seem to uphold the public's opinion that its leadership elite is probably no more skilled or visionary than any other group of people who might hold these jobs (e.g., artists, physicians, scientists, university professors, engineers). So the question is, if expertise and entrepreneurship fail as grounds for legitimacy, what is left to confirm the leadership of those who are in positions of power? The answer is some demonstration of moral rectitude by managers and administrators to show that they are more ethical, trustworthy, honorable, and accountable in the use of privilege than are members of any other hypothetical group. In short, members of this elite group should show that they are good stewards.

The literature on stewardship, however, points to just the opposite. Besides the abuses that we have already documented there is clear evidence that the American public is aware of the problem. Lipset and Schneider (1983) reported that numerous surveys show that variance in confidence is based in large part on variations in the perceived ethical standards of those leading each institution. These authors argue that the lack of trust rests on the belief that business and government leaders are concerned about themselves first and the public last. Leaders are seen as concerned with furthering their own self-interest through making as much money as possible.

A recent survey of 6000 business managers by Posner and Schmidt (1984) showed that, of 11 values, the top two in importance were organizational effectiveness and high productivity, and the bottom two were organizational value to the community and service to the public. In a separate study of 803 top-level public officials the same authors (Schmidt and Posner, 1986) found that effectiveness and productivity were respectively first and third, while service to the public and value to the community were respectively seventh and eighth. When rating the importance of various constituents, the general public was tenth on a list of 13 with clients, bosses, self, technical personnel, managers, and coworkers as more important. The evidence suggests that public and private administrators as a class appear to care little about their obligations to the general public.

Stewardship implies administrative accountability to many constituencies for the uses of privilege. As matters seem to stand now, administration is not accountable, at least to the extent that people have confidence in its regulation. Almost all government administrators and business managers are not subject to any type of recall by democratic voting procedures; they are insulated from market discipline by varying degrees of economic and governmental power concentration; and the application of the business judgment rule and sovereign immunity protects them from criminal and civil liability.

THEORETICAL BACKGROUND ON ACCOUNTABILITY

So far we have suggested that America has some significant problems that can be traced to the values and behaviors of legitimized leaders. The question of concern in this section is how such leaders can be held accountable for these behaviors.

The requirement that one be answerable for one's decisions and actions is an implicit, if not explicit, assumption of organizational systems. Accountability is an integral part of both the classical and current understanding of organization theory. However, the relevant research to date on this topic suggests two major conclusions. First, there is very little agreement about what actually constitutes accountability (i.e., What is it? What causes it? What are its consequences?). Moreover, there seems to be considerable agreement that various kinds of ineffective, dysfunctional, and counterproductive behaviors occur in organizations that are purported to be characterized by a lack of accountability. The purpose of the next few sections is to describe a model of accountability in organizations.

Definition

"Accountability" is defined as the extent to which a person feels that his or her behavior is going to be observed and evaluated by others, and that important rewards and punishments are contingent upon these evaluations. There are some important components of this definition that need elaboration. First, it focuses on behavior rather than outcomes (Ouchi and Maguire, 1975). Our concern is with the particular actions one chooses. Second, the focus is external. Accountability means that there is an external evaluative force (Tetlock, 1985). Internal evaluations may be important (Schlenker and Weingold, 1989), but our conceptualization of accountability implies an external evaluative mechanism. Third, external evaluations without contingent rewards are insufficient. Evaluation does not produce feelings of accountability unless important social, professional, or economic rewards are contingent on the evaluations.

The organizational objectives are to have people behave in ways that are goal-oriented (i.e., consistent with the organization's goals), fit with the task and setting, and are appropriate, honest, and ethical. Increased accountability feelings should increase these behaviors. However, in order to achieve these objectives, we must understand the environmental or situational causes of accountability feelings, how these external factors influence the cognitive process, and the consequences of these psychological deliberations.

Causes of Accountability

We believe there are three main contextual factors that increase feelings of accountability. First, there are laws, rules, and regulations. Organizations have legal constraints and prescriptions that influence the behavior of their members. These may vary from demands for data about expenditures, hiring practices, or environmental impacts to restraints on unethical behavior such as bribes or expense account abuses. Mitchell and Scott (1990) have discussed some of these laws and rules that are external and internal to organizations and prescribe appropriate behavior.

A second influence on, or cause of, accountability is the way in which performance is evaluated. When people know their performance (and subsequent rewards) is contingent on regular systematic evaluations, they feel more accountable. The specific evaluation system characteristics that seem to increase these feelings are the frequency of evaluations, the number of evaluators, the formality of the evaluation, and the openness of access to the results (Fry et al., 1987).

Third, and perhaps of most importance as causes of accountability, are mechanisms of social control. These mechanisms include observability factors (e.g., closeness of supervision), which result in evaluation apprehension (Ferris and Mitchell, 1987), as well as sent expectations by salient others (Ferris and Judge, 1991). Accountability is significantly influenced by our perceptions of what others expect (Tetlock, 1985), and how they will treat us if we deviate from those expectations.

Accountability and Cognitive Processing

The immediate step between the foregoing organizational or social factors that should enhance accountability and the behavioral and organizational consequences is the cognitive process engaged in by the individual. Whereas a number of theoretical perspectives could be used to describe these dynamics, we believe that control theory (Klein, 1989; Hyland, 1988) best captures the essence of this process. This approach suggests that people choose their behaviors based on a cybernetic-type model where there are behavioral standards, a comparison of current action against the standard, and pressure to self-correct behaviors when action-standard discrepancies occur. The literature on feedback systems (e.g., Taylor et al., 1984), self-assessment (e.g., Ashford, 1989), social learning, (e.g., Bandura, 1988), goal setting (e.g., Locke and Latham, 1990), and decisionmaking (e.g., Beach and Mitchell, 1990) all employ similar mechanisms to explain behavior.

From an organizational perspective, the prescriptions are clear. For people to make both correct (i.e., organizationally desired) and accurate assessments of their actions, they need (1) clear standards, (2) clear and salient priorities, (3) agreement about standards, and (4) accurate and timely feedback about their behavior. To the extent that it is unclear what is expected in terms of specifying behavioral expectations, prioritizing what is important, and getting similar expectations sent from all sources, people will not feel accountable. However, all of the above will fail unless there is also accurate and timely feedback. One must know both the standard *and* how one's behavior compares to the standard.

Consequences of Accountability

The consequences of accountability (or lack of) are significant and affect numerous areas of organizational functioning. Research has shown that varying levels of accountability and ambiguity result in the use of more political and nonapproved influence tacts (Baucus and Near, 1991; Fandt and Ferris, 1990). There is some indication that the unchecked acquisition of power leads to biases in performance appraisals of self and others (Kipnis, 1987). McAllister et al. (1979) demonstrated that accountability results in more analysis and thoughtful decision processes. Jones (1986) has shown that making top-level executives more accountable results in fewer lawsuits and less illegal behavior within the organization. Finally, Brief et al. (1991) showed how being held accountable affected the resolution of ethical dilemmas.

Thus, introducing factors that increase accountability to organizational and legal standards may prevent counterproductive outcomes and increase organizational effectiveness in a variety of ways.

RESEARCH ON ACCOUNTABILITY: STUDY COMPLETED

Given this concern with accountability, we conducted some research on the topic, close to home. More specifically, we looked at the accountability of professors and administrators in schools of business in the United States (Fry et al., 1987). We were interested in the organizational and situational factors that seemed to result in high accountability, as reflected in the way that performance was appraised. We will discuss one completed study, one study in progress, and one that is being planned to test the assumptions of our model of accountability.

As we mentioned in the development of our model of accountability, one mechanism that should increase accountability is performance appraisal. The appraisal mechanism and the way it is conducted can serve as powerful checks against abuses of power.

Background

Obviously the number of appraisal techniques, factors inherent in the process, the type of people being appraised, and the possible causes of variation in appraisal techniques are far too numerous to investigate in one study. In the following sections we briefly discuss the rationale for the components of the research: the dependent variables, the sample, and the independent variables.

Important Dimensions of the Appraisal Process

Numerous literature reviews have discussed the appraisal process (Kane and Lawler, 1979; Feldman, 1986; Latham, 1986; Landy and Farr, 1983; Bernardin and Beatty, 1984; Ilgen and Feldman, 1983; Kavanagh, 1981; Mohrman and Lawler, 1983). Some process variables that have received a lot of attention are the frequency of evaluation, who conducts the evaluation, how many people are involved, how formal the procedure is, and who has access to the information.

A broad set of criteria can be used to evaluate these appraisal process variables (e.g., the reliability and validity of the instrument, its usefulness of reward systems, its acceptance and fairness of the associated feelings of accountability). Using such comprehensive criteria and looking at the accumulated results over the last 20 years produces the following set of dimensions and principles:

1. Evaluation frequency: More frequent evaluations (e.g., up to once or twice per year) appear to be better than less frequent evaluations.
2. Number of raters: More than one evaluation is preferable and peers and subordinates should be used where appropriate.
3. Formality: Evaluations represented by specific criteria and written evaluations carried out at specified times are preferable to more random or informal methods.
4. Access to information: Accessibility to evaluations by the ratee and other people who need to know seems to result in a better appraisal than more secretive and closed procedures.

These are the dependent variables in the current study. More specifically, we measured the frequency of appraisal; the number of raters; whether the ratings were from superiors, peers, or subordinates; the formality of the evaluation; and the accessibility of the appraisal information. We should hasten to point out that while these variables were chosen because others have argued that they result in better appraisals (using broad criteria), the current study does not address the quality of the appraisal process directly. It simply tests whether these methods of holding one accountable vary as a function of structural and organizational characteristics.

Business Schools as the Focus of Study

Business school faculty and administrators were chosen for a variety of reasons. First, there has recently been voiced a concern over the direction of business schools in the United States (Porter and McKibbin, 1988). Of particular concern is how faculty and administrators are evaluated and held accountable to their various constituencies (Oviatt and Miller, 1989). Thus, gathering description information on how faculty and administrators are evaluated is of current importance.

Second, evaluation procedures in business schools are to some extent representative of such procedures in other university units and may also shed light on the wider topic of the evaluation of professionals in organizational contexts. Raelin (1985) has reported that 75 percent of all professionals reside in organizations and that professionals traditionally have extensive discretion, freedom, and external (to the organization) norms that govern their conduct. Professional bureaucracies (e.g., universities, law firms, hospitals, social work agencies) are seen as having a different organizational design and governance process from other large organizations (Mintzberg, 1983). Mintzberg argues that a high democratic governing structure is necessary so that professionals can maintain collective control over administrators. Performance accountability is one method of control, and measures the number of evaluators, their status, and the accessibility of information in schools of business should all reflect to some extent the issues raised by Mintzberg (1983). Thus, for both narrow practical reasons and broad theoretical reasons, the evaluation of business school faculty and administrators was of interest.

Structural, Organizational, and Contextual Factors Influencing Accountability and Appraisal

While numerous contextual factors could have been selected, we attempted to look at variables suggested in the literature that would affect the appraisal process and subsequent accountability. Our primary interest was to see whether people at different levels of the organization are evaluated differently. Tsui and Ohlott (1988) argue that higher levels may be harder to evaluate due to the ambiguity of the job description. On the other hand, Mintzberg (1983) very clearly believes that administrators in professional bureaucracies *should* be accountable to the professionals they represent. So a major variable of interest was the level of the job being evaluated, and specifically for business schools we were interested in the evaluation of faculty, chairpersons or heads, and deans. On the basis of the conflicting suggestions in the literature cited above, we had no hypotheses as to how administrators would be rated, relative to faculty in schools of business.

Our other contextual factors were chosen because they appeared to relate directly to our measures of the appraisal process or were theoretically related to the ideas of appraisal and accountability. For example, one of the most replicated findings in organizational research is that as organizations grow in size they tend to become more bureaucratic (Kimberly, 1976; Hsu et al., 1983). In particular, large organizations become more formalized in terms of rules, procedures, and written documentation such as policy manuals and job descriptions. Also, large organizations are more likely to respond to government requirements for compliance to EEOC (Equal Employment Opportunity Commission) and other fair-labor-practice legislation by adopting formal performance evaluations with specific criteria and written evaluations carried out at specific times for all personnel, including administrators. These findings would suggest that large business schools will have more formal appraisals than smaller schools.

Accreditation is also a variable that should influence appraisals. The American Assembly of Collegiate Schools of Business (AACSB) has as its mandate to ensure that standards are being met with respect to faculty expertise, teaching competence, course content, and so on. We would hypothesize that people in accredited schools would be more formally and frequently appraised by more raters than those in nonaccredited schools as a result of the "watchdog" function of the AACSB (Mission Statement, 1985).

Public or private ownership should be important as well. State institutions are subject to reviews and evaluations by legislators and federal government regulations. Public universities also fall under the statutory requirements of the disclosure laws. We would suspect that public institutions would have a greater number of evaluators, more formality, and accessibility of results than would private institutions.

Finally, unions may serve a watchdog function. However, the focus seems to be more on issues of justice and due process (Angell, 1978) than on performance appraisal. And in fact, unions have a long history of resisting evaluation conducted on grounds other than seniority. So, while the appraisal process may be different in union and nonunion schools, we had no prior judgments about what would occur.

In summary, the following study provides a description of performance appraisal practices in United States' schools of business. The structural and contextual independent variables are level of ratee, size of school, accreditation status, ownership, and unionization. The dependent variables are number of raters, level of raters, frequency of rating, formality of rating, and accessibility of results.

Method

A sample of presidents, deans, and department heads of business schools received questionnaires. Respondents were asked to describe the performance evaluation process for deans, department heads, and faculty in their schools. These data were checked for reliability and then analyzed to test for relationships between the contextual variables and the appraisal process variables.

Sample

We conducted a pilot study to assess the appraisal practices of professional educators and administrators occupying different hierarchical levels in schools of business within major colleges and universities. Questionnaires were mailed to four different respondents at each institution (president, dean, and two department heads) in a sample of 50 colleges and universities drawn randomly from the AACSB membership directory. The purpose of the study was to verify question clarity, examine understandability of the form, and estimate questionnaire return rate. Eighty-one responses were returned from 42 different schools, for a respondent return rate of 40.5 percent and a school return rate of 85 percent. No significant problems were reported with the questionnaire.

A larger study was then conducted by mailing the questionnaire to all remaining schools listed in the directory as "fully accredited" by the AACSB and to a randomly selected half of the schools listed as "not fully accredited." The questionnaire was mailed to three people occupying the positions of president, dean and a department head (randomly selected) in 461 schools, resulting in a total of 1383 possible respondents. The respondent return rate was 42 percent (581 returned) and the school return rate was 80 percent (at least one respondent from 369 of the schools). The pilot subjects are not included.

Measures

Multiple dependent variables were measured to assess appraisal procedures for deans, chairpersons, and faculty. These measures were: status of evaluation (who evaluates job performance—seven options discussed below), number of evaluators (two options: single or multiple evaluators), frequency of evaluation (two options: annually or more frequently, every

2 or more years), formality of evaluation (two options: written or not), and accessibility of evaluation results (two options: available to administration only or to multiple constituencies). The major independent variable of interest was the *position* being rated (not the position of the respondent) within the hierarchy. More specifically, presidents, deans, and chairpersons described the evaluation process for deans, chairpersons, and faculty. Other independent variables assessed were the size of the school (number of students), accreditation of the school (AACSB accredited or not), unionization within the school (unionized or not), and nature of the school's ownership (public or private). These variables were also used as moderators on "position within the hierarchy" to determine whether their influence differed across hierarchical levels.

The status-level measure needs further comment. Respondents identified evaluators in above, below, or equivalent positions according to hierarchical level. Respondents were requested to identify everyone who evaluated dean, department head, and faculty performance. The evaluators listed included "president," "dean's superior," "dean," "department head," "faculty committee," "faculty member," and "students," as well as a write-in opinion for positions not fitting the titles listed. Judges then categorized each position as being evaluated essentially from above, below, or mixed. Using this three-point scale, the raters reached almost complete agreement, and minor differences were resolved after further discussion.

Interrater Agreement

Multiple responses were received from 167 of the 369 schools that returned questionnaires. These responses were used to determine the interrater agreement of the independent and dependent variables. When there were three respondents, if they all agreed the school received a score of 1.00. If two of three agreed the score was .67 and we used the response of the two that agreed. If all three gave different answers, the score was .00 (occurred less than 1 percent of the time). We used the response of the person with the highest status in these cases. For pairs, if they agreed, the score was 1.00 and if they disagreed it was .00. Again we used the response of the person with the highest status when the score was .00. The average agreement for each of the variables was as follows: status of raters (.71), multiple evaluators (.70); evaluation frequency (.71), accessibility (.78), unionization (.93), accreditation (.87), ownership (.90). Note that the unit of analysis is the *school.* (The numbers for the dependent variables reflect averages over the three positions being rated.) Since the agreement is high for multiple response schools we felt comfortable in using single responses as valid indications of the school's evaluation practices for a school where there was only one respondent.

Analysis

The primary analyses used in this study were correlations and hierarchical regression with dummy variables coded for "position in the hierarchy." This technique involved a two-part analysis to check first for main effects of the independent variables, and then to determine which interactions were significant when the independent variables were entered as moderators.

Results

The intercorrelations for all variables are shown in Table 5.1. The dependent variables were moderately correlated. Since each of these variables represents different ways to make people accountable through appraisal (e.g., more raters, more raters from below, more frequent evaluations, more formal evaluations, and more accessible results) and are correlated,

Table 5.1
Intercorrelations among Study Variables

	1	2	3	4	5	6	7	8	9	10
1. Accountability practice	1.00	.39[a]	.31[a]	.16[a]	.19[a]	.10[a]	.06	−.10[a]	.07	.06
2. Use of multiple evaluators		1.00	−.17[a]	.17[a]	.12[a]	.18[a]	.06	−.10[a]	.09[a]	.04
3. Evaluation frequency			1.00	−.80	.03	−.24[a]	.09[a]	.20[a]	.02	.11[a]
4. Formality of evaluation				1.00	.07	.34[a]	.03	.07	.11[a]	.11[a]
5. Accessibility of results					1.00	.22[a]	.03	−.05	.02	.04
6. Position in hierarchy						1.00	.0[b]	.0[b]	.0[b]	.0[b]
7. Unionization							1.00	.01	.19[a]	.10[a]
8. Accreditation								1.00	.15[a]	.41[a]
9. Nature of ownership									1.00	.27[a]
10. Size										1.00

[a]$p<.001$
[b]A correlation coefficient of zero (0) logically occurs between "position in hierarchy" and the other contextual variables because no variation is present in each of the independent variables by hierarchical position; i.e., school unionization, accreditation, ownership, and size will be the same regardless of whether the hierarchical position is dean, department head, or faculty. (This nonvariance can also be explained as a consequence of transitioning between "levels of analysis.")

we will refer to those five variables in the aggregate as reflecting appraisal accountability. Among the independent variables, size was positively correlated with unionization, full accreditation, and public ownership.

Since the hierarchical regressions are available elsewhere (Fry et al., 1987) we will simply summarize these findings below. For the dependent variable rater status (with values ranging from 1 for mainly above to 3 for mainly below), there were significant main effects for faculty, accreditation, and unionization. The regression coefficient for faculty shows a very strong and positive departure from the appraisal practices for deans and department heads. In other words, faculty score about a half point higher on the rater status scale than do deans and department heads, indicating that faculty appraisal practices are more democratic (rated from below) than those of administrators. The regression coefficients also show that unionization and accredited schools appear to be more democratic in their rating procedures than unaccredited and nonunionized schools.

The regression results for the dependent variable "use of multiple evaluators" (1 = yes, 0 = no) also show that faculty display a strong departure from the results for deans and department heads. The proportion of faculty evaluated by multiple evaluators is higher by about 0.30 points than for administrators. Significant main effects for accreditation and nature of ownership also show a small increase in the likelihood of the use of multiple evaluators in public schools and a small decrease in the likelihood of the use of multiple evaluators in accredited schools, which was counter to our expectations.

The results for "formality of evaluation" (1 = written, 0 = nonwritten) are similar to the results for "accountability practice" and "the use of multiple evaluators." Comparing faculty to deans, faculty receive a higher proportion of formal evaluations. Public and larger schools are also more likely to have formal evaluations.

The results for "frequency of evaluation" show that both faculty and department heads are evaluated more frequently than deans. Also, unionized schools have less frequent evaluations.

Finally, the statistics for "accessibility of evaluation results" (1 = available to administration only, 2 = available to multiple constituencies) show that faculty appear to be more accountable by a strong margin than deans or department heads. Performance evaluation results are more likely to be made public for faculty than for administrators. No other significant effects were found for this dependent variable.

Overall, the regression results show strong convergence among all the dependent variables along several dimensions. Faculty clearly score higher than administrators on all five variables we used to measure the appraisal process. If, as an aggregate, these variables reflect some degree of accountability, then we can say that faculty are held more accountable than administrators. Also, size, accreditation, public ownership, and to a less extent, unionization appear to increase appraisal accountability, although there are differences in the influence of these contextual variable across levels in the hierarchy.

Discussion

Our results indicate that administrators (as compared to faculty) in the United States schools of business don't have particularly democratic appraisal practices. Contrary to Minztberg's (1983) hypothesis, our data suggest that ratings of performance of administrators involve fewer evaluators and are less democratic, frequent, formal, and accessible than faculty performance evaluations. Thus, administrator accountability overall and to the faculty (i.e., professionals) constituency is weak relative to the faculty's accountability.

Table 5.2 gives a summary of the significant main and interactive effects of the other contextual variables on the five appraisal process variables. These data also suggest that accountability is greater in larger, accredited, unionized, and public institutions.

None of these contextual variables significantly influenced the accessibility (availability of information) of evaluation results. Although the performance evaluation literature suggests that accessibility may be an important component of a valid and accepted performance appraisal system, it appears that public disclosure laws have not influenced this variable to date, and evidently, neither the unions nor the AACSB have taken action to make evaluation accessibility an important issue.

Table 5.2
Summary of Influence of Contextual Variables on Administrator Accountability

Administrator accountability	Size	Accreditation	Unionization	Ownership
1. Status of raters	Department head[a]	Main effect	Main effect	Faculty[a]
2. Multiple evaluators	Faculty[a]	Main effect	NS	Department head[a]
3. Formality of evaluation	Main effect	Faculty[a]	NS	Main effect
4. Evaluation frequency	NS	Faculty[a]	Main effect	NS
5. Accessibility	NS	NS	NS	NS

[a]Indicates a significant interactive effect of contextual X position variables on measures of administrator accountability.

However, these four contextual variables did differentially influence the other four appraisal process variables. As predicted, larger business schools had more formal performance appraisal systems at all levels. Larger schools also had more democratic accountability practices for department heads. In a counterintuitive finding, although faculty in general were more likely to have their performance appraised by multiple evaluators than administrators, this tendency was less pronounced in larger schools.

In support of our expectations, AACSB accreditation had a strong impact on the appraisal process variables. Accredited business schools are more likely to use multiple evaluators and are more democratic in their accountability practices than nonaccredited schools. Faculty in accredited schools are also evaluated less formally but more frequently than faculty in nonaccredited schools. The results also suggest that unionized business schools had significantly more democratic and frequent performance evaluations than nonunion schools at all levels in the hierarchy.

Finally, the business schools in public institutions tend to have more formal evaluations than in private institutions. Also, faculty in public schools experience a more democratic appraisal process than private school faculty. Department heads in public schools are more likely to be appraised by multiple evaluators than their counterparts in private schools. These results fit with our initial expectations.

These results clearly show that organizational and contextual variables influence performance appraisal practices. Each independent variable had main effects or interaction effects on at least two of the five dependent variables. Appraisal practices will vary systematically and in consistent ways as a result of the status of the person being rated, the organization size and external pressures for accountability produced by various constituencies (e.g., unions, legal or professional oversight bodies). Any comprehensive understanding of appraisal practices needs to incorporate these organizational and contextual factors.

To the extent that our findings are correct and representative, it appears as if Mintzberg's (1983) prediction that administrators are held accountable by professionals in professional bureaucracies is not supported in this sample. If one believes that accountability is essential for the effective operations of professional bureaucracies, then we may have a problem in our schools of business. The absence of this ingredient leaves open the possibility that the faculty's autonomy and discretion, which is seen as central to the effective application of the professionals' knowledge and expertise (Mintzberg, 1983), may not be adequately protected from the arbitrary and unjust use of administrative authority.

However, our findings simply show that the accountability of administrators *relative* to faculty is less strong. Various comparisons are needed to infer that administrators' accountability in schools of business is low in some absolute sense. First, similar research should be conducted in other schools and colleges within universities to investigate to what extent these results are sample-specific. It may be that appraisal practices vary greatly across campus colleges such as engineering, education, liberal arts, and other professional schools. Second, similar research is needed in other organizations (e.g., hospitals) considered to be professional bureaucracies to investigate to what extent our findings are unique to universities. These results would help in the interpretation of the present results.

Finally, the issues of appraisal process and accountability can be discussed at a broader and more normative level than the fairly narrow, descriptive approach taken in the current research. Numerous articles in the popular as well as professional literature have called for greater managerial and administrator accountability as a way to curb corruption and unethical behavior (Mitchell and Scott, 1987). However the links between specific appraisal techniques, this broader notion of accountability and subsequent behavior needs to be established. This is a potentially important and fruitful area for future research.

ACCOUNTABILITY AND INFLUENCE STRATEGIES: STUDY 2

Earlier we mentioned that research has suggested that nonaccountability may lead to the use of inappropriate influence tactics such as coalitions or ingratiation (Fandt and Ferris, 1990).

A second study, which is currently under way, is being conducted in collaboration with Gerald Ferris. The participants are 241 managers at a major oil company. The theoretical relationships of importance are between assessments of accountability and the use of different types of influence tactics.

Theoretical Background

Two main questions served as the foundation for this research. First, we were interested in attempting to assess accountability feelings directly and to observe how these feelings correlated with other less direct indicators of accountability. Besides using performance appraisal information as we did in study 1, we also looked at organization level, job ambiguity, and felt responsibility. Our hypotheses were that feelings of accountability were negatively associated with organization level and ambiguity and positively associated with responsibility and performance appraisal practices (e.g., frequency, formality).

Second, we wanted to see how these direct and indirect measures of accountability were related to the use of influence tactics. Kipnis et al. (1980) and Yukl and Falbe (1990) have developed scales to measure influence tactics that are less legitimate (e.g., coercion, coalition formation, ingratiations). We believe that lower accountability would be associated with the use of less legitimate strategies.

Method

A questionnaire was sent to about 400 managers (all levels) of the participating company. To date, we have received 241 back. The questionnaire is composed of two parts. The first part looks at the various indicators of accountability. As in study 1, appraisal accountability was assessed by looking at the formality and frequency of appraisal, number of raters, openness of ratings, and the extent to which one was rated from above or below. Direct feelings of accountability were measured by items such as "to what extent do you have to justify your work related decisions and performance to your supervisor" or "to what extent is your work performance visible and identifiable as *your* work performance." Ambiguity was measured by items such as "clear written goals and objectives exist for my job" or "there is an understandable sequence of steps that can be followed doing my work."

The second part of the questionnaire examined influence strategies. On the basis of interviews with the managers, we developed three vignettes to which the subjects responded. Each vignette described an influence setting and asked the respondent how they would react. One situation concerned the allocation of vacation time; a second concerned being selected to go to a professional meeting; and the third was about the assignment of office space.

Each respondent read each vignette. The person to be influenced variable was manipulated: his or her boss, a peer or a subordinate. The dependent variables were the influence strategy measures developed by Kipnis et al. (1980). These data are currently being analyzed.

STUDIES TO BE DONE

One laboratory study is planned where we will manipulate various causes of accountability. Included will be the presence or absence of close supervision and clear rules and regulation. Subjects will be involved in a problem-solving task involving the distribution of discretionary funds. The dependent variables will include assessment of psychological reactions (e.g., clarity of standards, feelings of accountability) and the behavioral outcomes (e.g., influence tactics, ratings of others, ethical behaviors). Similar laboratory studies and simulations will be conducted to further examine the complex relationship between the causes of accountability and its consequences.

ACCOUNTABILITY AND REFORM

We started this paper with a broad description of America's problems and confronted the "ethic of personal advantage." And we argued that leader legitimacy was being eroded. Obviously, one of our suggested remedies would be to increase accountability in both the public and private sectors. But our narrow empirical definition of accountability as performance review is not all that is needed to curb abuses and restore trust in the managerial elite. Reforms are needed that focus on other factors as well.

Most pertinent on the legal front is reform in the way that executives in business and government are held accountable for their decisions and actions. Since managers have the privilege of power they should be accountable for its use. But historically, individuals in managerial positions have been protected from accountability by the prudent business judgment rule in the case of the private sector and by sovereign immunity for managers in government jobs. In short, it is virtually impossible to establish personal managerial culpability in either civil or criminal actions. There are virtually no legal standards for assessing managerial malpractice, malfeasance, or nonfeasance. The most promising reforms may be achieved at this level in the judicial process.

We are not suggesting that every decision made by managers or civil servants be subject to retrospective consideration, taken with the benefit of hindsight. What we are saying is that much of the unethical behavior was done by people who knew at the time that their actions were a violation of federal or state laws or were contrary to their public trust and social responsibility. These are the actions for which individuals in management should be held accountable. Such actions most always involve the determination of the accused's intentions. Like it or not, judgments about those intentions can be rendered only in the court system. Consequently, increased litigation may be the price of individual executive accountability.

Another suggested reform aims at changing values through moral development. The research on this topic has repeatedly emphasized that higher levels of development reflect the ability to understand and empathize with perspectives different and perhaps more complex than one's own (Jones, 1991). Such new perspectives can help one to transcend the self-centeredness of the ethic of personal advantage. We believe that one of the main objectives of education is the development of student's moral character. Business schools are not exempted from this obligation, and it is one we should take seriously (Scott and Mitchell, 1986).

Our final set of reforms is aimed at both the values and the behaviors that specifically exist within the *organizational* context. America has been characterized as a sea of freedom filled with islands of organizational despotism (Scott, 1985). This metaphor implies a difference between the rights and liberties enjoyed by Americans as citizens versus those rights and liberties denied them as employees of organizations. We believe that such a disparity exists and, therefore, should be an object of reform; that is, reform of organizational governance and reform of systems of due process within organizations. Such reforms are both a challenge to the willful abuse of power that we claim has created America's blight and a mechanism for increasing a sense of shared community.

Some movement in this direction is evident by the increasing development and implementation of ethics programs in private corporations (Mathews, 1987; Cullen et al., 1989). However, many of these programs are being used as a tool of manipulation and the intent is often to increase cost-effectiveness rather than enhance character and moral development (Noreen, 1988).

But specifics with regard to moral development, organizational governance, and legal oversight are topics for another paper. Our purpose in the current manuscript is to highlight the need for research on accountability. We believe that such a focus is important not only because it will lead to greater legitimacy and heightened trust but also because it is part of a larger set of issues and body of reforms that are sorely needed.

Some believe it is already too late. MacIntyre concluded *After Virtue* (1981) by stating that "the new dark ages are already upon us" and "the barbarians have been governing us for quite some time." Perhaps MacIntyre is right. For the moment, however, we would argue that a national agenda led by enlightened managers could implement a program to change our course. Individual leaders do make a difference. Their autonomous moral choices can invigorate America and restore confidence in our ability to deal with the complex social, environmental, and economic questions of the twenty-first century.

References

Alaska oil field report cites unexpected harm to wildlife. *New York Times,* May 11, 1989.

American Assembly of Collegiate School of Business (1985). Accreditation Council Policies, Procedures, and Standards.

Angell, G. W. (1978). Management prerogatives and faculty rights. *Journal of Higher Education, 49*, 283–293.

Ashford, S. J. (1989). Self assessments in organizations: A literature review and integrative model. In L. L. Cummings and B. M. Staw (Eds.), *Research in organizational behavior* (Vol. 11, pp. 133–174). Greenwich, CT: JAI Press.

Bandura, A. (1988). Self regulation of motivation and action through goal systems. In V. Hamilton, G. H. Bower, and N. H. Frijida (Eds.), *Cognitive perspectives on emotion and motivation* (pp. 36–61). Dordrecht, Netherlands: Kluiver Academic Publishers.

Barnard, C. I. (1938). *The Functions of the Executive.* Cambridge, MA: Harvard University Press.

Baucus, M. A. and Near, J. P. (1991). Can illegal corporate behavior be predicted? An event history analysis. *Academy of Management Journal, 34*(1), 9–36.

Beach, L. R., and Mitchell, T. R. (1990). Image theory: A behavioral theory of decision making in organizations. In B. M. Staw and L. L. Cummings (Eds.), *Research in organizational behavior* (Vol. 12, pp. 1–41). Greenwich, CT: JAI Press.

Bernardin, H. J., and Beatty, R. W. (1984). *Performance appraisal: Assessing human behavior at work.* Boston, MA: Kent.

Brief, A. P., Dukerich, J. M., and Doran, L. I. (1991). Resolving ethical dilemmas in management: Experimental investigations of values, accountability, and choice. *Journal of Applied Social Psychology, 21*, 380–396.

Brief, A. P., Schuler, R. S., and Van Sell, M. (1981). *Managing job stress.* Boston: Little Brown.

Cameron, R. S., and Whetton, D. A. (1983). *Organizational effectiveness: A comparison of multiple models.* New York: Academic Press.

Cullen, J. B., Victor, B., and Stephens, C. (1989). An ethical weather report: Assessing the organization's ethical climate. *Organization Dynamics* (Autumn), 50–62.

Damaged wildlife indicates pollution in Great Lakes. *New York Times,* July 12, 1988.

Doig, J. W. (1983). The Wilsonian dichotomy and the public authority tradition. *Public Administration Review, 43*, 292–304.

Emphasis on private greed, rather than public service. *The Seattle Times,* January 15, 1989.

Environmental group ranks toxic polluters. *The Washington Post,* August 11, 1989.

Fandt, P. M., and Ferris, G. R. (1990). The management of information and impressions: When employees behave opportunisitically. *Organizational Behavior and Human Decision Processes, 45*, 140–158.

Feldman, J. M. (1986). Instrumentation and training for performance appraisal: A perceptual-cognitive viewpoint. In K. Rowland and G. Ferris (Eds.), *Research in personnel and human resources management* (Vol. 4). Greenwich, CT: JAI Press.

Ferris, G. R., and Judge, T. A. (1991). Personnel/human resources management: A political influence perspective. *Journal of Management, 17*, 1–42.

Ferris, G. R., and Mitchell, T. R. (1987). The components of social influence and their importance for human resources research. In K. M. Rowland and G. R.

Ferris (Eds.), *Research in personnel and human resources management* (Vol. 5, pp. 103–128). Greenwich, CT: JAI Press.

Fry, L. W., Scott, W. G., and Mitchell, T. R. (1987). Organizational and contextual causes of variation in the performance appraisal process used in schools of business. Presented at the National Meeting of the Academy of Management, Anaheim, CA (August).

Gasse, Y. (1980). Elaborations on the psychology of the entrepreneur. In C. Kent, D. Sexton and K. Vesper (Eds.), *New Venture Strategies* (pp. 55–73). Englewood Cliffs, NJ: Prentice-Hall.

Hsu, C., Marsh, R. M., and Mannari, H. (1983). An examination of the determinants of organizational structure. *American Journal of Sociology, 88,* 975–996.

Hyland, M. E. (1988). Motivational control theory: An integrative framework. *Journal of Personality and Social Psychology, 55,* 642–651.

Ilgen, D. R., and Feldman, J. M. (1983). Performance appraisal: A process focus. In B. Staw and L. L. Cummings (Eds.), *Research in organizational behavior* (Vol. 5). Greenwich, CT: JAI Press.

Jones, T. M. (1986). Corporate board structure and performance: Variations in the incidence of shareholder suits. In L. E. Preston (Ed.), *Research in corporate social performance and policy* (Vol. 8, pp. 345–359). Greenwich, CT: JAI Press.

Jones, T. M. (1991). Ethical decision making by individuals in organizations. *Academy of Management Review, 16,* 336–395.

Kane, J. S., and Lawler, E. E., III (1979). Performance appraisal effectiveness: Its assessment and determinants. In B. M. Staw (Ed.), *Research in organizational behavior* (Vol. 1). Greenwich, CT: JAI Press.

Kavanagh, M. J. (1981). Evaluating performance. In K. Rowland and G. Ferris (Eds.), *Personnel management: New perspectives.* Boston: Allyn and Bacon.

Kent, C., Sexton, D., and Vesper, K. (Eds.) (1980). *New venture strategies.* Englewood Cliffs, NJ: Prentice-Hall.

Kimberly, John R. (1976). Organizational size and the structuralist perspective: A review, critique, and proposal. *Administrative Science Quarterly,* 571–597.

Kipnis, D. (1987). Psychology and behavioral technology. *American Psychologist, 42,* 30–36.

Kipnis, D., Schmidt, S. M., and Wilkinson, I. (1980). Interorganizational influence tactics: Explorations of getting one's way. *Journal of Applied Psychology, 65,* 440–452.

Klein, H. J. (1989). An integrated control theory model of work motivation. *Academy of Management Review, 14,* 150–172.

Landy, F. J., and Farr, J. L. (1983). *The management of work performance.* New York: Academic Press.

Latham, G. P. (1986). Job performance and appraisal. In C. L. Cooper and I. Robertson (Eds.), *International review of industrial and organizational psychology.* Chichester, UK: Wiley.

Lewin, A. Y., and Minton, J. W. (1986). Determining organizational effectiveness: Another look and an agenda for research. *Management Science, 32,* 528.

Lipset, S. M., and Schneider, W. (1983). *The Confidence gap: Business, labor and government in the public mind.* New York: The Free Press.

Locke, E. A., and Latham, G. P. (1990). *A theory of goal setting and task performance.* Englewood Cliffs, NJ: Prentice-Hall.

Love yourself first; then (much later) love your neighbor. *Seattle Post Intelligencer,* May 7, 1989.

MacIntyre, A. (1981). *After virtue* (p. 71). North Bend, IN: University of Notre Dame Press.

Mathews, M. C. (1987). Code of ethics: Organizational behavior and misbehavior. In W. C. Frederick and L. E. Preson (Eds.), *Research in corporate social performance and policy: Empirical studies of business ethics and values* (Vol. 9, pp. 107–130). Greenwich, CT: JAI Press.

McAllister, D. W., Mitchell, T. R., and Beach, L. R. (1979). The contingency model of decision strategies: An empirical test of the effects of significance, accountability, and reversibility. *Organizational Behavior and Human Performance, 24,* 228–244.

Meindl, J. R. (1990). On leadership: An alternative to the conventional wisdom. *Research in Organizational Behavior, 12,* 159–203.

Mintzberg, H. (1983). *Structure in fives: Designing effective organizations.* Englewood Cliffs, NJ: Prentice-Hall.

Mitchell, T. R., and Scott, W. G. (1987). Leadership failures, the distrusting public, and prospects of the administrative state. *Public Administrative Review* (Nov./Dec.), 445–452.

Mitchell, T. R., and Scott, W. G. (1990). America's problems and needed reforms: Confronting the ethic of personal advantage. *Academy of Management Executive, 4,* 23–35.

Mohrman, A. M., Jr., and Lawler, E. E., III (1983). Motivation and performance-appraisal behavior. In F. Land, S. Zedeck, and J. Cleveland (Eds.), *Performance measurement and theory.* Hillsdale, NJ: Lawrence Erlbaum.

No time to relax, Earthlings, Greenhouse effect looms. *Seattle Post Intelligencer,* July 13, 1988.

Noreen, E. (1988). The economics of ethics: A new perspective on agency theory. *Accounting, Organizations and Society, 13,* 359–369.

Our fragile tower of greed and debt. *The Washington Post,* April 5, 1988.

Ouchi, W. G., and Maguire, M. A. (1975). Organizational control: Two functions. *Administrative Science Quarterly, 20,* 559–569.

Oviatt, B. M., and Miller, W. D. (1989). Irrelevance, intransigence and business professions. *Academy of Management Executive, 3,* 304–315.

Porter, L. W., and McKibbin, L. E. (1988). *Management education and development: Drift or thrust into the 21st century?* New York: McGraw-Hill.

Posner, B. Z., and Schmidt, W. H. (1984). Values and the american manager: An update. *California Management Review* (Spring), 202–216.

Raelin, J. A. (1985). The basis for the professional's resistance to managerial control. *Human Resource Management, 24*(2), 147–175.

Richest got richer and poorest poorer from 1979 to 1987. *New York Times,* March 23, 1989.

Schlenker, B. R., and Weigold, M. F. (1989). Self-identification and accountability.

In R. A. Giacalone and P. Rosenfeld (Eds.), *Impression management in the organization* (pp. 21–43). New York: Lawrence Erlbaum.

Schmidt, W. H., and Posner, B. Z. (1986). Values and expectations of federal senior executives. *Public Administration Review* (Sept./Oct.), 447–454.

Schumpeter, J. (1947). *Capitalism, socialism, and democracy.* New York: Harper Brothers.

Scott, W. E., and Mitchell, T. R. (1986). Markets and morals in management education. *Selections* (Autumn), 5–8.

Scott, W. G. (1985). Organizational revolution: An end of managerialism. *Administration and Society, 17,* 149–170.

Sloan, A. P. (1963). *My years with General Motors.* New York: Doubleday.

Taylor, M. S., Fisher, C. D., and Ilgen, D. R. (1984). Individuals reactions to performance feedback in organizations: A control theory perspective. In K. M. Rowland and G. R. Ferris (Eds.), *Research in personnel and human resources management* (Vol. 2, pp. 81–124). Greenwich, CT: JAI Press.

Tetlock, P. E. (1985). Accountability: The neglected social context of judgment and choice. In L. L. Cummings and B. M. Staw (Eds.), *Research in organizational behavior* (Vol. 7, pp. 297–332). Greenwich, CT: JAI Press.

Troubled seas: Global red tides of algae bring new fears. *New York Times,* May 3, 1988.

Tsui, A. S., and Ohlott, P. (1988). Multiple assessment of managerial effectiveness: Interrater agreement and consensus in effectiveness models. *Personnel Psychology, 41,* 779–803.

Violations of ozone standards rise, E.P.A. says. *New York Times,* May 4, 1989.

Why the underclass is still under. *New York Times,* November 16, 1987.

Yukl, G., and Falbe, C. (1990). Influence tactics and objectives in upward, downward, and lateral relations. *Journal of Applied Psychology, 75,* 132–140.

6

Leadership Perception: The Role of Gender and Culture

Roya Ayman
Department of Psychology
Illinois Institute of Technology

INTRODUCTION

The role played by perception in the process of leadership seems controversial. Some researchers have criticized the use of perception in leadership measurement (Phillips and Lord, 1986); however, exciting and promising new approaches such as transformational leadership (Bass, 1985) and charismatic leadership (Conger and Kanungo, 1988) have relied on data that are rooted in people's perception. In fact, most definitions of leadership have social perception inherent in them (Calder, 1977; Dachler, 1988).

This essay will briefly review the research demonstrating the significance of social perception in understanding leadership. The integration of findings on social perception and on the perception of leadership raises some issues and at the same time recommends directions for future research on leadership in an increasingly diverse work place. This paper will examine how social perception processes operate in leadership research with heterogenous samples. The implication of gender in leadership research, as well as related examples from cross-cultural leadership research, will be discussed.

The chapter has two objectives. The first is to analyze the methodological and theoretical complexities involved in perceptual measures of leadership. The second is to identify the psychological hurdles that people with different physical or cultural characteristics face when occupying positions of status, such as leadership. Such hurdles are exacerbated by perceptual processes. The review of research findings will be aimed at clarifying the role of values and expectations in perception and judgment of diverse people in leadership relationships. Since leadership occurs in a social setting, reference will also be made to situational factors, such as the nature of the social setting, amount of time the individuals have with one another, and the saliency of social roles, as well as the impact that the diversity of group members has on the perception of leadership process.

In order to identify the aforementioned psychological hurdles, an analytical examination will be made of the existing knowledge on leadership in settings that are socially heterogenous. In so doing, specific recommendations will be made for future research, in which either the culture or other characteristics of the participants are diverse. These recommendations will address the choice of variables and issues of research design in studies involving diverse populations. It is hoped that such an exercise will provide guidelines for both a systematic research program and a set of criteria for evaluating the design of studies. From the practitioner's perspective, some recommendations will also be made for managing diversity in today's multicultural society.

HISTORICAL REVIEW

Leadership has long been a focus of interest and study in civilizations all over the world. Through essays, parables, and epics, authors and poets have advised people on the ways to be an effective leader. For example, in Europe, Machiavelli (1977) wrote *The Prince;* in China, Confucius wrote essays (*The Sayings of Confucius,* 1955); and in twelfth-century Iran, Unsur u'l-Ma'ali (1963) wrote the *Qabus-Nameh.* The importance of leadership in building and maintaining a civilization is well acknowledged. However, through the centuries and in different parts of the world, the way this phenomenon was understood has varied. For example, in the late nineteenth century in Germany, Karl Marx (1906) explained leadership from a zeitgeist approach emphasizing that becoming a leader requires being at the right place in the right time. While about the same time in England, Thomas Carlyle (1907) approached leadership from the "great man" theory perspective, emphasizing that it is the unique characteristics of the individual that make the person a leader, that is, the "born leader."

In the twentieth century a new approach was added—the empirical, scientific method. To assure reliability in the information gathered, investigators developed various techniques of measuring leadership. Though the process of understanding and prediction of leader's behavior has improved, the time has come for an evaluation. We approach the end of the twentieth century faced with the recognition of a global society. A society that is diverse with multiple cultures and yet hopefully united in its goal of preserving peace while moving towards an ever advancing civilization. To understand leadership in such a diverse setting, it seems essential that we take a closer look at our techniques and at the inferences that flow from them.

Most of the leadership research in the twentieth century was based on various ways of measuring impressions, perceptions, or expectations of our about the leader. These perceptions were measured on those who were in the positions of leadership or were identified as prospects for such positions. That approach has been labeled "self-report." For example, when a leader described his or her behavior or attitude *in general* (i.e., across time and place), the resultant measure was considered a leadership trait. Such "traits" included intelligence, charisma, and self-esteem (Bass, 1990). On the other hand, if the leader was asked to describe his or her behavior in a given setting, it was labeled as leader behavior. Many studies of leader behavior employed the leader opinion questionnaire (LOQ), the leader behavior description questionnaire (LBDQ) (Cook et al., 1981; Fisher and Edwards, 1988), and the LEAD scale (Hersey and Blanchard, 1973) to measure the leader's self-perception. Some of these measures require the leader to describe his or her behavior in the past (e.g., LBDQ), while others inquire the respondent to state their expectations and wishes of how they would behave in the future (e.g., LOQ). The self-report studies have been criticized (Schrishiem and Kerr, 1977), yet the technique is still frequently used in research and practice.

In other situations leadership was measured by the "perception of others," such as the subordinates. The assumption of this line of research was that an increase in number of reports will enhance the reliability of the description of the leader's behavior. Since the fifties, with the introduction of the LBDQ and the subordinate behavior description questionnaire (SBDQ), this technique became the most prevalent source of information in the research on leadership (Bass, 1990). Although researchers were still using perception as their medium of data collection, the source had shifted from the self (i.e., the leader) to the other (i.e., the follower).

The two most frequently recognized sets of leadership behaviors are (1) behaviors focused on getting the task accomplished and (2) behaviors that are directed to maintaining group cohesion. A meta-analysis by Fisher and Edwards (1988) found a positive significant relationship between perceived leader behavior and outcome variables such as performance and various measures of satisfaction. More specifically, leaders who engaged in behaviors addressing the social and personal needs of their subordinates had positive or neutral, but not negative, group outcome, whereas leaders who engaged in behaviors focused on the task at times generated positive or negative consequences.

Scientists in pursuit of more error-free technique engaged in studying leadership through the perception of "independent observers" (e.g., Bales, 1955; Komaki, 1986; Korabik, 1990). Although these observers were well trained and focused on the leaders' behaviors in a specified short time period, (i.e., half an hour) they, nonetheless, were recording their perceptions. Later, the investigator might categorize these behavior observations through the filter of his or her own assumptions into more global behavior categories. Most of these observer-generated categories closely resembled those found in self- and other's reports.

Although these three major approaches (self-reports; subordinate reports; expert ratings) differ in the source of information, they are similar on another level; specifically, they all measure social perception. The fact that leadership measurement is perception-based should be neither surprising nor alarming. In the last decade some investigators have become concerned and criticized past research for its reliance on perception and its susceptibility to the inaccuracies in social perception. However, others have emphasized the importance of social perception in leadership, and the opportunities afforded by its study (Dachler, 1988; Lord and Maher, 1990; Meindl, 1990).

Leadership is a social interaction, and similar to all social interactions, perception and interpretation are critical to understanding the process (Martinko and Gardner, 1987). An observer may be more affected by what he or she *believes* occurred than by an absolute act of the leader that may be recorded objectively. Also, leaders actually have less access to the objective occurrence of acts that they had engaged in and are more dependent on what they thought they had said or done. These beliefs and thoughts are based on perceptual and attributional processes in which the leader engages, as an actor at one time and an observer at another time. Similarly, the follower or the team member, is also engaged in the same processes, concurrently as both an actor and an observer.

The end result of a decade of research on the perceptual approach to leadership was the development of implicit leadership theory (Lord and Maher, 1990). This research approach once again brought the social nature of human beings into focus. It argues that individuals process information through the complexity and intricacy of social perception coupled with social judgment (i.e., attribution theory). Implicit leadership theory has shed considerable light on the role of social perception in leadership processes.

Attributional approaches to leadership (Calder, 1977; Green and Mitchell, 1979; Martinko and Gardner, 1987) provided significant insight in the cognitive feedback loops that have an impact on social judgments and subsequent behaviors of the leader and subordinates (Chemers, 1987). In these models emphasis was placed on the judgment made by the perceiver, be it the leader or the follower. These two recent approaches in leadership research, implicit leadership theory and attribution theory, have acknowledged the influence of the social reality held by the participants in the leadership process.

In the next section a brief review of factors contributing to social perception will be reviewed. This will be followed by an analysis of the relation of these key factors in leadership perception.

SOCIAL PERCEPTION

In this section the processes of social perception and the factors that contribute to perception will be discussed. This brief review will highlight the factors that will subsequently be included in the discussion of the role of gender and culture in leadership.

Shiffrin and Schneider (1977) described two main processes of perception; automatic and controlled. The major distinction made between the two are that in automatic information processing the cognitive task occurs by the perceivers "without awareness, without intent, without effort and interference with other cognitive tasks" (Lord and Maher, 1990, p. 5). This may mean that the perceiver does not use all of the available cues to process the information and will be dependent on his or her schema [i.e., "a cognitive framework developed through experience that affects the way in which information about the external world is noticed encoded, stored, and remembered" (Baron and Greenberg, 1990, p. 145).] However, in controlled process perceivers are more attentive to the full array of cues available. Controlled processing also requires more time and attention, and thus may not be as efficient or parsimonious for the perceiver. It is important to acknowledge that parsimony is a fundamental principle of human cognitive functioning.

The factor that most affects perception is attention or selectivity in processing information. We primarily process the information about the environment that draws our attention, and we use this information to understand the environment.

The two elements that have the greatest effect on attention are the *saliency* of the perceived object or event and the *personal motives and attitudes* of the perceiver (Baron and Greenberg, 1990). "Saliency" refers to the nature of the stimulus, that is, characteristics of the object to be perceived. The more these characteristics are noticeable, the more they stand out and are salient. These characteristics are usually observable. They may be physical characteristics or verbal and/or nonverbal aspects of communication. On the other hand, "perceiver's motives and attitudes" refer to the frame of mind the perceiver brings to the setting. These attitudes may have been developed through years of socialization.

For example, in a situation where a perceiver, in a police station, observes a police officer who has long hair, the long hair is a salient cue. The saliency of long hair is due to two factors: (1) because most of the other police officers in that precinct are men with short hair and (2) because the perceiver is *expecting* a man who has short hair. Therefore, the long hair stood out. Both the existing norms or consensus and the perceiver's schema are contrary to the stimulus, namely, the police officer with long hair. By the way, when you read this example, was your initial expectation that the police officer was a man or a woman?

Let us examine the role of automatic and controlled processes in social perception. In the perception of people, two critical process of social perception are attribution and social information processing (or social cognition).

"Attribution" is the process by which an observer infers the causes of the actor's behavior. Attribution research has demonstrated that perceivers use previously learned social norms as the bases of judging whether a person's behavior is socially desirable or undesirable. In attributional theories, one factor that plays an important role is consensus; that is, judgments always involve the question of whether most people act in a particular way in a given situation. The perceiver is concerned with whether the behaviors or cues that he or she has perceived are normative (Jones and Davis, 1965; Kelley, 1967).

Therefore, "norms" provide a primary basis of social judgment used to infer a person's intention and characteristics from the perception of the person's overt actions. There is evidence that errors are often made in social judgment processes, and that these errors become more acute when the social norms and expectations are not held in common by the perceiver and the perceived.

"Social cognition" refers to the process by which perceivers sort, store, and remember information about their social interactions. Thus, during these cognitive processes the perceiver takes the information from the external environment, categorizes it and stores it in memory, and later retrieves it to understand the outside world.

For an individual to process information there needs to be a cognitive framework. Such a framework develops gradually and serves as the anchor to process new information. This framework is sometimes referred to as a "schema" or a "script." A "stereotype" is a schema regarding a specific group. A "script" is the specific pattern of appropriate behaviors learned regarding an event. For example, one may have a schema or script for a manager, that is, who this person should be (schema) or how this person should behave and be responded to (script). At the same time, one may have a schema or stereotype for any social object or subgroup (e.g., women).

These scripts and stereotypes, on one hand, guide our decisions in how to predict and respond to our experiences. On the other hand, they control our attention for both encoding information and retrieving information. If what we perceive is similar to what we expected, then we respond *automatically* using our habitual behavior on the basis of the scripts we have learned. However, it is believed that if the cues do not match our expectation we will use the controlled mode of information processing. In this mode, the perception process will be slow and effortful, and the perceiver has to consciously choose to regulate his or her information gathering (Shiffrin and Schneider, 1977). Although information processing in social perception is similar to perception in general, the factors that make social cues salient are more complicated.

What makes social perception different from object perception is the importance of context (Gergen and Gergen, 1981). In a social setting, factors like past history or anticipated future interaction with the individual, the nature of the setting and the roles of individuals, the nature of the task, and other potential variables constitute a social context. These factors are added to the perceiver's attitudes and the object's characteristics. Adding the complexity of context to Shiffrin and Schneider's (1977) automatic and controlled information processing leads us to an empirical question: "Do people change gears and shift into controlled mechanisms of information processing when faced with a social experience which is not as they expected?" An example may illuminate the complexity of the integration of context and perception.

If an individual has a stereotyped attitude toward women that differs from that for men, and when the individual's script for a manager is closer to the stereotype of men, what happens when a women manager gives this individual a reprimand or punishment for poor performance? As a manager, her behavior is within the scope of the script, but as a woman who is expected to be nurturant and compassionate, her behavior is out of role. In this situation, which is the schema that the individual will use to judge the woman manager?

A woman manager is also faced with this dilemma when she is deciding on how to behave. She is confronted with the two conflicting normative expectations—that of being a woman and of being a manager. In every situation, she has to decide which of these identities is more important. This decisionmaking process is not always conducted with full awareness. As a matter of fact, different women managers handle this situation differently.

On the basis of their interviews with 30 women managers, Korabik and Ayman (1989) found differences in leadership experiences among them. Those women managers who were more inclined to hold feminine values (e.g., emotional, considerate) and those who were more inclined to hold predominately masculine values (e.g., aggressive, independent) reported maladjustment and discomfort in managing their work group. However, women managers who were able to maintain a balance between being emotional and considerate versus independent and assertive seemed to report better adjustment as managers.

A recent court case involved a woman manager of an accounting firm who was denied partnership (Camara, 1989). The rationale for the decision was that her demeanor was too much like that of a man and that she did not wear enough makeup and jewelry. This woman, like many others, was faced with a dilemma. When the woman behaves in accordance with here sex stereotype, it is seen as "too soft," too much like a woman, while the script for her managerial role says "tighten the belt and act like a man." Thus, she has to make a choice. In the case of the woman manager in the accounting firm, she acted like a man, "an aggressive go-getter," and she was judged as "a dragon lady" (i.e., overly masculine).

Therefore, this example suggests that people do not shift gears from automatic to controlled information processing when confronted with multiple, conflicting cues. In the case mentioned above, people confronted with incongruencies, seemed to choose the most salient cue (i.e., sex), and used automatic cognitive processing. So, in the case of the woman manager, the observers chose the cue that she was a woman rather than she was a manager as the basis to judge her. While these questions regarding multiple and conflicting cues and information processing is a daily experience for many, research on this topic is meager. The issue of multiple conflicting schema is related not only to the observer, but also to the self-perception of women managers (Chusmir and Koberg, 1986). This topic deserves greater attention.

These examples illustrated some points that have been investigated by social psychologists regarding self-perception (Markus, 1977) and perception of others (Cantor and Mischel, 1977). However, until very recently, the research focused on a perceiver who was confronted with a discrepancy between a cue and held norms or expectations. In heterogeneous societies, leadership situations provide a more complex setting. The roles of the participants and their personal membership of a social group, as well as the nature of the setting all contribute to complexity in information processing. The perceiver is confronted with questions such as who has what role. In understanding this situation, which is more important; the person stereotype or the script for this role? Do I have to interact with this person later, and if so, in what capacity? If the later interactions would be as colleagues the behaviors of the two people will be very different than if they were planning to date each other. Therefore, to understand the role of perception in leadership it is important that various factors of the setting all be incorporated.

The next sections will briefly address the literature on stereotypes and implicit leadership theory leading to the examination of the research on gender and leadership. This review will provide evidence regarding how the existing schema for leaders and for women can create confusion.

STEREOTYPES

In society today, individuals in leadership positions come from many different social groups. Therefore, the perception of leadership is affected by both social stereotypes and leadership scripts, namely, implicit leadership theories. At this point, it may be valuable to define stereotypes and implicit theories.

Although stereotypes often have negative connotations, generically a stereotype has been defined as "a structured set of beliefs about the personal attributes of a group of people" (Ashmore and Del Boca, 1979, p. 222). Similarly, Ashmore and Del Boca assert that an implicit personality theory is a hypothetical construct, the components of which are personal attributes, particularly traits, and further that there is an assumption that people are unaware of the implicit theories that they hold. Ashmore and Del Boca (1979) also summarized some of the definitions of stereotypes presented by other authors: "stereotypes are one form of the implicit theories which individuals use to organize their experience of the world" (Wegner and Vallacher, 1977, p. 229). More specifically, "a stereotype is an individual's 'implicit theory' about a social group" (Hastorf et al., 1970, p. 229).

The research on stereotyping covers various social groups; however, a large body of empirical research has been on sex stereotyping. If gender (female vs. male) can be used as a social grouping, then femaleness or maleness reflect not only physical characteristics but also social roles and constructs (Deaux, 1984). In fact, people have distinct expectations for women and men, and like any other expectations, these can act as self-fulfilling prophecies. This line of research has shown that people tend to act on their expectation and thus channel or control others' behavior (see, e.g., Darley and Fazio, 1980; Skrypnek and Snyder, 1982). The self-fulfilling prophecy process has been further substantiated by demonstrating that subjects who are familiarized with a group's prototype or stereotype before encountering its members, relative to the naive subjects, engage in more prototype-based information processing and interaction (Smith and Zarate, 1990).

In heterosexual interactions the influence of stereotypes can have major consequences. There is evidence that shows that the presence of a strong stereotype for females and activities associated with them may have an impact on their interactions with men. The typical stereotype for women include nurturant, compassionate, and considerate characteristics, which are positive characteristics. It also includes characteristics such as being weak and subservient (Bem, 1974). There is evidence that shows that not only are women stereotyped as weak and not equal to men but also that any behavior and characteristic associated with women also are perceived as weak and unimportant. For example, being considerate and supportive is seen as a sign of weakness even though there is evidence in the management literature that a supportive and participative manager is effective. Feminine qualities such as interpersonal warmth are normatively perceived as less desirable and of lower status (Carli, 1990; Lockheed and Hall, 1976; Reid and Comas-Diaz, 1990). These studies have even demonstrated that when men engaged in activities that are seen as feminine, they are perceived as lowering their status.

In one study, experimenters placed men and women in interviewer and interviewee positions in an employment simulation. That is, there were men and women in both high-status (interviewer) and low-status (interviewee) positions. The results demonstrated that the interviewees smiled more often than the interviewers, did and across positions women smiled more than did the men (Deutsch, 1990). Thus, the act of smiling, which is enacted more frequently by women, is also related to the behaviors of those in lower-status positions. The attribution of status, therefore, is not dependent only on the position of an individual; it is also related to the incumbent's minority group membership.

In a meta-analysis, Driskell and Mullen (1990) ascertained that expectations associated with the status of a social group (e.g., race or gender) have a direct relationship to the observer's behavior; that is, the magnitude of position status characteristics (e.g., military rank, ability scores) and behavior will reach triviality if the effect of social group status is controlled. For example, if a nontraditional person (e.g., woman or minority) occupies a managerial position, it is the expectation that is associated with the nontraditional person's group stereotype rather than the expectations associated with the role of manager that will have a stronger impact on the social interaction. More specifically, being a woman or a minority-group member will lower the status associated with being a manager. Both women and members of minority groups have often stated that they have to work harder and be twice as good to get the recognition that a white male receives. The white male is given the benefit of the doubt not available to the nontraditional job occupant.

IMPLICIT THEORY AND LEADERSHIP

In reviewing social perception it becomes evident that a perceiver's values and attitude may affect the processes of information gathering and retrieval. The particular script or stereotype held by the perceiver regarding leadership therefore can affect the perception of a particular leader. In the last decade a series of studies have provided strong evidence for the effects of implicit leadership theories on the perception of leader's behavior. However, only a few studies have investigated what the factors are that influence the content of a person's implicit leadership theory.

Eden and Leviathan (1975) demonstrated the presence of implicit leadership theory in a respondent's descriptions of leaders. Subsequently, Lord and several other investigators substantiated that the presence of a dominant cue such as "effective leader" can distort or direct the respondent's description of a leader seen in a video tape (e.g., Cronshaw and Lord, 1987; Larson, 1982; Lord et al., 1978; Lord et al., 1984; Phillips and Lord, 1981, 1982). In these studies, investigators showed a group of raters a video tape of a problem-solving group. In these video tapes the leader followed a script that had a specific amount of structuring behavior, and the end result of the group activity was not clear. The investigators manipulated the perception of the leader's behavior by providing performance information before or after the viewing of the tape. In all cases, the raters were strongly influenced by the performance cues. Raters reported seeing considerate or structuring behavior consistent with their belief of what an effective or ineffective leader should have done in that situation, rather than describing what the leaders had actually done. When a schema such as "successful leader" is imposed on individuals, respondents use their implicit theory of the successful leader to encode or retrieve information regarding the leader's behavior.

Two lines of research will be reviewed to demonstrate that within a particular culture people hold a dominant implicit leadership theory and that various factors interplay in forming this schema. With regards to the content of peoples implicit leadership theory, research in the United States has demonstrated that a masculine image of ideal leaders is fairly dominant in the United States (Arkkelin, 1987; Lord et al., 1986; Powell and Butterfield, 1986). Between 1973 and 1989, several studies have examined the relative similarity of respondents' implicit theories for women, for men, and for managers (Schein, 1973, 1975; Schein et al., 1989). In all these studies there was greater similarity found between descriptions for men and managers than for women with either group. This masculine schema that is associated with managers seems to include characteristics such as aggressiveness, rationality, self-confidence, competitiveness, and independence (Fagenson, 1990). Recently, in a study of third-grade children, Ayman-Nolley et al. (1991) also found that, similar to adults, boys were more likely to hold a masculine stereotype of a leader than were girls. It appears that in the United States, the masculine script of a leader is well established, although young women may hold a less rigid image. A few studies have demonstrated some of the factors affecting implicit leadership theories held by people. For example, there is some evidence that respondents' leadership experience and the leader's domain of functioning (e.g., political) have an effect on descriptions of leaders (Foti et al., 1982). Others have demonstrated that respondents' sex and sex role have some bearing on their expectations of an ideal leader. The results of these studies have mostly shown that respondents who are sex-typed (e.g., women with high femininity and men with low femininity) expect their ideal leaders to be more directive and controlling (Ayman and Bronnenberg, 1992). There is some evidence that men and women with different value system, cultures, and work experiences have different ideal leadership expectations (O'Connell et al., 1991; Ayman and Hong, 1992). It seems evident, then, that an individual's past experiences due to culture, work experience, and subgroup membership among other factors interact to form the individual's implicit leadership theory.

In summary, past research has indicated that social cognition is an integral part of the leadership process. In this process the leader and the group members are both watchers and are watched. The existing research in leadership has been based heavily on this perceptual process. The review of social perception and implicit leadership theory research revealed that researchers studying leadership need to be more cognizant of perceptual processes.

In the past, the global society was segregated by geographic region and by division of labor for each social group. As the members of different subgroups will be interacting with each other more often in the workplace (see Morrison and Von Glinow, 1990), the importance of assumptions regarding leaders and people of different subgroups become more important. The following section is an analytical review of gender and leadership research. Since women as a subgroup have received more attention than other minorities in the last two decades, this body of research will be examined first. Subsequently, some of the issues discussed in this section will be related to the more general topic of culture and the perception of leadership.

GENDER AND LEADERSHIP: THE ROLE OF PERCEPTION (IMPLICIT THEORIES)

In the 1980s several approaches were taken to developing an explanatory structure to organize and summarize the gender research literature. Deaux (1984) presented a framework that conceptualized the literature into the demographic approach (i.e., focus on the physical sex of the subject), psychological approach (i.e., focus on the sex-role orientation of the subject), and the attributional–cognitive approach (i.e., focus on the sex as a social category that triggers implicit theories and stereotypes). She acknowledged that tasks and expectations play a key role in moderating gender effects.

In an earlier article, Riger and Galligan (1980) identified two dominant research paradigms in gender research in management. They were categorized as "person-centered" or "situation-centered" approaches. According to Riger and Galligan (1980), the approaches that included demographic or psychological understanding of gender differences were part of the first category, and the second category included issues such as the task, others' expectations and attitudes, and organizational policies that facilitate gender-free mobility and evaluation. Both review papers (Deaux, 1984; Riger and Galligan, 1980) have acknowledged the significant role of the person's characteristics, the nature of the task, and others' implicit theories in understanding gender effects. The following two sections will discuss some of the issues in each approach as they relate to study of leadership when leader sex is a variable.

Person-Centered

Several authors have reviewed the profile literature on gender differences in leadership. The initial review by Brown (1979), followed by two meta-analyses (Dobbins and Platz, 1986, Eagly and Johnson, 1991) seemed to agree that when the gender of leader was the only salient factor, as in laboratory studies, the results showed gender differences. However, in actual organizations women managers and their male counterparts did not differ in how they were perceived.

Three different interpretations can be advanced regarding the results of these meta-analyses:

1. In laboratory studies, the limited exposure of the group member or the rater to the leader can highlight the gender of the leader more than the position occupied. Thus, the rater could be more influenced by their sex stereotypes than by their leadership expectations.
2. In laboratory studies, the time spent with the leader ranges from a few seconds (in the case of vignettes) to a half an hour. There is a possibility that when people work together over a longer period, roles become more salient than the sex of the leader.
3. In field studies, the leaders are actual managers. It is possible that women managers in organizations have been selected for these positions because they fit the masculine managerial stereotype. Thus, it is not surprising that they are reported to behave similarly to men.

In a narrative review by Korabik (1990), the key issues that emerged were closely related to the Deaux–Riger and Galligan conceptualizations. Korabik (1990) discussed the significance of sex-role orientation in studies of gender difference in leadership. She argues that studies using biological sex assume that all women have been socialized to behave in a feminine role. Although that biological sex and sex-role orientation covary, Bem (1974) has argued that all men do not have masculine orientation nor all women, feminine orientation.

The relative importance of physical sex versus sex-role orientation should vary between studies in which effects are based on the self-report of the leader versus those that involve the perception of the leader by others. It can be assumed that in self-report one is more attentive to one's own psychological orientation, whereas other people's perceptions may be more affected by the saliency of the actor's physical characteristics. For example, Thomas and Littig (1985) found that gender had no significant effect on self-description of leadership using LOQ. Also, Chapman (1975) found no gender difference on leadership of military or civilian managers using least preferred coworker (LPC) scores. In both studies the leadership variable was measured through the leader's response.

However, the findings in studies on rating of male and female leaders by others have been more complex. There have also been fewer of these studies. Two approaches have been subordinates' ratings. In one approach, ratings are averaged across raters, and in the other approach subordinates are categorized and separated on some characteristic (e.g., gender, sex-role orientation). For the first approach, the results have been contradictory. For example, Baird and Bradley (1979) found differences in the male–female communication style as perceived by subordinates and Arnett et al. (1980) also concurred, but Petty and Bruning (1980) and Ragins (1989) did not support this finding. It is important to note that these studies use different definitions for managers' style (i.e., communication, use of power sources, or LBDQ). In these studies, personal characteristics of the rater that might have affected the ratings were not assessed.

The second approach demonstrated the influence of personal characteristics (e.g., sex role, locus of control) on held schema or expectations for leaders. For example, studies have shown that observers who believe that women should act feminine and men should act masculine, evaluate women and men leaders differently (Maurer and Taylor, 1991; Dobbins et al., 1988; Rice et al., 1980). As summarized by Korabik (1990), when the sex of the subordinate and the leader is included in the study, the results show that the subordinates' perception of leader's effectiveness was a function of both the subordinates and the leader's gender (e.g., Bartol and Butterfield, 1976; Petty and Lee, 1975; Rosen and Jerdee, 1973). Subordinates expressed more satisfaction with their leaders who behave sex-typed, specifically, men who are structuring and women who are considerate (Petty and Miles, 1976). In addition, Lord et al. (1980) demonstrated that raters' LPC scores, locus of control, and gender all affected the perception of leadership behavior and effectiveness. Therefore, there is a need for further programmatic research relating the source of information and the role of psychological characteristics and physical characteristics of the leader and follower.

Another line of research in gender difference and leadership have used vignettes or what is coined as a "paper person" (Gorman et al., 1978). In these studies the subjects are not relating their past experiences or their present activities, but are placed in a hypothetical situation asking them about their potential responses. The situation is removed from "real life." This exercise depends on subjects' imagination and perhaps familiarity with the situation. In addition, these situations lack emotional involvement, which may affect responses (Penner et al., 1991).

In the aforementioned reviews (Dobbins and Platz, 1986; Eagly and Johnson, 1991), experimental setting versus work setting has been kept separate. In all reviews there was an agreement that gender stereotypes are more salient and have a greater influence on ratings in experimental settings. In these settings women were seen as more considerate, as more deferent to men, and as more democratic (Eagly and Johnson, 1991). However, even these reviews, experimental studies were not separated on the basis of (1) paper person versus real people, (2) self-rating versus subordinate or observer rating, and (3) assigned leaders versus emergent leaders. In all the studies mentioned above, the focus of the investigations were person-centered (Riger and Galligan, 1980). Investigators focused on the leader and to a great extent ignored the situation in which the leader was functioning.

Situation-Centered

As mentioned in the review of social cognition, in addition to one's expectation (e.g., stereotype and implicit leadership theory) the context of interaction has a significant impact on information processing. Situational factors that could affect differences in leadership for men and women might be the time spent in the group, the nature of the task, the group composition, and the norms in the work group. In studies including situational factors, sometimes several of these factors were combined in one study. In other ones, only one situational factor was studied. In this section a selective review of the literature will demonstrate the impact of these factors.

Concerning the factor of time spent in the group, very little research has focused directly on this variable. However, by comparing studies conducted in laboratory setting, vignettes, and organizational settings, this issue has been indirectly addressed. The evidence collected in experimental settings demonstrated that masculine tasks and mixed-sex groups all contribute to gender differences in leader emergence and perception of leadership. In addition, research has demonstrated that women are treated differently when they are in leadership position in mixed-sex groups and have a harder time emerging as leaders in such groups. For example, when men and women worked on masculine task, dominant women deferred to their male peers (Carbonell, 1984; Megargee, 1969; Wentworth and Anderson, 1984), but when the task was feminine, the dominant person emerged as leader regardless of gender composition of the group (Carbonell, 1984; Wentworth and Anderson, 1984).

In general, in homogeneous groups (i.e., all male or female) the dominant person was recognized as the leader (Megargee, 1969). Anderson and Blanchard (1982) concluded that, while men and women did not differ in their participation, women were found to be engaged in more socioemotional behaviors than were men in mixed-sex groups.

Until recently, researchers did not investigate whether situations assumed to be similar are truly similar for men and women leaders. For example, do women and men perceive themselves as having the same amount of control in a leadership situation? In a recent laboratory study

Butler and Geis (1990) found that men and women confederate leaders were treated differently by their subordinates even though the confederates were following the same script. Observers recorded significantly more negative and critical nonverbal feedback to female leaders than to male leaders (Butler and Geis, 1990). Therefore, a condition that on the surface seemed similar for men and women (i.e., being the appointed leader) may prove to be functionally and psychologically quite different. This difference is subtle and sometimes unrecognizable even by the participants. However, it may have a dramatic impact on the ease in which men and women can lead.

The norms of the leadership situation also need to be considered, since they affect social perception. Norms could be determined by the general culture of a society or the culture of the work setting. In work settings the norms governing work behavior vary from one organizational culture to another (Schein, 1985). In situations where norms are set clearly and roles are explicit, the behaviors of the individuals are strongly directed by the demands of the situation and individual differences are less apparent. Mischel (1977) labeled these situations as having strong demands that do not allow for the effect of traits to be manifested. This may be a reason for a lack of differences between men and women managers in most work settings.

In this section I reviewed the literature on gender and leadership. From a person-orientation, it seems that future researchers have to be more careful about separating self-perceptions of leaders from others' perceptions. In addition, the involvement of the rater and the rater's characteristics in the leadership process should not be taken lightly. Added to level of involvement of the perceiver, that person's characteristics also contribute to the perception of leader's behavior and performance evaluation. In this section I demonstrated some of the factors in the work group that can also influence the effects of gender on leadership. In the following section the situation will be expanded to a societal level. With the presence of the diverse workforce in the Western countries and increase in number of multinational corporations, culture as a factor in perception of leadership has become more interesting to the practitioners.

CULTURE AND LEADERSHIP PERCEPTION

We have so far touched on the role of culture as it relates to the norms considered appropriate for men and women. In this section culture as value systems and behavior patterns of other social groups will be reviewed. In the last century many scholars have been engaged in cross-cultural research in leadership (e.g., Bass, 1990; Hui, 1990). These studies have compared managers' values or styles across national boundaries (e.g., Bass et al., 1979; Haire et al., 1963; Smith et al., 1989) or examined the manager's style and values within a single culture (e.g., Ayman and Chemers, 1983; Komin, 1988; Ling, 1989; Misumi, 1985; Sinha, 1984).

On a regional perspective there is considerable evidence that people of different regions hold different work-related values (Hofstede, 1984; Ronen and Shenkar, 1985; Schwartz and Bilsky, 1987). The more a region is homogeneous, the more accurately one can measure the group's values and its members' common expectations for the leader. In addition to homogeneity of values in a region, if a society has strong rules of conduct (i.e., norms), the individuals will all agree on the behavior patterns in a situation even if they do not hold similar values. This concept, which is not very different from Mischel's (1977) "strong demand situations," was the basis for Pelto's (1968) categorization of cultures. In this categorization, he called cultures "tight" (e.g., Korea) when their norms were strongly imposed and "loose" when the presence of norms were not as explicit (e.g., the United States).

Very few studies have examined values and expectations of leaders from different countries. Hofstede (1984) compared national patterns of work-related values, but his analyses employed data relevant to group rather than individual level of analysis. In addition, the study was conducted in a single multinational corporation, which may have had an impact on the results. However, some studies have compared the relation between values, experience, and expectations. For example, Ayman and Hong (1992) compared ideal leader expectations of two Korean samples (e.g., students and employees) and two similar samples from the United States. In this study not only did country of origin contribute to differences of images of the ideal leader, but also, gender, values, and work experience all interacted with each other in predicting the scripts for an ideal leader. O'Connell et al. (1991) compared the response of a Japanese sample to United States samples on ideal leader script. The results suggested that the two hold different scripts. In previous studies on Japanese schema for successful manager (DeFrank et al., 1985; Howard et al., 1983), respondents reported that management was a masculine job. However, the Japanese description of ideal leader was different from that of the respondents in the United States. Despite relating managerial success to masculinity, the Japanese subjects described the successful manager as kind, emotional, understanding, aware of others' feelings, and helpful. Other unicultural studies like those of Misumi (1985) in Japan and Sinha (1984) in India demonstrate that Japanese and Indians each have unique templates for identifying effective leaders.

To demonstrate that the people of a region may have common implicit leadership theory that affects their evaluation of their leader, we can compare two studies done in Iran. Ayman and Chemers (1983) analyzed the factor structure of ratings of leaders by Iranian subordinates and compared them with similar ratings reported by Chemers (1969). The two studies revealed similar factor structures. However, in the earlier study (Chemers, 1969), the Iranian respondents were describing American leaders, and in the later study (Ayman and Chemers, 1983) the raters and the leaders were both Iranian. This suggested that Iranian subordinates were using their culturally based schema in reporting their leaders' behavior, yielding factor structures quite different from those made by U.S. raters. In both Iranian studies, leaders who were perceived as "benevolently paternalistic" (i.e., both structuring and considerate) were also evaluated more favorably and had more satisfied subordinates.

More recently, Smith et al. (1989) examined the structure of the responses of Hong Kong, Japanese, English, and American subjects to a leader behavior questionnaire. They found that though the factors were similar across cultures, the behaviors contributing to each factor varied from one culture to another.

Triandis and Brislin (1984) have reviewed the benefits and implications of cross-cultural research. From a theoretical perspective, the unconfounding of leadership and cultural variables seems specifically valuable. From a practical perspective, leadership training seems critical in today's multicultural work setting. In the development of cross-cultural training, the role of perception, expectations, and attribution have received great attention (Brislin, 1981; Fiedler et al., 1971). Thus, studies in different countries can help to provide an atlas of diverse scripts for ideal leadership and to assess similarities or differences in the meaning of leadership styles in various cultures. Cross-cultural representation of leadership expectations can assist in training international managers and can provide a new perspective in leadership model building.

Social groups may be differentiated from each other on the basis of differences in appearance (e.g., Asians, Africans, Caucasians) or by differences in cultural values, attitudes and expectations. People that look different may hold similar values. For example, minority group members in the United States have values more similar to white Americans than do white Frenchmen with white Americans. On the other hand, people that look the same may have quite different values (e.g., Italians and Swiss). Physical appearance is obvious and most likely to affect perception by an observer (Deaux and Lewis, 1984; McArthur, 1982). However, values are internal and most likely to affect an actor's expectations, behavior, and reactions.

When people of different subgroups interact with each other, the perceptual issues become more complex. For example, if the leader and perceiver are from different subgroups, the norms by which they can make assumptions to guide their expectations may not be the same. The subgroups who have less observable difference may even confront more complications.

Of these characteristics, gender and physical characteristics (e.g., color) seem to be very strong cues, since they not only are physical but also carry social connotations. That is, when someone is confronted with these characteristics the target person's social group membership is easily identifiable and the stereotypes associated with that group become readily accessible. For example, in a leadership situation a woman or an African American person, even though he or she may have values and expectations that are similar to those of a white male, may not be given a chance to express themselves as such. Recent studies have provided evidence that physical cues engage the perceiver in automatic information processing (Devine, 1989; Branscombe and Smith, 1990). Therefore, the perceiver encountering a nontraditional manager focuses on the social group membership of the manager rather than the role expectations associated with the position.

In research on social interaction, the issue of multiple roles has been neglected for the most part (Zarate and Smith, 1990). I found only one study addressing the role conflict a woman manager may experience between being a woman and a manager (Chusmir and Koberg, 1986). The research on minorities is also quite limited, and the existing facts do not present conclusive evidence on how, for example, black men and women in management position handle multiple conflicting roles (Nkomo and Cox, 1989).

In organizational research, role conflict in the workplace has been the subject of numerous studies (Beehr and Bhagat, 1985). In these studies both multiplicity of role demands (i.e., role overload) and possible conflict are gauged. This line of work has not been extended to organizational role and social group membership. Although in organizational research role overload and role conflict may covary, in the case of social group membership and organizational role the differences become more critical.

To illustrate this point, two sets of conditions can be considered. Every manager occupies multiple roles; however, individuals in management positions (e.g., executives) who belong to social groups that are not traditionally occupants of these positions (e.g., women, African Americans) may experience additional sources of conflict. For example, when a black man is an executive, or a woman is a judge, not only are these individuals faced with multiple roles, but the roles trigger expectations which are in contradiction. For traditional managers the multiple roles may at the most become burdensome and time-consuming. For the nontraditional manager, the role conflict will be more subtle and more difficult. The sources of conflict may not be in the conscious awareness of the person at all times. However, a small incident can tip the balance and cause the nontraditional manager to experience racial or sexual discrimination.

An anecdote may illustrate how this conflict of schema may affect interaction. A black man who was a vice president of a large company arrived at the airport of a major city in the United States. He tried to get a taxi to get to town. After an hour of being ignored by several empty taxis passing by, he called his secretary and asked her to call a cab. The cab arrived in a short time, and he reached his destination. Although there may be many explanations for this man's experience, one that seems quite viable is that the taxi drivers passing by saw a black man, not an executive, and it was his color that was the cue they were responding to rather than his professional role. In other words, perhaps even unintentionally they (i.e., the taxi drivers) ignored all the positive CEO characteristics of the man, such as the possibility of a large tip, and perceived only the possible negative aspects of his status as a minority, such as having to take him into a dangerous neighborhood.

These conditions bring to mind questions that need further investigation.

1. When multiple roles are present, how does the actor and the observer deal with the information?
2. When multiple roles trigger expectations (i.e., implicit theories or stereotypes), which are in contradiction and which role dominates?
3. Is there a difference between the way the actor handles the conflicting roles and the way others deal with them?
4. Is the conflict less or more salient to the observer or to the self?
5. Is the observer more prone to using physical characteristics to categorize individuals while the actor is more likely to use the situation and the role that he or she is in?

Therefore, in cross-cultural and gender research, it is not clear which is more salient, the leadership role, gender, social group membership of the ratee, or the rater's assumption about the ratee's orientation. Further programmatic research is necessary to clarify the intricacies of role saliency and physical cues.

CONCLUSION

In this chapter information from several research areas such as social perception, implicit leadership theory, gender and leadership, and cross-cultural leadership was reviewed to highlight the significance of perceptual processes in leadership. The influence of schema and situational cues seem more critical among the individuals interacting when participants do not share the same expectations. These mismatches of perception have major implications for a society that is in transition to a pluralistic workforce (Morrison and Von Glinow, 1990).

Nontraditional managers (e.g., women or minorities) are faced with a setting where their own assumptions do not always accurately predict the appropriate behavior, and they may not have access to the expectations of others. The nontraditional manager caught between group identity and professional identity is struggling to maintain a cognitive balance for him- or herself. Recent research has demonstrated that non-traditional managers benefit from the ability to adjust to the situation. These studies have measured this ability either by using self-monitoring (Anderson and McLenigan, 1987) or androgyny (Korabik and Ayman, 1989; Sargent, 1983). Therefore, impression management skills combined with well-balanced self-identity seem useful for the nontraditional manager's success as a leader.

From a practical perspective, women as nontraditional managers are vulnerable to others' behaviors and judgments in order to maintain the necessary balance between group identity (feminine) and the role that has masculine characteristics. These identity issues have important implications for the issue of sexual harassment at work. At a time when women are struggling to maintain a balance between being professional and hanging onto a female identity, when a man makes a comment regarding the sexuality of a female manager, he makes her gender become the most salient cue. Saliency of an irrelevant cue such as the gender of the leader can off-set the delicate balance (Gutek et al., 1982) both in how the woman leader conducts herself and how her behaviors are judged. Thus, by sexual harassment the man gains control over the saliency of the situational cues. The saliency of gender roles is important for two reasons: (1) it influences the manner in which the individual is perceived by others (e.g., subordinates and superiors) and (2) it creates self-role discrepancies for actors.

As the economy of the world becomes increasingly more globalized, work groups and organizations are faced with interaction of people from different cultures. This is valid for both the expatriate manager working abroad and the manager working for a firm owned by people from a different culture. Understanding the diverse expectations naturally present in such multicultural settings is critical in order to avoid miscommunication. This diversity could include the cultural expectations of a leader or the expectation associated with the social group to which the leader belongs. Thus, one cannot overemphasize the implications of person perception in understanding and improving interactions in multicultural workplace (Oddou and Mendenhall, 1984). Such miscommunications have negative effects on both productivity and employee satisfaction.

As we move toward this pluralistic environment in all segments of our society, our research, theoretical models, and training programs need to also become more inclusive of the diversity inherent in the pluralistic environment. During this transition, subtle differences may create major problems. To capture these subtleties, a possible alternative for future research may be formation of cross-cultural research teams. This will allow for the development of a paradigm that can represent diverse perspectives necessary to reconcile the various pieces of the jigsaw puzzle of leadership process.

References

Anderson, L. R., and Blanchard, P. N. (1982). Sex differences in task and social-emotional behavior. *Basic and Applied Social Psychology, 3,* 109–139.

Anderson, L. R., and McLenigan, M. (1987). Sex differences in the relationship between self-monitoring and leader behavior. *Small Group Behavior, 18,* 147–167.

Arkkelin, D. (1987). Influence of gender schema on perceptions of the "good manager." Paper presented at the annual convention of the American Psychological Association, New York (August).

Arnett, M. D., Higgins, R. B., and Priem, A. P. (1980). Sex and least preferred coworker scale effects in leadership behavior. *Sex Roles, 6,* 139–152.

Ashmore, R. D., and Del Boca, F. K. (1979). Sex stereotypes and implicit personality theory: Towards a cognitive-social psychological conceptualization. *Sex Roles, 5,* 219–248.

Ayman, R., and Bronneberg, E. A. (1992). *Subordinates' gender, sex role, and expectations of ideal leader behavior.* Unpublished manuscript, Illinois Institute of Technology, Chicago.

Ayman, R., and Chemers, M. M. (1983). Relationship of supervisory behavior ratings to work group effectiveness and subordinate satisfaction. *Journal of Applied Psychology, 68,* 338–341.

Ayman, R., and Hong, S. (1992). *Gender and cultural effects on expectations of the ideal leader: A comparison between U.S.A. and Korea.* Unpublished manuscript, Illinois Institute of Technology, Chicago.

Ayman-Nolley, S., Ayman, R., Dowhower, D., and Dyer, M. (1991). Children's leadership concepts and emergence is affected by context and gender. Paper presented at the meeting of the American Psychological Society, Washington, DC (June).

Baird, J. E., Jr., and Bradley, P. H. (1979). Styles of management and communication: A comparative study of men and women. *Communication Monographs, 46,* 101–111.

Bales, R. F. (1955). Task roles and social roles in problem solving groups. In E. E.

Macoby, T. M. Newcomb, and E. L. Hartley (Eds.), *Readings in social psychology.* New York: Holt, Rinehart, Winston.

Baron, R. A., and Greenberg, J. (1990). *Behavior in organizations,* 3rd ed. Boston: Allyn and Bacon.

Bartol, K. M., and Butterfield, D. A. (1976). Sex effects in evaluating leaders. *Journal of Applied Psychology, 61,* 446–454.

Bass, B. M. (1985). *Leadership performance beyond expectation.* New York: Academic Press.

Bass, B. M. (1990). *Bass & Stogdill's handbook of leadership: Theory, research, and managerial applications,* 3rd ed. New York: Free Press.

Bass, B. M., Burger, P. C., Doktor, R., and Barrett, G. V. (1979). *Assessment of managers: An international comparison.* New York: Free Press.

Beehr, T. A., and Bhagat, R. S. (1985). *Human stress and cognition in organizations: An integrated perspective.* New York: Wiley.

Bem, S. L. (1974). The measurement of psychological androgyny. *Journal of Consulting and Clinical Psychology, 42,* 155–162.

Branscombe, N. R., and Smith, E. R. (1990). Gender and racial stereotypes in impression formation and social decision-making processes. *Sex Roles, 22,* 627–647.

Brislin, R. W. (1981). *Cross-cultural encounters: Face to face interaction.* New York: Pergamon Press.

Brown, S. M. (1979). Male versus female leaders: A comparison of empirical studies. *Sex Roles, 5,* 595–611.

Butler, D., and Geis, F. L. (1990). Nonverbal affect responses to leaders: Implications for leadership evaluations. *Journal of Personality and Social Psychology, 58,* 48–59.

Calder, B. J. (1977). An attribution theory of leadership. In B. M. Staw and G. R. Salancik (Eds.), *New directions in organizational behavior* (pp. 179–204). Chicago: St. Clair Press.

Camara, W. J. (1989). Supreme Court review case of sex bias in the workplace. *The Industrial-Organizational Psychologist, 26,* 39–41.

Cantor, N., and Mischel, W. (1977). Traits as prototypes: The effects on recognition and memory. *Journal of Personality and Social Psychology, 35,* 38–48.

Carbonell, J. L. (1984). Sex roles and leadership revisited. *Journal of Applied Psychology, 69,* 44–49.

Carli, L.L. (1990). Gender, language, and influence. *Journal of Personality and Social Psychology, 59,* 941–951.

Carlyle, T. (1907). *Heroes and hero worship.* Boston: Adams. (Original work published in 1841).

Chapman, J. B. (1975). Comparison of male and female leadership styles. *Academy of Management Journal, 18,* 645–650.

Chemers, M. M. (1969). Cross-cultural training as a means for improving situational favorableness. *Human Relations, 22,* 531–546.

Chemers, M. M. (1987). Leadership processes: Intrapersonal, interpersonal, and societal influences. In C. Hendrick (Ed.), *Group processes: Review of personality and social psychology* (pp. 252–277). Newbury Park, CA: Sage.

Chusmir, L. H., and Koberg, C. S. (1986). Development and validation of the sex role conflict scale. *The Journal of Applied and Behavior Science, 22,* 392–409.

Conger, J. A. and Kanungo, R. N. (1988). Behavioral dimensions of charismatic leadership. In J. A. Conger and R. N. Kanungo (Eds.), *Charismatic leadership: The elusive factor in organizational effectiveness* (pp. 78–97). San Francisco: Jossey-Bass.

Cook, J. D., Hepworth, S. J., Wall, T. D., and Warr, P. B. (1981). *The experience of work: A compendium and review of 249 measures and their use.* New York: Academic Press.

Cronshaw, S. F., and Lord, R. G. (1987). Effects of categorization, attribution, and encoding processes on leadership perceptions. *Journal of Applied Psychology, 72,* 97–106.

Dachler, H. P. (1988). Constraints on the emergence of new vistas in leadership and management research: An epistemological overview. In J. G. Hunt, B. R. Baliga, H. P. Dachler, and C. A. Schriesheim (Eds.), *Emerging leadership vistas* (pp. 261–285). Lexington, MA: Heath.

Darley, J. M., and Fazio, R. H. (1980). Expectancy confirmation processes arising in the social interaction sequence. *American Psychologist, 35,* 867–881.

Deaux, K. (1984). From individual differences to social categories: Analysis of a decade's research on gender. *American Psychologist, 39,* 105–116.

Deaux, K., and Lewis, L. (1984). The structure of gender stereotype: Interrelationships among components and gender label. *Journal of Personality and Social Psychology, 46,* 991–1004.

DeFrank, R. S., Matteson, M. T., Schweiger, D. M., and Ivancevich, J. M. (1985). The impact of culture on the management practices of American and Japanese CEOs. *Organizational Dynamics, 13,* 62–77.

Deutsch, F. M. (1990). Status, sex, and smiling: The effect of role on smiling in men and women. *Personality and Social Psychology Bulletin, 16,* 531–540.

Devine, P. G. (1989). Stereotypes and prejudice: Their automatic and controlled components. *Journal of Personality and Social Psychology, 56,* 5–18.

Dobbins, G. H., and Platz, S. J. (1986). Sex differences in leadership: How real are they? *Academy of Management Review, 11,* 118–127.

Dobbins, G. H., Cardy, R. L., and Truxillo, D. M. (1988). The effects of purpose of appraisal and individual differences in stereotypes of women on sex differences in performance ratings: A laboratory and field study. *Journal of Applied Psychology, 73,* 551–558.

Driskell, J. E., and Mullen, B. (1990). Status, expectations, and behavior: A meta-analytic review and test of the theory. *Personality and Social Psychology Bulletin, 16,* 541–553.

Eagly, A. H., and Johnson, B. T. (1991). Gender and leadership style: A meta-analysis. *Psychological Bulletin, 108,* 233–256.

Eden, D., and Leviatan, U. (1975). Implicit leadership theory as a determinant of the factor structure underlying supervisory behavior scales. *Journal of Applied Psychology, 60,* 736–241.

Fagenson, E. A. (1990). Perceived masculine and feminine attributes examined as a function of individual's sex and level in the organizational power hierarchy:

A test of four theoretical perspectives. *Journal of Applied Psychology, 75,* 204–211.

Fiedler, F. E., Mitchell, T., and Triandis, H. C. (1971). The culture assimilator: An approach to cross-cultural training. *Journal of Applied Psychology, 55,* 95–102.

Fisher, B. M., and Edwards, J. E. (1988). Consideration and initiating structure and their relationships with leader effectiveness. Paper presented at the annual meeting of the Academy of Management, Anaheim, CA (August).

Foti, R. J., Fraser, S. L., and Lord, R. G. (1982). Effects of leadership labels and prototypes on perceptions of political leaders. *Journal of Applied Psychology, 67,* 326–333.

Gergen, K. J., and Gergen, M. M. (1981). *Social psychology.* New York: Harcourt Brace Jovanovich.

Gorman, C. D., Clover, W. H., and Doherty, M. E. (1978). Can we learn anything about interviewing real people from "interviews" of paper people? Two studies of the external validity of a paradigm. *Organizational Behavior and Human Performance, 22,* 165–192.

Green, R. G., and Mitchell, T. R. (1979). Attribution processes of leaders in leader-member interaction. *Organizational Behavior and Human Performance, 23,* 429–459.

Gutek, B. A., Morasch, B., and Cohen, A. G. (1982). Interpreting social-sexual behavior in a work setting. *Journal of Vocational Behavior, 22,* 30–48.

Haire, M., Ghiselli, E. E., and Porter, L. W. (1963). Cultural patterns in the role of the manager. *Industrial Relations, 2,* 95–117.

Hastorf, A. H., Schneider, D., and Polefka, J. (1970). *Person perception.* Reading, MA: Addison-Wesley.

Hersey, P., and Blanchard, K. H. (1973). *Leader effectiveness and adaptability description-self.* Escondido, CA: Center for Leadership Studies.

Hofstede, G. (1984). *Culture's consequences: International differences in work related values.* Beverly Hills: Sage.

Howard, A., Shudo, K., and Umeshima, M. (1983). Motivation and values among Japanese and American managers. *Personnel Psychology, 36,* 883–898.

Hui, C. H. (1990). Work attitudes, leadership styles, and managerial behaviors in different cultures. In R. W. Brislin (Ed.), *Applied cross-cultural psychology* (pp. 186–208). Newbury Park, CA: Sage.

Jones, E. E., and Davis, K. E. (1965). From acts to dispositions: The attribution process in person perception. In L. Berkowitz (Ed.), *Advances in experimental social psychology* (Vol. 2, pp. 000–000). New York: Academic Press.

Kelley, H. H. (1967). Attribution in social psychology. In D. Levine (Ed.), *Nebraska Symposium on Motivation* (Vol. 15, pp. 192–238). Lincoln: University of Nebraska Press.

Komaki, J. L. (1986). Toward effective supervision: An operant analysis and comparison of managers at work. *Journal of Applied Psychology, 71,* 270–279.

Komin, S. (1988). Culture and work values in Thai organizations. In *Social values and effective organizations.* Symposium conducted in Taipei, Taiwan.

Korabik, K. (1990). Androgyny and leadership style. *Journal of Business Ethics, 9,* 9–18.

Korabik, K., and Ayman, R. (1989). Should women managers have to act like men? *The Journal of Management Development, 8,* 23–32.

Larson, J. R., Jr. (1982). Cognitive mechanisms mediating the impact of implicit theories of leader behavior on leader behavior ratings. *Organizational Behavior and Human Performance, 29,* 129–140.

Ling, W. Q. (1989). Pattern of leadership behavior assessment in China. *Psychologia, 32,* 129–134.

Lockheed, M. E., and Hall, K. P. (1976). Conceptualizing sex as a status characteristic: Applications to leadership training strategies. *Journal of Social Issues, 32,* 111–124.

Lord, R. G., Binnings, J. F., Rush, M. C., and Thomas, J. C. (1978). The effect of performance cues and leader behavior on questionnaire rating of leadership behavior. *Organizational Behavior and Human Performance, 21,* 27–39.

Lord, R. G., DeVader, C. L., and Alliger, G. M. (1986). A meta-analysis of the relation between personality traits and leadership perceptions: An application of validity generalization procedures. *Journal of Applied Psychology, 71,* 402–410.

Lord, R. G., Foti, R. J., and DeVader, C. L. (1984). A test of leadership categorization theory: Internal structure, information processing, and leadership perceptions. *Organizational Behavior and Human Performance, 34,* 343–378.

Lord, R. G., and Maher, K. J. (1990). Alternative information-processing models and their implications for theory, research, and practice. *Academy of Management Review, 15,* 9–28.

Lord, R. G., Phillips, J. S., and Rush, M. C. (1980). Effects of sex and personality on perceptions of emergent leadership, influence, and social power. *Journal of Applied Psychology, 65,* 176–182.

Machiavelli, N. (1977). *The prince* (R. M. Adams, Transl.). New York: Norton. (Original work published in 1513.)

Markus, H. (1977). Self-schemata and processing information about the self. *Journal of Personality and Social Psychology, 35,* 63–78.

Martinko, M. J., and Gardner, W. L. (1987). The leader/member attribution process. *Academy of Management Review, 12,* 235–249.

Marx, K. (1906). *Capital.* Chicago: Charles H. Kerr.

Maurer, T. J., and Taylor, M. A. (1991). How important is ratee sex in sex bias in evaluation? Paper presented at the annual meeting of the Society for Industrial and Organizational Psychology, St. Louis (April).

McArthur, L. Z. (1982). Judging a book by its cover: A cognitive analysis of the relationship between physical appearance and stereotyping. In A. H. Hastrof and A. Isen (Eds.), *Cognitive social psychology* (pp. 149–211). New York: Elsevier.

Megargee, E. I. (1969). Influence of sex roles on the manifestation of leadership. *Journal of Applied Psychology, 53,* 377–382.

Meindl, J. R. (1990). On leadership: An alternative to the conventional wisdom. *Research in Organizational Behavior, 12,* 159–203.

Mischel, W. (1977). On the future of personality measurement. *American Psychologist, 32,* 246–254.

Misumi, J. (1985). *The behavior science of leadership: An interdisciplinary Japanese research program.* Ann Arbor: University of Michigan Press.

Morrison, A. M., and Von Glinow, M. A. (1990). Women and minority in management. *American Psychologist, 45,* 200–208.

Nkomo, S. M., and Cox, T., Jr. (1989). Gender differences in the upward mobility of black managers: Double whammy or double advantage? *Sex Roles, 21,* 825–839.

O'Connell, M. S. Lord, R. G., and O'Connell, M. K. (1991). Differences in Japanese and American leadership prototypes: Implications for cross-cultural training. Paper presented at the meeting of the Academy of Management, San Francisco (August).

Oddou, G., and Mendenhall, M. (1984). Person perception in cross-cultural settings: A review of cross-cultural and related cognitive literature. *International Journal of Intercultural Relations, 8,* 77–96.

Pelto, P. J. (1968). The differences between "tight" and "loose" societies. *Transaction, 5,* 37–40.

Penner, L. A., Harris, S. L., Llobert, J. M., and Craiger, J. R. (1991). Studying social cognitions and decisions about female managers: Methodological considerations. *Equal Opportunity International, 11,* 3–9.

Petty, M. M., and Bruning, N. S. (1980). A comparison of the relationships between subordinates' perceptions of supervisory behavior and measures of subordinates' job satisfaction for male and female leaders. *Academy of Management Journal, 23,* 717–725.

Petty, M. M., and Lee, G. K. (1975). Moderating effects of sex of supervisor and subordinate on relationships between supervisory behavior and subordinate satisfaction. *Journal of Applied Psychology, 60,* 624–628.

Petty, M. M., and Miles, R. H. (1976). Leader sex-role stereotyping in a female-dominated work culture. *Personnel Psychology, 29,* 393–404.

Phillips, J. S., and Lord, R. G. (1981). Causal attributions and perceptions of leadership. *Organizational Behavior and Human Performance, 28,* 143–163.

Phillips, J. S., and Lord, R. G. (1982). Schematic information processing and perceptions of leadership in problem-solving groups. *Journal of Applied Psychology, 67,* 486–492.

Phillips, J. S., and Lord, R. G. (1986). Notes on the practical and theoretical consequences of implicit leadership theories for the future of leadership measurement. *Journal of Management, 12,* 31–41.

Powell, G. N., and Butterfield, D. A. (1986). The "good manager": Does androgyny fare better in the 1980's? Paper presented at the meeting of the Academy of Management, Chicago (August).

Ragins, B. R. (1989). Power and gender congruency effects in evaluations of male and female managers. *Journal of Management, 15,* 65–76.

Reid, P. T., and Comas-Diaz, L. (1990). Gender and ethnicity: Perspectives on dual status. *Sex Roles, 22,* 397–405.

Rice, R. W., Bender, L. R., and Vitters, A. G. (1980). Leader sex, follower attitudes toward women and leadership effectiveness: A laboratory experiment. *Organizational Behavior and Human Performance, 25,* 46–78.

Riger, S., and Galligan, P. (1980). Women in management: An exploration of competing paradigms. *American Psychologist, 35,* 902–910.

Ronen, S., and Shenkar, O. (1985). Clustering countries on attitudinal dimensions: A review and synthesis. *Academy of Management Review, 10,* 435–454.

Rosen, B., and Jerdee, T. H. (1973). The influence of sex role stereotypes on evaluations of male and female supervisory behavior. *Journal of Applied Psychology, 57,* 44–48.

Sargent, A. G. (1983). *The androgynous manager: Blending male and female management styles for today's organization.* New York: AMACOM.

The Sayings of Confucius (1955). (J. R. Ware, Transl.). New York: New American Library.

Schein, E. H. (1985). *Organizational culture and leadership.* San Francisco: Jossey-Bass.

Schein, V. E. (1973). The relationship between sex role stereotypes and requisite management characteristics. *Journal of Applied Psychology, 57,* 95–100.

Schein, V. E. (1975).The relationship between sex role stereotypes and requisite characteristics among female managers. *Journal of Applied Psychology, 60,* 340–344.

Schein, V. E., Mueller, R., and Jacobson, C. (1989). The relationship between sex-role stereotypes and requisite management characteristics among college students. *Sex Roles, 20,* 103–110.

Schmitt, N., and Saari, B. B. (1978). Behavior, situation, and rater variance in description of leader behaviors. *Multivariate Behavioral Research, 13,* 483–495.

Schrishiem, C. A., and Kerr, S. (1974). Psychometric properties of the Ohio State leadership scales. *Psychological Bulletin, 81,* 756–765.

Schrishiem, C. A., and Kerr, S. (1977). Theories and measures of leadership: A critical appraisal. In J. G. Hunt and L. L. Larson (Eds.), *Leadership: The cutting edge* (pp. 9–45). Carbondale, IL: Southern Illinois University Press.

Schwartz, S. H., and Bilsky, W. (1987). Toward a universal psychological structure of human values. *Journal of Personality and Social Psychology, 53,* 550–562.

Shiffrin, R. M., and Schneider, W. (1977). Controlled and automatic human information processing: Perceptual learning, automatic attending, and a general theory. *Psychological Review, 84,* 127–190.

Sinha, J. B. P. (1984). A model of effective leadership styles in India. *International Studies of Management and Organization, 14*(3), 86–98.

Skrypnek, B. J., and Snyder, M. (1982). On the self-perpetuating nature of stereotypes about women and men. *Journal of Experimental Social Psychology, 18,* 277–291.

Smith, E. R., and Zarate, M. A. (1990). Exemplar and prototype use in social categorization. *Social Cognition, 8,* 243–262.

Smith, P. B., Misumi, J., Tayeb, M., Peterson, M., and Bond, M. (1989). On the generality of leadership style measures across cultures. *Journal of Occupational Psychology, 62,* 97–109.

Thomas, V. G., and Littig, L. W. (1985). A typology of leadership style: Examining gender and race effects. *Bulletin of the Psychonomic Society, 23,* 132–134.

Triandis, H. C., and Brislin, R. W. (1984). Cross-cultural psychology. *American Psychologist, 39,* 1006–1016.

Unsur u'l-Ma'ali. (1963). *Qabus namah,* 2nd ed. Tehran, Iran: Foroogi.

Wegner, D. M., and Vallacher, R. R. (1977). *Implicit psychology.* New York: Oxford University Press.

Wentworth, D. K., and Anderson, L. R. (1984). Emergent leadership as a function of sex and task type. *Sex Roles, 11,* 513–524.

Zarate, M. A., and Smith, E. R. (1990). Person categorization and stereotyping. *Social Cognition, 8,* 161–185.

7

The Contingency Model in Cross-Cultural Perspective

Harry C. Triandis
Department of Psychology
University of Illinois at Urbana-Champaign

INTRODUCTION

Before Fiedler, for almost 40 years, psychologists struggled to find personality attributes that would predict effective leadership. Stogdill's (1948) review told them to stop looking, but they kept looking for another 20 years! Finally, Fiedler pointed out that it is the fit of the person to the situation that results in effective performance. Thus, after Fiedler we saw an enormous emphasis on interactions, on contingencies. While the pre-Fiedler period is characterized by one variable studies, trying to see what variable might discriminate the elusive "excellent leader" from the "aver-

Leadership Theory and Research: Perspectives and Directions

age leader," the post-Fiedler period was characterized by the examination of complexities. Contingency theories, of course, acknowledge the role of situational moderators, and culture is the greatest of all moderators.

In this paper an attempt will be made to place leadership theories in a cultural framework, and thus stimulate cross-cultural leadership research.

COMPLEXITIES IN CURRENT LEADERSHIP THEORIES

The proverbial traveler from Mars, faced with understanding current leadership theories, is likely to be overwhelmed by their complexities. Leader effectiveness depends on attributes of the job, leader and followers have to match; the difference in the skill levels of the leader and followers results in more decisions being taken by the leader; stress makes an intelligent leader ineffective, and when there is no stress there is a relationship between leader intelligence and effectiveness; if the subordinate has all the needed skills, the leader does not have to do much; if the job is boring, the leader must entertain the subordinates; if the job is a lot of fun, the best leader leaves the subordinates alone; if the leader has enough information to make a decision, the leader should decide, but if such information is lacking, it is better to ask the subordinates to contribute ideas; if the decision of the leader is likely to be accepted by the subordinates, it is okay for the leader to decide, but if it is not likely to be accepted, it is best to let the subordinates participate in decisionmaking. I could go on and on, but I am sure the reader could, also. Such findings are widely available in the literature, and they reflect a wide range of theories, not only Fiedler's but also Vroom and Yetton's (1973), House's (1971), and so on. I deliberately mixed up findings from several sources to indicate that there is something general about the notion of contingency.

In fact, as Smith and Peterson (1988) put it, "once the notion of One Best Way of Leadership is discarded, all subsequent theories must be contingency theories" (p. 156).

FIEDLER'S THEORY AS ONE CONTINGENCY THEORY

In examining cross-cultural leadership one could focus on any one of the contingency theories and examine the effects of culture on the theory. My choice of Fiedler's theory is based on my belief that it has a chance to be universal, with cultural variables functioning as parameters of the theory. In other words, as we develop a better understanding of cross-cultural leadership, we will develop theorems of the form: "If a culture is high in *X*, theory *Y* works as expected; if a culture is low in *X*, theory *Y* must be modified as follows."

The strongest point about Fiedler's contingency model is that it works. Meta-analyses such as those of (Peters et al., 1985; Strube and Garcia, 1981) indicate that over 100 tests of the model worked most of the time. Furthermore, changes inspired by the theory, such as the use of LEADER MATCH (Fiedler et al., 1977) to train leaders to become more effective, seem to follow predictions, and the theory makes predictions that are not at all consistent with common sense, and yet are supported empirically.

The weakest point of the theory is that we do not *really* understand what LPC (least preferred coworker) is. While the literature includes several attempts to explicate the meaning of LPC (Garvin and Rice, 1982; Rice, 1978; Rice and Chemers, 1975; Rice et al., 1982), LPC does not have well-established antecedents (e.g., this is the way you raise a child to have high or low LPC) and it is not cleanly linked to behavior, since behavior seems to be a complex function of stress and LPC (Fiedler, 1967). I think future research may provide such links, and I will make suggestions about this later in this chapter.

There is also much that we do not know about the model. Specifically, only a few studies have tested the model in other cultures, and so we do not know for sure whether the model is universal or works only in cultures similar to those of North America.

In the present paper I will assume the universal validity of the contingency model, and develop an extension of the model that takes into account cultural differences. I will begin by presenting some of the major dimensions of cultural variation, and then I will ask what predictions can be made from the model when the subjects are in a culture that is very different from the culture of the United States or northern Europe. This will suggest specific directions for future research.

CULTURAL VARIATIONS

There is a myriad of ways in which cultures differ. However, from a scientific point of view all these variations are of little interest. Just as in the physical sciences, we are not concerned with the prediction of every moving object, but can predict a good deal of the movement of objects by taking gravity and the specific weight of the medium within which the object is moving into account, so in this area we can concentrate on a few dimensions that are especially important, and ignore the rest.

There is reason to believe that the most important dimensions of cultural variation are (1) individualism versus collectivism and (2) uncertainty avoidance.

INDIVIDUALISM AND COLLECTIVISM

Meaning

The literature for the last 100 years has discussed contrasts that reflect this dimension. The terminology of Toennies (1957), *gemeinschaft versus gesellschaft,* sometimes translated into community versus society, captures some of the differences between collectivism and individualism. It reflects the relative emphasis on the collective (family, work group, tribe, nation, etc.) versus the individual in definitions of the self, in decisionmaking, in attitudes, values, and behavior. Similar ideas under the label of value orientations (Kluckhohn and Strodtbeck, 1961) contrasted the "relational" with the "individualistic" way of relating to other people. Discussions of social systems (Parsons and Shils, 1951), morality (Shweder, 1982; Miller et al. 1990), religion (Bakan, 1966), cognitive differentiation (Witkin and Berry, 1975), economic development (Adelman and Morris, 1967), modernity (Inkeles and Smith, 1974; Taylor, 1989), the structure of constitutions (Massimini and Calegari, 1979), cultural patterns (Hsu, 1983), and the self (Markus and Kitayama, 1991; Jansz, 1991) used similar terms. The individualism–collectivism terminology was proposed by Hofstede (1980) and has become the focus of considerable research.

The general topic is described under the label of "cross-cultural studies of individualism and collectivism" and has been reviewed by Triandis (1990). Empirical studies have been published by Triandis and his collaborators (e.g., Triandis et al., 1986, 1988a, 1990).

Individualism and collectivism are cultural "syndromes"; that is, they reflect attitudes, beliefs, norms, roles, self-definitions, and values that contrast two types of cultures. Industrial psychology has had a considerable history focusing on attitudes and values [e.g., Haire et al. (1966); England and Lee (1973); Whitely and England (1980); Hofstede (1980); England (1984), MOW International Research Team (1986); Bond's work as in The Chinese Cultural Connection, (1987)]. However, it has neglected other aspects of subjective culture (Triandis, 1972). The work on collectivism and individualism provides probes of one of the many important contrasts in subjective culture around the world, a contrast that finds northern and western Europe and North America, Australia, and New Zealand on one side, and southern Europe, Asia, Africa, and South America on the other side.

Attributes

First, I must emphasize that these two constructs are not polar opposites, in the sense that in one culture all people in all situations will have the attributes of collectivism. Rather, what we find is that there are two dimensions, correlated −.6 rather than −1.00 as a true bipolar structure would require, and in different cultures, depending on the situation, some or most of the attributes are individualistic or collectivist.

Spranger (1928) argued that systems of ethics differ depending on whether one deals with social (e.g., family life), economic, religious, aesthetic, political, or truth issues. Similarly, cultures that are collectivist in many situations (e.g., within the family, in work groups, in aesthetics, as when the state decides what is "good art," in science, in politics, in religion, in economic policy) are more collectivist (e.g., Mao's China) than cultures where many of these matters are decided by individuals. Similarly, we can identify many attributes that contrast collectivists and individualists, but it is rare that a culture would be consistently high in individualism or collectivism. Usually some combination of these attributes is collectivist or individualist, so that the definition of a culture as one or the other is polythetic, that is, it depends on the simultaneous observation of many attributes. Certain kinds of ecologies push cultures toward collectivism, but they do not necessarily do so on every attribute. Similarly, other ecologies and experiences push toward individualism.

It is useful to remember that culture is to society what memory is to individuals. It is the institutional memory of what has worked in the past, what was adaptive; these memories are widely shared, and become unstated assumptions about what is right or wrong, and about how people should think, feel, and behave. People act without thinking because behavior under the influence of culture is overdetermined; that is, all elements of subjective culture point in the same direction.

Second, there are individual differences. Even in highly individualistic cultures like the United States or northwestern Europe, there are "allocentrics" who have mostly collectivist attributes, and even in collectivist cultures, such as in the Far East there are "idiocentrics" who have mostly individualistic attributes (Triandis et al., 1985). One might expect allocentrics in individualistic cultures to join communes, and other collectives, and to feel "out of the stream," just as one might expect idiocentrics in collectivist cultures to abandon their group, and even migrate to individualistic cultures. Again, experiences that a particular individual has had during socialization will create patterns of habits (i.e. personality), that reflect idiocentric tendencies or allocentric tendencies. In every culture there are opportunities for both of these tendencies to develop.

A major contrast between collectivists and individualists is in what they pay attention to [see Triandis (1990) for a review of the evidence]. Collectivists cut the pie of experience by focusing on groups; individualists consider it obvious that the world consists of individuals. Collectivists define themselves by using group attributes (e.g., "I am Chinese"), see behavior as reflecting group influences (e.g., "I am not surprised he did this: What can you expect of a Japanese?"), see success as due to the help received from others (e.g., "I am what my coworkers helped me become"), and failure due to internal factors (e.g., "I did not try hard enough"). Individualists define themselves by reference to personality attributes (e.g., "I am reliable"), see behavior as reflecting internal factors (e.g., attitudes, personality) see success as due to their ability (e.g., "I am very intelligent"), and failure as due to external factors (e.g., "The task was difficult"). Triandis et al. (1990) present the empirical details.

Collectivists are context-dependent (Cohen, 1991). There is no such thing as a personality attribute that holds across all situations (Shweder and Bourne, 1984). Rather, Saddam is "*cruel* to his mother-in-law and *kind* to his mother." Collectivists focus on ascribed attributes of the other—family background, age, sex, and so on; individualists on achieved attributes—accomplishments. The other person's group identity is crucial to the collectivist. Groups are perceived as homogeneous, and ingroups are more homogeneous than outgroups. By contrast, individualists emphasize what makes a person different from others. They introduce their honored guests as "distinguished" and they see the ingroup as more heterogeneous than the outgroup (Quattrone, 1986).

Collectivists do not assume that attitudes are related to behavior (Iwao, 1988). Behavior must be "appropriate" and whether attitudes are or are not consistent is a trivial matter for them. After all, attitudes are an aspect of the person. Individuals are not important. Only groups are important. By contrast, individualists assume that attitudes predict behavior, and publish papers on the subject when they can't find the evidence!

Collectivists know and remember very little about themselves, but a great deal about others. Conversely, individualists know and remember much more about themselves than about others (Markus and Kitayama, 1991).

The important attributes of the self, for the collectivists, are the achievement of one'ss group, cooperation, endurance, abasement, endurance, nurturance, order and self-control (Hui and Villareal, 1989). The important attributes of the self, for individualists, are personal achievement, aggression to help in one's competition for scarce rewards, and exhibition.

The goals of collectivists emerge in group interaction, or are imposed by group authorities. The goals of individualists are generated by themselves to reflect their personal needs. When group and personal goals are in conflict, the collectivists give priority to the group goals; the individualists find it acceptable to give priority to their personal goals.

Communication is different in these two kinds of cultures (Cohen, 1991). Collectivists are more concerned about others understanding them than whether they are enjoying themselves during the communication; individualists are self-focused in their communication (i.e., as long as they feel good about themselves, it does not matter if the other person does not understand). Individualists are more concerned with the "I" than with the "we," communicate more or less the same way regardless of context, and prefer to communicate horizontally (to equal-status peers). Collectivists (Hsu, 1983) prefer vertical communications (e.g., father–son).

Decisions are taken by vote among individualists and by consensus among collectivists. This means that collectivists spend more time deciding than implementing a decision, while the opposite is the case with individualists. Collectivists emphasize the harmony of the relationship within the ingroup, so they do not confront, but instead use a lot of "maybe," "probably," while individualists see nothing wrong with some confrontations that will "clear the air" and tend to use extreme terms such as "terrific," "the biggest."

Since collectivists know a lot about the people they communicate with, and can assume considerable similarity with ingroup members, they often communicate elliptically, giving just a few clues, and letting the listener "fill in the gaps." In fact, some think that to draw conclusions is to insult the listener. Sometimes the communication sounds to outsiders as rather idiosyncratic and seems linked to the particular relationship (i.e., consists of private language).

Collectivists ask "What makes me the same as my group?"; individualists ask "What makes me different from others?" Collectivists focus on the needs of others, while individualists focus on their needs, rights, and capacities. Collectivists favor interdependence, security, obedience, duty, ingroup harmony, hierarchy, and personal relationships. Individualists emphasize independence, doing their own thing, pleasure, achievement, competition, autonomy, and fairness (Triandis et al., 1990).

The major worry of collectivists is that they might be ostracized. The major worry of individualists is that they might become dependent on others.

Collectivists have few ingroups and are highly concerned about the integrity and well-being of these groups. Individualists have many ingroups and are highly concerned only about the integrity of their immediate family. The influence of the one or two ingroups of the collectivists is profound and widespread; the influence of the ingroups of the individualists is superficial and limited to specific behaviors (Triandis, 1990).

A major attribute of collectivists is that they behave very different when they are dealing with an ingroup other than with an outgroup other (Triandis, 1972, 1990). The definition of who is ingroup is culture-specific. For example, it may be only the family, or only the tribe, or it can be very broad (e.g., Japan). Which ingroup is activated at a specific point in time depends on the situation. If the ingroup is attacked or challenged, it becomes the major focus of cognitions. Ingroups can be visualized as concentric circles, with the inner circles exerting more influence than the outer.

In collectivist cultures it is difficult to enter ingroups, but once one has been accepted social behavior is intimate, and smooth (Triandis et al., 1988b). On the other hand, social behavior with outgroups is at best indifferent, and often hostile, and distrusting. Given the struggle among outgroups, collectivists are extremely hospitable toward "guests" who are viewed as potential ingroup members, and thus might strengthen the ingroup in its struggle with outgroups. In individualist cultures the difference between ingroup and outgroup behaviors is less pronounced, and the ingroup tends to be defined more broadly (e.g., those who have the same attitudes or values as I do).

In summary, collectivist social behavior is a function of "who the other person is"; individualist social behavior is a function of "what the other person thinks (attitudes) and does (achievements)." Individualists are personal-goal-oriented, and communicate the same way, regardless of context. Collectivists are group-goal-oriented and much more sensitive to context.

PROBABLE DETERMINANTS OF INDIVIDUALISM

There is evidence that the more affluent (gross national product per capita) the society, the more individualistic it is (Hofstede, 1980). Affluence allows people to be economically independent of their ingroups, and such independence often leads to emotional and attitudinal as well as goal independence. In addition, social mobility, urban residence, and other attributes of cultures seem to be linked to individualism. The upper classes in most cultures (ancient or modern) are individualistic. A representative sample of Poles showed the more educated, those with higher incomes, those who lived in cities, and the men to be more individualistic than the lower social classes, rural dwellers, and the women (Daab, 1991).

Jobs that require individual action (e.g., writing a book) result in individualism. Hunters and food gatherers in preliterate societies are more individualistic than agriculturalists. Conversely, when one has limited resources it is helpful to have an ingroup that can help during difficult moments; those who live in the same place, and in rural environments are likely to pay attention to group norms and be more collectivist; jobs that require cooperative action (e.g., building an irrigation canal) result in collectivism.

THE IDEAL LEADER

Of Collectivists

The image of the ideal leader is likely to be different in these two kinds of cultures. It follows from the descriptions just provided that the ideal collectivist leader is paternalistic, taking good care of the ingroup. Such a leader would support, solve personal problems, and generally show maintenance and consideration behaviors. Thus, "acting like a good boss" in collectivist cultures means being nurturant, supportive, "like a father" (Ayman and Chemers, 1983). Furthermore, what is a desirable behavior for a boss in one culture may be undesirable in another. Smith and Peterson (1988) reported that indirect criticism (such as talking about an absent subordinate) is considered "inconsiderate" in individualistic cultures, such as the United States and Britain, and "considerate" in the Far East. While the nurturant leader may be very well liked in order for the leader to be effective, it is important that that person also be production-oriented. Thus, Misumi (1985) reports that the leader who is both nurturant and production-oriented is most effective.

Of Individualists

The ideal leader for individualists is the one who allows them to do their own thing, but is supportive when they need help. It is one who will respect and admire their distinctiveness, who accepts their search for pleasure and achievement, and helps them win interpersonal competitions.

ATTRIBUTES OF POWER DISTANCE

Hofstede (1980) distinguished collectivism and power distance (seeing high-status people as extremely different from low-status people), although empirically the two dimensions were correlated (.67). Subsequent research has shown that most collectivist samples are high in power distance, although there are examples where the two attributes are uncorrelated (Billings, 1989, 1991). To simplify the present discussion, I will not pay attention to the possible separate status of these two dimensions, and will assume that collectivism and high power distance are linked. Thus, I will not provide a separate "ideal leader profile" for high-power-distance cultures. However, one can guess that high power distance would be especially related to charismatic leaders, who are "extraordinary" individuals, and the ideal leader may well be expected to be such an extraordinary person.

Summary

To aid in memory, here are some of the main contrasts discussed above:

Collectivists	Individualists
Unit of analysis	
The group, the collective	The individual
Attributions for success	
Help given by collective	Ability
Attributions of failure	
Lack of effort	Difficult task, bad luck
Self is defined in	
Ingroup terms	Trait terms
When individual and group goals are in conflict	
Group goals win	Individual goals win
Attitudes and norms	
Favor interdependence	Favor independence
Values	
Security, obedience, duty, ingroup harmony, hierarchy, personalized, intimate relations	Pleasure, achievement, competition, freedom, autonomy, fairness
Ingroups	
Few, very important	Many, not too important
Social behavior	
Very different if the other is ingroup vs. outgroup. Intimate, ingroup harmony important. Can be hostile to outgroups	Somewhat different if the other is outgroup. Friendly, but not deep Fairness toward outgroup

ATTRIBUTES OF UNCERTAINTY AVOIDANCE

As mentioned in the Introduction, the two most important dimensions of cultural variation may be individualism and uncertainty avoidance. Hofstede (personal communication, 1991) argues that his fourth dimension, masculinity–femininity, is also very important, but so far there has been little empirical work on this dimension. Thus here we will only discuss, in addition to collectivism, the uncertainty avoidance dimension.

Hofstede (1980) identified a dimension that was linked to willingness to take risks versus valuing certainty, security, and structure. He also thought that the dimension linked to Pelto's (1968) concept of tightness. Tight cultures require people to behave exactly as specified by norms; loose cultures allow some latitude in behavior. Sanctions are provided in tight cultures (e.g., Japan) quite readily for minor deviations (e.g., a high-school girl having a perm), while larger deviations are tolerated in loose cultures (e.g., a high-school girl with an Afro hairdo in the United States).

Discussions of Hofstede's work, in cross-cultural psychology circles, suggested that it is not cultures that are high or low in uncertainty avoidance, but situations-in-cultures. Specifically, it seems important to consider whether the norm is generated via group interaction, or is a law that has been written down. Also, it makes a difference whether the norm applied to specific members of the ingroup or to people in general.

In the case of loose cultures, very severe sanctions apply when a law that applies to all individuals is broken (e.g., the person wrote a bad check), or a written agreement has not been followed (e.g., broken contract). On the other hand, the sanctions are not as extreme when a behavior affects only a few people (e.g., unmarried couple living together) or is not written down (e.g., oral agreement to buy something). Conversely, in tight cultures oral agreements that are broken result in severe sanctions (e.g., ostracism by the whole ingroup), and deviation from written laws (e.g., traffic violations) are tolerated. Thus, tightness, like individualism, is situation-specific, and we need to pay attention to what is the behavior *and* the situation, and count the number of situation/behaviors that result in severe sanctions.

Tightness requires that norms be very clear; otherwise, one cannot provide sanctions for deviation from norms. Also the culture has to be homogeneous, so that people will have no doubts about which norm is applicable. Loose cultures tend to be at the intersections of major cultural traditions (e.g., Thailand at the intersection of Chinese and Indian cultures) or are very pluralistic (e.g., the United States). When more than one culture is present, it is difficult to impose a particular norm. Often individuals decide for themselves whether to follow the norm, so looseness should be correlated with individualism. However, we do not have such data as yet.

FISKE'S RELATIONAL ORIENTATIONS

The dimensions of individualism, collectivism, power distance, and uncertainty avoidance, discussed above, match with a typology of social behaviors provided by Fiske (1991). This typology represents a most impressive integration of theory from all the social sciences. A major advantage of Fiske's theory is that it is linked with much of the already existing social science theory, as well as to empirical findings. On the empirical side, for instance, we have (see Triandis, 1978) evidence that social behavior is seen as different along the dimensions of association versus dissociation, superordination versus subordination, intimacy versus formality, and overt versus covert behavior, in all cultures (Lonner, 1980). While these dimensions are extracted in diverse cultures via factor analysis, they constitute the skeleton and Fiske provides the flesh of the beast that is called "social behavior" around the world. Furthermore, his theory results in a typology of four kinds of leaders that appear to be optimal for cultures that emphasize particular orientations.

Fiske argues that there are four and only four independent, relational orientations, which he calls "community sharing," "authority ranking," "equality matching," and "market pricing." These orientations are cultural universals, in that they exist in every culture in some situations. In each culture we find a unique configuration of these orientations in particular situations.

Community sharing is characterized by a sense of belonging to a group, thinking more in "we" than in "I" terms, having a shared identity; isolation, abandonment, and loneliness are feared; resources are distributed according to need; marriage is for love so that the two spouses experience a total "oneness"; gift giving is frequent; social behavior is intimate, nurturant, altruistic, caring, unselfish, generous, and sharing (one gives what one can and takes what one needs); there is concern for the ingroup, protection of the ingroup, and willingness to fight the outgroup, racism, and genocide; work is a collective responsibility; there is emphasis on the land; relationships are perceived as eternal; decisions are taken by consensus; children learn by modeling adults; and the self if relational and includes group identities. Hofstede's collectivism largely overlaps with this orientation.

Authority ranking is a relationship system based on asymmetric power. Boss versus subordinate; one marries for status; top-level person gives gifts; subordinates do what boss says; noblesse oblige, subordinates show respect, deference, loyalty, and obedience; boss decides. The impertinent are punished; land belongs to the high-status people (e.g., royal lands); precedence is important in how one walks, eats. Wars extend the authority of the boss.

Hofstede's power distance largely overlaps with this orientation. As we have seen above, I take the position that the .67 correlation between collectivism and power distance [empirically obtained by Hofstede (1980)] makes separate discussion of this dimension unnecessary, so I present collectivism as a cultural pattern that includes high power distance, and where authority ranking is a way of life. Other students of collectivism (e.g., Cohen, 1991) agree with this view.

However, Fiske [in concert with many anthropologists (e.g., Billings, 1989, 1991)] argues that there are collectivist cultures with low authority ranking, and hence the two dimensions are orthogonal. I accept this. However, the cultures where this happens are preliterate, and it seems that in contemporary major cultures the correlation is about .7, as found by Hofstede (1980). I find the simplification of dropping one dimension worthwhile.

Equality matching is based on reciprocity, equality, and equal distribution of resources. One marries an equal; gifts of equal value are distributed; justice and fairness are important concerns; work is shared equally, land is divided equally; people take turns going through a door, one person one vote; self is separate and distinct, and like all other selves; misfortune should be distributed equally; revenge is common.

Market pricing is characterized by analyses of the "profits" and "costs" of an interpersonal relationship. Resources are distributed according to each person's contribution. People marry for money; gifts are exchanged according to their contribution to the relationship, achievement is important, there is freedom for people to do their own thing, people are willing to do almost anything for money, there are a lot of ratios computed (e.g., tax), people often are paid according to how much they produce, land is an investment, concern for rate of return per unit of time is high, the market decides many things, there are rational bureaucracies, the self is defined by one's occupation, the greatest good for the greatest number makes sense; there are mercantile wars, exploitation of the workers, and computation of kill ratios during war. This orientation overlaps with individualism.

Note that both community sharing and authority ranking link with collectivism, and equality matching and market pricing link with individualism.

The important point of the Fiske system is that each culture has a unique way of using the four orientations. For example, in the United States market pricing is used widely, but marriage is based on community sharing and equality matching. *So, in each culture situations are "constructed" out of the four basic elements.* I called the Fiske system, when I introduced Fiske to psychologists, "the periodic table of social science."

What are the ideal leaders of each orientation? In community sharing, this is the nurturant leader, who says "take what you need, we all work together until the job is done, to each according to needs and from each according to abilities." In authority ranking this is the charismatic leader, who says "those who have the least rank do all the dirty work" and no good member of the culture argues with that view! In equality matching this is the leader who does what the subordinates do, and there is an equal share of the profits. In market pricing this is the leader who rewards those who contribute the most.

CULTURE AND THE CONTINGENCY THEORIES

Almost all the data of contingency theories come from individualistic, low-uncertainty-avoidance cultures. In fact, what is remarkable about Misumi's (1985) theory is that it is *not* a contingency theory. The high-production/high-maintenance (PM) leader is best under a wide range of situations, samples, and tasks. One has to look hard (e.g., the low-achievement subjects) to find a condition when another type of leader is needed.

Given the facts about cultural variations, perhaps each contingency theory must be modified, to show that when one moves to cultures that are collectivist, or high in uncertainty avoidance, the normal "laws" of the theory change.

If this perspective is used, how will the contingency model work in different cultural contexts? The answer is "we do not know," because there is too little evidence. However, there are some Japanese studies suggesting that Japanese social psychologists obtained some results compatible with predictions of the model (Hashiguchi and Fujita, 1978). One of the derivations of the Fiedler theory, developed by Chemers (Chemers et al., 1985) has been replicated in Japan (Shirakashi, in press). Such findings justify that we start with the assumption that the contingency model is universally valid, and then proceed to find specific cultural variables that limit its generality in specific situations.

That strategy was used by Ayman (1984) and Chemers (1987) who reported (Ayman and Chemers, 1991) that the contingency model worked among Mexican managers who were low in self-monitoring (Snyder, 1974), but did not work among those high in self-monitoring (Chemers and Ayman, 1985). It emphasizes an earlier point—there are variations in personality within culture that need to be considered when examining how a particular leadership theory operates. One interpretation of this finding is as follows: Mexico is a collectivist culture (Hofstede, 1980), and in collectivist cultures, as we have seen, there is little relationship between internal factors (attitudes, personality) and behavior. This tendency must be more pronounced among high self-monitors, who would be paying more attention to the local culture, and hence there was no relationship between

LPC and performance among high self-monitors. Furthermore, since self-monitors behave according to Mexican norms they were rated more favorably than low self-monitors.

In other words, the meaning of the leadership situation changes from culture to culture, and if we are to make predictions about how the contingency model will work in other cultures, we need to examine the links between the model on one hand and the cultural variations on the other hand.

Before we engage in this activity it is desirable that we remember some fundamentals about Helson's (1964) level of adaptation theory, which has received considerable support in social psychology (e.g., Sherif et al., 1965). Level of adaptation is like a neutral point on continua of experience. Remember the basic findings: people whose occupations required moving heavy objects judge most objects in the world to be "light"; people whose occupations required them to move light objects, perceive most of the same things to be "heavy." Similarly, if we are raised, in a culture where people frequently take risks we are likely to see more of the situations in the world as "low-risk," because we are likely to have a level of adaptation that is relatively high, with respect to the concept of risk.

Now, Fiedler's three situational dimensions have some conceptual relationship to the dimensions of cultural variation we have discussed. The model's "leader–member relations" has a conceptual link with collectivism. From our previous discussion it follows that leader member relations are likely to be good if the leader belongs to the same ingroup as the followers, and bad if the leader belongs to the outgroup of the followers. Leader member relations should be good in collectivist cultures when a leader acts in a nurturant way, and there is a lot of community sharing. In fact, community sharing reminds one of the Ohio State dimension of consideration, which often is linked to satisfaction with the boss.

But if the leader is a member of the outgroup, or is not nurturant, we expect that in collectivist cultures the situation is likely to be in Fiedler's Octant 8: only a very-low-LPC leader can be at all effective.

The model's "task structure" has much in common with uncertainty avoidance. A leadership situation with much task structure should be compatible for people high in uncertainty avoidance, since such people like structure, and avoid uncertainty. Following the logic of level of adaptation theory, in high-uncertainty-avoidance cultures most situations will be seen as low in task structure, therefore, the contingency model would predict (unless there are extraordinarily good relations and high power) the need for a high-LPC leader.

The model's "leader power" dimension clearly has something to do with power distance, since we can expect that in high-power-distance cultures the leader will have been given much power by the social systems. Thus, we can expect cultures with much authority ranking to have many leadership situations with high power and those with high equality matching to have few leadership situations with high power. In the high-authority-ranking cultures most leaders will be seen as having low power, and in the high-equality-matching cultures, most leaders will be seen as having high power.

Finally, we can expect cultures that use a lot of market pricing to have leaders who pay a lot of attention to performance and reward it accordingly.

In summary, if we take into account the argument about shifts in level of adaptation, we can predict that people in collectivist cultures will expect a lot of community sharing and authority ranking; hence more situations in the world at large will be seen by them as low in those attributes. This should lead to dissatisfaction with many situations, and thus the leader will find him- or herself in the middle of the model's situational control variable; hence the high-LPC leader would be more effective in collectivist cultures. We predict, then, that in collectivist cultures nurturance will be an important attribute of effective leaders. When the leader is not nurturant, we expect a very poor situation, and it is doubtful that even a low-LPC leader will be able to manage such a situation. In short, in such cultures, when we find leaders who are satisfactory, they will be nurturant as well as interested in getting the job done (Ayman and Chemers, 1983). Similarly, Sinha has reported that in India the leader who is most effective starts by being nurturant, and *then* suggests how the work is to be done (Sinha, 1986).

Note that this essentially says that there is no need for contingency theories in collectivist cultures. This is consistent with Misumi's position: The good leader is high in both production (P) and maintenance (M) in all situations. Misumi (1985) reports consistently that the PM leader (high in both) is better than the pm (low in both) or the pM or Pm leader.

Incidentally, he also makes the important point, that the perceived quality of P changes when the leader is high in M as opposed to low in m. In the case of an M leader, P is seen as "planning"; in the case of an m leader, P is seen as "pressure for production."

Such interactions suggest that the meaning of behavior changes within the context of other behaviors. We also know that how a behavior is perceived does differ with culture (Triandis et al., 1968). As already mentioned, Smith and Peterson (1988) show that "to criticize privately, directly" is seen as "considerate" in individualistic cultures and as "inconsiderate" in Japan, where the expectation is that people will be criticized indirectly (receive the information from a peer rather than directly from the boss, since they will loose too much face if it comes from the boss). This raises the following question: Are the behaviors that are associated with high LPC or low LPC different across cultures?

FUTURE RESEARCH

The previous question would be a good place to start future research. In addition, we can predict, on the assumption that the contingency model is valid cross-culturally, a number of relationships. First, the more collectivist the culture, the more will an ingroup leader be expected to have good leader–member relations. However, this prediction must hold "other things being equal" and may not hold when power distance is very high. Specifically, when power distance is very high, the leader can get away with being bossy. One is reminded of Bond et al. (1985), who found that in Hong Kong a boss can insult a subordinate with fair impunity. Nevertheless, in collectivist cultures if the leader is not a legitimate member of the ingroup (e.g., kin), even slightly poor leader–member relations will result in the leader being perceived as belonging to an outgroup. That would lead to very poor situational control, and a situation where, according to the contingency model, only low-LPC leaders would function at all. This analysis, then, leads to a testable prediction: The more collectivist the culture, the more likely it will be to find "effective" leaders who are either quite nurturant but also concerned with the task (i.e., PM in Misumi's terms) *or* extremely task-oriented (Pm). The latter profile reminds us of some African dictators of the Idi Amin variety.

Task structure will be expected to be higher in cultures high in uncertainty avoidance, such as Japan, than in cultures low in uncertainty avoidance, such as Singapore. Thus a leader's situation that is marginally low in structure will be seen as very low in structure in Japan. If leader–member relations are good, one would expect a low-LPC leader to be less effective in Japan, because the number of situations that will be perceived as low task structure will be large. Hence this prediction: in Japan most leaders would be in the middle range of the leader control variable of the contingency model; in other words, to be effective, they would have to be high-LPCs. Since few leaders are disinterested in the task, that essentially means that they must be PM leaders, as Misumi has found. However, in Hong Kong, which is low in uncertainty avoidance, we would not expect this relationship to hold as strongly.

Leader power is likely to be higher in high-power-distance cultures, such as Venezuela. A situation in which the leader has less than absolute power is likely to be perceived as a "low-power" situation, and predictions from the contingency model should use the low-power cells of the model.

As mentioned earlier, if we are to understand the meaning of LPC completely, we should be able to link specific child-rearing patterns to LPC. One hypothesis, derived from our discussion above, is that child-rearing antecedents of individualism and collectivism may also be the antecedents of low and high LPC, respectively. Affluence, urban living, individualized child-rearing (typical of only children), and frequent rewards for working alone (e.g., individual play) should predispose to low LPC. This is because we know they link with individualism, and individualism is linked with emphasis on achievement, on the task. On the other hand, poverty, rural living, large numbers of siblings, and frequent rewards for team play (e.g., football) should predispose toward high LPC. This is because these conditions lead to collectivism, and collectivism is linked to concerns for interpersonal solidarity. Research on this hypothesis may finally provide a clear answer about the meaning of LPC. The task orientation may be a reflection of an aspect of individualism, while the person-orientation may be a reflection of satisfying team experiences.

In other words, what is being proposed can be summarized as follows:

1. The contingency model is valid cross-culturally, but predictions from the model will require taking into account whether the culture is collectivist, high in uncertainty avoidance, or high in power distance.
2. In collectivist cultures the contingency model will work only with low self-monitors, and there will be more situations defined as having "poor leader–member relations" than in individualistic cultures, so effective leaders will have to be more nurturant and supportive and do more community sharing in more situations in such cultures than in individualistic cultures.
3. In high-uncertainty-avoidance cultures more situations will be defined as "low task structure" than in low-uncertainty-avoidance cultures. Thus, the "low-task-structure" cells of the model will have to be used more frequently in the former than in the latter cultures.
4. In high-power-distance cultures more situations will be defined as "low-power" than in low-power-distance cultures. Hence, the low-power cells of the contingency model will have to be used more frequently in making predictions of effectiveness from the contingency model in high than in low-power-distance cultures.

If these predictions are supported, the utility of the contingency model will be enlarged, and leadership theory will reach new heights of effectiveness.

References

Adelman, I., and Morris, C. T. (1967). *Society, politics and economic development: A quantitative approach.* Baltimore: Johns Hopkins Press.

Ayman, R. (1984). The effects of leadership characteristics and situational control on leadership effectiveness. In M. M. Chemers (Chair.) Leadership Effectiveness in Mexico. Symposium conducted at the International Congress of Psychology, Acapulco, Mexico (August).

Ayman, R. and Chemers, M. M. (1983). The relationship of supervisory behavior ratings to work group effectiveness and subordinate satisfaction among Iranian managers. *Journal of Applied Psychology, 68,* 338–341.

Ayman, R. and Chemers, M. M. (1991). The effect of leadership match on subordinate satisfaction in Mexican organizations: Some moderating influences of self-monitoring. *International Review of Applied Psychology, 40,* 299–314.

Bakan, D. (1966). *The duality of human existence.* Chicago: Rand McNally.

Billings, D. K. (1989). Individualism and group orientation. In D. M. Keats, D. Munroe, and L. Mann (Eds.), *Heterogeneity in cross-cultural psychology,* (pp. 92–103), Lisse, The Netherlands: Swets & Zeitlinger.

Billings, D. K. (1991). Genus individualism/communalism: Persistent sightings of an untamed beast. Paper presented at the annual meetings of the Society for Cross Cultural Research, Isla Verde, Puerto Rico (February).

Bond, M., Wan, K., Leung, K., and Giacalone, R. A. (1985). How are responses to verbal insult related to cultural collectivism and power distance? *Journal of Cross-Cultural Psychology, 16,* 111–127.

Chemers, M. M. (1987). Leadership processes: Intrapersonal, interpersonal, and societal influences. In C. Hendrick (Ed.), *Group Processes, Review of Personality and Social Psychology.* Newbury Park, CA: Sage.

Chemers, M. M., and Ayman, R. (1985). Leadership orientation as a moderator of the relationship between performance and job satisfaction of Mexican managers. *Personality and Social Psychology Bulletin, 11,* 359–367.

Chemers, M. M., Hay, R. B., Rhodewalt, F., and Wysocki, J. (1985). A person-environment analysis of job stress: A contingency model explanation. *Journal of Personality and Social Psychology, 49,* 628–635.

Cohen, R. (1991). *Negotiating across cultures.* Washington, D.C.: United States Institute of Peace Press.

Daab, W. Z. (1991). Changing perspectives on individualism. Paper presented at the Helsinki meeting of the International Society of Political Psychology (July).

England, G. (1984). Work centrality in Japan and USA. Paper presented at Meetings of Academy of Management, Boston.

England, G., and Lee, R. (1973). Organizational size as an influence on perceived organizational goals: A comparative study among American, Japanese, and Korean managers. *Organizational Behavior and Human Performance, 9,* 48–58.

Fiedler, F. E. (1967). *A theory of leadership effectiveness.* New York: McGraw-Hill.

Fiedler, F. E., Chemers, M. M., and Mahar, L. (1977). *Improving leadership effectiveness: The leader match concept.* New York: Wiley & Sons.

Fiske, A. (1991). *Structures of social life: The four elementary forms of human relations.* New York: Free Press.

Garvin, D., and Rice, R. W. (1982). Subjective meaning of the LPC scale: The view of respondents. *Basic and Applied Social Psychology, 3,* 203–218.

Haire, M., Ghiselli, E. E., and Porter, L. (1966). *Managerial thinking: An international study.* New York: Wiley.

Hashiguchi, K., and Fujita, M. (1978). Leadership. In J. Misumi (Ed.), *Social psychology in Japan.* London: Sage.

Helson, H. (1964). *Adaptation-level theory.* New York: Harper & Row.

Hofstede, G. (1980). *Culture's consequences.* Newbury Park, CA: Sage.

House, R. J. (1971). A path-goal theory of leadership. *Administrative Science Quarterly, 16,* 321–338.

Hsu, F. L. (1983). *Rugged individualism reconsidered.* Knoxville, TN: University of Tennessee Press.

Hui, C.H., and Villareal, M. (1989). Individualism-collectivism and psychological needs: Their relationship in two cultures. *Journal of Cross-Cultural Psychology, 20,* 310–323.

Inkeles, A., and Smith, D. H. (1974). *Becoming modern.* Cambridge, MA: Harvard University Press.

Iwao, S. (1988). Social psychology's models of man. Isn't time for East to meet West? Invited address to the International Congress of Scientific Psychology, Sydney, Australia (August).

Jansz, J. (1991). *Person, self, and moral demands: Individualism contested by collectivism.* Leiden, The Netherlands: DSWO Press.

Kluckhohn, F., and Strodtbeck, F. (1961). *Variations in value orientations.* Evanston: Row Peterson.

Lonner, W. (1980). The search for psychological universals. In H. C. Triandis and W. W. Lanbert (Eds.), *Handbook of Cross-Cultural Psychology* (Vol. 1, pp. 143–204). Boston: Allyn and Bacon.

Markus, H., and Kitayama, S. (1991). Culture and self: Implications for cognition, emotion, and motivation. *Psychological Review, 98,* 224–253.

Massimini, F., and Calegari, P. (1979). *Il contesto normativo sociale.* Milano: Angeli.

Miller, J. G., Bersoff, D. M., and Harwood, R. L. (1990). Perceptions of social responsibilities in India and the United States: Moral imperatives or personal decisions? *Journal of Personality and Social Psychology, 58,* 33–47.

Misumi, J. (1985). *The behavioral science of leadership.* Ann Arbor: University of Michigan Press.

MOW International Research Team (1986). *The meaning of work: An international perspective.* New York: Academic Press.

Parsons, T., and Shils, E. A. (1951). *Toward a general theory of action.* Cambridge, MA: Harvard University Press.

Pelto, P. J. (1968). The difference between "tight" and "loose" societies. *Transactions* (April), 37–40.

Peters, L.H., Hartke, D. D., and Pohlmann, J. T. (1985). Fiedler's contingency theory of leadership: An application of the meta-analysis of Schmidt and Hunter. *Psychological Bulletin, 97,* 274–285.

Quattrone, G. A. (1986). On the perception of a group's variability. In S. Worchell and W. G. Austin (Eds.), *Psychology of Intergroup Relations.* Chicago: Nelson-Hall.

Rice, R. W. (1978). Construct validity of the least preferred coworker scale. *Psychological Bulletin, 85,* 1199–1237.

Rice, R. W., and Chemers, M. M. (1975). Personality and situational determinants of leader behavior. *Journal of Applied Psychology, 60,* 20–27.

Rice, R. W., Marwick, N. J., Chemers, M. M., and Bentley, J. C. (1982). Task performance and satisfaction: Least preferred coworker (LPC) as a moderator. *Personality and Social Psychology Bulletin, 8,* 534–541.

Sherif, C. W., Sherif, M., and Neubergall, R. E. (1965). *Attitude and attitude change.* Philadelphia: Saunders.

Shirakashi, S. (in press). Job stress of Japanese managers: A contingency model analysis. *Journal of Applied Social Psychology.*

Shweder, R. A. (1982). Beyond self-constructed knowledge: The study of culture and morality. *Merrill-Palmer Quarterly, 28,* 41–69.

Shweder, R. A., and Bourne, E. J. (1984). Does the concept of person vary cross-culturally? In R. Shweder and R. LeVine (Eds.), *Culture theory: Essays on mind, self, and emotion.* (pp. 158–199). New York: Cambridge University Press.

Sinha, J. B. P. (1986). Concepts and controversies in Indian organizational psychology. Invited Address, International Congress of Applied Psychology, Jerusalem (July).

Smith, P. B., and Peterson, M. F. (1988). *Leadership, organizations and culture.* Newbury Park, CA: Sage.

Snyder, M. (1974). Self-monitoring of expressive behavior. *Journal of Personality and Social Psychology, 30,* 526–537.

Spranger, E. (1928). *Types of man: The psychology and ethics of personality.* (P. J. W. Pigors, Transl.) Halle (saale): Max Niemeyer Verlag.

Stogdill, R. M. (1948). Personal factors associated with leadership: A survey of the literature. *Journal of Psychology, 25,* 35–71.

Strube, M. J., and Garcia, J. E. (1981). A meta-analytical investigation of Fiedler's contingency model of leadership effectiveness. *Psychological Bulletin, 90,* 307–321.

Taylor, C. (1989). *Sources of the self: The making of modern identity.* Cambridge, MA: Harvard University Press.

The Chinese Cultural Connection (1987). Chinese values and the search for a culture free dimension of cultures. *Journal of Cross-Cultural Psychology, 18,* 143–164.

Toennies, F. (1957). *Community and society.* (C. P. Loomis, Transl.) East Lansing: Michigan State University Press.

Triandis, H. C. (1972). *The analysis of subjective culture.* New York: Wiley & Sons.

Triandis, H. C. (1978). Some universals of social behavior. *Personality and Social Psychology Bulletin, 4,* 1–16.

Triandis, H. C. (1990). Cross-cultural studies of individualism and collectivism. In J. Berman (Ed.), *Nebraska Symposium on Motivation, 1989* (pp. 41–133). Lincoln: University of Nebraska Press.

Triandis, H. C., Leung, K., Villareal, M., and Clack, F. (1985). Allocentric vs idiocentric tendencies: Convergent and discriminant validation. *Journal of Research in Personality, 19,* 395–415.

Triandis, H. C., Bontempo, R., Betancourt, H., Bond, M., Leung, K., Brenes, A., Georgas, J., Hui, C. H., Marin, G., Setiadi, B., Sinha, J. B. P., Verma, J., Spangenberg, J., Touzard, H., and de Montmollin, G. (1986). The measurement of etic aspects of individualism and collectivism. *Australian Journal of Psychology, 38,* 257–267.

Triandis, H. C., Bontempo, R., Villareal, M. J., Asai, M., and Lucca, N. (1988a). Individualism and collectivism: Cross-cultural perspectives on self-ingroup relationships. *Journal of Personality and Social Psychology, 54,* 323–338.

Triandis, H. C., Brislin, R. W., and Hui, C. H. (1988b). Cross-cultural training across the individualism-collectivism divide. *International Journal of Intergroup Relations, 12,* 269–289.

Triandis, H. C., McCusker, C., and Hui, C. H. (1990). Multimethod probes of individualism and collectivism. *Journal of Personality and Social Psychology, 59,* 1006–1020.

Triandis, H. C., Vassiliou, V., and Nassiakou, M. (1968). Three studies of subjective culture. *Journal of Personality and Social Psychology, Monograph Supplement, 8,* (4), 1–42.

Vroom, V., and Yetton, P. W. (1973). *Leadership and decision-making.* Pittsburgh, PA: University of Pittsburgh Press.

Whitely, W., and England, G. (1980). Variability in common dimensions of managerial values due to value orientation and country differences. *Personnel Psychology, 33,* 77–89.

Witkin, H. A., and Berry, J. W. (1975). Psychological differentiation in cross-cultural perspective. *Journal of Cross-Cultural Psychology, 6,* 4–87.

8

Managing Cultural Diversity on the Individual, Group, and Organizational Levels

Renate R. Mai-Dalton
School of Business
University of Kansas

INTRODUCTION

Since the publication of Workforce 2000 (Johnston and Packer, 1987) numerous businesses have stressed with additional vigor the need to manage a diverse workforce. The authors of the report indicate that during the 1990s, 85 percent of the net growth of the U.S. labor force will consist of people of color, white women, and immigrants. By the year 2000, blacks will make up 12 percent, Hispanics 10 percent, and Asians 4 percent of the total workforce (Kiplinger and Kiplinger, 1989). Women are expected to make up 48 percent (*Businessweek,* 1988). Morrison and Van Glinow (1990) point out that between 1984 and 1995 some of the fastest growing occupations will include managerial, executive, professional, and technical positions, which are higher-skilled positions not traditionally held by women and minorities. Thus, the increased need for human resources in these jobs might also require the accelerated inclusion of women and minorities. The well-documented upcoming changes in the demographic composition of the U.S. population require that steps be taken to successfully integrate culturally diverse individuals into our workforce.

Such a movement also provides an opportunity to facilitate the integration of additional minority groups that have struggled for full acceptance in high-status occupations (e.g., Native Americans, the disabled, gays and lesbians, religious minorities), but that have not been typically included in such integrative efforts. Others have made similar suggestions and add that a broadening of the studied groups would benefit research in intergroup relations (Stephan, 1987). For the purpose of this chapter, the term *minorities* will refer to individuals who are not members of the dominant group and could be minorities because of gender, race, ethnicity, national origin, religion, disability, or sexual orientation.

The argument is frequently made that the United States is one of the few countries that has a wealth of people with different backgrounds. If managed correctly, such diversity could be an advantage both for personal growth of its citizens (Copeland, 1988a) as well as for an increase of productivity in its businesses (Cox and Blake, 1991). However, if not managed correctly, U.S. organizations may become less competitive with organizations in other countries. This chapter will deal with some of these issues. Specifically, it will (1) describe a multicultural model that should underlie our philosophy regarding the management of cultural diversity; (2) describe issues that arise in the management of diversity on the individual, group, and organizational levels; and (3) discuss the kind of leadership that will be required to guide a culturally diverse workforce.

THE MULTICULTURAL MODEL

Berry (1986) describes how different societies adopt different models that guide the relationships between members of various subgroups. He contrasts the mainstream–minority model with the multicultural model and explains how the choice of one model over the other influences the relationships between individuals in a given society. For instance, in 1971 the Canadian government officially adopted the multicultural model as its national policy. The practical consequences for Canadians are that their government encourages individuals from various ethnic and racial backgrounds to share their heritage with the rest of the population. Such sharing has two advantages: (1) individuals from different cultures develop pride in their heritage and have the opportunity to retain it and (2) other Canadians have an opportunity to learn about different cultures and will lead a richer life. In contrast to the Canadian example, the U.S. government officially pursues a mainstream–minority policy (*E Pluribus Unum* is the premise). It encourages all citizens to assimilate and to strive to become more like mainstream Americans. Thus, Americans are encouraged to subordinate their cultural heritage to that of the mainstream population. Despite this government policy, it is true that de facto multiculturalism is evident in many areas. It is argued here that despite the fact that the U.S. government is not expected to change to the Canadian policy, U.S. organizations should do so in order to manage their culturally diverse populations successfully. I am advocating this position because minority group members experience less acculturative stress in countries that use the multicultural model than in countries where the mainstream–minority model is used. The multicultural model will also facilitate the use of all human resources in organizations and, if managed correctly, will improve divergent input and creativity. These points will be discussed further below.

What are the differences between these two models? Berry (1986, 1990) asserts that in the mainstream–minority model, minority groups of various kinds are seen as subordinate to the dominant mainstream population and the expectation is that minorities will eventually assimilate into mainstream society. Influence flows from the mainstream to the minority population. Berry explains that in this model the implicit assumption is that minorities somehow "need fixing." In contrast, the multicultural model assumes that minority groups are an integral part of the overall population. (See Fig. 8.1 for an adaptation of Berry's figure to that for the U.S. population.) This would indicate that each minority group is similarly respected and the contributions of its members are given equal weight to that of any other group. A bidirectional influence takes place. For organizational environments, this means that individuals with different backgrounds would be encouraged to express thoughts and ideas that are special to their particular culture. It would enable them to contribute their unique strengths, such as their insights into work-related problems as these relate to their own life experiences as well as share their views based on the values that their particular culture might hold strongly. In contrast, individuals who function under the mainstream–minority model perceive that they are not acceptable the way they are, and will or cannot share their skills and abilities. As a result, they will experience severe stress.

Berry (1990) describes the stress that individuals experience as a result of acculturation. *Acculturation* can be defined as the process of change that individuals go through as they come in contact with another culture. Berry posits four kinds of acculturation: integration, assimilation, separation, and marginalization. The first two correspond to the multicultural and mainstream–minority models. Thus, integration takes place when members of a minority group are permitted to retain their cultural heritage in addition to becoming a part of the overall population. Assimilation takes place when the individuals immerse themselves or are forced to immerse

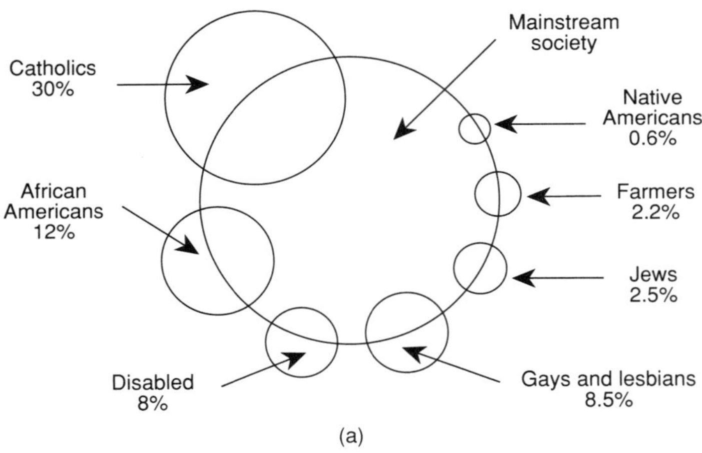

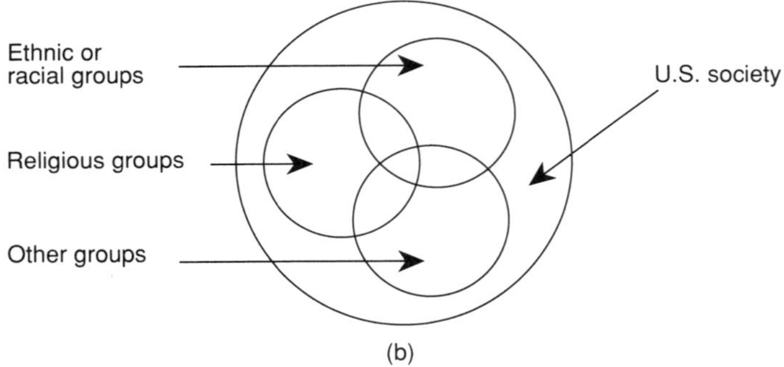

Figure 8.1 Two models of intergroup relations. (a) Mainstream–minority model; (b) multicultural model. (Adapted from Berry, 1986.)

themselves in the mainstream culture and do not focus on the culture they were initially from. Acculturative stress, in general, can result in poor mental health, feelings of alienation, and psychosomatic illnesses. However, Berry (1990) asserts that "the stress of persons experiencing acculturation in plural societies to be less than those in monistic societies that pursue a forced inclusion or assimilationist ideology" (p. 249). In addition, Berry feels that individuals who *want* to be part of the overall society, but are prevented from doing so by societal policies, will also experience greater acculturative stress than will individuals who do not have such a desire.

For organizations, this means that the multicultural or pluralistic approach to managing employees will result in lower levels of stress for minority employees and higher levels of performance. It further means that if these employees are permitted to infuse thoughts and ideas from their specific cultural backgrounds into their work, the organizations will gain divergent inputs that can lead to more creative and effective problem solving. This issue will be further discussed in the section that deals with managing diversity on the group level.

The psychological impact of the assumptions of the mainstream–minority model is not unique to minority-group members. All individuals who must work under such assumptions will suffer from stress and behavioral changes. Thus, majority-group members placed in minority-like situations show similar affects. This can be easily demonstrated.

During the past 8 years, I have asked the students in my introductory organization behavior classes to place themselves into situations where they are the minorities. They may not take anyone with them and have to do this exercise on their own (Mai-Dalton, 1984–1985). As part of this assignment, mainstream students have gone to self-selected environments where *they* were "minorities" among African Americans, Native Americans, the disabled, Jews, gays and lesbians, and others. About 90 percent of the time, these students report that the new environment influences them in such a way that they behave differently and experience elevated levels of anxiety.

For instance, a white young man who had gone to play basketball with a group of African Americans, whom he had occasionally observed while he was walking his dog, describes it this way:

> I went to the park, took my basketball, and waited for the group to arrive. While I was shooting, I was feeling some anxiety. After each shot I'd look down the road to see if anyone was coming. Just about when I was somewhat relieved by the thought that they weren't coming, a car pulled up with them in it. My heart began to beat a little faster. There were six of them in the car. That meant I was an odd-man and probably wouldn't get to play. As they walked on the court, a couple of them greeted me by nodding their heads. I responded in the same manner. No conversation took place. This was disappointing; I was hoping to mix in with them right away. It became more apparent to me now just how cohesive this group was. I could sense a cold feeling from the group. They were not rude but they certainly weren't friendly, either.
>
> During a break after they had played their second game, I walked over and asked: "Would anybody want to sit out a game and take a break?" For what seemed to be the longest five seconds in my life they looked at each other and didn't respond. Finally, the 6'4" guy answered: "Yeah, I'll sit out. Take my

> place." This guy was definitely the group's leader. Everyone looked to him for the answer rather than speaking out for themselves.
>
> Having played a couple of years of college basketball, I certainly felt I could hold my own against these guys. After the first few points of the game, I began to wonder if I would ever get a chance to show them I could play. My teammates didn't pass me the ball.

This short excerpt demonstrates that the well-intentioned student, who had placed himself into a situation where he was the minority, had a difficult time both to cope with his own perceptions of not being accepted and being able to behave in his usual capable manner in this different environment. The situation also did not permit him to share his competence.

A second sample reinforces the point that such experiences are not unique to situations with racial minorities, but are also occurring with "invisible minorities" that are seldom included in the cultural diversity literature. Here is an excerpt of a paper I received from a student who went to a gay bar:

> On the way over to the club, I experienced some stress-related symptoms. The frequency of urination increased substantially, chest pains developed and their intensity increased the closer I got to the club. I circled the block two times and then finally parked about four blocks away. Before entering the club, I made sure no one was standing around or driving by. After I had entered the bar, the atmosphere seemed like any other bar, except for the occasional holding of hands and hugging between males. The nervousness and chest pains went away after about 10 minutes. . . . Going to the club gave me some insight on what it is like to be a minority. Even though I dislike homosexuality, I still felt a need to belong to the surroundings. I felt isolated sitting by myself and wanted to be able to engage in conversations with other people at the club.

Since none of the bar patrons could have known the sexual orientation of the student, it is clear that the stress and behavioral changes he experienced were the results of his own perceptions. Thus, even when minorities might not be openly discriminated against, their own feelings of ambiguity and estrangement can trigger stressful situations.

These two examples demonstrate that most individuals who must function in situations where they feel alone and estranged will experience increased levels of stress and might not be able to show the competence they are capable of. If these effects can be demonstrated so easily on majority-group members who only briefly find themselves in a minority situation, it can be imagined how much stronger the effects can be for minority-group members who function in such environments during most of their working lives. It would be both in the interest of such workers and their organizations to avoid such stress.

MANAGING DIVERSITY

In order for organizations to adequately manage a diverse workforce and to avoid an environment that can hinder employee performance, they need to identify the processes that negatively influence individuals from different backgrounds. These processes operate on at least three levels of the organization: (1) the individual employees and their perception of the multicultural environment; (2) groups and the dynamics that influence their work; and (3) organizational structure and policies and their effect on individuals and groups. Organizations must identify and remove negative influences on each of these levels and find ways to facilitate high performance in a diverse workforce. The following section will outline important processes on each of these levels that have been reported in the literature along with some suggested solutions.

Individual Level

Much research documents the stress that individuals experience when trying to function in a multicultural environment. Research has been conducted with at least three different populations: immigrants who have come to the United States from different countries (Bhagat, 1985), mainstream individuals who have gone to different countries and experienced a minority status there (Brislin, 1981), and U.S. resident minority groups who operate in the mainstream U.S. culture (Ford, 1985). Across all three populations there is evidence that stress, created by cultural differences, prevents them from functioning up to their abilities. In addition, there is evidence that cross-cultural contacts not only influence the minority-group members but also induce anxiety and stress in majority group members who supervise or work with minorities (Thiederman, 1991).

Ford (1985) reviewed the literature of how minority professionals are affected by job-related stress. He particularly analyzed five empirical studies with samples that included African American males and females, Native Americans, and Mexican Americans. He concluded that minority professionals (1) experience more stress than do their nonminority counterparts, (2) experience less stress relative to one another when they are given emotional and structural support at their places of work, and (3) experience less stress when they are supervised by nonwhites. In addition, he cites a study by Cobbs (1981) that identified specific characteristics of the work environment for minorities that are indicative of job stress. These include the perceptions that (1) the organization has lower performance expectations for minority-group members, (2) these individuals have less access to important information, (3) these individuals experience unwarranted promotion and earnings ceilings, and (4) these individuals feel that they have a lack of role models and mentors. Similar points are made in a later study by Morrison and Von Glinow (1990).

Thiederman (1991) refers to stress that comes from culture shock, defined as "a state of mind that occurs when people find themselves immersed in a strange culture" (p. 5) and describes situations that immigrants encounter at their places of work. For instance, it is difficult for immigrants to know how to behave because they are not aware of the new cultural rules that might apply and are not reinforced for the same behaviors as they were previously accustomed to. These dynamics result in psychological states that will have a negative impact on their performance. For instance, the workers might develop feelings of inadequacy, loneliness, and frustration. The result of these might be that they will be unwilling to try new tasks, contribute new ideas, and interact with new coworkers. In addition, the different behaviors of the immigrants might also affect the managers who supervise them. Since managers in the United States are usually trained to supervise workers that come from a similar culture, they will become disoriented because the workers are not responding to them in the expected manner. In addition, many managers have the expectation that workers should assimilate and behave like mainstream employees. When this does not happen, the managers might experience the same feelings that described the immigrants. Neither of them will be able to perform up to their abilities in such an environment.

Bhagat (1985) also refers to the stress that immigrants experience and what the consequences of such stress might be for organizations. He cites stress from (1) differences in values, norms, roles, and attitudinal orientation; (2) negative stereotypes about immigrants that might be prevalent in the new culture; (3) lack of knowledge about organization-specific politics; (4) overworking in order to fulfill all expectations; and (5) the difficulty of retaining their cultural heritage while feeling a need to adopt the new mainstream values. The researcher hypothesized that unless the above issues can be adequately resolved, immigrants might show low organizational commitment and job satisfaction and will not perform well in their jobs.

The foregoing research from various writers indicates that minority employees from many different backgrounds are affected by stressors on the job that result in reduced performance. White supervisors of minority employees might also experience stress if they are not trained to deal with individuals from nonwhite backgrounds.

The stressors for minority employees seem to be associated with factors originating from within the minority employees themselves and factors rooted in the organizational environment. The former include a lack of knowledge about the new culture, conflict experienced because of different value systems between their own heritage and the new culture, and an eagerness to be successful that might result in over exertion. Organizational factors include negative stereotypes that might be held about minority employees; biased decisions with respect to promotions and earnings; and the lack of role models, access to job-relevant information, and knowledge of organization-specific politics. The stressors for white supervisors seem rooted in a lack of knowledge about the culture of the individuals with whom they are working.

From the above it seems obvious that organizations must learn how to decrease the stress for both minority employees and their white supervisors. The literature suggests various strategies, which will be described below.

Several researchers point out that a supportive work environment is vital in the reduction of stress for minority employees. Such support must be endorsed by top management (Brislin, 1981) and provided on a day-to-day basis by supervisors (Ford, 1985). Ford identified several kinds of social support at the workplace, including emotional and structural. His research shows that a lack of emotional support is related to chronic and episodic stress and job burnout while a lack of structural support is related to frustration with the work environment. If we assume that job burnout leads to turnover of the affected employees, we can conclude that the absence of emotional support at the workplace will lead to turnover. An absence of structural support would leave the employee frustrated with the job and result in low motivation and effort.

Bhagat (1985) also emphasizes the importance of social support in reducing stress in the work environment of minorities. He particularly mentions the need for emotional support and the need to provide appropriate cultural information to workers to enable them to better cope with their work environment.

Thiederman (1991) focuses on the white supervisor and recommends that that individual become familiar with the culture of minority workers, including being informed about their value system, expectations, and desires. A supervisor will be able to communicate and motivate workers from different backgrounds only on appreciating their uniqueness.

These research findings translate into a need for training both minority employees and their nonminority supervisors in the cultural aspects of the affected minority groups and to design organizations in such a fashion that they are mindful of the needs of their minority employees. The section on organizational aspects of managing diversity will refer to specific training programs that some organizations have developed.

Before moving on to the next section, it might be worthwhile to note the advantages to the individual employee that can be expected if organizations could initiate and facilitate successful cross-cultural interactions. Brislin (1981) reports on changes that have taken place in individuals who had been exposed to different cultures: (1) they became more "world-minded" in their thinking and recognized that solutions to problems should consider contributions from other cultures, (2) they felt more in control of their lives and recognized that they could influence their environment, and (3) they became more achievement-oriented and set reasonable standards for themselves and worked toward them. Some additional advantages of multicultural exposure are more speculative but include an increase in creativity, and an ability to adapt in difficult situations and to analyze these more objectively. There are also possible disadvantages to becoming multicultural. These include a loss of personal authenticity and contempt of people who do not have a multicultural background (Adler, 1977).

Group Level

The nature of the work that must be accomplished in most organizations requires that individuals work together in groups. This is the case for many reasons. For instance, individuals might not possess all the information needed to solve existing problems or to make necessary decisions, and the division of labor that is possible through group work permits organizations to do work more efficiently. In an extensive literature review of teamwork, Bass (1982) reports that nearly 90 percent of all companies with 250 or more employees rely on committee work. A survey of several thousand readers of the *Harvard Business Review* indicates that 50 percent of lower-middle management, 76 percent of upper-middle management, and 81 percent of top-management readers served on standing committees in their organizations. Most of them believed that committee work improves decision making, enhances creativity, and serves to coordinate work between departments. Most of the readers also believed that committees waste too much time. Given the frequency of teamwork in organizations, it is clear why it is important to facilitate good team functioning.

With respect to the management of culturally diverse, heterogeneous workteams, additional factors might have to be considered that do not apply to less diverse, homogeneous teams. Bass (1982) stresses that in order for each individual to be able to contribute his or her talents to the team effort, each individual's talent must be matched with a given role requirement on the team. He further asserts that the greater the interdependence of individuals with diversified skills, the greater the opportunity for a better or worse performance than could be expected of independent group members. This is so because greater diversity in groups could result in either positive outcomes (i.e., increase solution creativity) or negative outcomes (i.e., increase conflict among group members).

Research on small groups has focused on at least three major topics, as they relate to cultural diversity: (1) what factors influence group productivity (Bass, 1982); (2) how majority- and minority-group members influence group work (Levine and Russo, 1987), and (3) how to improve intergroup relations (Stephan, 1987). Each of these will be addressed below. However, before doing so, it is important to note that much of the small-group research that refers to diverse or heterogeneous groups was not conducted with individuals of different racial, ethnic, religious, etc., backgrounds. Instead, diversity or heterogeneity was in most studies defined as subject groups with different values, attitudes, educational backgrounds, professional positions, and so on than the majority of the group members. Thus, in order to utilize some of the findings of small-group research the assumption must be made that individuals from diverse backgrounds, as defined in this chapter, also exhibit differences in values, attitudes and ideas, based on their different life experiences.

Factors That Influence Group Productivity

Bass (1982) refers to McGrath and Altman's (1966) research that had identified state and action variables and their relationship to team productivity. He points out that in addition to these important variables, a more complex model is needed that includes how interaction processes between group members modify the relationship between state and action variables and group productivity. The following section will briefly review the state, action, and interaction process variables and how group performance might be enhanced or hindered by them.

The state variables that Bass (1982) describes include properties of group members (biographical characteristics, abilities, and task-relevant proficiencies), position of group members (social and task importance), properties of the group (group capabilities, status of interpersonal relations, and structure), and conditions imposed on the group (e.g., nature and difficulty of the task, time limitations). The action variables include how group members share information, consult with each other, and the frequency and length of their communications. Interaction processes, which the author feels modify the influence of state and action variables on team productivity, include how well the group works as a team, focuses on a single goal, and secures full participation from each group member. These latter processes are influenced by the heterogeneity or homogeneity of group membership and the nature of the task that the group must accomplish.

Research evidence indicates that diverse groups experience more conflict earlier in their existence than homogeneous groups. Individuals from different backgrounds will take longer to know each other well enough to function smoothly as one team and might have a more difficult time to determine one goal for the group and establish trust and confidence to obtain full participation from each group member. However, once these processes have been developed, diverse groups can be expected to generate more creative, novel solutions to complex and difficult problems than homogeneous groups. On the other hand, homogeneous groups will be fully functioning faster than diverse groups and will do well on simple tasks (Hoffman, 1961). Because of the more difficult interaction processes, it appears that diverse groups experience higher turnover, and it might be more difficult for organizations to keep their creative, innovative groups together (Bantel and Jackson, 1989).

Majority and Minority Influence

Research on the influence of majority-group members has evolved over a period of 50 years or so. Typically, the term *majority* was defined as the group of individuals who holds one position on an issue while a smaller group of individuals, the minority, holds another position on the same issue. Lately, this research has been extended to different samples where *minorities* could refer to a few women in a predominantly male group or a single African American in an otherwise white group. Most of the work was also conducted in laboratory rather than in field settings.

Levine and Russo (1987) point out that the research on majority and minority influence progressed along at least three stages:

1. Festinger (1950) focused on how the majority influences minority-group members. Such influence became known in the literature as conformity research.
2. Moscovici and Faucheux (1972) changed the focus to the influence of minority-group members on members of the majority. Such influence was termed *innovation*.
3. Moscovici (1976) recognized that most likely both the majority and the minority-group members can become either the source or the target of influence. His theory is known as the *conflict model*. Such theoretical position is congruent with the assumptions of the multicultural approach to diversity in that it allows for mutual influence of parties with different backgrounds. It might be important to learn under what circumstances majorities and minorities can affect changes in small-group settings.

The variables that have received the most attention in this research are the consistency of minority opinion and the differences in the outcome when the majority or the minority-group members exert influence.

Nemeth and Wachtler (1983) suggest that the majority exerts influence on minority-group members. This is the case because minorities are dependent for information about reality on the majority-group members and on their social approval. Disconfirming information and the withdrawal of social support could result in substantial stress for the minority-group member, and the threat of such stress induces conformity. The dynamics of minority influence are quite different. It is believed that the behavioral style that minorities use to convince majority-group members of the correctness of their position is important in their success or failure to influence the majority. It seems important for minority-group members to express consistency and confidence in their position. Such behavior will create cognitive and social conflict for majority-group members: cognitive conflict, because majority-group members might be startled by the insistence of the minority about the correctness of the presented information; social conflict, because such insistence results in a confrontation of group opinions and demands the solution of the conflict. Empirical evidence shows that the outcomes of majority and minority influences are different. Group members who are exposed to majority influence change their opinions publicly in order to maintain the social support of the majority group members. They do not, however, seem to agree with such opinion change privately. On the other hand, group members who are exposed to the influence of minorities might not change their opinions in public but reevaluate their position privately and agree with the position of the minorities on a personal level.

It is interesting to note how Nemeth and Wachtler (1983) describe the process of minority influence. They write:

> At first, the disagreeing minority is regarded with derision. When the minority refuses to compromise but, rather, insists on its position with consistency, he/she is perceived less negatively and, in fact, is accorded dynamic perceptions of confidence. . . . If the minority is that confident, if they are willing to incur the unfavorable consequences of nonconformity, perhaps there is something to their position. The consideration of that viewpoint and its correlate of reconsideration of one's own viewpoint is, we believe, a starting point for creativity. (p. 49)

Thus, the authors believe and their research confirms that the influence of minority-group members not only results in the acceptance or rejection of their opinions, but introduces a new, novel way of looking at an issue or situation that results in solutions that had not been considered previously. Minority influence stimulates the thought processes of majority-group members to become more complex and enables the overall group to think of an issue in a comprehensive and creative fashion. To suppress such thought processes by suppressing minority opinion, or by not managing nontraditional employees effectively, would deprive organizations of these workers' very best potential contributions.

How to Improve Intergroup Relations

Research that concerned itself with the improvement of relations between racially different groups was stimulated at the end of World War II when the troops returned home and relations between the races came sharply into focus. During the war, black and white soldiers had fought side by side but were no longer equal when they returned to their social settings in the United States. It was at that time that the contact hypothesis was formulated (Stephan, 1987). It essentially states that frequent contacts between different social groups will reduce the conflict between them (Nelson, 1989). Subsequently, researchers identified contact characteristics that improved group relations. These were reviewed by Stephan (1987) and are described below.

The research deals with the concept of ingroups and outgroups (e.g., minority individuals) and finds that in addition to equal-status contact, an equal balance of ingroup and outgroup members is desirable in small-group settings. When such numerical balance exists, the ingroup members will not especially focus on outgroup members and the possibility of a biased interpretation of their behavior will be diminished. It is further desirable that outgroup members behave in a vivid, nonstereotypical manner to disconfirm preestablished biases that ingroup members might hold. Long-term, genuine contacts are necessary for the improvement of intergroup relations, and these contacts should be made in a spirit of cooperation. Authority figures must value and support such contacts, and the interactions should have a social rather than a task orientation. In addition to these general findings, Stephan (1987) listed all of the variables that have been included at various times in the contact hypothesis. His table (pp. 24–25) shows a total of 56 variables, and he wonders whether the profusion of variables has prevented the search for those factors that might be the most important in affecting intergroup relations. He refers to cross-cultural research and indicates that knowledge of intergroup differences is important to good relations between culturally different groups (Brislin, 1981). However, it has also been shown that training programs to improve intergroup relations in domestic settings emphasize group similarities (Stephan, 1987). Thus, a two-pronged approach to improving intergroup relations seems indicated. There should be emphasis on teaching about specific cultural differences and a focus on similarities between groups, such as concentration on one group goal.

From the findings of the foregoing three strains of group research, some conclusions can be drawn as to the management of diversity in groups. First, the interaction processes in diverse groups are at least initially more complicated and time-consuming than those in homogeneous groups. Once these processes have been established smoothly, the best performance with diverse groups can be expected on complex tasks that require creative and novel solutions. The dynamics whereby such solutions are generated seem to evolve from the richness of ideas in diverse groups that come to the fore as minority-group members challenge and question the opinions and ideas of majority-group members. It appears that the behavioral style that is used by minority-group members to express themselves influences their ability to sway majority-group member opinion. Minorities must be consistent and confident in the presentation of their ideas. Finally, the contact hypothesis of intergroup relations has generated research that suggests how interactions between culturally different groups and individuals can reduce prejudices and biases. It is important for such groups to have long-term, equal-status contacts that consist of genuine, social interactions with an opportunity for majority-group members to experience the uniqueness of minorities. The knowledge of what kind of work diverse groups can complete most effectively and how diverse groups and their members can become accepted in organizations are important information for organizations who want to utilize all their employees appropriately. Such information can then be used to design strategies and training programs for the successful integration of a diverse workforce.

Organizational Level

The management of diversity, if it is to be successful, must ultimately be orchestrated at the organizational level. The insights that have been gained from research at the individual and group levels must be utilized to design policies and programs that are initiated, supported, and implemented by top management. Such efforts must begin with a clear pronouncement of the corporate position on cultural diversity, as has been done by such firms as Digital Equipment and Proctor and Gamble (Copeland, 1988b) before any additional programs can evolve. The point has been made earlier in this chapter that the philosophical approach to managing cultural diversity must be based on the multicultural approach because of the negative psychological impact of the mainstream–minority model on minorities. The mainstream–minority model is incongruous with the position that every individual in the organization must be given an equal opportunity and equal respect. A further consequence of the endorsement of multiculturalism, as pointed out by Triandis (1991), is the recognition that under such a philosophy both minority *and* majority employees need attention and training. By the same token, it must be recognized that organizations must function as overall entities, and as such must operate in some unified fashion. This means that the differences that are attended to, based on culturally different employees, must at some point be pulled together to function as a unified whole. How this is to be done is the challenge for any organization that wants to manage cultural diversity effectively.

Cox (1991) pointed out that the nature of organizations has changed over time. He uses an evolutionary approach and categorizes organizations in terms of stages toward their development of becoming multicultural. He asserts that organizations could be in the monolithic, plural, or multicultural stage. Monolithic organizations were prototypical in the United States before the 1970s. They consist of a homogeneous workforce where white males occupy managerial, high-status positions, while women and racioethnic minorities occupy nonsupervisory, low-status positions. Partially because of the civil rights and feminist movements, most monolithic organizations became transformed into plural organizations. The latter attempt to include women and minorities on more levels in the organization and sometimes provide mechanisms, such as training programs for managers to deal with nontraditional workers to facilitate workforce integration. However, the underlying premise of the plural organization is still the need for individuals with different backgrounds to assimilate into the organization. It does not stress the value of diversity. In contrast, the multicultural organization has this value at its core and "deliberately capitalizes on its diversity" (Morrison and Von Glinow, 1990, p. 204). The adoption of a policy to value diversity must be followed by changes in many areas of the organization.

Cox (1991), Geber (1990), and Copeland (1988b) propose several areas that organizations must pay attention to when multicultural organizations are to be created. These include (1) raising awareness of pluralism and providing pluralism training, (2) facilitating structural integration of minorities, and (3) facilitating full integration of minorities in informal networks. Some of the specific tools that can be used to address each of these areas, as suggested by the above researchers, will be described below. In addition, examples will be cited as to which U.S. corporations currently use these tools.

Raising Awareness and Providing Training

Top management must provide leadership in establishing processes that impress on all organizational members the importance of valuing diversity. These processes typically include raising awareness of the issue and providing skill building training for employees. Copeland (1988b) describes how the president and the board of directors of Ortho Pharmaceutical participated in training to manage diversity. The training taught them about their own attitudes about race and gender, how their actions influenced the organization, and what each person could do to effect change. The CEOs then followed this up by establishing a "culture change process" that provides the same kind of training to individuals at the various supervisory levels.

The necessity of awareness training becomes clear when one knows that surveys in organizations indicate that most managers have not had contact with individuals from other cultures or races before reaching adulthood. In addition, universities in this country fail to prepare college business students adequately on how to manage cultural diversity in the workforce (Copeland, 1988a). Research conducted on cross-cultural work interactions is also relatively rare (Black and Mendenhall, 1990). All of these findings reinforce the fact that awareness training may be a necessity in most organizations before skill-specific training can be administered.

Skill-building training can introduce a variety of skills. Most researchers advocate that such training must include specific information about values, norms, and acceptable behaviors of minority and majority groups (Brislin, 1981; Thiederman, 1991; Loden and Rosener, 1991). Since not every employee can be taught everything about every culture, it would be important for each corporation to design tailor-made training programs that impart culture-specific information about the diverse groups that are represented in its organization. Hewlett Packard uses such an approach in that it focuses its cultural differences program on its white, Mexican, Indochinese, and Filipino employee groups. Skill training also can include language training that stresses the value of languages other than English. Thus, in addition to the more common approach of teaching English as a second language to minority employees, firms such as Esprit De Corp, Economy Color Card, and Pace Foods give their employees an opportunity to learn Spanish, Italian, or Japanese, as is appropriate to their specific corporate environment. McDonnell Douglas focuses on gender issues and the use of role-playing exercises to teach their male and female employees about differences in work-related behaviors.

Structural Integration of Minorities

This area can include corporate efforts to recruit, select, and promote employees from diverse backgrounds and to establish special task forces or focus groups to give minorities an opportunity to be heard. Organizations that are doing so point to the need of matching their workforce diversity with that of their customers. For instance, Avon recognized that its customer base is multicultural and initiated the recruitment of a workforce that matches the customer base. Other firms pay special attention to the need of promoting minorities. Honeywell's president meets quarterly with the chair of the executive steering committee to learn about the progress the firm makes in developing its culturally diverse workforce. Mobil identifies and selects high-potential women and minorities for line positions that typically lead to top-level positions in the company (Copeland, 1988b; Schachter, 1988).

In order to ensure input from all employees and to let them know that their opinions are valued, *USA Today* insists on having members from culturally diverse groups represented on all of its committees, and Avon, Equitable Life Assurance, Intel, and U.S. West use advisory groups that have access to top management to provide input to their organizations (Cox, 1991). Digital Equipment has long been known for its "valuing differences" program and uses "core groups" to stimulate discussions among its culturally diverse workforce. The discussions focus on both the advantages of the program for the participants' own growth and the advantages of the program for the corporation with respect to productivity and profitability (Walker, 1989). Phillip Morris has established task forces that focus on the administrative side of organizations. The "affirmative-action committee," as the task force is called, monitors the policies and practices of the organization for incidents of unfairness. It is a particular strength of the committee that it consists of senior managers and minority employees (Cox, 1991). Senior managers have the power to address injustices within the system with some clout, while the presence of minority employees probably sensitizes senior managers to any diversity-related problems.

Structural integration also necessitates that organizations build the valuing of diversity into their performance evaluation and reward structures. Cox (1991) points out that Fannie Mae, Baxter, Coca-Cola, and Merck all evaluate their managers on the progress they make toward the effective management of diversity and tie salary increases to this evaluation. Exxon seems most specific in that it requires that its division managers review at least 10 women and minority men with respect to their career development plans.

Many organizations have also recognized that their reward systems must be tailored to employees with special family needs. For instance, many workers find themselves responsible for both children and their own aging parents. Some corporations are trying to be responsive to this need of their workers. Johnson and Johnson and Stride-Rite have instituted programs that help with child and elder care (Fusco, 1989; Rodgers and Rodgers, 1989).

All of the above efforts must, of course, be supported by the organization with the necessary resources to carry out the programs and evaluate their effectiveness. Such support could consist of establishing departments that monitor the progress of the managing cultural diversity efforts or the hiring of individuals who are responsible for overseeing the progress that is made.

Integration of Minorities in Informal Networks

Many firms are aware of the importance of giving minorities access to informal networks, such as including them in social events and providing them with mentors that might "show them the ropes." For instance, Digital Equipment found that many women were uncomfortable with frequenting bars after their sales meetings, as their male coworkers did, and that some minority employees felt uncomfortable about coming to sales meetings at country clubs. The situation was improved considerably when a new norm was established that placed breakfast meetings in hotels in the cities where all employees felt comfortable and welcome (Copeland, 1988a).

Mentoring programs for the retention of black and female managers were established by Proctor & Gamble (Copeland, 1988b) and Chemical Bank and General Foods (Cox, 1991). The usefulness of this concept has found some support in the literature (Nkomo and Cox, 1989). However, some researchers reject the traditional form of mentoring as a tool for managing diversity. Loden and Rosener (1991) assert that mentors were better suited for homogeneous (monolithic) organizations and are not useful for multicultural ones. These researchers point out that mentors typically selected upcoming, younger employees that they perceived to be similar to themselves and who could become their successors. The mentoring concept was used as a tool to keep the dominant elite in place. In contrast, when mainstream mentors are paired with employees with different backgrounds, the match is oftentimes seen as artificial. The "chemistry" does not click, and the relationship does not proceed along the traditional mentor–mentee lines. Loden and Rosener (1991) suggest that in multicultural organizations the better way to promote culturally diverse employees is to provide them with informal coaching and tutoring programs. The reasoning is that such programs are not based on the assumptions that one must learn rules that are known to only a few insiders—the mentors—who can pass them on. Instead, informal coaching and tutoring focus on technical, interpersonal, and managerial skill development that would be beneficial to all employees.

As the foregoing examples indicate, many organizations have recognized that the managing of cultural diversity will be one of their important tasks during the coming years. Many corporations have come to their specific programs and efforts through "eye-opening" incidents that occurred more or less by happenstance. As a result, one or the other program was born. What is needed in most organizations is a comprehensive approach to managing diversity. This could be done best by information exchanges and the utilization of human resource professionals who are experts in the area. Motorola seems to be one of the firms that has developed a comprehensive plan to manage its diverse workforce. The company formed a task force that interviewed 400 employees in focus groups and asked them about their needs and frustrations. It then turned to 50 corporations and inquired about their efforts to manage their diverse workforces. Thus, information was gathered both from internal and external sources to arrive at Motorola's plan to manage its workforce diversity. From it evolved the Cross-Industry Diversity Network that consists of human resource professionals from different organizations who are meeting to exchange information about their different efforts (Geber, 1990). Such an organization could be an important first step to a cross-country, cross-cultural management effort.

LEADERSHIP IN MULTICULTURAL ORGANIZATIONS

As has been learned from the foregoing section, many organizations are concerned about managing their culturally diverse workforces effectively. In order for them to be successful, they will have to get a clear understanding of what kinds of leaders are needed for such an effective management. The leadership research of the past 70 years or so has made much progress, but the upcoming demographic changes in organizations and the possible requirement of a different type of leadership have not been anticipated and have rarely been taken into consideration. The exceptions are work by Loden and Rosener (1991) and Harris and Moran (1989), who have attempted to identify characteristics of leaders who can successfully manage a culturally diverse workforce.

Loden and Rosener (1991) discuss the trend during the past years toward a more participative leadership style. They define participative leaders as ones who empower their employees by involving them in the daily work of the organization. They point out, however, that the leadership of a culturally diverse organization must go beyond participation. They recommend that a new form, pluralistic leadership, is needed. Such leadership assumes that the organizational culture must be changed to incorporate individuals with different backgrounds and must be driven by collaboration between minority and mainstream employees. Gordon and Loden (1989) conducted a survey with 450 employees from a cross section of organizations. It consisted of six leadership dimensions that had been found to be important for pluralistic leaders. The dimensions had evolved from interviews with over 200 employees in 20 private and public institutions. The survey participants were asked about the relative importance of each of the dimensions for leaders who supervise a diverse workforce. Four dimensions refer to the leaders' values and attitudes; two dimensions refer to roles that effective leaders must play. Each dimension was rated as important and will be described below.

- Organization vision and values that recognize and support diversity. Pluralistic leaders have long-term plans to include culturally diverse employees at all levels of the organization. They express their vision by including in their physical environment various symbols and traditions that reinforce the value of diverse populations.
- Ethical commitment to fairness and the elimination of "isms." Pluralistic leaders base such a commitment on both economic and moral considerations, and moral considerations precede economic ones. The elimination of ageism, ethnocentrism, heterosexism, racism, sexism, and other kinds of discrimination must be openly advocated by pluralistic leaders, even if such behavior elicits criticism from mainstream colleagues.
- Broad knowledge of dimensions of diversity and awareness of multicultural issues. Pluralistic leaders should have "basic knowledge of the six core dimensions of diversity, including age, ethnicity, gender, physical ability/qualities, race, and sexual/affectional orientation" (p. 187). Such knowledge must then be applied by the use of inclusive language, the adaptation of communication styles to different population groups, and signs of respect for cultural differences.
- Openness to change. Pluralistic leaders encourage criticism from their employees and show a willingness to change their behavior. The ability to accept feedback was rated most important by survey participants. In addition, pluralistic leaders must show empathy with culturally different employees. Empathy was seen as leading to trust and openness between individuals.
- Mentor and empowerer of diverse employees. Pluralistic leaders take an active role in creating opportunities for their diverse employees that utilize their unique talents. They also provide honest, constructive performance feedback and provide coaching when necessary. They reward managers who show respect toward culturally different employees and who encourage their contributions at all organizational levels.

• Catalyst and model for personal and organizational change. Pluralistic leaders further the interests of diversity on organization, community, and worldwide levels and challenge others when they observe prejudice by them. Pluralistic leaders see their work as far-reaching and important.

Gordon and Loden (1989) indicate that the above dimensions were judged as more important by minority survey participants than by white men and feel that sensitivity to these dimensions must be increased by the latter group. The researchers complete their report with the following observation: "To the extent that today's leaders . . . adopt the pluralistic leadership model as their own, they will stand a far better chance of weathering the inevitable storms of change and succeeding in the future" (p. 194).

Harris and Moran (1989) have also arrived at characteristics that describe multicultural leaders. They based their findings on interviews with and speeches, and writings of corporate executives. Their book is entitled *Managing cultural differences*. Their focus is broader than that of Loden and Rosener (1991) since they apply their work to domestic as well as international aspects of managing diversity. Harris and Moran introduce 10 concepts that underlie their book, many of which overlap with Loden and Rosener's research. The concepts are to be seen as "the essence for leadership and excellence in human . . . affairs, and should be incorporated into the development of global managers" (p. 9). Some of the leader characteristics that Harris and Moran identify include the need for leaders to be able to comfortably work in a pluralistic environment. As such, they must understand the impact of different cultures on behavior and be willing to adjust their leadership styles. They must be knowledgeable of cultural patterns and be able to use such knowledge to improve organizational performance. The writers place particular emphasis on the need for pluralistic leaders to obtain cultural synergy. This is defined as the ability to build on differences between people to enrich their activities in organizations and to arrive at richer, more complex solutions to problems. Like Loden and Rosener (1991), the pluralistic leader has the role of mediator between people from different backgrounds and must synergize the work of others and facilitate needed organizational changes. In addition to being responsible for the leadership of others, the pluralistic leader also must take responsibility for the organization as a whole and "is to promote the right combination of the system's elements . . . the interacting equal forces of people, goals, structures, and technology" (p. 116). Finally, multicultural leaders must share their insights, skills, and knowledge with their colleagues to introduce their leadership philosophy to their own and other organizations. Thus, both groups of researchers seem to have arrived independently at similar leadership characteristics that will benefit multicultural organizations.

The reader might ask how difficult it would be to secure leaders with the characteristics described in the foregoing section. The answer might not be as difficult as it at first seems. Geber (1990), in referring to the skills necessary to manage diversity, points out that good managers have used them for a long time. They consist of good interpersonal skills, such as active listening, coaching, and giving feedback. The good pluralistic leader probably applies these skills while being aware of the cultural differences of each of his or her coworkers and, thereby, empowers them to contribute their unique strengths to the organization. Geber states that "Managing diversity . . . is not so much your behavior as a manager but your behavior as a human being" (p. 30). I propose that this thought is the bottom line of this chapter.

We have now examined the research on managing cultural diversity in terms of the necessary underlying philosophy about minority and majority relations and how a diverse workforce is impacted by various factors and dynamics on the individual, group, and organizational levels. What rings through in all examples are several basic desirable characteristics of human relationships. These include an openness to cultural differences, a knowledge of what these differences in specific situations consist of, and the acceptance and use of differences in improving organizational performance. Many researchers and writers have felt a need to justify the efforts of organizations to manage their diverse workforces in economic terms and somewhat hesitatingly also asserted that organizations have a moral obligation to treat all their members justly. The many corporate failures, based on ethical misconduct of their members during the last decade worldwide, should have taught all leaders who formulate long-term corporate strategies that the emphasis on ethical conduct, including the respectful, fair treatment of all members, are as important to conducting a business as the bottom line. The latter will probably be the important by-product of living responsibly toward all of an organization's constituents. Maybe the changing demographics in this country will make it socially acceptable to emphasize moral and economic considerations in leading organizations equally.

CONCLUSION

This chapter highlighted the research that deals with managing a multicultural workforce on the individual, group, and organizational levels. It was asserted that any such effort should use the multicultural model. This model minimizes acculturative stress on the minority workforce and improves organizational performance.

The section on managing a multicultural workforce on the individual level pointed out that both minorities and their majority supervisors are impacted by acculturative stress. Such stress can be reduced when a support system is available that is sensitive to the needs of all workers. Such a system can be created by appropriate support from top management and awareness and skill training.

The section on managing cultural diversity at the group level dealt with the dynamics that take place when individuals from different backgrounds try to work together. It was found that heterogeneous groups will, initially, take more time to become productive but offer an opportunity for complex, in-depth thought processes that can lead to greater creativity than homogeneous groups will generate. Organizations who know how to manage multicultural groups will turn their contributions into a strength rather than a liability.

The section on managing diversity at the organizational level outlines programs that organizations currently are using to address some of the issues discussed on the individual and group levels. It appears that most large organizations are well aware of the changing demographics of their workforces and are taking steps to cope with these changes. However, most organizations have yet to introduce comprehensive programs that address all aspects of managing diversity. These include awareness and skill training and changes in the organizational structure to integrate minorities and to provide minorities with access to informal networks. There are some signs, however, that organizations are catching on. The foundation of the Cross-Industry Diversity Network is one such sign. It has the potential to turn into an important force for providing multicultural information to organizations who are searching for a comprehensive approach to managing their workforces.

Finally, the chapter closes with describing the kind of leader who is needed to guide a culturally diverse workforce. Such leaders must have good human relations skills that include knowledge about various cultural differences. They also need the moral fortitude to challenge coworkers who have not learned yet to include workers from diverse backgrounds into the mainstream of organizational life or who hold prejudices against individuals who are different from themselves. In addition to having good human relations skills and moral fortitude, these pluralistic leaders need to feel a responsibility toward their organizations as a whole and match the needs of employees with the needs of the organization to find a balance that makes best use of a multicultural workforce.

Where do we go from here? Given the multitude of programs that are taking place in various organizations, it is necessary to evaluate to what extent they have the desired outcomes. In addition to evaluating training programs, the contextual variables in each organization must be assessed in order to determine how they might influence the success of training programs. Such contextual variables could include employer commitment to cultural diversity issues and proportion of various minorities on each level of an organization. Morrison and Von Glinow (1990) suggest conducting research across organizations that would enable management to select training programs that are found effective in organizations with comparable environments. In addition, it seems important to identify variables that describe characteristics of organizations that are applicable across cultures. For instance, the literature indicates that good support systems help employees to deal with acculturative stress. If a number of such unifying concepts can be identified, then the managing of a multicultural workforce can be simplified.

References

Adler, P. (1977). Beyond cultural identity: Reflections upon cultural and multicultural man. In R. Brislin (Ed.), *Culture learning: Concepts, applications, and research.* Honolulu: University of Hawaii Press, 1977.

Bantel, K. A., and Jackson, S. E. (1989). Top management and innovations in banking: Does the composition of the top team make a difference? *Strategic Management Journal, 10,* (summer), 107–124. (Special issue.)

Bass, B. (1982). Individual capability, team performance, and team productivity. In M. D. Dunnette and E. A. Fleishman (Eds.), *Human performance and productivity: Human capability assessment.* Hillsdale, NJ: Lawrence Erlbaum.

Berry, J. W. (1986). Multiculturalism and psychology in plural societies. In L. H. Ekstrand (Ed.), *Ethnic minorities and immigrants in a cross-cultural perspective.* Lisse: Swets & Zeitlinger.

Berry, J. W. (1990). Psychology of acculturation. In R. W. Brislin (Ed.), *Applied cross-cultural psychology.* Newbury Park, CA: Sage.

Bhagat, R. S. (1985). Acculturative stress in immigrants: In T. A. Beehr and R. S. Bhagat (Eds.), *Human stress and cognition in organizations.* New York: Wiley.

Black, J. S., and Mendenhall, M. (1990). Cross-cultural training effectiveness: A review and a theoretical framework for future research. *Academy of Management Review, 15*(1), 113–136.

Brislin, R. W. (1981). *Cross cultural encounters.* New York: Pergamon Press.

Businessweek (September 19, 1988). For American business, a new world of workers, p. 112.

Cobbs, P. (1981). Challenge of the 80's. Corporations, credentials, and race. Invited address presented at the Black Alumni Conference. Harvard Graduate School of Business, Boston (February 27–28).

Copeland, L. (1988a). Valuing diversity, Part 1: Making the most of cultural differences at the workplace. *Personnel* (June), 52–60.

Copeland, L. (1988b). Valuing diversity, Part 2: Pioneers and champions of change. *Personnel* (July), 44–49.

Cox, T., Jr. (1991). The multicultural organization. *Academy of Management Executive, 5*(2), 34–47.

Cox, T. H., Jr., and Blake, S. (1991). Managing cultural diversity: Implications for organizational competitiveness. *Academy of Management Executive, 5*(3), 45–56.

Festinger, L. (1950). Informal social communication. *Psychological Review, 57,* 271–282.

Ford, D. L., Jr. (1985). Job-related stress of the minority professional. In T. A. Beehr and R. S. Bhagat (Eds.), *Human stress and cognition in organizations.* New York: Wiley.

Fusco, M. A. Castronovo. (1989). Employment relations programs. *Employment relations today* (autumn), 259.

Geber, B. (1990). Managing diversity. *Training* (July), 23–30.

Gordon, T. A., and Loden, M. (1989). *Pluralistic leadership survey.* Copyrighted by Loden Associates, Inc., and Interface Associates. All rights reserved.

Harris, P. R., and Moran, R. T. (1989). *Managing cultural differences.* Houston, TX: Gulf Publishing.

Hoffman, L. R. (1961). Conditions for creative problem solving. *Journal of Psychology, 52,* 429–444.

Johnston, W. B., and Packer, A. H. (1987). *Workforce 2000.* Indianapolis: Hudson Institute.

Kiplinger, A. A., and Kiplinger, K. A. (1989). *America in the global 90s.* Washington, DC: Kiplinger Books.

Levine, J. M., and Russo, E. M. (1987). Majority and minority influence. In C. Hendrick (Ed.), *Review of personality and social psychology* (Vol. 8, *Group processes).* Newbury Park, CA: Sage.

Loden, M., and Rosener, J. B. (1991). *Workforce America!* Homewood, IL: Business One Irwin.

Mai-Dalton, R. R. (1984–1985). Exposing business school students to cultural diversity: Becoming a minority. *The Organizational Behavior Teaching Review, 9*(3), 76–82.

McGrath, J. E., and Altman, I. (1966). *Small group research: A synthesis and critique.* New York: Holt, Rinehart and Winston.

Morrison, A. M., and Von Glinow, M. A. (1990). Women and minorities in management. *American Psychologist, 45*(2), 200–208.

Moscovici, S. (1976). *Social influence and social change.* New York: Academic Press.

Moscovici, S., and Faucheux, C. (1972). Social influence, conformity bias, and the study of active minorities. In L. Berkowitz (Ed.), *Advances in experimental social psychology,* (Vol. 6, pp. 149–202). New York: Academic Press.

Nelson, R. E. (1989). The strength of strong ties: Social networks and intergroup conflict in organizations. *Academy of Management Journal, 32*(2), 377–401.

Nemeth, C. J., and Wachtler, J. (1983). Creative problem solving as a result of majority vs. minority influence. *European Journal of Social Psychology, 13,* 45–55.

Nkomo, S. M., and Cox, T. H., Jr. (1989). Gender differences in the upward mobility of black managers: Double whammy or double advantage? *Sex Roles, 21*(11/12), 825–839.

Rodgers, F. S., and Rodgers, C. (1989). Business and the facts of family life. *Harvard Business Review, 67*(6), 121–129.

Schachter, J. (1988). Firms begin to embrace diversity. *Los Angeles Times,* April 17, pp. 1, 14, 16–18.

Stephan, W. G. (1987). The contact hypothesis in intergroup relations. In C. Hendrick (Ed.), *Review of personality and social psychology* (Vol. 9, *Group processes and intergroup relations),* Newbury Park, CA: Sage.

Thiederman, S. (1991). *Bridging cultural barriers for corporate success.* Lexington, MA: Lexington Books.

Triandis, H. C. (1991). Diversity training. Paper given as part of the Science Weekend of the meetings of the American Psychological Association, San Francisco (August 17).

Walker, B. (1989). How the valuing differences approach evolved at Digital Equipment Corporation. Paper presented at the Annual Academy of Management Meeting, Washington, DC. Preconference Roundtable: Managing the diversity of women of color and white women.

9

Toward a Dynamic and Systemic Theory of Groups: An Integration of Six Temporally Enriched Perspectives

Joseph E. McGrath and Deborah H Gruenfeld
Department of Psychology
University of Illinois at Urbana-Champaign

INTRODUCTION

As many have noted, small-group research experienced a system crash in the middle or late 1960s. Most interpretations of that crash attribute it in part to certain weaknesses in the conceptual, methodological, and substantive content of small-group research at that time, weaknesses that were merely one manifestation of how the entire field of social psychology had evolved over the previous half century (see, e.g., Hackman and Morris, 1972; Hare, 1976). Although these limitations are now widely noted and understood, small-group research has not by any means regained center stage as an area of study in mainstream social psychology—thus foiling the optimistic predictions of Steiner (1974), McGrath (1978); McGrath and Kravitz, (1982), and others. According to Levine and Moreland (1990), however, the field is actually alive and well, but simply living elsewhere—sometimes under other names—in the higher-rent districts of business schools, communications departments, and military research agencies.

The commonly noted limitations of traditional small-group research tend to converge on two issues: the artificial nature of the groups studied and the concomitant lack of consideration for the appropriate context in which actual groups function. Specifically, there has been a strong preference for studying short-lived, artificially concocted groups, usually in laboratory settings. The physical, sociocultural, and temporal aspects of the context within which "real" groups operate has been treated with overwhelming neglect.

To the extent that these preferences still mark the ethos of current mainstream psychology, it may not be surprising that group research has shifted its location and sometimes changed its name (to "team research," "collaborative work," and the like). However, there are a number of recent theoretical treatments of groups that manage to depart from, or transcend, those traditional shortcomings (i.e., the habit of studying ad hoc groups, in short-term, artificial settings out of context). In these new conceptualizations, the group and its activities are defined in terms of their location in some temporal, physical, and cultural setting. In addition, these theories all have an emphasis both on temporal aspects of context, and on temporal aspects of the patterning of group behavior—suggesting that these theories are dynamic as well as systemic, an almost unheard-of combination in past group research.

We will discuss six such formulations here. They share strong temporal and contextual emphases but are otherwise quite varied in perspective. The phenomena they are designed to explain and explore range from the production of yearly ceremonies by entire communities, to the development of small groups and their environments, over the entire life spans of those entities, to the socialization of members into groups, to the patterning of complex decision paths, characterized by sequences and clusters of specific behaviors.

Individually, each of these approaches provides a strong theoretical frame for studying an important subset of topics within the group research domain. Together, they offer partially overlapping but mainly complementary points of view. It is our belief that their systematic integration might provide a powerful, overarching framework for understanding groups, a framework that is both broader and at the same time more detailed than has yet been constructed in the group area.

The aim of this paper is to begin the process of tying these six formulations together into such a single, coherent, comprehensive formulation. We will begin our treatment here by introducing one of those conceptualizations—a theory dealing with time, interaction, and performance in groups (TIP theory) (McGrath, 1991)—which will be used as a template for that integration. We will present the key ideas of TIP theory, followed by a brief description of each of the other five approaches. We will then attempt to relate the basic conceptions and assumptions of those six theories within an overall schema.

Five important caveats are in order before beginning our discussions of the six group theories. First, we do not purport to treat any of these bodies of work comprehensively. Our treatment is selective in two ways. On one hand, we are deliberately selective, giving emphasis to the parts that seem to bear a clear relation to TIP theory and to the substantive domain that is of concern here. On the other hand, we are probably selective in other, unintended ways, because we deal here only with a limited portion of the total corpus of those authors' works.

Second, in developing this chapter, and requesting comment on our formulations from the other theorists and from other colleagues, we have come to recognize what may well be the scholar's equivalent of the so-called standard attribution error. In a number of specific places, we had interpreted the range of other scholars' work relatively narrowly, treating only the conceptions that appear explicitly in their published work (and only in the portions of it with which we were familiar); whereas we tended to interpret the range of our own work much more broadly, taking into account ideas embodied in our intentions, plans, and work in progress, as well as in our published work. We have tried to modulate, if not eliminate, this attribution bias in the present version of the chapter.

Third, by choosing these six theories for inclusion, we do not intend to imply that they are the *only* bodies of work that reflect dynamic and systemic treatments of groups, or that they are the only ones worth considering in such an integrative treatment. There are, of course, other theories of groups that are of great value. Our sins of omission in this regard arise from combination of (1) the limits of our knowledge of the literature; (2) our inability to formulate clearly the relations between a given theory and those presented here; and/or (3) our intention to emphasize theories for which temporal factors are explicitly made a focus of attention. Thus, for example, we have not included the excellent theoretical formulations about groups by J. R. Hackman (e.g., Hackman, 1985, in press)—even though our own work has drawn heavily on them—because the main themes of Hackman's work seem more explicitly concerned with issues of work-group design and effectiveness than with issues of group process over time.

Fourth, because of space limitations, our treatments of all six theories are very brief, and necessarily omit both vital details and enlightening nuances. We apologize for those omissions, to both those theorists and to readers; and we cite appropriate references to encourage readers to learn of the theories first-hand.

Finally, this paper is based on the premise that building toward a single, integrated formulation regarding groups is a good thing to do. But the idea of creating such an overarching, integrated theory is by no means uncontroversial. All of the theorists whose work is treated here have expressed reservations, if not skepticism, as to both the feasibility and the desirability of such a single integrated theory of groups. We share their skepticism. Nonetheless, we choose to set aside our doubts on the grounds that the attempt to build such an integrated picture (even if not fully successful) will be worthwhile in itself. At the least, it will yield useful insights on, and raise worthwhile issues about, each of the individual theories, as well as provide new perspectives on the substantive domain that they encompass.

A Time, Interaction, and Performance (TIP) Theory of Groups

Projects, Functions, Modes, and Paths

Research associated with TIP theory (e.g., Futoran et al., 1989; Kelly, 1988; Kelly et al., 1990; Kelly and McGrath, 1985, 1988; McGrath, 1978, 1984, 1990, 1991; McGrath and Kelly, 1986, 1992; McGrath et al., 1984; McGrath and Rotchford, 1983) views groups as contributing to multiple functions. Group activities make contributions to (1) the systems in which they are embedded (e.g., an organization), (2) their component parts (i.e., their members), and (3) the group itself, as an intact, continuing social structure. In TIP theory, those three functions are called, respectively, the group's *production* function, its *group well-being* function, and its *member-support* function.

Ordinarily, at any one time, a group will be engaged in activities contributing to all three functions, with respect to at least one, and often more than one, ongoing project. [This formulation draws on ideas from Hackman (1985); Little (1983); Weick (1976); and others.] In this conceptualization, projects are organized or focused purposes, or missions, that are accomplished by carrying out various tasks and steps. Such activities are assumed to represent one or another of four activity modes: mode I, which entails inception and acceptance of a project (*goal choice*); mode II, which entails solution of technical issues (*means choice*); mode III, which entails resolution of political or value conflicts (*policy choice*); and mode IV, which entails execution of the performance requirements of a project (*goal attainment*).

Modes of activity apply to all projects. They transcend group functions; that is, there is a distinctive but parallel set of mode sequences, or *time–activity paths*, for projects related to the production function, the group well-being function, and the member-support function (see Fig. 9.1).

Modes are potential, not required, forms of activity. Modes I and IV (inception and execution) are involved in all (completed) group projects; modes II (technical problem solving) and III (conflict resolution) may or may not be involved in any given group activity.

The *direct path*—from mode I inception (opportunity for production, interaction, and/or participation) to mode IV execution (actual production, interaction, and/or participation), without engaging in any mode II or III activities—is the *default path* for all functions on most group projects. TIP theory assumes that a group will use the default path if it can, and in any case will use the least complex path that its purposes, resources, and circumstances will allow.

From the perspective of this framework, group activity always entails an interplay of functions, modes, and projects. A given group may use different paths for different functions on each of multiple concurrent projects. An important assumption in TIP theory is that such complexity of paths, modes, and functions is by no means evidence of inefficiencies or "process losses" (see Steiner, 1972), with regard to effective group functioning. Rather, when a group engages in any path more complex than the

Modes	Functions: Production	Well-being	Member support
Mode I: inception	Production demand/opportunity	Interaction demand/opportunity	Inclusion demand/opportunity
Mode II: problem solving	Technical problem solving	Role network definition	Position/status attainments
Mode III: conflict resolution	Policy conflict resolution	Power/payoff distribution	Contribution/payoff relationships
Mode IV: execution	Performance	Interaction	Participation

Figure 9.1 Modes and functions.

default path, it does so for good and sufficient reasons—reasons that, while they might seem unimportant, uninteresting, or elusive to the researcher, are certainly meaningful and perhaps necessary from the perspective of the group.

Along these lines, groups that follow complex paths may be engaging in one or more of three important activities: (1) giving attention to the well-being and member-support functions, as well as to the production function; (2) attempting to resolve technical and/or political problems within the production function, of which the researcher may be unaware; or (3) engaging in some project other than (or in addition to) the one the experimenter is tracking. In TIP theory, it is assumed that use of such complex paths *may* presage long-run effectiveness on the part of the group as an intact, functioning social system, even if it comes at a small cost in short-run performance rate on the group's assigned task. [See Poole and Roth (1988a,b) for an alternative, perhaps complementary, perspective on phase sequence issues.]

Temporal Issues

According to TIP theory, *complex temporal patterning* of behavior is pervasive in group contexts. For example, organizations typically manage the flow of work in groups by institutionalizing procedures for (1) scheduling, (2) synchronization of activities, and (3) allocation of temporal (and other) resources (McGrath and Rotchford, 1983). At a fairly macro level, procedures often evolve to address the problem of efficiently matching periods of time with bundles of activities, under conditions where all periods of time are not interchangeable and where many bundles of activities are not entirely flexible as to when they may be done. At a more micro level, some behavior in small groups and in organizations can be accounted for in terms of social entrainment processes—that is, patterns of synchronization, both of group members' behaviors with one another, and of group behavior with "external" events.

Lack of fit between organizational strategies and individual responses to them can give rise to residual temporal problems that have to do with (1) establishing and enforcing deadlines, (2) establishing and enforcing norms to get smooth dynamic teamwork, and (3) regulating the flow of task and interpersonal interaction to resolve inefficient or inequitable demand–capability matches. These residual problems often get played out in group contexts as well. They become ubiquitous issues in regard to all three functions, for groups that are doing multiple concurrent projects in real time.

TIP theory implies that changes in group membership, task type, and operating circumstances will have powerful effects on the time–activity paths taken by groups, and hence on the speed and quality of their task performance. To date, empirical research associated with the TIP model has investigated how group interaction and task performance are affected by such factors as (1) type, difficulty, and temporal qualities of tasks (see Kelly, 1988; Kelly and McGrath, 1985; Kelly et al., 1990; McGrath et al., 1984) and (2) technological enhancements of the group's communication and task performance systems (e.g., use of computers) (see Hollingshead and McGrath, in press; McGrath and Hollingshead, 1992).

Concluding Comments

Although TIP theory offers a detailed framework for understanding time, interaction, and performance in groups, much can be learned by relating TIP theory to other systemic and dynamic theories that can provide conceptual elaborations and extensions at both micro and macro levels. For example, TIP theory notes but does not explore a number of aspects of group process, group socialization, decisionmaking, and the conditions under which temporal markers can serve as signals for external entrainment of group behavior. The five theories to be summarized in the next section address many of these issues in some detail; and they also address some other issues that TIP theory does not treat at all. If these theories can be integrated with TIP theory into a single integrated formulation, the resultant product will provide a broader and more richly articulated conceptualization of groups in temporal context than does any one of the theories alone. We turn now to that task (see also Fig. 9.2).

FIVE TEMPORALLY ORIENTED PROGRAMS OF RESEARCH ON GROUPS AND THEIR RELATIONS TO TIP THEORY

Decision Development and Adaptive Structuration in Groups (Poole)

M. Scott Poole and his coworkers at Minnesota and Illinois (e.g., Poole and DeSanctis, 1989; Poole and Roth, 1988a,b) have proposed and found extensive support for a "contingency" model of decision development in groups. The model depicts group activity as an active process by which information from the embedding context—the rules and resources available to the group—is adapted to construct decision paths. Unlike traditional models of group decision behavior, the adaptive structuration model holds that "unitary sequence models"—which depict group process in terms of a uniform, fixed sequence of stages that follow a logical order (e.g., a set of stages of "rational decisionmaking")—do not provide a very in-

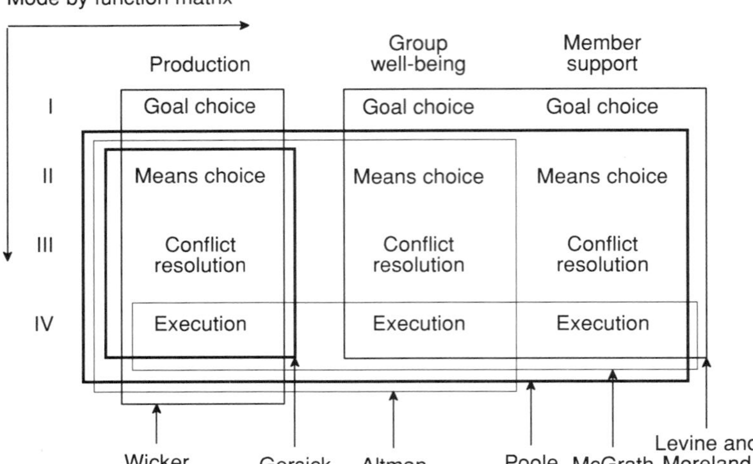

Figure 9.2 Fit of theories to TIP theory matrix. (Realms of group activity addressed explicitly in associated empirical work.)

formative description of much of what groups actually do. Poole argues, and shows empirically, that situational contingencies (such as high levels of conflict, task difficulty, time pressure, or internal group problems) lead groups of different types, performing different tasks, to follow different decision paths—nearly all of which are much more complex, dynamic, and apparently "disorganized" than traditional models would suggest.

Poole's studies have included small (roughly four to six members) groups doing tasks indigenous to those groups (e.g., groups of students selecting a topic for a term project, physicians performing a medically relevant program planning task, and an energy-conservation committee making decisions on various projects). Analyses are performed on coded transcripts of the verbal activities of such groups. These analyses show, in various ways, that the decision paths of small groups can be predicted as a function of the contingency variables noted above.

In particular, Poole's model characterizes group decision development as several continuously evolving tracks of activity, intertwining over time, punctuated by breakpoints that mark changes in the development of the strands. The unit of analysis is the "interact," an act–response pair of coded statements. Each interact is coded as conveying information about *task process, group relations,* and/or *topical focus.*

On both conceptual and empirical fronts, Poole's work shares much common ground with TIP theory. To begin with, both programs of research address group process at the relatively micro level of sequences of individual acts. Both study small work groups, collaborating on relatively short problem-solving tasks (e.g., tasks that are completed within a single experimental session). Both incorporate the notion that interpersonal or socioemotional activities are an integral part of such group performances. Both theories also use data from specific periods in the life of the work group, and make no explicit attempt to map the group's whole life cycle, except to note that the groups will use information from their own histories as a resource in the process of completing their tasks, and are likely to recycle through various kinds of activities (problem-solving phases for Poole, modes of activity for McGrath) over the course of their work. The central relations of interest in both programs of research concern interaction among members and performance of the group while carrying out one focal task or project.

Conceptually, there are parallels as well. Poole's notion that dual sets of phases of activity always operate simultaneously in group decision activities resembles TIP theory's insistence that groups are always engaged in all three of their functions simultaneously (see Fig. 9.1). In addition, both formulations regard various potential contingency factors (such as amount of conflict) as affecting the complexity and organization of decision paths.

In this regard, Poole's research activities can be viewed as covering most of the mode-by-function terrain laid out by TIP theory. That is, the work deals directly with modes II, III, and IV of the production and group well-being functions, with some attention to the member support function (see Fig. 9.2).

Thus, adaptive structuration theory and TIP theory share a lot of common ground, but at the same time each provides an elaboration of the other. Moreover, both formulations draw inferences regarding a number of more macro-level features that provide a complex embedding context for a given acting group—features that are focal to the work of some of the other theorists that are to be described later in this paper. What is more, both adaptive structuration theory and TIP theory draw upon and depend on those macro-level features as a major part of their causal or explanatory representation. Thus, both theories can benefit, not only by building on each other but also by being carefully integrated with (and embedded within) the more macro-level formulations yet to be described.

Punctuated Equilibrium and Time-Based Transitions in Groups (Gersick)

Gersick, like Poole, studies small groups collaborating on problem-solving, or work-related tasks. Gersick uses groups with a single, predetermined project requiring the construction of a concrete product (e.g., the soundtrack for a radio commercial) by a predetermined deadline. She has studied both naturally occurring groups (Gersick, 1988) and groups concocted for experimental purposes (Gersick, 1989). In her discussion of group interaction and behavior, she emphasizes the interplay between group performance and environmental contingencies by focusing on group attention to outside resources and requirements. Specifically, Gersick shows how groups use their awareness of external temporal markers, or deadlines, to pace themselves. This emphasis reflects a belief that a group's ability to recognize, tap, and adapt to the resources in its environment is often pivotal to its progress.

Gersick finds that development in groups follows a pattern of "punctuated equilibrium." This pattern is characterized by three relatively short but intense and crucial transition periods, separated by two relatively long periods of more or less "normal" work activity. It is the transitions, or periods of revolution, that are the occasions for the group's most important choices, rather than the periods of "normal" work, or "inertia," that they separate.

The middle transition stage is of most interest. Gersick finds a remarkably strong and often transforming transition period in group activities that occurs at precisely the temporal midpoint of each group's expected existence. Most groups begin their work with little explicit consideration for strategy, goals, and procedures (see Hackman et al., 1977). One might say they follow the default path defined by TIP theory. But each work group that Gersick has studied shows a sharp transition phase at the midpoint of its expected lifespan. This transition breaks the group's momentum, so to speak, and provides the opportunity (seized by most of the group's Gersick has studied) to examine all aspects of its own past work carefully, to reconsider its goals, and often to revise both goals and strategy dramatically.

Gersick's data are derived from verbatim transcriptions, of every meeting of each group studied, over the group's entire lifespan. She has studied both naturally occurring groups, over timespans of several months, and experimental groups working for a single 2-hour session. All activities are categorized as pertaining either to (1) management of the work process or (2) contributions to the final product. Subcategories are used to code time-pacing comments and resource-requirement comments, among other types of statements. Among other findings, Gersick shows that groups' attention to time is not uniformly distributed throughout the lifespan, and that while groups appear to view time as a resource during certain stages, time becomes mainly a source of pressure in others.

Gersick's theory of punctuated equilibrium shares some qualities with

TIP theory, although it does not overlap with the TIP framework to the extent that Poole's work does. It is narrower in some respects, and broader in others, than TIP. Like McGrath and Poole, Gersick studies small work groups, and begins with an analysis of micro-level activity, or interaction. However, note that, for Gersick, the total project and the total life span are coextensive; hence group development takes place in the same time frame as project completion.

Whereas TIP theory and the adaptive structuration model incorporate distinctions between work-related and social activities, Gersick makes no attempt to differentiate between the two. In this sense, her work is localized within the production function of the TIP mode-by-function matrix. The distinction between task- and process-related activities, however, does reflect the notion of modes, as defined by TIP. Her distinction might be translated as contrasting mode IV (execution) with modes II and III (means choice and conflict resolution; see Fig. 9.1).

Gersick's notions of shifts in the modes of group activity link her work with both the time–activity paths of TIP theory and the decision paths of Poole's adaptive structuration theory. For example, her description of the group's midlife transition can be viewed as a shift from an unexamined pursuit of the default path to a more complex time–activity path for the production function, including recycling through activities associated with modes II and III. Gersick's work can also be connected to the part of TIP theory that emphasizes entrainment processes. The group attending to the midpoint of its expected life is an instance, par excellence, of how an external "pacer" can function as an entrainment signal that modifies the phase and periodicity of subsequent group behavior sequences.

Hence, the theory of punctuated equilibrium provides some of the concepts by which we can "link" the more micro-level experimental paradigms of McGrath and Poole with more longitudinal or developmental perspectives on groups. The remaining three provide an expanded and embellished framework for this integration, all at more macro levels.

Patterns and Determinants of Group Socialization (Moreland and Levine)

The conceptual core of Moreland and Levine's approach is an interest in how the group evolves, as a *joint* function of member orientation to the group and group orientation to its members, over time (Levine and Moreland, 1985, 1990; Moreland and Levine, 1982, 1984, 1988). This evolution is characterized as a process of *socialization*, involving three psychological dynamics, each of which can be viewed both from the member's and from the group's perspective: *evaluation, commitment,* and *role transition*. The socialization process involves five ordered "stages" (investigation, socialization, maintenance, resocialization, remembrance), separated by four transitions (entry, acceptance, divergence, exit). Each stage is characterized by a specific set of activities that are assumed to describe the reciprocal relations among the group and its individual members.

The main focus of Moreland and Levine's work is on what TIP theory calls the member-support function, although they do give some attention, as well, to development of the group as an intact system (i.e., to the group well-being function). In that latter regard, they argue that socialization processes are best understood in reference to the group's location within its own developmental cycle, and vice versa (Moreland and Levine, 1988). In outlining the course of group development, they adopt a variant of Tuckman's modified stage sequence (Tuckman, 1965; Tuckman and Jensen, 1977): forming, storming, norming, performing, and adjourning. Their interest is less in stages of group development, however, than in examining how the type and prevalence of various socialization activities may vary systematically across these different stages.

Moreland and Levine explicitly address all four modes of TIP theory for two of the group functions. They give some emphasis to what TIP theory calls the group well-being function, but most emphasis to what TIP theory calls the member-support function. They also recognize the interdependence of all three functions. For example, they suggest that task or production related goals and needs can shape evaluations within a group, affecting feelings of commitment and prospects for role transition. In addition, they have examined how changes in member composition, problem identification, and innovation in groups are related to socialization activities. Some of their recent work has focused on how training programs in organizations might be improved by taking group socialization practices into account. Such broad mode-by-function emphases are rare in group research.

Moreland and Levine's work also marks a clear departure from an emphasis on group process at the micro level. In contrast to the other models considered thus far, they attend to the more macro-level processes and stages in development and socialization and, working with the group's entire lifespan, incorporate the assumption that most long-term groups work on many tasks rather than just one project within that lifetime. Along these lines, Moreland and Levine address not only the pattern of group activity over its life span but also the patterns of activity that characterize specific developmental periods subsumed therein. They encompass a relatively macro temporal unit; but they examine behaviors spanning much shorter temporal durations. In addition, they separate, conceptually, the group itself from its assigned projects or substantive tasks. Thus, the conceptualization highlights activities associated with the evolution and maintenance of the group as a social unit, rather than any externally oriented production objectives the group may have. Taken as a whole, then, the conceptualization provides the means for determining not only what groups do and which paths they choose or construct but also how the group itself changes as it navigates these paths.

The focus on macro units of time and activity, the emphasis on evolution and change of the social unit, and the interest in the social aspects of group process are among the most important contributions of the work of Moreland and Levine to the field of small-group research. Integrating their model with those of McGrath, Poole, and Gersick lends valuable breadth to the scope of phenomena thus far considered.

Life Cycles of Behavior Settings (Wicker)

Wicker is interested in the life cycles of behavior settings—those time, place, thing, milieu combinations within which much complex human behavior takes place (Wicker, 1987; Wicker and King, 1988). The explicit focal unit of his work is a particular behavior setting, such as a gas station or a grocery store, and all the activities it encompasses, from its inception to its demise.

Wicker proposes four stages in the life cycles of behavior settings: (1) *preconvergence,* the period prior to founding a setting; (2) *convergence,* the period during which a setting is being organized and begins to operate; (3) *continued existence,* the indefinite lifetime of a setting; and (4) *divergence,* the period during which the setting disintegrates. Each of these is characterized by sets of important topics and events. Settings themselves are characterized by two distinct facets: *resources* (such as people, equipment, and space) and *internal dynamics* (including the interplay of individual, group, and setting-level events).

The main topics and events of Wicker's stages bear close resemblance to those presented in TIP theory, although they do not overlap completely. Wicker's stages cover all four modes of TIP theory, but the behavior-setting formulation puts most emphasis on the modes of the production function (see Fig. 9.2). Some of the events of the preconvergence stage (e.g., assembly of resources, gathering of knowledge and formulation of plans) reflect activity in TIP theory's mode I (inception); some of the events in the convergence and continued existence stages (e.g., negotiations by staff; sensemaking activities; differentiation of functional activities) reflect mode II and III activities of the various functions; and some of the events of the divergence stage (e.g., coping with deficiencies) reflect perturbations that are likely to accompany breakdowns of mode IV, and subsequently be manifest in complex recycling through time–activity paths.

However, in behavior-setting theory, those events are referenced not to the modes of activity for a single function, with respect to one project being enacted by one group, but rather to a particular stage of development of a particular behavior setting, presumably applying to all projects subsumed within that behavior setting, and to all sets of actors who inhabit it. In this sense, it could be argued that TIP's time–activity paths cycle and recycle through (or within) Wicker's behavior-setting phases.

Like Moreland and Levine, Wicker is interested in group lifespan development, but whereas Wicker emphasizes the work-oriented or functional component of the phenomena (the production function in TIP theory), Moreland and Levine emphasize the social unit's development and transformation (the group well-being and member-support functions in TIP theory).

Wicker's approach differs from Moreland and Levine's, as well as the other authors discussed so far, in another important way. True to the Barker (1968) behavior-setting tradition, Wicker gives the internal qualities of groups a very limited explicit place in his formulations. In fact, Wicker's approach does not really constitute a theory of groups at all, but a theory of places and environments that groups (i.e., sets of people) produce, inhabit, and change. He nevertheless has much to say about the patterned behavior in the purposive work of organized sets of people—that is, about interaction and performance of aggregations that TIP theory (and the others) would call work groups.

Wicker's conceptions provide a much more detailed treatment of the task and technological features of group performance than most of the other theories. At the same time, they provide a much less richly articulated treatment of the group well-being and member-support functions than do Poole, McGrath, or Moreland and Levine. Behavior-setting theory offers an opportunity to extend the integrated theory both in developmental terms and in terms of the "task" and "context" parts of the formulation.

Transactionalism in Community Contexts (Altman)

Altman's work is by far the most macro of the theories here considered. It deals with community or cultural practices subsuming months, years, or longer, and involving relatively large and complex sets of events and behaviors. In fact, like Wicker, his work is not really a theory of groups, although it certainly contains a great deal of material about groups. For Altman, specific groups would be "parts" or "members" of the social unit being studied.

Altman and colleagues work from a transactional worldview (Altman and Rogoff, 1987; Werner et al., 1988, 1989). In that view, phenomena are holistic unities made up simultaneously of (1) people and psychological processes, (2) their physical and social environments, and (3) a variety of temporal qualities. While these three sets of considerations are conceptually separable for discursive purposes, they are inherently intertwined in concrete systems. Each helps define the others. Phenomena can be understood only be treating all of these together, holistically.

This view puts special emphasis on the dynamic aspects of such holistic phenomena, and thus deals in some detail with their temporal qualities. Altman and colleagues specify a set of temporal qualities that are intrinsic to such human social phenomena: *salience, scale, pace, sequence,* and *rhythm.*

In the research associated with the transactional approach, Altman chooses specific social settings because of their cultural and temporal, rather than their task or productive, significance. For example, Altman has conducted case studies of yearly rituals or ceremonies that are performed by various communities, such as a neighborhood Christmas celebration and a Pueblo Indian house-blessing ceremony. Both of these discussions are characterized by attention to the temporal qualities (listed above) of the ceremonies, and all the subcategories of activities that lead to their production.

Because Altman begins his investigation at a point in time beyond when the social unit is considering choices about whether to participate in these ceremonies, or whether to enact them at all, he thereby skips over an analysis of activities associated with TIP theory's mode I; but he treats the other three modes thoroughly. As to functions, he gives central focus to the group well-being function (for the community as the relevant focal unit), and deals substantially with the production function—although the motivations for production arise at cultural rather than individual or group levels. Individuals are viewed as integral parts of the phenomenon of interest, rather than entities whose experiences are to be given focal attention in their own right; thus Altman does not treat the member-support function (that is, member in relation to group) in its usual form. But in other work Altman gives considerable attention to member–member relations; and he treats the relation between individual and community (which is Altman's focal unit) as a dialectic that pervades human activity and experience. Thus, Altman's research activities can be seen as covering modes II through IV of all three functions (see Fig. 9.2).

Altman's approach embodies another sort of culmination of the previously described theories: It is thoroughly systemic in its causal logic. The notion that group phenomena can be conceived as sets of separate variables becomes successively less appropriate over the progression from McGrath and Poole, to Gersick, to Moreland and Levine, and to Wicker. Altman takes this progression to its conclusion. True to the spirit of a transactional approach, Altman describes all of the elements inherent in the events he studies as inextricably embedded in one another. From his perspective, it does not make sense to sort acts according to a set of categories; the meaning of any given act is completely dependent on the context in which it occurs.

All the other theories considered here, including TIP theory, nestle within the domain staked out in Altman's work. Altman's transactional approach deals directly with phenomena that involve the macro-level units (social, behavioral, and temporal) that TIP theory and the others treat as "context" within which the phenomena of interest are embedded. Hence, incorporating Altman's ideas into this integration serves a dual function: It deals explicitly with factors and issues that the other theories relegate to the (relatively unexamined) category of "context"; and it thereby provides the opportunity to expand the domain to which the theory applies.

SOME CONCLUDING COMMENTS

Considering these six research programs in relation to one another, the result suggests that research on groups can be made more precise and informative if each approach can be understood with regard to the areas it excludes, as well as those it covers. This integration can be used, for example, to generate various intriguing cross-theory questions for research, such as

1. How do activities of TIP theory's production function relate to Moreland and Levine's stages of group–member socialization?
2. Do the midpoint transition patterns Gersick finds in her work groups also characterize the longer, recurrent projects of Altman's groups, and the much shorter task performance periods of the groups in Poole's and McGrath's studies?
3. How do TIP theory's mode I activities (project acquisition) moderate the patterns observed by Poole, Gersick, and Altman?
4. How do Moreland and Levine's socialization phases relate to the life-cycle phases of Wicker's behavior settings?

Some Steps toward Integration of the Theories

Some Useful Facets of the Domain

To carry this integrative treatment further, it is useful to make explicit a set of interrelated concepts that pervade these formulations. First, there is a distinction between references to the activity of a focal unit toward which the inquiry is addressed, on one hand, and references to features of the context within which that unit and its activity is embedded on the other. Those two can be seen as *text* and *context.* There are major differences among the theories treated here in terms of what sort of unit is chosen as the focal unit for study. There are differences, as well, in which aspects of context are given emphasis, and how and to what degree those contextual features are seen as affecting the focal unit and its activities.

There are also certain major facets of both the focal unit and its embedding context that must somehow be taken into account in any theoretical formulation, and these theoretical perspectives give differing degrees and kinds of emphasis to them. There is a *social unit facet,* an *activity facet,* and a *temporal facet.* In relation to the embedding context, those three facets refer to the sociocultural, the physical–technical, and the temporal–historical aspects of context, respectively. As Altman insists, these three aspects are separable for analytic purposes, but they are inextricably intertwined in concrete systems. In relation to the focal unit, those same three facets refer to the group (or other social unit) itself, to the content and process of that group's interaction and performance, and to the temporal patterning of its activity. These, too, are separable for analytic purposes but intertwined in concrete systems.

These six concepts—the social, physical, and temporal aspects of context, on one hand, and the group, its activity, and its temporal patterning, on the other hand, together constitute an intricately interrelated set of constructs that frame the formulations in this domain. Since the six theories here considered give different degrees of emphasis to these different constructs, that substantive frame can help us examine some of the relations among those theories (see Fig. 9.3).

The set of constructs shown in Figure 9.3 encompasses the main concerns of this attempted integration. Our purpose in this paper has been to examine formulations about groups that are both systemic (i.e., concerned with *context*) and dynamic (that is, concerned with *time*). We will therefore close this chapter by considering, in turn: (1) some ways in which these theories differ in terms of the groups and activities they have chosen as their focal unit for study, (2) the ways in which considerations of context are related to that focal unit; and (3) some ways in which these theories differ in how they address matters of time.

	Referents	
Facet	Focal unit	Embedding context
Social unit	Group	Sociocultural context
Activity	Interaction and performance	Physical–technological context
Time	Temporal patterning of activity	Temporal–historical context

Figure 9.3 Some facets of the domain.

Treatments of the Focal Unit and Its Embedding Context

One interesting comparison among the six theories centers on what each theory's main focal unit of study is, and how that unit is related to other key concepts of its embedding context.

Moreland and Levine. Their treatment focuses on study of all of the behavior of a given group, and its members, throughout that group's lifetime. They examine that behavior as the group acts within a range of task structures or behavior settings; that is, as it recurrently becomes an acting group executing various projects. "Group activity" includes both how the unit treats individual members, and how individuals treat the group. The group is both the vehicle for and the product of the task; stage of socialization determines the nature of group activity, and group activity leads to transitions among stages. In this framework, there is an emphasis on cycling and transitions. Context is defined mainly in temporal terms, focusing on the group's history, or stage of development, although issues of external threat, the influence of outsiders, and opportunities presented for participation in other groups on intragroup relations have also been explored to some degree.

As they carry out their study, at any given point in time Moreland and Levine are dealing with a particular group—one whose behavior is shaped by and has meaning because of that group's place within its own developmental history. For example, the way in which the group evaluates given acts of a given member depends in part on that member's status in terms of group socialization, and in part on the stage of development of the group itself.

Wicker. Wicker adopts a similar approach to that of Moreland and Levine, but points it in another direction. He adopts as his focal unit a given behavior setting, and tracks the behavior of the inhabitants of that setting (groups and individuals) over the lifetime of that setting. At any given time in his study, he is dealing with the equivalent of one or more group(s) (and/or individuals). The behaviors of the inhabitants of the setting, and the meanings of those behaviors, are shaped by their place in the developmental cycle of that behavior setting.

In Wicker's framework, the setting's inhabitants (i.e., groups and individuals) are an integral and inextricable part of the phenomena that are to be explored. The setting is characterized by stages, but the notion of specific individual variables acting in a linear causal chain does not apply. Indeed, the inhabitants, their activities, time, and the context are all mutually codetermining. Context is treated in terms of not only temporal but also sociocultural and technological characteristics. The behavior setting's purpose (or "program") assumes an especially important contextual role.

Gersick. Gersick chooses as her focal unit of study a group that has been constructed to carry out a specific project within a specific time period—that is, she chooses a "task force" (McGrath, 1984) rather than a "team." She then studies the temporal patterning of that group's behavior, as that patterning is triggered and/or modified by (i.e., externally entrained to) temporal features of the group's embedding context.

From this perspective, she examines the temporal flow of all of the behavior of a particular group-in-context, for cases in which the group's project, its technological system, its personnel, and its timeframe are already given. Context is defined primarily in terms of its temporal aspects, so time is viewed as an independent variable in that sense. However, group activity and development, which are seen as being paced by aspects of the temporal context, are also described temporally, in terms of the pacing or timing of certain activities. Gersick represents the phenomena she observes in terms of phases and transition periods, and she includes the group's attention to time as a key feature of her conceptualization and research. So temporal issues are utilized as dependent variables, as well as independent variables, in this formulation.

Altman. In effect, Altman's focal unit is the collection of all of the groups (and individuals) who are involved in the coordinated pursuit of a cultural-level project. He studies the temporal qualities of the behavior that those groups exhibit in that endeavor—with the timing and meaning of the behaviors shaped by (i.e., entrained by) temporal markers in the cultural context external to those groups.

One difference between Altman's and Gersick's formulations is that, whereas Gersick attempts to cull patterns of group progress that can be extracted from their context, and taken to underlie group activity in general, Altman's transactional perspective prevents him from attempting to separate the patterns of activity he observes from the groups and contexts they characterize.

In this sense, his approach resembles Wicker's. Altman focuses on study of the temporal qualities of all of the behavior of a set of groups-in-context, for cases in which all of those groups and individuals are interdependent parts of a larger social organization that is involved in a major cycle of collective behavior. Unlike Wicker, however, Altman's groups pursue projects that are not so much production driven as time driven. That is, activities are carried out *when appropriate,* and *until no longer appropriate,* rather than being driven by production goals and attainments.

Poole. Poole chooses as his focal unit of study the temporal patterning of behavior of a group (e.g., the stages and cycles involved in its decision path) as it goes about carrying out a given project(s). Poole's groups consist of a set of individuals undifferentiated as to roles, who interact in the process of completing work-related decision tasks. The product of interaction that is of interest to Poole is not only the group's final decision, or solution to a problem, but also the complex path over time that their discursive activity forges as they do that task, and the structured pattern of interaction that they thereby create.

Time, therefore, serves mainly as a dependent variable in Poole's work. The temporal forces involved are intrinsic to, or endogenous within, that focal unit. Context is defined in terms of the type of group, the type of task, and the history that is created throughout the course of interaction.

McGrath. TIP theory pursues two different foci with respect to focal units. Like Poole, some work relating to TIP theory (e.g., work using the TEMPO interaction coding system) has as its focal unit of study the temporal patterning of a group's behavior as those patterns unfold endogenously. But, like Gersick, other work pertaining to TIP theory—notably the work dealing with external entrainment of task performance rates and quality—studies the temporal patterning of behavior of a group as that temporal pattern is influenced by temporal markers in the embedding context external to that group.

Some Further Comparisons. Groups that are chosen as the focal unit for study may vary in size, composition, history, and expectations. These formulations differ in a number of ways related to those matters, including (1) whether groups are thought of as having primarily work-related (cf., Poole, Gersick, Wicker) or social (Moreland and Levine, Altman) concerns; (2) whether they share one or another type of history (Poole) or are in the process of creating such a history (Wicker, Gersick); (3) whether they anticipate an indeterminate collective future (Wicker, Moreland and Levine), or know exactly when their disbanding will occur (Gersick) or when the activities in which they are engaged will be completed (Altman). These formulations also differ in terms of how they view the purpose of the group. A group may be viewed as a vehicle for task accomplishment, in which case the role of any individual member, or the relations among them, may be relatively inconsequential (e.g., McGrath's work on entrainment). Alternatively, a group may be viewed as a "container" in which bundles of activities (tasks) occur, using a perspective that highlights issues of process (e.g., Poole). Or, groups may be viewed as the "product" of the "task" itself (e.g., Moreland and Levine).

These formulations also differ in terms of how much they emphasize the temporal and historical aspects, the physical and technological aspects, and the social and cultural aspects of the embedding context. For example, Gersick defines context mainly in terms of its temporal aspects: the group's own history, and temporal markers (deadlines) arising in the embedding sociocultural and technological system. Similarly, Altman defines context in terms of the sociocultural environment, the composition of the community, and temporal features (e.g., the time of year). The group's activities are interpreted in terms of their symbolic meanings, which derive from those external qualities. Moreland and Levine, Poole, and Wicker use stages or phases of activity to refer to the temporal context that is endogenous or internal to the group. But they define other aspects of context differently. Wicker emphasizes the physical and technological environment (e.g., the physical setting and the type of behavior setting being created); Poole and Moreland and Levine refer to the effects of group composition characteristics and other aspects of the social environment.

These theories also differ in terms of a more basic question about the relation of focal unit, activities, and context: the issue of whether group activities can be separated cleanly from context variables, and understood primarily in terms of *generic* meanings (McGrath, Poole); or whether, instead, activities and context are inextricably related and mutually defining (Moreland and Levine, Gersick, Wicker, and Altman), and hence have *situated* rather than generic meanings. An integrated formulation must take both of those viewpoints into account.

Treatments of Time

We have already noted several ways in which these theories treat temporal matters differently, including the question of the temporal scope or scale of the phenomena being studied and the degree to which temporal aspects of context are considered. Several other temporal issues warrant mention here.

First, it is worth making explicit the distinction between temporal features intrinsic to the behavior of any given focal unit (endogenous temporal factors), and temporal features of the context within which that focal unit exists and acts (exogenous temporal factors). That distinction has already been embedded, implicitly, in preceding discussions, and is captured in the idea that time is reflected both in temporal context (time as "independent variable," so to speak), and in the temporal patterning of behavior (time as "dependent variable") (see Fig. 9.3).

Although all six theorists would doubtless recognize the importance of both kinds of temporal factors, some of the theories here considered give more emphasis to one than the other. Three of these theorists—Poole, Moreland and Levine, and Wicker—are alike in that they give major emphasis to temporal patterning endogenous to the focal units they choose for study. They differ from one another, of course, in terms of what that focal unit is and therefore in terms of what kinds of endogenous patterning each considers. But, although they all recognize the importance of temporal aspects external to the group, they do not really give much explicit attention to these exogenous temporal factors.

In contrast, Gersick, Altman, and McGrath differ from the other three theorists—and are like one another—in this important respect. They each deal with temporal patterning of behavior within focal units under circumstances in which the temporal patterning itself is driven, or triggered, or entrained by temporal markers external to that focal unit. They differ from each other in terms of the level of the focal unit to which they attend. Altman is concerned with a very broad class of behaviors and purposes of several groups; Gersick attends to patterns of behavior that evolve as a single group carries out its one main project. McGrath, in his entrainment work, deals with a still more micro-level unit—a group dealing with (a series of) specific recurrent tasks.

These three theories also are like each other and differ from the other three (and from most group theory) in terms of the degree to which their formulations *question the assumptions of the dominant Newtonian view of time.* Altman, Gersick, and McGrath treat time from a transactional perspective (McGrath and Kelly, 1986) as though the meaning of time inhered in relations among events and observers—as if time were epochal, phasic, relative, and experiential, rather than homogeneous, smooth and directional in its flow, absolute, and abstract as the Newtonian perspective would have it. Altman explicitly argues that time is both linear (i.e., directional) and cyclical. He (and others) emphasize complex patterning. Altman, especially, gives much emphasis to simultaneous consideration of stability and change; he treats it as an ever-operating dialectic that pervades human experience.

Some Requirements for an Integrated, Dynamic Theory of Groups in Temporal Context

An adequate comprehensive theory of groups ought to encompass all of the conceptual territory dealt with by these six theories. It ought to deal with groups in all of their complexity—taking into account how their history, purpose, composition, and internal dynamics are related to their behavior. It should address the context within which groups are embedded, by considering both how that context can define and influence behavior and how behavior can define and influence the context in which it occurs. And, it should account for temporal aspects of these phenomena, recognizing that there is a continual interplay of stability and change over time, at both micro and macro levels.

That comprehensive theory should deal with interaction and performance in ways that link different levels of micro and macro consideration (as does Gersick). One way of doing this is to provide temporally defined contingency paths (as Poole does with his contingency paths, and as McGrath does in terms of time–activity paths). These need to be specified both in micro-level detail and, simultaneously, at the level of activities pertaining to task performance, to member–group relations, and to operation and maintenance of the group-qua-group (i.e., the production, support, and well-being functions), treating these dynamically as embedded in a physical, sociocultural, and temporal context.

At the micro level, that theory must recognize that groups produce and reproduce patterns of behavior by adaptive structuration, as they follow more or less complex time–activity paths in carrying out multiple functions for one or more projects. It must also recognize that *acts have both generic and situated meanings,* and it should try to resolve that dialectic tension by identifying the group, task, and context factors on which those meanings are contingent.

In short, such a comprehensive, dynamic theory of groups will have to deal with all of the issues that arise at each of a number of levels of consideration, in the operation of groups over time and in context. We recognize, of course, that it is not really practical for all researchers to conduct each of their research projects as longitudinal, developmental, and integrative studies that address all of these issues. Nevertheless, having a systematic framework that can place the temporal and contextual features of each particular study in a broader, integrative perspective could provide valuable guidance for the comparative interpretation of results obtained in different studies dealing with different specific groups in different specific contexts. We hope this presentation can be a step toward establishment of such a systematic framework about groups.

Acknowledgments

This paper was prepared for presentation at the Fourth Annual Claremont McKenna College Leadership Conference: *The Future of Leadership Research: A Tribute to Fred Fiedler,* February 1991. Research discussed in this paper was supported in part by National Science Foundation grants BNS 85-06805, BNS 87-05151, and IRI 89-05640 (J. E. McGrath, Principal Investigator). We wish to acknowledge contributions to these research programs by Janice R. Kelly, Purdue University; Gail Clark Futoran, Texas Tech University; David A. Harrison, Texas University at Arlington; Scott W. VanderStoep, University of Michigan; Dennis Stewart, University of Miami of Ohio; Andrea B. Hollingshead, University of Illinois. We also want to acknowledge the invaluable comments on an earlier draft of this chapter by Irwin Altman, Martin Chemers, Connie Gersick, John Levine, Richard Moreland, M. Scott Poole, and Allan Wicker; and to express our appreciation for the help we received from Tim Buckley, Susan Grant, Sharon Furiya, Joe Lualhati, and Mark Peecher, who joined us in a seminar in which we worked through many of the ideas dealt with in this paper. Correspondence regarding this paper should be sent to Joseph E. McGrath, Psychology Department, University of Illinois, 603 W. Daniel St., Champaign, IL 61820.

References

Altman, I., and Rogoff, B. (1987). World views in psychology: Trait, interactionist, organismic, and transactionalist approaches. In D. Stokols and I. Altman (Eds.), *Handbook of environmental psychology*. New York: Wiley.

Barker, R. G. (1968). *Ecological psychology: Concepts and methods for studying the environment of human behavior.* Stanford, CA: Stanford University Press.

Futoran, G. C., Kelly, J. R., and McGrath, J. E. (1989). TEMPO: A Time-based system for analysis of group interaction process. *Basic and Applied Social Psychology, 10,* 211–232.

Gersick, C. J. G. (1988). Time and transition in work teams: Toward a new model of group development. *Academy of Management Journal, 31,* 9–41.

Gersick, C. J. G. (1989). Marking time: Predictable transitions in task groups. *Academy of Management Journal, 32,* 274–309.

Hackman, J. R. (1985). Doing research that makes a difference. In E. E. Lawler, A. M. Mohrman, S. A. Mohrman, G. E. Ledford, T. G. Cummings, & Assoc.

(Eds.), *Doing research that is useful for theory and practice*. San Francisco: Jossey-Bass.

Hackman, J. R. (in press). Group influences on individuals in organizations. In M. D. Dunnette and L. M. Hough (Eds.), *Handbook of industrial and organizational psychology* (Vol. 3). Palo Alto, CA: Consulting Psychologists Press.

Hackman, J. R., Brousseau, K. R., and Wiess, J. A. (1977). The interaction of task design and group performance strategies in determining group effectiveness. *Organizational Behavior and Human Performance, 16,* 350–365.

Hackman, J. R., and Morris, C. G. (1972). Group tasks, group interaction process, and group performance effectiveness: A review and proposed integration. In L. Berkowitz (Ed.), *Advances in experimental social psychology,* (Vol. 8). New York: Academic Press.

Hare, A. P. (1976). *Handbook of small group research,* (2nd ed.) New York: The Free Press of Glencoe.

Hollingshead, A. B., and McGrath, J. E. (in press). The whole is less than the sum of its parts: A critical review of research on computer-assisted groups. In R. Guzzo and E. Salas (Eds.), *Team decision making in organizations*. San Francisco: Jossey-Bass.

Kelly, J. R. (1988). Entrainment in individual and group behavior. In J. E. McGrath (Ed.), *The social psychology of time: New perspectives* (pp. 89–110). Newbury Park, CA: Sage.

Kelly, J. R., Futoran, G. C., and McGrath, J. E. (1990). Capacity and capability: Seven studies of entrainment of task performance rates. *Small Group Research, 21*(3), 283–314.

Kelly, J. R., and McGrath, J. E. (1985). Effects of time limits and task types on task performance and interaction of four-person groups. *Journal of Personality and Social Psychology, 49,* 395–407.

Kelly, J. R., and McGrath, J. E. (1988). *On time and method.* Newbury Park, CA: Sage.

Levine, J. M., and Moreland, R. L. (1985). Innovation and socialization in small groups. In S. Moscovici, G. Mugny, and E. Van Abermaet. *Perspectives on minority influence* (pp. 143–169). Cambridge, MA: Cambridge University Press.

Levine, J. M., and Moreland, R. L. (1990). Progress in small group research. *Annual Review of Psychology, 41,* 585–634.

Little, B. R. (1983). Personal projects: A rationale and method for investigation. *Environment & Behavior, 15,* 273–309.

McGrath, J. E. (1978). Small group research. *American Behavioral Scientist, 21*(5), 651–674.

McGrath, J. E. (1984). *Groups: Interaction and performance.* Englewood Cliffs, NJ: Prentice-Hall.

McGrath, J. E. (1990). Time matters in groups. In J. Galegher, R. E. Kraut, and C. Egido (Eds.), *Intellectual teamwork: Social and technical bases of collaborative work* (pp. 23–61). Hillsdale, NJ: Lawrence Erlbaum.

McGrath, J. E. (1991). Time, interaction, and performance (TIP): A theory of groups. *Small Group Research, 22,* 147–174.

McGrath, J. E., and Hollingshead, A. B. (1992). Putting the "group" back in "group support systems": Some theoretical issues about dynamic processes in groups with technological enhancements. In L. M. Jessup and J. E. Valacich (Eds.), *Group support systems: New perspectives* (pp. 78–96). New York: Macmillan.

McGrath, J. E., and Kelly, J. R. (1986). *Time and human interaction: Toward a social psychology of time*. New York: Guilford Press.

McGrath, J. E., and Kelly, J. R. (1992). Temporal context and temporal patterning: Toward a time-centered perspective for social psychology. *Time and Society, 1*(3), 199–220.

McGrath, J. E., Kelly, J. R., and Machatka, D. E. (1984). The social psychology of time: Entrainment of behavior in social and organizational settings. In S. Oskamp (Ed.), *Applied social psychology annual* (Vol. 5, pp. 21–44). Beverly Hills, CA: Sage.

McGrath, J. E., and Kravitz, D. (1982). Group research. *Annual Review of Psychology, 33,* 195–230.

McGrath, J. E., and Rotchford, N. L. (1983). Time and behavior in organizations. In L. Cummings and B. Staw (Eds.), *Research in organizational behavior* (Vol. 5, pp. 57–101). Greenwich, CT: JAI Press.

Moreland, R. L., and Levine, J. M. (1982). Socialization in small groups: Temporal changes in individual-group relations. In L. Berkowitz (Ed.), *Advances in experimental social psychology* (Vol. 15, pp. 137–192). New York: Academic Press.

Moreland, R. L., and Levine, J. M. (1984). Role transitions in small groups. In V. Allen and E. Van de Vliert (Eds.), *Role transitions: Explorations and explanations* (pp. 181–195). New York: Plenum Press.

Moreland, R. L., and Levine, J. M. (1988). Group dynamics over time: Development and socialization in small groups. In J. E. McGrath (Ed.), *The social psychology of time: New perspectives* (pp. 151–181). Newbury Park, CA: Sage.

Poole, M. S., and DeSanctis, G. (1989). Understanding the use of group decision support systems: The theory of adaptive structuration. In C. Steinfield and J. Fulk (Eds.), *Theoretical approaches to information technologies in organizations.* Beverly Hills, CA: Sage.

Poole, M. S., and Roth, J. (1988a). Decision development in small groups IV: A typology of group decision paths. *Human Communication Research, 15*(3), 323–356.

Poole, M. S., and Roth, J. (1988b). Decision development in small groups V: Test of a contingency model. *Human Communication Research, 15*(4), 549–589.

Steiner, I. D. (1972). *Group process and productivity*. New York: Academic Press.

Steiner, I. D. (1974). Whatever happened to the group in social psychology? *Journal of Experimental Social Psychology, 10,* 84–108.

Tuckman, B. W. (1965). Developmental sequences in small groups. *Psychological Bulletin, 63,* 384–399.

Tuckman, B. W., and Jensen, M. A. C. (1977). Strategies of organizational socialization. *Organizational Dynamics, 7,* 18–36.

Weick, K. E. (1976). Educational organizations as loosely coupled systems. *Administrative Sciences Quarterly, 21,* 1–19.

Werner, C. M., Altman, I., Oxley, D., and Haggard, I. (1989). People, place, and time: A transactional analysis of neighborhood social networks. In W. Jones and D. Perlman (Eds.), *Advances in interpersonal relationships.* New York: JAI Press.

Werner, C. M., Haggard, L. M, Altman, I., and Oxley, D. (1988). Temporal qualities of rituals and celebrations: A comparison of Christmas Street and Zuni Shalako. In J. E. McGrath (Ed.), *The social psychology of time: New perspectives* (pp. 203–232). Newbury Park: CA: Sage.

Wicker, A. W. (1987). Behavior settings reconsidered: Temporal stages, resources, internal dynamics, context. In D. Stokols and I. Altman (Eds.), *Handbook of environmental psychology* (Vol. 1, pp. 613–653). New York: Wiley.

Wicker, A. W., and King, J. C. (1988). Life cycles of behavior settings. In J. E. McGrath (Ed.), *The social psychology of time* (pp. 183–200). Newbury Park, CA: Sage.

10

Team Research in the 1990s

Daniel R. Ilgen
Departments of Psychology
and Management
Michigan State University

Debra A. Major
Department of Psychology
Michigan State University

John R. Hollenbeck
Douglas J. Sego
Department of Management
Michigan State University

INTRODUCTION

One of the remarkable strengths of Fred Fiedler's leadership research is its endurance and viability. For over four decades he and his students have been actively engaged in empirical research and theory development as it relates to leadership in small groups or teams. Unfortunately, over the same period of time, behavioral scientists have not shown the same level of commitment to the pursuit of understanding the behavior of persons in teams and team effectiveness, particularly teams that produce goods and services in organizations. Our focus is on these types of teams.

Teams are an integral part of work. Thus, it is not surprising that a great deal of behavioral science research and theory has been devoted to the study of teams. Yet, as we have implied, the interest has not produced a smooth growth curve in activity or increased knowledge about team functioning. Quite the opposite has happened. The late 1940s through the middle 1960s saw a flurry of research activity on teams and groups. By the late 1960s and early 1970s, the activity level had slowed down. One of the leading scholars on small-group/team performance asked in the early 1970s, whatever happened to team-like constructs in social psychology (Steiner, 1974). At the same time, Steiner predicted a resurgence of interest by the end of the 1970s (Steiner, 1974). In the middle 1980s, he acknowledged his failure at predicting the future and went so far as to suggest that many of the behavioral science paradigms and research methods in vogue at the time were actually inhibiting the study of small groups or teams.

By the late 1980s teams again came to the fore, but the interest was generated outside social psychology and sociology, where the previous research had been greatest in the past. Levine and Moreland (1990) concluded their *Annual Review* article on small-group research with a section labeled, "Groups are alive and well, but living elsewhere" (p. 620). Consistent with their point of view were the cries for innovative work on small groups or teams coming from a Carnegie–Mellon conference on work groups (Goodman, 1986a), Hackman's (1990) book on teams that work, and the appearance of a comprehensive review of small groups, not in *Psychological Bulletin* but rather in the *Journal of Management* (Bettenhausen, 1991). Cover stories in *Time* and *Fortune* in 1990 (*Time,* 1990; *Fortune,* 1990) provided clear support for the conclusion that the interest was not simply limited to academics.

Much of the current interest in teams has stemmed from their role in the workplace. In this setting, a major concern is with the ability of people, working in teams, to effectively accomplish team tasks. In an effort to understand and construct effective work teams, attention, quite naturally, turned to the accumulated literature on teams and teamwork for answers to current team needs. In large part, this knowledge base proved disappointing (Goodman, 1986a; Hackman, 1990). In spite of the volume of work, there was surprisingly little that generalized to the kinds of problems faced by ongoing teams in work environments with a strong emphasis on effective team performance.

In this chapter we attempt to look from the present to the future, speculating on the nature of research and research needs related to teams in the decade ahead. We will first describe some of the current forces toward the increased interest in teams and teamwork. This is followed by a brief (and very selective) review of past research for the purpose of identifying some of the factors we believe have led to the gaps in our current knowledge base. From that we will provide a few suggestions for trying to avoid past limitations. However, before turning to the main tasks of the chapter, we shall first more precisely define what we mean by a team.

WHAT IS A TEAM?

Groups versus Teams

The distinction between teams and groups is not clear and is often arbitrary. Service and production focused organizations often refer to sets of individuals convened for the purpose of accomplishing some specified tasks as work *groups*. Clusters of individuals with similar duties and responsibilities in the military are called *teams,* as are those involved in competitive sports. When the purpose of the unit is to sell goods and services, sets of individuals with identical duties and responsibilities in some organizations are referred to as *sales teams* and others as *sales groups*. Thus, the label in use is not sufficient to conclude that a group or a team possess the characteristics of one, the other, or both.

Almost all of the psychological literature on aggregates of people occurs under the rubric of small groups. Virtually all discussions of small groups are based on aggregates of people that possess three attributes. A recent review by Steiner (1986) concludes that a small group consists of (1) two or more individuals who (2) interact with each other and (3) are interdependent in some way. To this set of attributes, McGrath (1984) added time. He cogently argued that groups have a past, a present and a future and that the past and the future influence the present, no matter how brief the past or future may be. The longer the past or the more that the persons anticipate needing to interact in the future, the more likely it is that past and anticipated future conditions will influence the behavior among group members in the present.

Definition of a Team

From our perspective, teams share the four characteristics described above with small groups. However, the definition of a team includes one additional critical component having to do with the collective's goals or objectives. Teams exist for some task-oriented purpose. They may design or assemble automobiles, plan political campaigns, or play baseball. Although social processes are important to team performance, unlike any small group, a team does not exist for purely social reasons. Five people who meet every Saturday for lunch are certainly a small group, but rarely would they be considered a team.

Teams have explicit goals and, with few exceptions, team members are aware of these goals. Thus, when we speak of teams in work-oriented organizations, we add a fifth defining characteristic over and above the four conditions for small groups, that of shared goals. This characterization of teams conforms most closely to the definition of Morgan et al. (1986), who define teams as, "distinguishable sets of two or more individuals who interact interdependently and adaptively to achieve specified, shared and valued objectives" (p. 3).

When teams exist within organizations producing goods and services, a very salient feature related to the relationship among team members is that of status or power differences among the team members. The presence of organizational and team goals almost without exception creates some need for control which is often manifested in some power differentials among organization and team members. Even in the absence of explicit status and power differences, these differences emerge over time among task-performing groups (Schneier and Goktepe, 1983). As a result, stable work team members are rarely, if ever, equal in status or power, and leadership is an important part of effective team functioning. Thus, as we consider work teams and research on them in the 1990s, we cannot overlook the role of leaders and leadership.

Ambiguities Surrounding Teams

Although the definition above is reasonably straightforward, a number of less concrete issues should be mentioned before leaving descriptive concerns. Confusion arises because, in the literature to date, the labels *team* and *group* have been used interchangeably. Therefore, care must be taken when reviewing the team and particularly the small group literature if the purpose for the latter is to generalize to teams as defined here.

Another issue concerns team membership and the "fuzzy" boundaries surrounding them (McGrath, 1984). There are both intra- and interperson questions regarding team membership. From the intraperson perspective, people may be members of many teams, but they are rarely the exclusive property of any one collective. Indeed, how much of a person belongs to a team is not very meaningful or specifiable. Katz and Kahn (1978) spoke of "partial inclusion," recognizing the fact that association with a team, or in their case, an organization, represented a commitment of only a part of a person's potential resources. Similarly, individuals may belong to more than one team at the same time, but rarely do they actively function in more than one at any given moment.

Determining at what times and in what ways an individual should be considered a team member is only part of the inclusion problem, the intraperson part. The other is between individuals. For some teams membership is clear, as is the case of a work team assigned a specific task and physically located in a well-defined area. In other cases, members may vary in the duties they perform for the team and the amount of time they dedicate to the team, making it difficult to decide who is and is not a member of the team. Does a member have to be physically present to be considered part of the team? What if the individual is present, but does not actively participate in the team's activity? These issues of membership have not been resolved in the past nor will they be in the future. Their resolution, more frequently than not, will be decided on the basis of conditions facing a particular team in question.

The final ambiguity has to do with just how large or small a team can be. There is little consensus on the size of a small group. Most researchers, however, would agree that teams are small enough for all team members to be aware of each other. However, even this requirement sometimes needs to be qualified, such as is the case of teams where the members are spread out over a large geographic area.

Most definitions of small groups and teams include dyads. Yet, it is recognized that two-person groups may be fundamentally different from other small collectives. Coalition formation, for example, is often important in teams but is not relevant in dyads; when a collective consists of only two people, coalition formation is not possible. The same is true of "majority" and "minority" distinctions when majority and minority are designations based on within-team (intrateam) subgroups. The nature leadership is also more obscure when the team size is limited to two persons. Even Graen's dyadic theory of leadership (Dansereau et al., 1975; Graen and Scandura, 1987) that focuses directly on the dyadic relationship between a leader and his or her subordinates focuses attention on teams where the leader is developing and maintaining more than one dyadic relationship.

For our purposes here, we will arbitrarily exclude dyads from our definition of teams because many of the characteristics unique to dyads are beyond our interest, and many of the constructs of interest to us do not apply to dyads. Rather than invoking exact size specifications, we will opt to leave the size question open.

EARLY TEAM RESEARCH

The scientific approach to the types of groups that fit the subset defined as teams, can be traced back many years to multiple sources. Much of the early psychological work fell within the group dynamics movement initiated most directly by Kurt Lewin in the 1930s and 1940s (see Lewin, 1948, 1951, 1953; Lewin et al., 1939). Another major influence was the compilation of the social psychological research done as part of the war effort in World War II that appeared in the *American Soldier* (Stauffer, 1949). McGrath (1984) observed that this early team research was born of a strong desire to focus the application of social science on significant real-world problems. Early successes both in terms of the practical significance of some of the initial findings and in terms of the theoretical issues that were raised stimulated a surge of interest in team research throughout the decades of the 1950s and 1960s and into the 1970s. Topics such as leadership, persuasion, conformity, coalition formation, and team performance were aggressively pursued.

In 1984, McGrath provided a useful taxonomy of small-group [team] research up to that time. Figure 10.1 presents the primary dimensions of that taxonomy. Both the rows and the columns of Figure 10.1 are dichotomized into two mutually exclusive categories. The individual cells created by the intersection of the two dichotomized dimensions contain ex-

		Nature of groups	
		Composed	Natural
Nature of tasks	Natural		Families, sports teams
	Imposed	Communication networks, ad hoc lab groups	Team training exercises

Figure 10.1 Primary dimensions of McGrath's taxonomy of types of small groups used in research. [Adapted from J. E. McGrath (1984), Fig. 4.3, p. 49.]

emplars of research representing the intersection of row and column characteristics. One cell is blank. No research exists for it because, by definition, composed groups are not "natural" ones either in character or in terms of the tasks performed by them.

The primary dimensions of McGrath's taxonomy are those of nature of the groups and the task. With respect to nature of the groups (columns of Fig. 10.1), the distinction is between naturalistic settings in which a wide variety of teams exist for all kinds of purposes. In contrast, composed groups exist primarily for research purposes. The groups are completed so the groups can be studied often under controlled conditions.

In a similar fashion, McGrath viewed team tasks from the standpoint of those that were naturally occurring ones and those imposed on the teams by researchers. The result created four cells where teams represented by the lower left-hand corner of the figure were operating under highly controlled conditions in terms of both the settings in which the interactions took place and the task on which the team members worked. In contrast to this, the upper right-hand corner represented teams operating under low levels of control in natural settings with naturally occurring tasks.

Not obvious from the figure is the fact that far more published research was and is done on teams in the lower left-hand quadrant than in the upper or lower right. There is a common explanation for this; conducting research on teams is never easy, but it is considerably easier, in general, to construct laboratory teams than it is to find naturalistic teams to study, particularly naturalistic ones working on natural tasks. Without discounting this feasibility explanation, there is, in our opinion, one other factor that supported and supports the disproportionate frequency of research in the lower left-hand corner of the figure. It has to do with the orientations of those who do research on teams.

For the most part, research on teams is initiated and carried out by behavioral scientists whose primary orientation is that of a scholar. As a result, research is often designed to investigate the viability of hypotheses deduced from a particular theory or developed to pit one theoretical deduction against another. These scientists have been well trained in the logic and research strategies of the scientific method. Thus, in contrast to the emphasis of early researchers such as Kurt Lewin, who had a strong desire to show that behavioral science research could be useful for addressing practical problems (McGrath, 1984), over time the goals of the research were tipped toward showing that one theory was more viable than another. In other words, the focus for doing research on teams shifted to that of developing theory rather than developing solutions to problems facing teams in ongoing settings. This shift in focus was reasonable and understandable given the nature of the people attracted to conducting research on teams and the fact that more controlled research was less costly. At the same time, the result was less emphasis on the practical problems faced by teams in real-world settings.

RECENT EMPHASES ON TEAMS

The 1980s saw a resurgence of interest in teams and teamwork. The interest arose from at least three sources: competitive economic concerns, advances in communications technology, and highly visible team failures. Each of the three major forces is discussed in greater detail below.

Competitive Economic Issues

The United States faces substantial competition from countries that strongly believe in the concept of work teams (e.g., Japan and Sweden). As U.S. industries attempt to regain a prominent position in key industries (e.g., automobile manufacturing), more emphasis is being placed on designing and implementing effective work teams (Hackman, 1990). Sweden's Volvo plants continue to serve as one of the best examples of the implementation of effectively functioning work teams. Since the early 1980s, Volvo employees have worked in teams instead of on traditional assembly lines. The work teams are responsible for assigning job duties, scheduling work, and quality control. In many cases the team assembles the entire automobile (*Business Week,* 1989). The organization-wide results are remarkable, with reports of high morale, decreased absenteeism (*Business Week,* 1989), and less turnover (Krepchin, 1990). It's no wonder that other companies have attempted to replicate the Volvo model.

General Motors' Saturn plant represents a large-scale effort to employ self-managing work teams. While it is still too soon to tell whether the Saturn automobile will be a boom or bust, the team concept behind the Saturn plant has met with varying degrees of support and suspicion from the business community. Proponents of the concept contend that success at Saturn will serve as a model for helping the United States recapture its competitive edge in the automotive industry (Fischer, 1991; Solomon, 1991). Critics assert that the United States lacks the drive, imagination, and expertise to make effective work teams a reality in automotive manufacturing (Peters, 1991; *Business Week,* 1990). This argument is based, in large part, on cultural expectations. In particular, it is argued that the individualistic focus in the United States is likely to work against strong team identification and the willingness to be committed to team performance.

Throughout the 1980s, the United States has attempted to utilize a tool most widely used by the Japanese, the quality circle (QC). Although there are many variations in practice, the typical QC team consists of a small group of employees who meet to discuss issues such as quality, productivity, and costs (Miller, 1989). The implementation of quality circles, or any type of work team, has profound implications for traditional areas of human resource management, such as selection (Lawler, 1990; Owens, 1991), training (Dulworth et al., 1990; *Industry Week,* 1989) and compensation (Smith, 1991). These effects are likely to become more pronounced the more widespread the use of teams is within the organization. Research to date has not provided much guidance on the system wide effects of the interaction between team structures and human response management practices.

Communications Technology

Advances in communications technology is a second major force that will drive team research in the 1990s. The widespread use of audio teleconferencing and recent advances in video teleconferencing allow for the possibility of work teams comprised of members from dispersed locations. Team members will be able to work "face to face" without being physically present.

Electronic mail provides the opportunity for spontaneous interaction among physically remote team members. It also creates the capability for quick and spontaneous communication, without requirements for meeting at a specific time and place. Audio teleconferencing has the added advantage of allowing reciprocal communication and immediate feedback. Via audio teleconferencing team members can engage in active discussion, an advantage over the message leaving limitations of electronic mail (Gillette, 1991). Team members need to participate at the same time, but geographic locations can be widespread.

Video teleconferencing is perhaps the most exciting technological communications advancement. While companies such as IBM and Hewlett Packard have taken advantage of the technology for years, others are exploring the advantages of video teleconferencing as the cost of equipment decreases (Feldman, 1991). Video teleconferencing literally brings team members together for face-to-face interaction across widely dispersed geographic locations. Similarly, team members can share and discuss pictorial and graphic illustrations via a video conferencing network.

Advances in communications technology create the possibility for a new kind of team. These are teams that are highly interactive, and in a sense face to face, yet geographically remote. These team situations may pose one of the most radical challenges to leadership. If we assume that these teams, like all teams in the past, are likely to develop status hierarchies that will create or demand some form of leadership within the team, it is not clear how the leadership will be displayed. This may be one area where the literature on substitutes for leadership may be valuable for identifying the content of leadership types of functions (e.g., Kerr and Jermier, 1978; Podsakoff et al., in press). The current literature to our knowledge has little to offer in the way of advice about how to best utilize technologically mediated teams or what can be expected of their performance.

Team Failures

The last major catalysts for team research are the highly visible team failures of recent history. "Human error" has resulted in the loss of human life and created incidents with international ramifications. Two military disasters attributable at least in part to faulty team processes, the *Stark* and *Vincennes* incidents, will be discussed in more detail below.

In May 1987, the *USS Stark* was hit by two missiles launched in error by an Iraqi plane (*Time,* 1987a,b; *Newsweek,* 1987). The ship was severely damaged and 37 crew members were killed. This tragedy could have been avoided, or the damage at least diminished, had the *Stark* reacted quickly and used its defenses. The crew on board had 1 or 2 minutes between the detection of the missile launch and impact. Although time was short, it was long enough to implement defensive maneuvers had any been attempted. The crew simply failed to react under the intense stress and pressure.

In the summer of 1988, the *USS Vincennes* mistakenly shot down an Iranian civilian airliner carrying 290 passengers (*Newsweek,* 1988; *U.S. News and World Report,* 1988). Several factors may have contributed to this tragedy. Here, we will focus on those that are most related to team processes.

Several events may have primed the *Vincennes* crew to expect trouble from hostile aircraft. First, the *Stark* incident was still fresh. As discussed above, American lives were lost and the frigate was severely damaged by two missiles launched by an Iranian aircraft. Second, the *Vincennes* had experienced a series of threatening events within an hour of the airliner tragedy. The sequence of events began when three small Iranian boats fired on a U.S. helicopter. The *Vincennes* had to fire on the boats, sinking two and damaging one. Five minutes later, the airliner, which would later be shot down, was detected departing from a nearby airfield.

Undoubtedly the crew aboard the *Vincennes* was under a great deal of stress given its recent experiences. The stress was probably compounded by the ambiguous information radar equipment provided about the unidentified aircraft. Perhaps the team was under so much pressure that procedures that would have been obvious otherwise, were neglected. For example, one crew member looked through the airline guide to determine whether a commercial flight was scheduled during that time, but he overlooked the particular flight that had taken off only 17 minutes behind schedule. Finally, no one contacted the airport to inquire about commercial traffic in the area.

Several points from the preceding two examples are relevant. Real-world teams must make critical decisions under suboptimal conditions. Stress and pressure can lead to a breakdown in critical communication and team processes. Many teams are likely currently taxed beyond their capabilities with little guidance on how to improve performance under adverse conditions. The need for information regarding team effectiveness and team decisionmaking far outweighs what is currently available.

TEAM RESEARCH IN THE 1990s

The resurgence of interest in teams and teamwork brought on, in part, by the conditions just described, naturally led to a search for research findings to guide the practices and procedures for establishing such teams. In many respects, the knowledge base represented by Fig. 10.1 was found lacking. We suggest that a major contributor to the disappointment with the existing literature was the fact that much of it was concentrated in the lower left-hand corner of Fig. 10.1 and was focused almost entirely on testing relatively narrow propositions derived primarily from one particular theory. In saying this, let us quickly add what we are not saying. We are not suggesting research should not be guided by theory or that theory development is unimportant. Quite the contrary. We are simply responding to the content balance across the total team research domain. In our opinion, the balance was tipped farther from the upper right-hand corner of Fig. 10.1 than was desirable when the need arose to attempt to use what was known to address problems of teams operating over time in ongoing organizations.

We are also not saying that the problem was necessarily one of research setting. In particular, it was not an issue of laboratory versus field, as these types of issues often get construed. We strongly believe that laboratory research is often extremely valuable for advancing knowledge about team effectiveness just as some field research is of little value. The issue again is one of balance and an effort to carefully address limits and levels of external validity regardless of the setting in which the research takes place.

From our perspective, the problem for current researchers is to conduct research on teams that provides information useful for developing and maintaining effective teams operating under conditions that are and will be faced in the near future. The challenge this problem presents is to identify critical team issues at the present time and to conduct research that avoids some of the limitations of earlier research. There are, in our opinion, two critical issues. The first of these involves identification of the content of team issues to be studied. The second deals with how these issues are studied. We shall refer to the two dimensions of the problem as those of "content" and "process."

Content of Team Research in the 1990s

One way to try to speculate on what will be some of the important content issues for any discipline is to look to reviews and innovative discussions of work that has appeared in the recent past. Fortunately for us, there are a number of excellent sources. In particular, Goodman (1986a) provided a compilation of chapters from a number of the leading small-group scholars who addressed the issue of designing effective work groups (teams) at a Carnegie–Mellon University conference, Levine and Moreland (1990) reviewed the recent literature on small groups in the *Annual Review of Psychology,* and Bettenhausen (1991) provided an excellent review of small-group research, addressing specifically some future needs for it to contribute more effectively to a knowledge base valuable to those who are most concerned about managing teams. Finally, Hackman (1990) edited a book reporting a number of team research projects conducted in the field and focused on creating conditions for effective teamwork.

From these sources and others, the following four topics would appear to be particularly important today and in the near future: (1) project or quasi-independent teams, (2) tasks and technology interfaces with teams, (3) team decisionmaking, and (4) team rewards. It is interesting to note that several of the content issues identified in the literature have ties to the real-world forces generating interest in teams, such as those discussed in the previous section. All have implications for leadership in small teams. Each will be discussed in turn.

Quasi-independent Teams[1]

In the last 10 to 15 years, teams have moved to center stage in the design of organizations. A response to the loss of market share to Japanese firms was to look to the structure of Japanese work units to attempt to discover

[1]From a purely descriptive standpoint, autonomous or self-managing work teams would have fit as a title for this section nicely. However, these labels and others (e.g., quality circles, team building) that fit our focus here have come to have meaning all their own in the team literature. In order to avoid the excess meaning that goes with the labels in use, we chose the above. The reader can be assured that there is no attempt or desire on our part to coin yet another term for teams of the type that we discuss here.

methods and procedures that might account for the differences in quality of products produced in the two countries. One of the "innovations" identified from that search was the use of work teams called "quality circles," which, ironically, had been advocated a number of years earlier by an American, ignored by U.S. industry, and picked up by a number of successful Japanese industries (Cole, 1979). Although the format and structure of quality circles varied a great deal, they were teams of workers (typically 5 to 10 people) at the shop floor level who were given an opportunity to discuss problems of production in their immediate work environment and some responsibility for proposing solutions to the identified problems and carrying them out.

From quality circles, team advocates expanded the domain of responsibilities assigned to teams and shifted organizational structures away from a strict hierarchy to a structure with more responsibilities and authority distributed somewhat lower in the organization to work teams. Teams in such structure go by many names, but they are best known as "autonomous work groups" or "self-managed teams." A key feature of these teams is a high degree of control by team members over their day-to-day work activities, such as the way jobs are done and how they are distributed across team members, as well as over recruitment, selection and training of team members (Wall et al., 1986). As mentioned in the previous section, GM's Saturn plant is one "real-world" example of self-managed teams in action.

In spite of the strong support of autonomous work teams by those writing to managers (e.g., Rosen, 1989; Tjosvold, 1986, 1989) and the popular support that has arisen around them (e.g., the cover stories of *Time* and *Fortune* in 1990), empirical support for their utility is mixed. In a very-well-done longitudinal field experiment of a large, nonunionized, British manufacturing company, Wall et al. (1986) found that autonomous work teams enhanced intrinsic job satisfaction, but they did not affect job motivation, organizational commitment, work performance, or voluntary turnover. At the organizational level, there was some indication of productivity increases because of a reduction in labor costs due to the need for fewer supervisors. On the balance, both workers and managers appreciated the autonomous work teams, but the latter also recognized that there were some major costs in terms of personal stress arising from maintaining and managing with a less centralized control structure.

Although structurally the use of autonomous work teams often leads to a reduction in formal supervisory positions, this does not mean that the leadership functions traditionally associated with the supervisory positions disappear. On the contrary, we would argue that leadership is still needed within the teams to accomplish team goals. Furthermore, in the absence of clear authority structures, teams, over time, will develop them on their own as is evidenced by past work with small groups (Schneier and Goktepe, 1983). Labeling a team a "self-managed" or "leaderless" work team is not likely to decrease our concerns for leadership. In fact, issues of authority and leadership are often quite difficult with these kinds of teams (Hackman, 1990). This may be because efforts are made to decrease or remove visible signs of authority, but the needs for some of the leadership functions served by clear authority structures still remain making it less obvious to the team members how they should address these needs.

Hackman (1990), in his concluding chapter to an edited book reporting 27 case studies of work teams, most of which possessed many of the characteristics of quasi-independent teams in organizational settings, identified some common themes that occur across many of the teams and also provided a list of commonly occurring obstacles to team effectiveness. These are listed below.

Themes

1. Teams develop a temporal rhythm that has a powerful influence on how they respond to demands over time.
2. A self-fulfilling prophecy (labeled a "self-fueling spiral" by Hackman) develops in teams such that early successes seem to lead the team to behave like a winner and do well over time; the pattern tends to be reversed following early failure.
3. Teams develop their own authority structure within the team, and this process is potentially difficult.
4. Team values and the general character of the team is strongly influenced by the nature of the tasks they perform.[2]

Obstacles

1. When team structures are created in organizations, there is a tendency to label a unit as a quasi-independent team but to require it to function as a managed group with team members reporting to a leader–manager in a very structured fashion.
2. At the other extreme, quasi-independent teams are established with no stable means of dealing with authority.
3. Little guidance is given to the team as to its purpose and how it might function when the team is established.
4. Challenging team objectives are specified but too little support is given for accomplishing the objectives.

[2]This issue will be addressed later in the chapter.

5. There often is too little emphasis on training team members to function in a team.

The dilemma facing the use of quasi-independent work teams in organizations is that their popularity is outstripping our knowledge about them. Practitioners, in our opinion, are far too willing to sing their praises and then to press forth to incorporate such teams in their organizations. The research findings are much more cautious. In the next few years, there is clearly a need to explore what does and does not work well with quasi-independent work teams. The list of issues raised by Hackman (1990) and cited above provides a good starting point for further investigation.

Tasks and Technology

Hackman (1990) makes the seemingly intuitively obvious observation that the character of teams is affected by the nature of the tasks that they perform. He goes on to say that over time the values of team members appear to become increasingly aligned with the kinds of things with which the team works. Thus, we would expect that the values of five-person teams loading trucks with illegal drugs would differ from five-person teams loading rice for displaced hurricane victims.

As intuitively obvious as the above may appear, there has been a tendency to downplay or ignore the role of the products produced while performing tasks in a small group on team member beliefs, values, and behavior. In many cases, the task is simply seen as a means of standardizing conditions in which team behaviors can be observed. Often the task is held constant so nothing is learned about the effects of task products. An example of the latter is the use (overuse) of the NASA moon problem in laboratory research on teams simply as a way to create interactions among persons. When the task has received careful attention, that attention is usually focused on kinds of behaviors that are required to do the task and the types of interactions that are generated when the task is used (see Hackman and Morris, 1975) rather than the reciprocal effects of the products that are produced on the producers themselves. Further attention to task products deserves more attention.

In ongoing organizations, tasks are embedded in larger technical systems, and these technological system demands affect both the nature of task structures and the likely impact of the tasks on teams (Goodman, 1986b). Put another way, the tasks confronted by teams in organizations are typically confounded with the technology within which those tasks exist. In spite of this naturally occurring confound, little attention in the past has been paid to the technology (Goodman, 1986b).

With respect to leadership, the *content* of team tasks and task products has been ignored primarily because of a legitimate desire to find task dimensions at a higher level of abstraction than content. Consider the contingency model of leadership (Fiedler, 1967), in which team tasks are indexed according to their level of task structure. Teams with similar task structure, leader position power, and leader–member relations are considered the same with respect to task regardless of their task products. It seems reasonable to expect that even when teams share these three major characteristics of the model, if their products are as diverse as producing wins or losses in basketball games, providing services in a butcher shop, or hitting targets on an artillery firing range, some of the variance in team performance not explained by the model may be captured by consideration of the nature of team products. The same could be said of all leadership models, in our opinion.

There is some, albeit small, indication that technologies are receiving a little more attention in the immediate past, and there is good reason to believe that technological variables deserve more attention in the team research of the 1990s. First, Goodman's (1986b) chapter provides a nice start for suggesting some of the interactions between tasks and technologies that are important regarding team effectiveness. Second, there is a growing literature dealing with teams and one particular technological issue—that of electronic communication through computer networks. McGrath and Gruenfeld's chapter in this volume (Chap. 9) directly addresses that issue. In our opinion, technological effects on team behavior are ripe for further exploration.

Team Decisionmaking

A critical product of many teams is a decision or judgment. In some cases, this may be the only product such as is the case for a jury. A well-established research base exists for jury decisions with excellent empirically based models (see Gerbasi et al., 1977; Penrod and Hastie, 1979; Davis and Kerr, 1986). Typically, a consensus rule is described or proposed, and teams (real or mock juries) are observed with respect to the extent to which they use the rule as function of conditions that may influence the use of the decision rule. Researchers have been interested in both the processes that are used by juries to make decisions and the decisions themselves (the outcomes of the decision).

Although team decisionmaking is concerned with both the process and the outcomes of teams, the outcome has been limited primarily to consensus. Juries reach or do not reach verdicts. The verdicts are the team outcomes—consensus outcomes. Specific content issues, such as the likelihood of consensus when capital punishment is involved, are very important, but the content is primarily of interest in a domain different from that of research on juries from the jury functioning standpoint. Generalizing to other kinds of problems such as those faced in work teams in organizations is not readily apparent from jury decision content.

Our own work on distributed decisionmaking under conditions of stress illustrates team decisionmaking research where both the process and the outcome are important. It also addresses some of the team decisionmaking issues raised by disasters such as the *Stark* and *Vincennes* incidents. In an adaptation of individual decision models, Ilgen et al. (1991) presented four-person teams with a series of decisions. Teams had available to them nine pieces of information. A weighted combination of the pieces of information created the rule for determining what is and is not the correct decision for the team. Neither all the rules nor all the pieces of information were available to any one member; thus a team decision could be reached without sharing information and expertise (knowledge of rules) among the members prior to making a decision. Finally, when such decisions are made by expert teams with assigned leaders, leadership issues are likely to play an important role in the quality of the decisions that are reached by the teams.

A concrete example of a distributed decisionmaking task under conditions of stress would be that faced by four persons in an emergency room. Here a decision could be made about whether to admit a victim of a street fight. The decision makers might be a friend of the person him or herself, an emergency room physician, a police officer, and an admitting nurse. In a laboratory simulation, team members learn the nature of the team task, practice on it, and then work together for extended periods of time. Both the process and the quality of team decisions can be traced and observed as the teams perform the simulation on a networked computer system with four workstations.

Rewards

Power, negotiation, conflict resolution, and coalition formation are just a few of the topics that address the way in which rewards are distributed among team members. Considerable attention has been given to all of these topics in the small-groups literature. Yet, to our knowledge, little of this research was done with teams in ongoing work organizations. In particular, a major boundary condition in work settings is that team members agree to participate in the teams in exchange for explicit rewards, one of which is almost always money. The amount of financial return and the way in which it and other extrinsic rewards are administered are bound to have a major impact on team functioning. If, for example, rewards are based on merit and merit is based on an individual performance rating that leaves little room for assessing contributions to effective team performance, then the effectiveness of teams composed of individuals whose raises are based on such an appraisal system is likely to suffer.

Ilgen (1988) observed that it was ironic that the growth of interest in teamwork and work teams in the middle 1980s coincided with a similar growth in entrepreneurial activity—an activity that so dogmatically stresses individualism. In our opinion, unless research on teams and teamwork in ongoing organizations addresses explicitly the nature of the rewards under which individual team members function as a result of the larger organization in which they are employed, knowledge gained about teams and their use in organizations will be severely limited.

When rewards in teams are addressed with respect to leadership, the leader is typically seen as one who dispenses rewards to team members in ways that enhance member task motivation. House's (House, 1971; House and Mitchell, 1974) path–goal model is the clearest example of such a model. Yet, for the most part, it is a view of leadership that treats leaders as critical elements in the members' environments, but focuses on individual member behavior. To our knowledge, little research exists that attempts to tie leadership and rewards and keep the primary focus at the team level without decomposing the team into leaders and team members. Today's more interactionist point of view demands greater attention to team-level phenomena when combining leadership and reward concerns.

Guzzo and his colleagues (Guzzo, 1986; Shea and Guzzo, 1984) presented a model of team effectiveness that explicitly addressed rewards. According to this model, team effectiveness was directly a function of the way in which team members interacted to accomplish the task, and members' interaction was related primarily to the degree of interdependence among them fostered by the nature of the team task(s) and the extent to which member outcomes were interdependent. Primary among member outcomes was that of pay and other valued rewards. Guzzo argued that regardless of whether the members were likely to work well together depended on whether the reward structure within which they operated was likely to facilitate or get in the way of working together. Although the model provided a nice framework from which to view team effectiveness and a central role to the importance of rewards in the team process, it has, to our knowledge, not been followed up empirically. Yet, if teams are to be integrated into present organizational structures, we feel that attention to rewards, either from the perspective of Guzzo's work or others, must receive more careful attention.

Process: Doing Team Research for Knowledge Transfer to Work Teams

Our position in this chapter is that the knowledge base for teams and teamwork, represented by the scientific literature available by the early 1980s and classified by McGrath in his review of 1984 (McGrath, 1984) (see Fig. 10.1), has had limited applicability for the design and implementation of work teams in the 1990s.

Accepting the limited applicability assertion, we have asked what might be done to avoid some of the previous limitations. The items listed below are items that appear most critical to us at the present time. The list is neither exhaustive nor entirely unique. Others, for example, McGrath (1986) identified similar issues when addressing ways to study work groups in organizations. Furthermore, it should not be construed to be a discussion of issues to be addressed by one particular study or even, necessarily, a specific individual's research program. Rather, it is to be viewed from the collective level—the collective of the domain of all team research with individual research studies on teams constituting the elements.

Tolerate Diversity

The need for diversity in participants, settings, behaviors, methods, measures, and even paradigms is an old observation apparently far easier to express than to live by. However, the need to stress diversity could hardly be greater than it is in team research. We have already stated that one of the reasons for the limitations in past team research, in our opinion, was its lack of diversity as represented by the preponderance of research in the lower left-hand portion of Fig. 10.1.

Fortunately, the ability to respond to the need for diversity is better today than it has ever been in the past. At one time, diversity meant primarily creating some variance in a field of inquiry in settings (laboratory and field) or, usually confounded with settings, between experimental and correlational designs (Cronbach, 1968). Today, at all phases of the research process, more opportunities exist for diversity. The examples begin with means for collecting data. For example, Gersick (1989) describes a procedure of generating what she calls "meeting maps." This process is an evolutionary one in which the data that are used as observations of the team or group activity are defined, in part, by the unique characteristics of the teams or groups being observed rather than forced on the team by an a priori structure provided by the investigator. Do we believe that this is the only, or even the best way to gather data from teams? Of course not. But it offers an additional method that addresses some of the weaknesses and criticisms of other data collection methods. As such, when the whole set of methods are considered, the method can be evaluated against a standard of value added rather than a standard of absolute value.

Diverse methods are also more readily available with respect to testing theoretical models. Davis and Kerr (1986) describe what they call "thought experiments" as a way to develop models for studying team performance. These thought experiments lead to the laying out of precise mathematical models that can then be used in conjunction with empirical data to judge the utility of the model. The authors have successfully followed a variant of this approach in their previous work with juries (and mock juries) (Davis et al., 1977). Although relatively rare in the team research of behavioral scientists, systems analysts, mathematicians, and others who conducted research on command and control teams use very similar paradigms (e.g., Pattipati et al., 1980).

Finally, the opportunity for data analytic techniques that begin to address some of the complex problems of causal inferences and longitudinal designs have never been greater. LISRL (Joreskog, 1973) and the use of survival analyses for longitudinal data (Singer and Willett, 1991) are just a few of the multiple methods that are available to study teams today and were not available only a few years earlier.

Take Boundaries Seriously

Boundary conditions are those conditions in any particular research study that restrict or qualify the conclusions that can be drawn from that study; they are the conditions that set limits on generalizability of research results. It is well accepted that all research (i.e., a particular research study) is flawed in some ways. What is less well accepted is the willingness to face up to potential limitations in the design phase of the research by fully exploring potential limitations in generalizability or the willingness to discuss the specific nature of the limitations of completed research.

The challenge for all researchers is to identify the variables that create potential boundaries with regard to the constructs of interest and then to design research in a way that will address these boundary conditions. The focus of design should be on needed generalizations to the domain of people, behaviors, and situations of interest. For example, on the topic of supervisory performance appraisal, Ilgen and Favero (1985) proposed that a sense of the need to interact with the appraisee in the future was an essential boundary condition that needed to be present if research knowledge about appraisals was to generalize to appraisals obtained from supervisors of their subordinates in ongoing work settings. Fromkin and Streufert (1976), Mook (1983), and others have enumerated a number of issues related to boundary conditions in laboratory research.

With respect to generalizing to teams functioning in ongoing organizations, the most critical boundary conditions, in our opinion and the opinion of others, relate to the fact that such teams have some degree of permanence with a past, present, and future. McGrath (1986) addresses this, stressing the need to recognize that work teams are intact social systems existing in a context that involves time and place. Hackman (1990) defines the boundaries for organizational work groups (teams) as those of (1) intact social systems with (2) one or more tasks to perform, and (3) existing in an organizational context.

Given these kinds of boundary conditions, the challenge for team researchers is to design research that will allow reasonable generalizations to teams that have the above characteristics. To do this does not mean that only research conducted in a particular setting is legitimate. In particular, it does not mean that all research must be done in the field. It also does not mean that all laboratory research must create "realistic" field conditions, conditions that Mook (1983) describes as "mundane realism." It does mean that the essential dynamics of the conditions as they could be expected to impact on key constructs being studied in the research should be created in some fashion. To do this, there are no easy answers or general solutions that can be offered for all research. However, for investigators to carefully consider these issues before the design of every study should make it less likely that the research data generated by the field of inquiry would drift too far from the phenomena that generated the interests in the research in the first place.

Beware of Levels of Analyses

Teams, by their nature, are aggregates of individuals. Only recently have behavioral scientists become aware of the need to be sensitive to a number of issues raised by what has become known as the "levels of analysis issues" (Dansereau and Alutto, 1990; Roberts et al., 1978; Rousseau, 1985). Two sets of issues are important for teams. The first of these is that constructs of interest in research typically exist at a particular level by the way in which they are defined, but the ways they are measured often are not consistent with their level.

Consider for the moment the construct of cohesion in teams. Cohesion is a team-level construct. At the individual level, cohesion makes no sense; whatever the definition of cohesion, it has something to do with the bonding between two or more persons and cannot go on at the individual level. Therefore, care must be taken to define the construct at the level appropriate for it, theoretically, and to measure it in a way that is consistent with that definition. It is, for example, not appropriate to ask team members about their individual satisfaction with the team and then average all team members' satisfaction and assume that this is cohesion.

A second problem with levels is that, independent of the theoretical nature of the variables, it is often possible to produce statistical artifacts by inappropriately aggregating data across levels. The point here is not to go into all the ways that such artifacts can occur but to warn that team research is particularly vulnerable to these kinds of problems because of the fact that teams exist at a level between individuals and organizations. Furthermore, variables from both the lower (individual) and higher (organizational) levels are likely to impact on team functioning. Therefore, in any one research study, variables from multiple levels are likely to be involved. This makes sensitivity to levels issues very important in team research.

CONCLUSION

More than other areas of interest, team research has been initiated from real-world concerns. Today is no different than before. The exciting factor today is that teams are cropping up in many places as central to the successful accomplishment of important organizational goals. The frightening issue is that expectations are exceeding both the knowledge base and, more than likely, the ability of teams to deliver. The challenge is to provide research knowledge that is valuable for guiding the development and implementation of teams in ways that will, to the best of our knowledge, do well. The team research community has been faced with that challenge before, and the data came up short. Our challenge today is to attempt to avoid some of the problems of the past and to generate future research data that more closely addresses the effectiveness of teams embedded in ongoing organizations. We have suggested some ways to do that taking into account the types of content issues that appear to be more important today and in the near future and to suggest some issues to which researchers should be particularly sensitive as they conduct their research.

Acknowledgments

Writing of this chapter was supported, in part, by Grant No. N00014-90-J-1786 from the Office of Naval Research as part of the technical base research for the Cognitive and Neural Sciences Division. Although the support for this work is gratefully acknowledged, the ideas expressed herein are those of the authors and not necessarily endorsed by the supporting agency.

References

Bettenhausen, K. L. (1991). Five years of groups research: What we have learned and what needs to be addressed. *Journal of Management, 17,* 345–381.

Business Week (1989). Volvo's radical new plant: "The death of the assembly line? (August), 92–93.

Business Week (1990). Here comes GM's Saturn. (April), 56–62.

Cole, R. E. (1979). *Work, mobility, and participation: A comparative study of American and Japanese industry.* Berkeley, CA: University of California Press.

Cronbach, L. J. (1968). The two disciplines of scientific psychology. *American Psychologist, 12,* 671–684.

Dansereau, F., Jr., and Alutto, J. A. (1990). Level-of-analysis in climate and culture research. In B. Schneider (Ed.), *Organizational climate and culture* (pp. 193–236). San Francisco: Jossey-Bass.

Dansereau, F., Jr., Graen, G. B., and Haga, W. J. (1975). A vertical dyad linkage approach to leadership within formal organizations: A longitudinal investigation of the role-making process. *Organizational Behavior and Human Performance, 13,* 46–78.

Davis, J.H., and Kerr, N. L. (1986). Thought experiments and the problem of sparse data in small-group performance research. In P. S. Goodman (Ed.), *Designing effective workgroups* (pp. 305–349). San Francisco, CA: Jossey-Bass.

Davis, J. H., Kerr, N. L., Stasser, G., Meek, D., and Holt, R. (1977). Victim consequences, sentence severity, and decision processes in mock juries. *Organizational Behavior and Human Performance, 18,* 346–365.

Dulworth, M. R., Landen, D.L., and Usilaner, B. L. (1990). Employee involvement systems in U.S. corporations: Right objectives, wrong strategies. *National Productivity Review, 9,* 141–156.

Feldman, R. (1991). Field experiences with videoconferencing. *Business Communications Review, 21,* 45–49.

Fiedler, F. E. (1967). *A theory of leadership effectiveness.* New York: McGraw-Hill.

Fischer, B. (1991). Finishing out the century. *Journal for Quality and Participation,* 48–52.

Fortune. (1990). Who needs a boss? (May) 52–60.

Fromkin, H. L., and Streufert, S. (1976). Laboratory experimentation. In M. D. Dunnette (Ed.), *Handbook of industrial and organizational psychology* (pp. 415–466). Chicago: Rand McNally.

Gerbasi, K. C., Zuckerman, M., and Reiss, H. T. (1977). Justice needs a new blindfold: A review of mock jury research. *Psychological Bulletin, 84,* 323–345.

Gersick, C. J. G. (1989). Marking time: Predictable transitions in task groups. *Academy of Management Journal, 32,* 274–310.

Gillette, D. (1991). Teleconferencing: A better way to meet. *Journal of Information Systems Management, 8,* 76–79.

Goodman, P. S. (1986a). *Designing effective workgroups.* San Francisco: Jossey-Bass.

Goodman, P. S. (1986b). Impact of task and technology on group performance. In P. S. Goodman (Ed.), *Designing effective workgroups* (pp. 120–167). San Francisco, CA: Jossey-Bass.

Graen, G. B., and Scandura, T. A. (1987). Toward a psychology of dyadic organizing. In L. L. Cummings and B. M. Staw (Eds.), *Research in Organizational Behavior* (Vol. 9, pp. 175–208). Greenwich, CT: JAI Press.

Guzzo, R. A. (1986). Group decision making and group effectiveness in organizations. In P. S. Goodman (Ed.), *Designing effective workgroups* (pp. 34–71). San Francisco, CA: Jossey-Bass.

Hackman, J. R. (Ed.) (1990). *Groups that work (and those that don't).* San Francisco, CA: Jossey-Bass.

Hackman, J. R., and Morris, C. G. (1975). Group tasks, group interaction process, and group performance effectiveness: A review and proposed integration. In L. Berkowitz (Ed.), *Advances in experimental social psychology*. New York: Academic Press.

House, R. J. (1971). A path-goal theory of leadership. *Administrative Science Quarterly, 16,* 321–338.

House, R. J., and Mitchell, T. R. (1974). Path-goal theory of leadership. *Journal of Contemporary Business, 3*(4), 81–97.

Ilgen, D. R. (1988). Small groups and teams in work organizations: Barriers to successful use. In R. S. Schuler, S. A. Youngblood, and V. M. Huber (Eds.), *Research in personnel and human resource management.* (Vol. 4, pp. 340–349), Greenwich, CT: JAI Press.

Ilgen, D. R., and Favero, J. (1985). Methodological limitations of social psychological literatures for the understanding of performance appraisal processes. *Academy of Management Review, 10,* 311–321.

Ilgen, D. R., Major, D. A., Hollenbeck, J. R., and Sego, D. J. (1991). *Decision making in teams: Raising an individual model to the team level* (Technical Report No. 91-2). East Lansing: Michigan State University, Departments of Psychology and Management.

Industry Week (1989). Hybrid incubator hatches workers (August), 27–30.

Joreskog, K. G. (1973). A general method for estimating a linear structural equation system. In A. S. Goldberger and O. D. Duncan (Eds.), *Structural equation models in the social sciences.* New York: Seminar Press.

Katz, D., and Kahn, R. L. (1978). *The social psychology of organizations,* 2nd ed. New York: Wiley.

Kerr, S., and Jermier, J. M. (1978). Substitutes for leadership: Their meaning and measurement. *Organizational Behavior and Human Performance, 22,* 375–403.

Krepchin, I. F. (1990). Report from Sweden: The human touch in automobile assembly. *Modern Materials Handling, 45,* 52–55.

Lawler, E. E. (1990). The new plant revolution revisited. *Organizational Dynamics, 19,* 4–14.

Levine, J. M., and Moreland, R. L. (1990). Progress in small group research. *Annual Review of Psychology, 41,* 585–634.

Lewin, K. (1948). *Resolving social conflict: Select papers on group dynamics.* New York: Harper.

Lewin, K. (1951). *Field theory and social sciences.* New York: Harper.

Lewin, K. (1953). Studies in group decision. In D. Cartwright and A. Zander (Eds.), *Group dynamics: Research and theory,* 1st ed. Evanston, IL: Row, Peterson.

Lewin, K., Lippett, R., and White, R. (1939). Patterns of aggressive behavior in experimentally created "social climates." *Journal of Social Psychology, 10,* 271–299.

McGrath, J. E. (1984). *Groups: Interaction and performance.* Englewood Cliffs, NJ: Prentice-Hall.

McGrath, J. E. (1986). Studying groups at work: Ten critical needs for theory and practice. In P. S. Goodman (Eds.), *Designing effective work groups* (pp. 362–391). San Francisco: Jossey-Bass.

Miller, T. R. (1989). The quality circle phenomenon: A review and appraisal. *Advanced Management Journal, 54,* 4–7, 12.

Mook, D. G. (1983). In defense of external validity. *American Psychologist, 38,* 379–387.

Newsweek (1987). A tragedy in the gulf. (June) 16–22.

Newsweek (1988). Seven minutes to death. (July) 18–24.

Owens, T. (1991). The self-managing work team. *Small Business Reports, 16,* 53–65.

Pattipati, K. R., Kleinman, D. L., and Iphrath, A. R. (1980). From OCM to ODM—an optimal decision model of human task sequencing performance. *IEEE Proceedings of the International Conference on Cybernetics and Society,* 121–126.

Penrod, C., and Hastie, R. (1979). Models of jury decision making: A critical review. *Psychological Bulletin, 86,* 462–492.

Peters, T. (1991). Total quality leadership: Let's get it right. *Journal for Quality and Participation,* 10–15.

Podsakoff, P. M., Niehoff, B. P., MacKenzie, S. B., and Williams, M. L. (in press). Do substitutes for leadership really substitute for leadership? An empirical examination of Kerr and Jermier's leadership model using new measures and analytical procedures. *Organizational Behavior and Human Decision Processes.*

Roberts, K. H., Hulin, C. L., and Rousseau, D. M. (1978). *Developing an interdisciplinary science of organizations.* San Francisco: Jossey-Bass.

Rosen, N. (1989). *Teamwork and the bottom line.* Hillsdale, NJ: Lawrence Erlbaum.

Rousseau, D. M. (1985). Issues of level in organizational research: Multi-level and cross-level perspectives. In L. L. Cummings and B. M. Staw (Eds.), *Research in organizational behavior* (Vol. 7, pp. 1–38). Greenwich, CT: JAI Press.

Schneier, C. E., and Goktepe, J. R. (1983). Issues of emergent leadership: The contingency model of leadership, leader sex, and leader behavior. In H. H. Blumberg, A. P. Hare, V. Kent, and M. F. Davies (Eds.), *Small groups and social interaction* (Vol. 1, pp. 413–421). Chichester, UK: Wiley.

Shea, G. P., and Guzzo, R. A. (1984). A theory of work group effectiveness. Unpublished manuscript, The Wharton School, University of Pennsylvania.

Singer, J. D., and Willett, J. B. (1991). Modeling the days of our lives: Using survival analysis when designing and analyzing longitudinal studies of duration and the timing of events. *Psychological Bulletin, 110,* 268–290.

Smith, F. W. (1991). Empowering employees. *Small Business Reports, 16,* 15–20.

Solomon, C. M. (1991). Behind the wheel at Saturn. *Personnel Journal, 70,* 72–74.

Stauffer, L. (1949). *The American soldier: Studies in social psychology in World War II.* Princeton, NJ: Princeton University Press.

Steiner, I. D. (1974). What ever happened to the group i social psychology? *Journal of Experimental Social Psychology, 10,* 94–108.

Steiner, I. D. (1986). Paradigms and groups. In L. Berkowitz (Ed.), *Advances in Experimental Social Psychology, 19,* 251–259.

Time. (1987). A shouted alarm, a fiery blast. (June), 20–22.

Time. (1987b). Why did this happen? (June), 17–19.

Time. (1990). The right stuff. (October), 74–84.

Tjosvold, D. (1986). *Working together to get things done: Managing for organizational productivity*. Lexington, MA: Lexington Books.

Tjosvold, D. (1989). *Managing conflict.* Minneapolis, MN: Team Media.

U.S. News and World Report. (1988). Where is the light at the end of the Gulf? (July). 12–16.

Wall, T. D., Kemp, N. J., Jackson, P. R, and Clegg, C. W. (1986). Outcomes of autonomous workgroups: A long-term field experiment. *Academy of Management Journal, 29,* 280–304.

11

Four Revolutions in Behavioral Decision Theory

Lee Roy Beach
Department of Management and Policy
University of Arizona

It generally is assumed that one of the duties of a leader is to make decisions. Since the 1940s, research and theory have been concerned with the adequacy of these decisions and with ways of improving them. Work in operations research and management information systems has focused on systematic, usually quantitative, methods of improving specific classes of decisions. Behavioral decision research has focused on understanding how decisions in general normally are made, both because such understanding is interesting in its own right and because it can provide guidance for aiding and improving decisionmaking.

Attempts to use behavioral decision theory and research to understand and aid organizational decisionmaking have not been particularly successful. In large part this is because the theory and research are prefaced on a surprisingly narrow view of what constitutes a decision and of the conditions under which decisionmaking normally takes place. The result has been a growing dissatisfaction with this narrow view and its failure to illuminate decisionmaking as it actually occurs in organizations (or in the private lives of individual decisionmakers, for that matter). The purpose of this chapter is to describe the ongoing evolution of behavioral theory and

Leadership Theory and Research: Perspectives and Directions

research as it slowly, and rather hesitantly, broadens its view and addresses decisionmaking in a more realistic manner.

BACKGROUND

Fifty years of research on unaided human decisionmaking has produced four major revolutions in how we view the day-to-day decisionmaking of reasonably bright, reasonably conscientious, reasonably reasonable people—either in their roles as leaders or in their private lives. The early view was that all decisions were properly regarded as choices that, after extensive evaluation of the available options, were guided by the desire to maximize expected utility. *Expected utility* was defined as the product sum of the utilities of all of the possible outcomes associated with an option and the probabilities of each of those outcomes occurring should that option be selected. *Choice* was defined as selecting a single option from among the available options. *Maximization* was defined as choosing the option with the highest expected utility.

The first revolution came from recognition that evaluation seldom is extensive (e.g., Simon, 1955; Tversky and Kahneman, 1974). The second revolution came from recognition that decisionmakers possess a variety of different strategies for making choices, many of which have quite different aims than the maximization of expected utility (e.g., Beach and Mitchell, 1978; Payne, 1976). The third revolution, which is still in progress, comes from recognition that choices occur relatively rarely; that behavior largely is preprogrammed. Decisions are required primarily when the programs fail, and even then the decisions may consist of something other than simply choosing the best from a set of options (Beach and Mitchell, 1987, 1990; Klein, in press). The fourth revolution, which is just beginning, comes from recognition that in order to make further progress behavioral decision research must abandon its single-minded allegiance to the economic view of decisionmaking and pay more attention to relevant developments in modern cognitive, organizational, and systems theory and research (Beach, 1990).

Many readers will be familiar with the first revolution—represented by research on satisficing and heuristics and biases. Fewer will be familiar with the second and third revolutions—represented by research on phased decisionmaking, contingent processing, and screening. Fewer still will be aware of the brewing fourth revolution—noneconomic, cognitive, decision theory and research. The purpose of this essay is to describe the less-familiar second and third revolutions and to identify the harbingers of the fourth.

To anticipate what follows, the currently emerging picture of decisionmaking reveals that it takes place in two steps—and each step is a different kind of decision. The first step consists of *screening* out unacceptable or inappropriate options; if only one option survives, it is selected. If more than one option survives, the process moves to the second step, *choosing* the best of the survivors of the first step. Examination of the decision processes at each step shows that screening decisions are made using a distinctly different strategy than are choice decisions.

The strategy used in screening decisions is rapid but fairly crude. It merely requires the option to measure up on various relevant criteria. There is, in fact, some tolerance for failure, but if the option falls too short, it is rejected. This strategy is noncompensatory, which means that failing to meet a criterion cannot be compensated for (cannot be balanced out) by exceeding the mark on one or more other criteria. Moreover, when only one option survives the screening step, the decision process stops—the survivor becomes the decided-upon option, and there is no choice step.

While studies of screening find that a single decision strategy is used for all screening decisions (Beach et al., 1988a; Beach and Strom, 1989; Potter and Beach, 1990; van Zee et al., 1992), studies of choice show that different decision strategies are used for different choice decisions (Lussier and Olshavsky, 1979; Olshavsky, 1979; Park, 1978; Payne, 1976, 1982). The decisionmaker's selection of a strategy for a particular choice is contingent on the characteristics of the choice itself, the demands of the situation in which the decision arises, and the skills and abilities of the decisionmaker (Christensen-Szalanski, 1978, 1980; Huffman, 1978; McAllister et al., 1979; Payne, 1976, 1982; Payne et al., 1988; Smith et al., 1982; Waller and Mitchell, 1984). In short, the screening step is accomplished using a single strategy that demands only limited evaluations of options, but the choice step, when it occurs at all, is accomplished by any of a number of different strategies.

Building upon the first and second revolutions, this two-stage view of decisionmaking marks the third revolution in behavioral decision theory: that screening and choosing are substantially different processes. Moreover, the two-stage view makes it clear that because it dictates the set of options from which choices can be made, screening is no less important to decisionmaking than is choice, and in fact it may be more important. The two-step view dethrones choice as the reigning characterization of decisionmaking and as the primary focus of research. In what follows we will begin by examining arguments for the existence of two steps in decisionmaking. Then we will expand on the arguments by examining separately the research on screening and the research on choice strategies.

ARGUMENTS FOR THE PROMINENCE OF SCREENING IN DECISIONMAKING

Personal observation and private experience both argue for a two-step decision process. Choices, when they are made at all, are made among the members of a circumscribed set of options. The choice set is only a subset of the conceivable possibilities—one does not choose a spouse by considering the relative merits of all of one's acquaintances who are both unmarried and of the opposite sex (let alone all persons with such qualifications in the immediate locale, the nation, or the world). Even when it may appear that the choice set naturally is small, there always are other options, however far-fetched, that could be considered. For example, when deciding between heart surgery or medication to deal with clogged arteries, killing oneself is a possible third option, although it is unlikely to be included in the choice set. True, the idea of suicide might occur to the decisionmaker, but in most cases it would be rejected before it became a serious contender. In short, some options, particularly the outlandish, the reprehensible, or the unthinkable, never make it into the choice set. Therefore, screening, the process by which some options are admitted and some are not, is logically prior to choice, is separate from choice, and is fundamental to choice because it dictates what is included in the choice set.

Conclusions based on observation and experience are strengthened by objective descriptions of what decisionmakers actually do (e.g., Isenberg, 1984; Mintzberg, 1975; Selznick, 1957). An especially clear analysis is provided by Eddy and Clanton (1982), who examined 50 case reports published in the *New England Journal of Medicine* from 1974 to 1979. Each report outlined the available information and how it was used by physicians in the course of deciding what caused the patient's illness. From these cases the authors extracted a general pattern that reveals two clear stages in the process of deciding upon a diagnosis.

Eddy and Clanton (1982) found that before decisionmaking begins, fragments of presenting information are aggregated into familiar symptoms (respiratory failure, severe hypoxia, infection). Then one or two pivotal symptoms are selected, usually symptoms that are generally recognized as diagnostic. The other symptoms are temporarily ignored while the decisionmaker compiles a list of diseases that could have caused the pivotal symptoms. Then decisionmaking begins as the diseases on this list are screened by serially comparing them with all of the nonpivotal symptoms; if the credibility of the disease falls below some threshold, it is rejected; otherwise it is retained. If this process screens out all but one disease, that disease is the diagnosis. If more than one disease survives screening, a diagnosis must be chosen from among the survivors. Choice often can be facilitated by securing additional information (perhaps an additional test) that will eliminate some of the survivors. But, if more than one still remains, the final decision requires comparison of their relative merits as possible causes of the patient's illness and choice of the best bet. In short, once the symptoms are identified and a list of options compiled, the first step in the decision is to screen out unreasonable options (diseases) on the basis of their incompatibility with the presenting symptoms. If more than one option survives this process, the second step is to choose from among the survivors on the basis of the relative merit of one over the others for accounting for the symptoms.

The laboratory provides additional evidence for the two-step nature of decisionmaking. The landmark study was done by John Payne (1976). Subjects were required to examine information about options (apartments) in order to make a choice among them. The number of options and the amount of information about them was varied and the subjects' decision strategies were inferred from the order in which they examined the information. It was found that for simple decisions, few options and little information, subjects appeared to balance the pros and cons of each option against the pros and cons of the other options in an effort to determine which was best. However, when the decision was at all complex, more options and more information, subjects appeared first to screen out the less desirable options and then to make a choice from among the survivors by comparing the latters' relative pros and cons.

Payne's (1976) results were of particular interest to investigators of consumer choice. Lussier and Olshavsky (1979) replicated his results in the context of choices among portable typewriters. Olshavsky (1979), studying choices among apartments, and Crow et al. (1980), studying choices made by industrial buyers, also replicated Payne's results. Additionally, Lussier and Olshavsky (1979) and Olshavsky (1979) and Olshavsky (1979) showed that subjects differentially weight information to such an extent that the less important information sometimes had no impact at all on the decisions.

All these studies found that screening could best be described as a conjunctive strategy that required the option to meet certain criteria in order to survive to become part of the choice set, although sometimes subjects examined only the information that was relevant to the most important criteria and sometimes the conjunctive rule was not applied very strictly.

Payne (1976) interpreted his results as reflecting subjects' attempts to reduce the information processing demands of complex decisions (p. 384). That is, he made no fundamental differentiation between screening and choice; screening merely was a way of simplifying the choice task. Lussier and Olshavsky (1979) made the differentiation, but in spite of this, the tendency has been to regard screening as just another simplifying heuristic that permits decisionmakers to reach a decision without undue strain (e.g., Park, 1978; Slovic et al., 1985). However, as we shall see, this interpretation of screening mistakenly trivializes the role that it plays in decisionmaking.

RESEARCH ON SCREENING

Screening is a special case of sorting and categorizing. In the latter the target is evaluated in terms of both its similarities and its dissimilarities to categorical exemplars or prototypes (Oden, 1987). In contrast, the empirical evidence suggests that screening is based exclusively on evaluation of a particular kind of dissimilarity (incompatibility) between the characteristics of an option and private or organizational criteria (Beach and Strom, 1989).

Although screening, as a general conjunctive strategy, was included as a step in earlier models of consumer choice (Lussier and Olshavsky, 1979; Park, 1978), only recently has the mechanism been theoretically developed and research begun. Theoretical development has occurred in the context of image theory (Beach, 1990; Beach and Mitchell, 1987, 1990; Mitchell and Beach, 1990; Mitchell et al., 1986), which is a new, two-step theory of decisionmaking. The mechanism for the screening step is called the *compatibility test*, and the mechanism for the choice step is called the *profitability test*. The compatibility test is a single strategy that is used for all screening decisions. The profitability test is a multiplicity of strategies, the use of any single one of which is contingent on the circumstances.

The components of the compatibility test's strategy are as follows:

Violations When an attribute of an option fails to meet the critical value on a relevant criterion or is in some other way incompatible with the criterion (Beach, 1990), a violation is said to occur. The option's overall compatibility with the criteria decreases as a function of the (weighted) number of violations the decisionmaker attributes to it in the course of screening it.

Rejection threshold The rejection threshold is the minimum compatibility that the decisionmaker will tolerate before rejecting the option.

Decision rule If the (negative) weighted sum of the violations exceeds the (negative) rejection threshold, the option is rejected, otherwise it is accepted.

Compatibility is measured by

$$C = \sum_{t=1}^{n} \sum_{c=1}^{m} W_c V_{tc}; \qquad V_{tc} = -1 \text{ or } 0, .00 \leq W \leq 1.00$$

where compatibility C is zero when the option has no violations and decreases (is more and more negative) as the number of violations increases; t is a relevant attribute of the option; c is a relevant criterion dimension; V_{tc} is a violation of criterion c by attribute t of the option; and W_c is the importance weight for each of the c relevant criteria—W_c is between and including .00 and 1.00. Thus, while the violations are all-or-none (-1 or 0), violations of some criteria may count more than others (W_c) and compatibility is a continuous scale between 0 and $-mn$, where m is the number of relevant criteria and n is the number of the attribute's relevant attributes (an attribute may violate more than one criterion).

The compatibility test evaluates candidates sequentially, and thus one at a time, and it only screens them; it does not choose, except by default when there is only one survivor of the test. In addition, the test gives negative weight to violations but gives no weight to nonviolations, rejection is determined solely by violations. This means that the traditional concept of maximization as a decision rule does not apply. Therefore, the acceptability of the option must be determined by another standard, the rejection threshold.

Research on the Compatibility Test

A clue to the primacy of violations in screening is illustrated by comments from Payne's (1976) subjects as they evaluated alternative apartments to rent. For example,

> Apartment E. The rent for apartment E is $140. Which is a good note. The noise level for this apartment is high. That would almost deter me right there. Ah, I don't like a lot of noise. And, if it's high, it must be pretty bad. Which means, you couldn't sleep. I would just put that one aside right there. I wouldn't look any further than that. (p. 375)

Or,

> I'm going to look at landlord attitude. In H it's fair. In D it's poor. B it's fair, and A it's good. In L the attitude is poor. In K it's poor. In J it's good, and in I it's poor. So, one of them . . . is poor. So, that's important to me. . . . So, I'm not going to live any place where it's poor. (p. 379)

Stronger evidence about the pivotal role of violations comes from a study (Beach and Strom, 1989) in which subjects were presented descriptions of jobs. Jobs were inspected one at a time and the information about each was presented sequentially. Each piece of information either violated or did not violate one of 16 criteria and the order in which the violations and nonviolations occurred in the sequence was manipulated. Subjects were instructed to look at successive pieces of information about a job until they could decide whether to reject it. In effect, they were instructed to screen the jobs, consigning the survivors to the choice set. The results showed that rejection of the jobs was almost wholly accounted for by violations and that nonviolations did not compensate for violations.

Subjects seldom examined all of the information about a job. Rather, there was a rejection threshold of four to five violations that was consistent across jobs. There was weak evidence for some kind of acceptance threshold when fewer than four violations were observed. (Without some sort of acceptance threshold the decisionmaker would never accept even a perfect option; but rather would continue searching indefinitely for reasons to reject it.) However, the acceptance threshold was quite variable, in contrast to the stable rejection threshold.

Other research on the compatibility test also has shown that violations are pivotal in screening decisions (Potter and Beach, in press; van Zee et al., 1992), as well as rated acceptability (Beach et al., 1988a) and rated attractiveness (Rediker, 1988) of options. Moreover, van Zee et al. (1992) demonstrated that the information used in screening has virtually no influence on subsequent prechoice evaluations of surviving options or the choice from among them. Subjects apparently regarded screening and choice as two different tasks; they treated information used in the former as largely irrelevant to the latter.

Beach et al. (1988a) had executives of three large commercial firms describe the values that guided their respective organization's business decisions. For each firm separately, the reported values were used as criteria and a series of options for introducing a new product line were designed. Different options violated more or fewer of the criteria. The options were then presented to the executives who were asked to rate each of them in terms of their compatibility with the firm, i.e., how acceptable they would be to the executive's firm as a way of introducing the new product. The prediction was that the ratings would be determined by each option's number of violations. It was found that in all three firms the predicted ratings were indistinguishable from the executives' ratings. That is, an outside observer would be indifferent between knowing the number of violations or asking an executive about the acceptability of a particular option for a given firm (Turing, 1950). Similarly, in the context of a laboratory study of decisions about business acquisitions, Rediker (1988) found a correlation of $r = -.95$ ($p < .01$) between the number of violations attributed to options and subjects' ratings of the attractiveness of those options for acquisition.

The most recent study in this series is somewhat tangential but instructive. Potter and Beach (in press) told decisionmakers that the survivors of their screening efforts had become unavailable for choice and that no new options were forthcoming even though a single option had to be selected. This required them to rescreen the previously rejected options in order to select an option. As one might expect, most decisionmakers merely singled out the least incompatible of the rejects rather than forming a new choice set. Surprisingly, however, it was found that rescreening involved not just an adjustment in the rejection threshold sufficient to allow rejected options to become survivors, it also involved an adjustment in the weights (W_c) of the criteria. The end result was that by adjusting the weights, the threshold did not have to be adjusted as much as it otherwise would have—shades of cognitive dissonance! The authors' conjecture was that having to lower one's standards (threshold) is stressful, but the stress can be reduced by rationalizing that the criteria were not all that important, anyway.

RESEARCH ON CHOICE

Choice has been the ultimate focus of most behavioral decision research, usually in the context of investigating the expected utility maximization model. However, when they have bothered to look, researchers have found that decisionmakers use a variety of choice strategies, and that rather than being the sole strategy used, the expected utility maximization strategy is not even the primary strategy used. [In one laboratory study subjects did not base choices on expected value even when they were instructed about it and even when it was computed for them for each option (Lichtenstein et al., 1969).] Recent research has looked more closely at this variety of choice strategies and at the contingencies that promote use of one rather than another.

In image theory (Beach, 1990; Beach and Mitchell, 1987, 1990), choice is accomplished using the profitability test. Unlike the compatibility test, the profitability test is not a single strategy. Instead, it is the decisionmaker's repertory of choice strategies, and these may be quite different from one decisionmaker to another. The purpose of the compatibility test is to screen out unacceptable options. The purpose of the profitability test is to choose the best of whatever options, if any, survive the compatibility test. In many cases "best" means the option that promises more of some desirable outcome, hence the term "profitability" for the test.

The forerunner of the profitability test was Beach and Mitchell's (1978) strategy selection model. This model was proposed as a way of accounting for both Payne's (1976) findings and the common observation that decisionmakers approach choices in a variety of ways (Mintzberg, 1975; Selznick, 1957). When image theory was developed, the strategy selection model was modified slightly to fit into the new theory as the profitability test.

The strategy selection model is a contingency model (Fiedler, 1967). Selection of a choice strategy is contingent on both the characteristics of the decisionmaker and the characteristics of the choice problem. The decisionmaker possesses a unique repertory of choice strategies from which one is selected for use on the choice at hand. The model is concerned with the factors that determine the decisionmaker's selection of one strategy rather than another. That is, the model is concerned with the metadecision about how to go about making a choice decision: should one toss a coin, ask a friend, imagine possible scenarios, weigh pros and cons, do a cost/benefit analysis, calculate expected utilities?

According to the model, the selected strategy is the one for which the potential benefits (the possible consequences of making the right choice balanced against the possible consequences of making the wrong choice) most greatly exceed the potential costs of using the strategy (the amount of time, effort, and money required to execute it). The consequences of making a right or wrong choice are dependent on the nature of the choice problem itself: whether the choice is similar to a decision that has been made in the past, whether the arguments for and against the options are clearly understood, whether there are numerous options, and whether these options involve many actions and/or many possible outcomes. Additionally, the consequences of the choice depend on the characteristics of the environment in which the choice is embedded: whether the choice is or is not irreversible, whether it can be implemented incrementally, its significance (including the consequences of its success or failure), whether the decisionmaker is or is not accountable for the outcome, and whether time or money constraints have been imposed. The cost of using a strategy depends on the execution time and effort it demands, as well as by the knowledge, ability, and motivation of the decisionmaker. Complex strategies tend to be more costly to use than simple ones.

To make this bit more intuitively understandable, consider a choice problem that is familiar, fairly clear, rather simple, reversible, incremental, and not very significant, for which the decisionmaker is not particularly accountable, and for which there are no time or money constraints. Clearly the consequences of making the wrong choice are not very serious. In such circumstances, the decisionmaker is not going to be motivated to use a strategy that requires a lot of time and effort. Thus, strategies like computation of expected utility or even extensive cost-benefit analysis seem unnecessarily "costly," given the nature of the choice problem. Much more reasonable are simple, quick-and-dirty strategies like simply following advice or imagining what might happen if one or the other option were chosen. Were the conditions surrounding the choice reversed, a more "costly" strategy would make sense.

Suppose you were choosing a research assistant from a pool of previously screened applicants. This is a familiar kind of decision. It is fairly clearcut. It is simple. You can change assistants if things do not work out. Implementation probably is not incremental, although it could be if you insisted on a trial period before making a final decision. Although the choice is significant, it is not earth-shaking. You are not particularly accountable to anyone else about the ultimate success of the choice or about how it is made, although you want to avoid appearing arbitrary, sexist, or anything else negative. You may have a deadline, but it probably is not absolute. And, the money involved is the amount of the assistant's salary, which probably is both fixed and not very much.

Choosing an assistant under these circumstances would not be particularly harrowing, and you could use any number of rather simple strategies. Perhaps the advice of someone who has worked with the applicants. Or even the first applicant to apply. Or the applicant who pesters you the most (or the least). Or the one that you can imagine getting on with the best. Certainly you would be unlikely to invest in a formal, pencil-and-paper analysis that meticulously compared their various strengths and weaknesses or that resulted in construction of a detailed decision tree. In short, your choice strategy would match the demands of the choice problem and the environment in which it was embedded.

Research on the Selection Model (the Profitability Test)

Christensen-Szalanski (1978, 1980) formalized the Beach and Mitchell (1978) model and derived a series of precise predictions that he proceeded to test. The tests were supportive of the model and lead to a simple conclusion: Within the limits of their repertories and abilities, decision-makers select choice strategies that are commensurate with choice tasks—they do not haul out their "big guns" for trivial choices or vice versa. Among the big guns that they seldom haul out is the expected utility maximization strategy.

Common sense suggests that the strategy selection model and Christensen-Szalanski's (1978, 1980) results are right. However, there is still the question of how the contingencies of the choice problem and of the choice environment influence selection of a choice strategy.

McAllister et al. (1979) began investigation of task contingencies in a series of experiments that manipulated problem significance, choice reversibility, and decisionmaker accountability. Subjects were given business choices to make and were provided with strategies with which to make them. The strategies differed in the time and effort required to execute them. It was found that significance, irreversibility, and accountability all influenced strategy selection, and that there were no interactions. The more significant and irreversible the choice, and the more highly accountable the decisionmaker, the more complex (requiring more time and effort) were the strategies the subjects selected to make the choices.

Huffman (1978) performed similar studies varying problem familiarity and complexity, choice significance and reversibility, and decisionmaker accountability. Overall, her results showed that the perceived appropriateness of using costly complex strategies is determined by the characteristics of both the choice problem and the choice environment; the more demanding the characteristics of both, the more appropriate it is to use a complex choice strategy. Moreover, it was found that while decisionmakers regard the complex strategies as more likely to result in a correct choice, they clearly recognized that they were costly to use, a result also obtained by Christensen-Szalanski (1978, 1980).

These studies were followed by two more: Smith et al. (1982) found that time constraints (a characteristic of the environment) affect decisionmakers' confidence in their ability to execute complex strategies properly, and thereby affect strategy selection. Waller and Mitchell (1984) found that ambiguity and greater significance of the choice to the decisionmaker (characteristics of the problem) resulted in selection of more costly, complex strategies.

It is interesting to note in passing that after examining the results of 45 studies from 41 published papers, Ford et al. (1989) conclude that one reason so many studies have observed decisionmakers using simplistic choice strategies is that the experiments give them no reason to do otherwise. They argue that this is what would be expected on the basis of the strategy selection model.

Finally, after conducting a series of simulations and a related experiment involving real decisionmakers, Payne et al. (1988) conclude that

> The experimental results clearly demonstrate a shift in processing strategies with variation in context. People demonstrated an ability to shift processing to take advantage of problem structure so as to reduce processing load while maintaining accuracy (p. 545). . . . people adapted to time pressure by accelerating processing, increasing the selectivity of processing, and moving toward more attribute-based processing. (p. 546)

A move to attribute-based processing implies a shift to simpler choice strategies as time constraints increase, which agrees with the predictions of the strategy selection model and with results on the effects of deadlines obtained by Christensen-Szalanski (1980) and by Smith et al. (1984).

THE FOURTH REVOLUTION

The first two revolutions, resulting from recognition that evaluation is limited and that decisionmakers have multiple choice strategies, together with the ongoing third revolution, dethronement of choice and recognition of the importance of screening, have resulted in a description of decisionmaking that is markedly different from the conventional description of just a few years ago. However, these revolutions are only preliminary to the revolution that is at hand.

Not only are unaided decisions often based on limited evaluation; not only are decisions made in many different ways; not only are decisions largely determined by screening; it also appears that decisionmakers face far fewer real decisions than previously has been thought. Indeed, decisionmaking in general, and choice in particular, may play a surprisingly minor role in any inclusive account of human behavior.

To argue that people avoid decisions, especially important decisions (Janis, 1988; Janis and Mann, 1977), somewhat misses the point. The fact is, many decision tasks recur with sufficient frequency that the decisionmaker need only make decisions when they are encountered for the first time and can rely on past experience thereafter. That is, once a decision leads to a successful procedure for dealing with the task, that procedure can be retained for use when the task is reencountered. Indeed, in many cases the decisionmaker never even makes those early decisions—someone instructs the decisionmaker about what to do in that particular situation. This, of course, is the whole point of training.

Image theory (Beach, 1990; Beach and Mitchell, 1990) incorporates the existence of preformulated procedures, calling them "policies." The idea is that when a decision task is encountered, the decisionmaker uses its features to probe memory (Beach, 1964; Hintzman, 1986) to determine whether this specific situation, or one like it, has been encountered before. If it is recognized, the procedure that was decided on previously is part of the memory and can be used again if it was successful (or modified if it was unsuccessful or only marginally successful). This ready-to-hand procedure is a policy for dealing with that particular task (Beach, 1990; Mitchell and Beach, 1990).

Only if the encountered decision task is unlike any previous task, or if the existing policy was unsuccessful and cannot be remedied, is the decisionmaker forced into making a decision about what to do. It is here that the decisionmaker engages in two-step decisionmaking, and it clearly does not happen very frequently. By the time decisionmakers become adults, they have encountered so many different decision tasks, and have been trained to deal with so many more, that any new task is likely to be similar to a recognizable task. This means that a policy is nearly always available, if only for use as a starting point for formulating a new policy, thus rendering a new decision unnecessary.

It primarily is in unfamiliar circumstances, a changing environment, or a new environment such as a new job, that previously successful policies may not work. However, the decisionmaker seldom is aware of their shortcomings until they fail—thus the awkward behavior of people who are out of their element; they expect previously successful behavior to work in the new setting. When the behavior proves inadequate or inappropriate, they must search for or craft a new policy. Image theory provides for this in a mechanism for monitoring the implementation of policies (and new decisions) and for revising them when they show signs of failure.

The idea of preformulated decisions in the form of policies ties decisionmaking in general, and image theory in particular, to work on scripts (Golambos, 1986; Schank and Abelson, 1977), scenarios (Jungermann, 1985), and knowledge representation (Dinsmore, 1987; Pennington and Hastie, 1986, 1988). Moreover, the many years of research on learning, before it so resolutely divorced itself from recognizable human experience, spoke to what we now call policy formulation and use. Learning, especially skill learning, consists of formulating and perfecting a procedure for successfully accomplishing a task—presumably by a series of decisions and revisions in light of feedback (reinforcement). Stimulus and response generalization are learning theory terms for recognition that a task is sufficiently similar to an earlier task to call for a similar procedure. *Extinction* is the term for recognition that the procedure is unsuccessful. This is not the place for translation of learning theory jargon into decision theory jargon, nor for reviewing the ties between decisionmaking and scripts, scenarios, or knowledge representations (For such, see Beach, 1990, 1991.)

The point is, there is a very large literature that addresses policy formulation and policy use by individuals, the sheer volume of which indicates the importance of policy in human behavior. In fact, policy probably accounts for most of most people's behavior, and decisionmaking becomes necessary only when policy fails on those rare occasions when a unique situation arises, necessitating formulation of a new policy. Moreover, even when decisionmaking actually takes place, it usually stops with screening; choice is necessary only when screening passes more than one option and there is a need to break the tie.

The prevalence of policy-based behavior has been examined by Gary Klein and his colleagues in the context of "natural" decision settings, only they use the term *recognition-primed* decisions rather than policy-based behavior. Klein (in press) summarizes the findings of five field studies of decisionmaking by fire fighters, tank platoon leaders, and design engineers. First, the proportion of decisions identified as "recognition-primed" ranged from 39 to 80 percent. Second, the more experienced the decisionmakers were, the higher the observed percentage of "recognition-primed" decisions. Third, examination of predecision deliberation showed that decisionmakers who had a good deal of experience with the situation focused on situational assessment rather than on options, and decisionmakers who had less experience did exactly the opposite.

Klein (in press) draws a parallel between these results and findings in problem-solving research where experts focus on recognizing the structure of problems so that familiar solution techniques can be brought to bear, while novices focus on the surface characteristics of problems, frequently failing to find a solution.

In an extension of Klein's research, Thorsden et al. (1990) examined decision points in the course of the planning of a military exercise. As it turned out, there were only 27 distinct points, of which 26 appeared to be made on the basis of recognition of the problem and retrieval of a solution from memory. Only one decision involved weighing the relative merits of alternative options. Of course, military training is aimed at providing experience with a broad range of problems that might be encountered during actual operations and supplying plausible solutions to these problems. Therefore, policy-based behavior may be more common in the military than elsewhere. Moreover, in Klein's analyses no distinction is made between recognition-primed (policy-based) decisions and screening decisions, so many of the decisions identified as recognitional may in fact be screening decisions. However, we suspect that policy-based behavior, which passes for decisionmaking, is much more common than generally is appreciated and that decisions in the form of screening and choice are, relatively, uncommon.

Fiedler and his associates (Fiedler and Garcia, 1987: McGuire, 1987) also have examined policy, although they have not used this term. Fiedler and Garcia's (1987) cognitive resource theory turns on a simple finding: Stress, particularly boss stress, appears to decrease the ability of leaders to use their creativity and intellect in problem solving and forces them to fall back up on experience (policy). It probably is the case that this often causes no difficulty. However, when experience is not wholly adequate and creativity and intellect are required to get the job done properly, the leader may be unable to provide what is needed.

The problem appears to lie in the allocation of limited intellectual resources—when stressed, the leader devotes valuable resources to worrying about how his or her boss will evaluate performance, thereby reducing the resources available for creatively solving problems. If the leader has adequate experience on which to fall back, all may be well and the group may succeed in its task. However, if experience is lacking, or if the leader persists in trying to be creative in the face of inadequate cognitive resources, it is unlikely that all will be well and that success is possible.

Research by a student of Fiedler's, Mark McGuire (1987), highlights what goes on. ROTC (Reserve Officers Training Corps) students were given a task to perform under the watchful eye of a uniformed army officer or under the supervion of another student. The presumption was that the officer's presence would induce stress, a presumption that turned out to be sound. Moreover, the students were given an IQ test that differentiated between problem soving ability (fluid intelligence) and knowledge (concrete intelligence). It was found that stress interfered with the use of problem solving ability, but that use of knowledge, of experience, was unimpaired.

Of course, the work of Fiedler and his colleagues has been directed particularly to how leaders use their cognitive resources under stress, primarily boss stress. However, the results speak to the policy issue because they show that policies are durable under stress while decisionmaking is not. Leaders who are under stress behave as though their cognitive resources are restricted (see also Nichols-Hoppe and Beach, 1990). As a result they, perhaps wisely, fall back on experience (policies) rather than trying to come up with new solutions to problems (decisionmaking). If the policies they possess are equal to the task, success is possible. If the policies are inadequate, or if the leader attempts to be decisive under stress, the likelihood of failure increases. In short, decisionmaking is rather fragile, and when things get tight it often is best to rely on policy—providing of course that the policy is itself adequate.

In summary, most behavior is guided by past experience in the form of preformulated policies. Failure, or absence, of a policy calls for a decision about what to do. Seldom are there many available options to decide among, but in any case the first step is to screen them to cull out those that obviously are inadequate or inappropriate. If there are no survivors, more options must be found (and screened) or the rejects must be rescreened. If there is only one survivor, it is the decided-upon option. Only if there are two or more survivors does choice come into things at all, and then merely to break the tie by selecting the option that offers the most promise of success. Even at that, because the choice set contains only those options that survived screening, the options from which the choice must be made tend to be fairly similar to one another. As a result, it often may not be particularly crucial which one is chosen—any one may prove sufficient. In short, choice, the most thoroughly studied and elaborately modeled aspect of decisionmaking, is perhaps the least common and sometimes the least important aspect of the entire process.

The Next Revolution

Each of the three revolutions discussed above has shifted conventional thinking about decision behavior further away from the economic paradigm and closer to a psychological description.[1] The fourth revolution is the logical next shift in that direction.

Everything discussed thus far is a harbinger of the fourth revolution. In addition, two other events suggest that the revolution already is under way. These events are two recent conferences held specifically to discuss dissatisfaction with the present state of behavioral decision theory and research and to explore alternatives. The first conference was held at Leiden University, The Netherlands, in April 1988 (Beach, 1988b). Attended almost exclusively by European and American academics, the pretext for the conference was to consider the appropriateness of the expected utility maximization strategy for unique, short-run decisions (Lopes, 1981). There is evidence that the strategy is not appropriate—not on theoretical grounds (Lopes, 1981; Oden, 1988) and not on empirical grounds (Adelbratt and Montgomery, 1980; Keren and Wagenaar, 1987; Wagenaar, 1988).

Indeed, as the conference proceeded it became clear many participants were of the opinion that the expected utility maximization strategy applies in only the most limited circumstances. This strategy reduces all decisions into choice dilemmas (gambles) in which each option is reduced to valued

[1]The reader may consider the body of research on heuristics and biases (Kahnemen et al., 1979; Tversky and Kahneman, 1974) to constitute a tie between behavioral decision research and theory and cognitive research. While it is true that the opportunity exists, or at least existed, for heuristics and biases to provide such a tie, it has not happened. Biases merely are descriptions of the deviations of observed subjectively judged values from the values that the researcher deems to be correct, usually justified by some statistical model. Heuristics are the hypothesized causes for the biases. As such, they would appear to be the theoretical component of the heuristic and bias literature. However, for reasons that are not altogether clear, heursitics never were elaborated and developed theoretically. The result is that they are theoretically shallow and remain unlinked to broader psychological concepts, including concepts in cognitive science. Although heuristics are beloved by decision researchers and by the authors of introductory psychology textbooks, they have not been taken very seriously by cognitive scientists, with the result that they have had virtually no impact on mainline cognitive theory.

outcomes and probabilities. This view was regarded by conferees as too restrictive to encompass the variety of decisions that real decisionmakers encounter in the course of their private lives and their occupations. (Owning a hammer does not make every problem a nail.) The primary psychological characteristics of gambles are irreversibility (once a decision is made, one cannot back out) and uncontrollability (one cannot influence the outcome). The research shows that decisionmakers do not characterize many of their own decisions in this way, and when they do, they regard those decisions as difficult and stressful. Instead, they view most decisions as points in a managed flow of acts and events that has continuity with the past, defines the present, and is directed toward achievement of goals in the future. The latter characterization is critically different from the way in which economic theory characterizes decisions. No doubt attempts could be made to stretch the expected utility logic to accommodate this broader view of decisions, in the spirit of prospect theory (Kahneman and Tversky, 1979) or regret theory (Bell, 1982; Loomis and Sugden, 1982). But doing so misses the point. The recurring need to patch up the economic logic is a symptom of its inadequacy. At this point it is difficult to justify retention of the economic logic even to preserve the continuity of the research it has engendered or to save the infant decision aiding industry. Although conferees were ambivalent about abandoning economic logic, it appeared to many that the logic no longer is sufficient for the task that behavioral decision theory and research has set itself.

The second conference, held in Dayton, Ohio, in September 1989, was less anguished than the Leiden conference (Klein and Calderwood, in press). Many of these conferees were systems engineers, design engineers, human factors researchers, or in other ways involved in the design of command and control systems and other information systems that heavily involve humans making crucial decisions. Among these people there was strong agreement that the existing behavioral decision literature largely is irrelevant to understanding and aiding real-world decisionmaking. They complained of the lack or correspondence between what they read in academic journals and what they observe on their jobs. Their call was for a more "naturalistic" theory that would help them understand the cognitive processes by which decisions are made in the course of people's daily activities. As the discussion progressed, it became clear that any attempt to answer this call is de facto to embark on yet a fourth revolution in behavioral decison theory and research.

The story of behavioral decision theory and research is the story of a fading love affair with economics. Because economics is about decisions, it is not surprising that behavioral decisionmaking was among the first to succumb to the charms of economic theory. First, but not last. Most social sciences are flirting with the "imperial science," some in hope that its simplicity and apparent precision will rub off, others in hope it will provide a unified theory of behavior. Having been among the first thus seduced, it is fitting that behavioral decision researchers be among the first to acknowledge that these hopes are in vain. Then we must place our hope elsewhere. We must look beyond economics to return to our psychological roots in the cognitive and organizational sciences, and, by recognizing our natural kinship with systems engineering and information science, to broaden the definition and scope of our enterprise. Three revolutions were required to drive this lesson home, but perhaps it has been learned. The rumble in the distance is the next revolution.

References

Adelbratt, T. and Montgomery, H. (1980). Attractiveness of decision rules. *Acta Psychologica, 45*, 177–185.

Beach, L. R. (1964). Recognition, assimilation, and identification of objects. *Psychological Monographs, 78,* 22–37.

Beach, L. R. (1990). *Image theory: Decision making in personal and organizational contexts.* Chichester, UK: Wiley.

Beach, L. R. (1991). Epistemic strategies: Causal thinking in judgment and forecasting. In G. Wright and F. Bolger (Eds.), *Expertise and decision support.* London: Plenum Press.

Beach, L. R., and Mitchell, T. R. (1978). A contingency model for the selection of decision strategies. *Academy of Management Review, 3*, 439–449.

Beach, L. R., and Mitchell, T. R. (1987). Image theory: Principles, goals, and plans in decison making. *Acta Psychologica, 66*, 201–220.

Beach, L. R., and Mitchell, T. R. (1990). Image theory: A behavioral theory of decisions in organizations. In B. M. Staw and L. L. Cummings (Eds.), *Research in organizational behavior* (Vol. 12). Greenwich, CT: JAI Press.

Beach, L. R., Smith, B., Lundell, J., and Mitchell, T. R. (1988a). Image theory: Descriptive sufficiency of a simple rule for the compatibility test. *Journal of Behavioral Decision Making, 1,* 17–28.

Beach, L. R. and Strom, E. (1989). A toadstool among the mushrooms: Screening decisons and image theory's compatibility test. *Acta Psychologica, 72,* 1–12.

Beach, L. R., Vlek, C., and Wagenaar, W. A. (1988b). *Models and methods for unique versus repeated decison making* (Leiden Psychological Reports: Experimental Psychology, EP04-88). Leiden, The Netherlands: Leiden University, Psychology Department.

Bell, D. (1982). Regret in decision making under uncertainty. *Operations Research, 30,* 961–981.

Christensen-Szalanski, J. J. J. (1978). Problem-solving strategies: A selection mechanism, some implications, and some data. *Organizational Behavior and Human Performance, 22,* 307–323.

Christensen-Szalanski, J. J. J. (1980). A further examination of the selection of problem-solving strategies: The effects of deadlines and analytic aptitudes. *Organizational Behavior and Human Performance, 25,* 107–122.

Crow, L. E., Olshavsky, R. W., and Summers, J. O. (1980). Industrial buyers' choice strategies: A protocol analysis. *Journal of Marketing Research, 17,* 34–44.

Dinsmore, J. (1987). Mental spaces from a functional perspective. *Cognitive Science, 11,* 1–21.

Eddy, D. M., and Clanton, C. H. (1982). The art of diagnosis: Solving the clinicopathological exercise. *The New England Journal of Medicine, 306,* 1263–1268.

Fiedler, F. E. (1967). *A Theory of Leadership Effectiveness.* New York: McGraw-Hill.

Fiedler, F. E., and Garcia, J. E. (1987). *New approaches to effective leadership.* New York: Wiley.

Ford, J. K., Schmitt, N., Schechtman, S. L., Hults, B. M., and Doherty, M. L. (1989). Process tracing methods: Contributions, problems, and neglected research questions. *Organizational Behavior and Human Decision Processes, 43,* 75–117.

Golambos, J. A. (1986). Knowledge structures for common activities. In J. A. Golambos, R. P. Abelson, and J. B. Black (Eds.), *Knowledge Structures.* Hillsdale, NJ: Erlbaum.

Hintzman, D. L. (1986). 'Schema abstraction' in a multiple-trace memory model. *Psychological Review, 93,* 411–428.

Huffman, M. D. (1978). *The effect of decision task characteristics on decision behavior* (Technical Report No. 78-16). Seattle, WA: University of Washington, Department of Psychology.

Isenberg, D. J. (1984). How senior managers think. *Harvard Business Review* (Nov.–Dec.), 81–90.

Janis, I. L. (1988). *Crucial Decisions.* New York: Free Press.

Janis, I. L., and Mann, L. (1977). *Decision-making: A psychological analysis of conflict, choice, and commitment.* New York: Free Press.

Jungermann, H. (1985). Inferential processes in the construction of scenarios. *Journal of Forecasting, 4,* 321–327.

Kahneman, D., and Tversky, A. (1979). Prospect theory: An analysis of decision under risk. *Econometrica, 47,* 263–291.

Keren, G. B., and Wagenaar, W. A. (1987). Violation of utility theory in unique and repeated gambles. *Journal of Experimental Psychology: Learning, Memory, and Cognition, 13,* 29–38.

Klein, G. A. (in press). Recognition-primed decisions. In W. Rouse (Ed.), *Advances in man-machine systems research* (Vol. 5). Greenwich, CT: JAI Press.

Klein, G. A., and Calderwood, R. (Eds.) (in press). *Decision making in action: Models and methods.* Norwood, NJ: Ablex.

Lichtenstein, S., Slovic, P., and Zink, D. (1969). Effect of instruction in expected value on optimality of gambling decisions. *Journal of Experimental Psychology, 79,* 236–240.

Loomis, G., and Sugden, R. (1982). Regret theory: An alternative theory of rational choice under uncertainty. *The Economic Journal, 92,* 805–824.

Lopes, L. L. (1981). Decision making in the shortrun. *Journal of Experimental Psychology: Human Learning and Memory, 7,* 377–385.

Lussier, D. A., and Olshavsky, R. W. (1979). Task complexity and contingent processing in brand choice. *Journal of Consumer Research, 6*, 154–165.
McAllister, D., Mitchell, T. R., and Beach, L. R. (1979). The contingency model for selection of decision strategies: An empirical test of the effects of significance, accountability, and reversibility. *Organizational Behavior and Human Performance, 24*, 228–244.
McGuire, M. A. (1987). *The contribution of intelligence to leadership performance on an in-basket test.* Unpublished master's thesis. University of Washington, Seattle, WA.
Mintzberg, H. (1975). The manager's job: Folklore and fact. *Harvard Business Review* (July–Aug.), 49–61.
Mitchell, T. R., and Beach, L. R. (1990). " . . . do I love thee? Let me count . . . " Toward an understanding of intuitive and automatic decision making. *Organizational Behavior and Human Decision Processes, 47*, 1–20.
Mitchell, T. R., Rediker, K. J., and Beach, L. R. (1986). Image theory and its implications for organizational decision making. In H. P. Sims and D. A. Gioia (Eds.), *The Thinking Organization*. San Francisco: Jossey-Bass.
Nichols-Hoppe, K. T., and Beach, L. R. (1990). The effects of test anxiety and task variables on predecisional information search. *Journal of Research in Personality, 24*, 163–172.
Oden, G. C. (1987). Concept, knowledge, and thought. *Annual Review of Psychology, 38*, 203–227.
Oden, G. C. (1988). Heuristic decision strategies in unique versus repeated gambling. Paper presented at the Leiden Conference on Models and Methods for Unique Versus Repeated Decision Making, University of Leiden, The Netherlands (April).
Olshavsky, R. W. (1979). Task complexity and contingent processing in decision making: a replication and extension. *Organizational Behavior and Human Performance, 24*, 300–316.
Park, C. W. (1978). A conflict resolution choice model. *Journal of Consumer Research, 5*, 124–137.
Payne, J. W. (1976). Task complexity and contingent processing in decision making: An information search and protocol analysis. *Organizational Behavior and Human Performance, 16*, 366–387.
Payne, J. W. (1982). Contingent decision behavior. *Psychological Bulletin, 92*, 382–402.
Payne, J. W., Bettman, J. R., and Johnson, E. J. (1988). Adaptive strategy selection in decision making. *Journal of Experimental Psychology: Learning, Memory and Cognition, 14*, 534–552.
Pennington, N., and Hastie, R. (1986). Evidence evaluation in complex decision making. *Journal of Personality and Social Psychology, 51*, 242–258.
Pennington, N., and Hastie, R. (1988). Explanation-based decision making: Effects of memory structure on judgment. *Journal of Experimental Psychology: Learning, Memory and Cognition, 14*, 521–533.
Potter, R. E., and Beach, L. R. (in press). *Decision making when the acceptable options become unavailable. Organizational behavior and human decision processes.*

Rediker, K. J. (1988). *The influence of strength of culture and decision optionality on strategic decision making: An exploratory application of image theory.* Unpublished doctoral dissertation, University of Washington, Seattle.

Schank, R. C., and Abelson, R. P. (1977). *Scripts, plans, goals and understanding.* Hillsdale, NJ: Erlbaum.

Selznick, P. (1957). *Leadership in administration: A sociological interpretation.* Evanston, IL: Row, Peterson.

Simon, H. A. (1955). A behavioral model of rational choice. *Quarterly Journal of Economics, 69*, 99–118.

Slovic, P., Lichtenstein, S., and Fischoff, B. (1985). Decision making. In R. C. Atkinson, R. J. Herrnstein, G. Lindzey, and D. Luce (Eds.), *Stevens' handbook of experimental psychology*, (2nd ed). New York: Wiley.

Smith, J. F., Mitchell, T. R., and Beach, L. R. (1982). A cost-benefit mechanism for selecting problem solving strategies: Some extensions and empirical tests. *Organizational Behavior and Human Performance, 29*, 370–396.

Thorsden, M., Galushka, J., Klein, G. A., Young, S., and Brezovic, C. (1990). *A knowledge elicitation study of military planning* (Technical Report No. 876). Yellow Springs, OH: Klein Associates.

Turing, A. M. (1950). Computing machinery and intelligence. *Mind, 59*, 433–460.

Tversky, A., and Kahneman, D. (1974). Judgment under uncertainty: Heuristics and biases. *Science, 185*, 453–458.

van Zee, E. H., Paluchowski, T. F., and Beach, L. R. (1992). The effects of screening and task partitioning upon evaluations of decision options. *Journal of Behavioral Decision Making, 5,* 1–25.

Wagenaar, W. A. (1988). *Pardoxes of Gambling Behavior.* Hove, UK: Erlbaum.

Waller, W. S., and Mitchell, T. R. (1984). The effects of context on the selection of decision strategies for the cost variance investigation. *Organizational Behavior and Human Performance, 33*, 397–413.

12

An Integrative Theory of Leadership

Martin M. Chemers
Department of Psychology
Claremont McKenna College

INTRODUCTION

The leadership literature has often been described as fragmented and contradictory (Calder, 1977; Chemers, 1983, 1987; Fiedler and House, 1988). A lack of integration across theories and approaches ultimately diminishes the utility of research findings for both scientist and practitioner. A successful integration should illuminate common findings and provide a platform for the next generation of theory and research. Such an integration is possible and long overdue.

The objectives in this chapter are to (1) identify the major issues in the leadership literature that contribute to a sense of contradiction and divergence, (2) present a framework for organizing our current knowledge that emphasizes the functions of leadership, (3) provide a new theory that integrates those functions of leadership, and (4) suggest some new directions for research.

There are as many definitions of leadership as there are theorists. "Leadership" is defined here as a process of social influence and "effective

Leadership Theory and Research: Perspectives and Directions

leadership," as the successful application of the influence to mission accomplishment. In other words effective leaders are able to obtain the cooperation of other people and to harness the resources provided by that cooperation to the attainment of a goal.

The most prominent points of contention in the contemporary leadership literature revolve around two important questions: (1) Are the effects of leadership objective and real or socially constructed and illusory? and (2) If leaders do have real and substantial effects on the performance of groups and organizations, is there one best way for leaders to be effective, or is the nature of effective leadership contingent on task, organizational, and cultural mediators?

The assumption guiding the first half century of leadership research was that the effects of leadership on group and organizational outcomes were real and objective. This assumption has been under attack for a decade and a half. In 1975, Eden and Leviatan (1975) reported the effects of implicit leadership theories on ratings of leader behavior. Subsequent research indicated that judgments of leadership behavior and effectiveness were affected by cognitive biases that distorted or exaggerated the leader's responsibility for group performance (Lord et al., 1978; Lord and Mahar, 1989; Phillips and Lord, 1981).

A more severe indictment of leadership theory was made by Calder (1977), who argued that leadership was nothing more than a convenient attributional fiction for assigning the misunderstood variance in group or organizational performance. While less strident in tone, Meindl's (Meindl, 1990; Meindl and Ehrlich, 1987) "romance of leadership" work reflects the same view, specifically, that variability in group performance is misattributed or overattributed to the effects of leadership because of dispositional biases and implicit theories emphasizing the importance of leadership in the determination of organizational outcomes.

While these demonstrations of the effects of cognitive biases on perceptions of leader behavior and performance are quite convincing, any comprehensive review of the leadership literature (Chemers, 1987; Fiedler and House, 1988; Yukl, 1981) points out numerous individual studies and entire research programs in which leaders' personality or behavioral differences are reliably predictive of variability in objectively measured indices of group performance. At least some of the observed effects of leadership are more than social constructions.

Given that leaders have real effects on organizational performance as well as on the thoughts and emotions of followers, what determines the nature of these effects? The empirical leadership literature of the last 30 years has been dominated by contingency approaches that view the relationship between leader actions and group outcomes as moderated by situational variables (Fiedler, 1967; Fiedler and Chemers, 1974; House and Mitchell, 1974; Hunt, 1984; Vroom and Yetton, 1973; Yukl, 1981).

A considerable body of research supports the validity of contingency approaches (Field and House, 1990; Peters et al., 1985; Strube and Garcia, 1981). Yet theorists continue to present arguments favoring universally effective leadership patterns. Popular books targeted for lay audiences imply that the essential elements of effective leadership are appropriate for leaders in all or most situations (Bennis and Nanus, 1985; Kouzes and Posner, 1987).

For example, Bennis and Nanus conducted in-depth, relatively unstructured interviews with 60 private-sector and 30 public-sector leaders with reputations for outstanding organizational performance. When these leaders were asked to describe the basis of their success, common themes emerged. A compelling vision that is articulately communicated, trustworthiness, and self-confidence were seen as universal aspects of the leadership styles of these presumably highly effective leaders.

Studies that rely heavily on retrospective self-reports of managers or subordinates, are prone to various methodological difficulties (e.g., self-serving biases, memory distortions). However, more careful research has generated somewhat similar conclusions. Bass (1985) conducted research on "transformational" leaders identified through the reports of subordinates. Transformational leaders were able to change their subordinates' orientations toward their job from one of self-interest to true commitment. Subsequent interviews identified an inspirational vision, intellectual stimulation and challenge, and personalized consideration of followers as the keys to highly productive leader–follower relationships. A quantitative measure of transformational, transactional, and laissez-faire leadership was constructed reflecting the elements identified in the earlier interviews. Research relating subordinate reports on this measure to superior evaluations and objective performance measures has provided some support for the validity of these common elements of highly effective leadership (Hater and Bass, 1988).

In summary, leadership research has provided evidence (at varying levels of credibility) that supports both subjective and objective views of the effects of leadership, and that verifies that both specific situationally contingent and broadly generic causal forces are at work.

LEADERSHIP AS A MULTIFACETED PROCESS

Can leadership theory reconcile these contradictions and provide a comprehensible core of knowledge to guide future research? A first step would involve the recognition that leadership processes are multifaceted and different aspects of leadership may be explained by different causal relationships. Like the proverbial committee of blind men clutching an elephant, different perspectives lead to different conclusions. It might be illuminating to open our eyes and directly confront the nature of these different perspectives and the processes that play central roles in each.

The factors that loom most prominently in defining effectiveness in each aspect are sufficiently different from each other to create the impression that divergences in research findings are irreconcilable. Adding to the confusion is the current tendency to group together research paradigms that employ similar variables or methods, but which study very different underlying processes.

For example, several contingency approaches to leadership argue that leader motivations or behavioral styles interact with situational variables to determine effectiveness, such as Fieldler's (1967) contingency model, Vroom and Yetton's (1973) normative decision theory, and House's path–goal theory (House and Mitchell, 1974). These theoretical approaches overlap to some degree in terms of the leader behaviors studied (e.g., structuring, directive behavior versus considerate or participative behavior) and in terms of the situational variables considered (e.g., degree of structure in tasks to be accomplished). However, these apparent similarities hide important differences in the approaches. One important difference concerns the specific outcomes the contingent relationships are hypothesized to affect. In one model the outcome might be subordinate satisfaction (path–goal theory), in another subordinate willingness to implement a group decision (normative decision theory), and in the third, objective group performance (contingency model).

Likewise, the situational variables may share denotative labels, but differ dramatically in connotation. For example, in path–goal theory, the term *task structure* refers to the degree to which the *subordinate* understands and is capable of responding to task demands. It is assumed that the supervisor understands and can instruct the subordinate to provide structure. In the other two approaches, it is the *leader's* lack of structure or information that is at issue. Thus, in one situation, effective coaching is the process under study, while in the other case it is problem solving or decisionmaking.

A similar sort of confusion is created by the miscategorization of the study of cognitive processes in leadership. Research approaches that employ attributions as a central construct are sometimes lumped together despite important differences. What is important to understand about how observers decide if a person is a leader is quite different from the processes by which a supervisor assesses whether punishment or training is likely to be more efficient in correcting the performance of an unsuccessful subordinate.

By grouping together research findings that address the same underlying processes, we stand a better chance of seeing the commonalities among them as well as identifying the points of disagreement. Although they are not mutually exclusive, three major aspects of the leadership process can be isolated. These will be labeled *image management, relationship development*, and *resource utilization. Image management* refers to those aspects that affect the perception of the leader by others. *Relationship development* encompasses the leader's efforts to establish an exchange that motivates followers' efforts and guides those efforts in productive directions. *Resource utilization* concerns the ability of the leader to make the most effective use of his or her own energies and the talents, efforts, and resources of subordinates in the accomplishment of organizational objectives. This three-facet conceptualization can provide a rubric for combining individual theories and disparate findings into an integrated body of knowledge.

Image Management

Status is a concept that is central to leadership. Individuals who are seen as valued members of a group have greater influence on beliefs and opinions of others and are accorded greater latitude to affect group processes. Leaders can only function if they are accorded the status and authority to direct others. Hollander's (1958) research on "idiosyncrasy credits" established that leader legitimacy flows from the perception that the leader is competent to help the group toward goal attainment and trustworthy enough to remain loyal to collective interests and objectives. Perceptions of legitimacy are based both on direct observations of the leader's behavior as well as on inferences relating the leader to group outcomes. Because legitimacy is tied to perception, it is heir to all the distortions that bias cognitions.

Research indicates that perceptions of an individual's "leaderliness" are partially governed by the extent to which the traits and behaviors of the individual match the cognitive "prototypes" (Cantor and Mischel, 1979) held by observers (Lord and Mahar, 1989). If the leader's projected image overlaps sufficiently with the observer's prototype, the observer will attribute to the leader all the characteristics related to the prototype. Thus, effective leaders will attempt to act in ways that are compatible with the prototypes held by relevant observers. The traits that characterize a leader vary somewhat across leadership domains, such as business, political, military, religious (Lord and Mahar, 1989), and across cultural or national groupings (Hofstede, 1981). The ability of a leader to match these varying expectations may be the result of the leader's perceptiveness at recognizing the exemplars of the category for a particular audience.

Similarly, if leaders are associated with positive group outcomes such as high productivity, causal attributions for those outcomes are assigned to the leader (Calder, 1977). Furthermore, the more extreme the outcomes, whether positive or negative, the more likely and extreme is the degree of attribution of responsibility (Meindl, 1990). When groups, organizations, or societies perform especially well or especially poorly, the observer's tendency is to assign responsibility for these outcomes to the leader (Meindl and Ehrlich, 1987). This tendency may also vary by culture depending on the implicit theories of cause held by the group. For example, we might expect the strongest tendency toward dispositional attributions to leaders among the highly individualist cultures of western Europe and North America that see individual action as responsible for collective outcomes.

When leaders are able to project an image highly consistent with the followers' expectations for leadership and to associate themselves with very positive outcomes or the potential for positive outcomes, they may be seen as possessing leadership qualities of extraordinary magnitude. House's (1976) work on charismatic leadership indicates that leaders who desire to be seen as specially gifted expend considerable energy in managing their image for followers.

Image management is a particularly critical leadership strategy for political leaders who frequently interact with many of their followers only from a distance. By engaging in portrayals of competency (e.g., reviewing troops, signing legislation) and trustworthiness (e.g., attending religious services, kissing babies) and by taking credit for positive outcomes (e.g., success in foreign relations, a reduction in unemployment) while avoiding the responsibility for failure, they can enhance their legitimacy with the electorate.

In a study of American presidential success, Simonton (1987) makes attribution theory the central explanatory construct. Recent research indicates that political leaders whose public utterances are confident and optimistic fare much better than those whose speeches reveal doubts and concern (Zullow et al., 1988). Not surprisingly, politicians attempt to manipulate the public perception of their responsibility for positive and negative national outcomes through mechanisms such as increasing the complexity of explanations for the causes of such events (Tetlock, 1981).

Because the processes underlying image management are primarily perceptual and cognitive, they are extremely susceptible to bias and distortion. This aspect of leadership can rightfully be regarded more as social construction than objective reality. Nonetheless, it is important to recognize that the perceptions of a leader's behavior and influence on tangible outcomes, while open to manipulation and distortion, may also be rooted in real effects. Leaders do, after all, differ in levels of competency and trustworthiness, and their decisions may, in fact, have objectively more positive or negative results with respect to goal attainment. These objective differences will, to some degree, have an influence on perceptions of competency and trustworthiness.

Relationship Development

The exchanges or transactions by which leader and followers develop a relationship has been the crux of traditional leadership research. This complex dimension of leadership effectiveness ultimately affects the followers' loyalty, commitment, and motivation to engage in group activities.

Leaders and followers approach their relationship with needs that require mutual fulfillment. Needs are oriented both toward the rational goals of the group and each individual's interest in group success, as well as toward the more personal emotional needs of each person (Schein, 1985). These needs while not always rational nor completely conscious are the critical moderators of the relationship. The processes of need fulfillment and relationship development in leadership can be understood as they are manifested and negotiated in three major areas: coaching, attribution, and transactional exchange.

Coaching and Guidance

Leaders provide subordinates with direction and support that help them to accomplish their goals. This area is within the purview of theories such as the path–goal theory (House and Mitchell, 1974; House and Dessler, 1974) and situational leadership theory (Hersey and Blanchard, 1977). These models attempt to specify the ways in which leader actions interact with followers needs to affect follower motivation and satisfaction.

Roughly speaking these models argue that leader actions should complement other sources of guidance and support available in the environment. Thus, directive or instructive leader behavior will have the most beneficial effects when subordinates are unable to accomplish assigned tasks without help. Supportive behaviors will result in higher levels of subordinate satisfaction when other aspects of the environment, such as a boring or aversive task increase the subordinate's need for support. When other aspects of the environment can substitute for the leader's actions in fulfilling subordinate needs, those actions are seen as less necessary for even negative (Kerr and Jermier, 1978).

Also, characteristics of the subordinate such as personality will influence their reactions to environmental or task demands and leader behaviors. Working in the path–goal approach, Griffin (1981) has shown that subordinates high in the need for growth and challenge in their job do not respond positively to structuring behavior by a supervisor, even in highly unstructured and ambiguous task situations. Hershey and Blanchard (1977) conceptualize many issues of subordinate characteristics under the concept of maturity, which roughly equates to subordinate motivation and ability to be self-directed. As subordinates increase in maturity, that is, as they develop task knowledge and job commitment, the supervisor should direct less, delegate more.

Attribution

A second aspect of the relationship development is communication between leader and follower. Because of the necessity for the leader to recognize the subtle interactions of person and situation, perception and communication underly the psychological exchanges embedded in the processes of coaching and guidance. A considerable body of research has shown the important role that leader attributions about the causes of subordinate performance play in the coaching process (Green and Mitchell, 19879; Mitchell and Wood, 1980). Like actors in other social relationships, leaders attempt to understand the causes of the behavior of their subordinates in order to predict future behavior and to affect that behavior. The rules that govern attributions about subordinates are similar to those in other social situations (Jones and Davis, 1965; Kelley, 1967). When a subordinate performs in a way that consistent across situations and different from the way that other subordinates perform, the subordinate is more apt to be regarded as personally responsible for the performance.

What is different or more pronounced about leader attributions is related to two factors. First, the actions of subordinates have important implications for the fulfillment of the needs and goals of the leader. Leaders with poorly performing subordinates are regarded as poor leaders. This enhances the leader's need to ascribe responsibility for poor performance to subordinate dispositions, especially when the results associated with that performance are extreme. Brown (1984) has pointed out that leaders are often making attributions about whole groups of subordinates (e.g., a work team). When an entire team performs poorly, negative evaluations of the leader may be enhanced.

The potency of attributional processes for leader-follower relationships is multiplied by the second factor. Leaders are supposed to take action to maintain, change, or remedy subordinate performance. Thus, attributions become the basis for subsequent action (Dobbins, 1985; Mitchell and

Wood, 1980). Misperceptions or ego protective attributions can begin a spiral of poor communication and a deteriorating relationship. For example, a leader may ascribe subordinate poor performance to a lack of effort on the subordinate's part, because the leader does not want to acknowledge responsibility for inadequate training or support. On the basis of the attribution of low effort, the leader chooses to punish or threaten the subordinate to improve future performance. The likely progression of this scenario is not hard to imagine.

Transactional Exchange

Finally, the third major aspect of research on relationship development is concerned with the broader, more abstract, and more global assessment of the exchange. Hollander (1978) has argued that the notion of fairness or equity is central to social exchange process. Graen and his colleagues (Graen and Shiemann, 1978) have examined the "rolemaking process" in leadership and offer the observation that leaders establish individual transactional relationships with each subordinate, termed "vertical dyadic linkages." These linkages may vary drastically in quality. For example, in a high-quality exchange, a leader may like and respect a subordinate, have great confidence in her ability and commitment, make very positive attributions about the causes of her performance. This assessment of the subordinate leads to interesting assignments for her, supportive interactions, and opportunities for her growth and development. On the other hand, the leader may have much less positive perceptions of another subordinate and give him a much less positive exchange. Research indicates that subordinates in high-quality exchange evidence more positive attitudes and behavior toward the superior and the organization.

Approaching this same issue in a slightly different way, Bass and his associates have identified the central elements of highly positive exchanges and argue that at a certain level, these exchanges undergo a qualitative change. The change is from a "transactional" relationship characterized by the exchange of rewards for efforts (contingent reward) to a "transformational" relationship that actually changes the subordinate's orientation from a self-interested calculation of personal goal attainment to a true commitment to organizational goals. Leaders who interact with their subordinates in ways that are seen by the subordinates as being intellectually challenging, sensitively considerate and supportive, and expressing an inspirational vision of their collective mission are classed as transformational. Such leaders are viewed in very positive terms by both subordinates and superiors and are frequently associated with very productive groups and organizations (Hater and Bass, 1988).

One might quibble about whether the characteristics of Bass's outstanding leaders are really qualitatively different from those of transactional leaders or just represent the most effective use of the behaviors and strategies common to their transactional counterparts. Nevertheless, transcendant leadership in the sphere of relationship development is the result of a highly perceptive leader, in tune with the capabilities and needs of followers, and able to supply followers with the requisite level of challenge, support, and guidance necessary to elicit maximal follower loyalty, commitment, and effort.

Cultural differences play an important role in defining the relationship between leader and follower. Differences in values will be reflected in different needs for both the leader and the follower. What is considered fair and appropriate behavior will vary. For example, Hofstede (1981) has described the expectations held by followers in different cultures with different values about power. Members of societies high in "power distance" values accept large differences in power of different individuals and consider those differences normal and appropriate. Cultures low in power distance hold more egalitarian beliefs. Subordinates in high power distance cultures (e.g., Greece, Japan) have strong dependence needs, expect their superiors to act autocratically, and prefer a leader who is somewhat paternalistic. The leader behaviors that lead to high motivation in such a subordinate would be very different from effective leader behaviors for more egalitarian subordinates who seek high levels of personal autonomy and independence.

The bases of leader–follower exchange relationships are interpersonal perceptions. Good-quality relationships can exist independently of the tangible outcomes of group process. That is, a leader might be *seen* as visionary, fair, and supportive even when the group is not performing well. Rooted in perception and largely divorced from performance, relationship development is primarily a social construction and is very susceptible to subjectivist influences. This does not mean that these perceptions are unimportant. The reactions of followers depend on these perceptions of the leader.

Resource Utilization

The effective deployment of the resources of the leader and of the group will largely determine how much the motivation and commitment of leader and follower are translated into group performance. In this aspect of leadership, the literature favors contingency formulations, supporting the assumption that different kinds of behaviors or strategies will have differential effects on group outcomes depending on situational parameters.

The interaction of person and situation manifests effects on both the individual and the group. In other words, when an individual has a good fit between their personality or needs and the situation, the person is energized and can make better use of personal resources like knowledge or intelligence.

Chemers and his colleagues have shown that a fit or "match" between leader personality and situational demands is associated with low levels of stress and high levels of leader confidence and satisfaction. In a contingency model guided study of university academic department chairs, Chemers et al. (1985) found that chairs whose leadership orientation was matched with the level of situational control in their jobs reported less stress and stress-related illness. In an extensive followup study of high-school administrators, Chemers et al. (1986) replicated the findings of the university study. Principals and assistant principals who were in match with their jobs reported less stress and illness and higher levels of job satisfaction.

Chemers et al. (1991) followed a similar paradigm in a laboratory study of student leaders. Leaders whose orientation was in-match with the task environment reported more positive moods, higher assessments of their own influence in the group, and a perception of more harmonious relationships among group members. In-match leaders were also rated as more effective by their followers and by objective observers. In short, leaders whose personalities, abilities, or leadership styles, are in good fit with the demands of the environment seems to be happier, more confident, and more optimistic about their group activities.

Similar results are found when the focus is on objectively measured group performance rather than on the psychological responses of the leader. Research has shown that when leader personality, behavior, or decision style match the requisite demands of the task or organizational environment, groups perform more effectively and group members experience greater satisfaction. Extensive meta-analysis and validation studies support the person–situation match effects of Fiedler's (1967, 1978; Fiedler and Chemers, 1984) contingency model (Peters et al., 1985; Strube and Garcia, 1981) and Vroom and Yetton's normative decision theory (Field and House, 1990).

Both of these models suggest that effects of specific leader behaviors will be moderated by situational characteristics. In both models, the most important situational characteristics are the degree of clarity, structure, and information in the task to be accomplished or the decision to be made, and the amount of follower support on which the leader can depend. The critical leader behavioral variable in the Vroom–Yetton model is the degree of subordinate participation in decisionmaking. In Fiedler's contingency model, the key person variable is the leader's motivational focus on task success or interpersonal harmony.

Unlike most of the effects discussed thus far, resource utilization outcomes are much less susceptible to social construction. Research in this area typically follows a paradigm involving performance outcomes that are objectively measured, or at least external and independent of the measurement of other variables in the model, namely, leader characteristics or situational parameters. For example, in many tests of Fiedler's contingency model, measures of the leader's personality, measures or manipulations of situational variables, and performance measures are taken from separate and independent sources (e.g., see Chemers and Skrzypek, 1972). Where various aspects of the causal relationship are independently measured and outcome measures objectively compiled (e.g., tons of steel per shift, games won by a basketball team, accuracy of surveying), social constructions or common perceptions cannot account for the observed relationships.

Some Conclusions

The foregoing analysis has provided us with potential opportunities for reconciling different perspectives, but also requires further integration. We have seen that at the most positive pole of each aspect of leadership, certain commonalities exist between the scientific and the popular literature and between the one best way and the contingency perspectives.

The zenith of the image management dimension is occupied by a leader who gives the impression of competent, trustworthy, and visionary leadership. Likewise, the highest plane of the relationship/exchange aspect reveals a leader who motivates at extremely high levels through vision, trustworthiness, and concern for followers. Finally, the resource utilization aspect's most effective levels are occupied by leaders who operate with high levels of commitment and confidence engendered by a match of personality and situation.

Both popular and scientific conceptions, then, yield vision, trust, and confidence as important factors. However, even though these qualities may appear universal at the level of their perception, they may be rooted in complex contingency relationships. Being "in-match" with the environment may produce confidence and optimal use of the leader's capabilities. Likewise, although the perceptions of leadership effectiveness are highly susceptible to social construction and distortion, group and organizational effectiveness are also tied to objective criteria. If we could understand the relation of perception to performance and reconcile the universal and contingent aspects of leadership, the resultant integration could provide a vehicle for broader understanding and suggest future research directions.

A COMPREHENSIVE THEORY OF LEADERSHIP EFFECTIVENESS

In the previous sections, the essential processes underlying effective image management, relationship development, and resource utilization were discussed. In the pages that follow, these processes will be integrated into a comprehensive theory of leadership effectiveness.

Leadership processes are sufficiently complex that all perspectives cannot be presented here simultaneously. The model that will be discussed below makes accommodations to that limitation. Group effects are presented from a leader oriented point of view. The leader is treated as the central actor in the group context. However, the relationships among leader, followers, and the group as an entity are acknowledged to be reciprocal and intertwined. Moreover, the processes discussed here are presented in a linear fashion with a static, slice-in-time orientation. In fact, these processes are multidimensional, reverberating systems, dynamic over time.

The overall model of this integrative theory is presented in Figure 12.1. The model attempts to integrate individual, dyadic, group, and organizational interactions. The model is divided into three zones. Each zone represents a predominant interface of persons and environment. Each zone is guided by a predominant causal principle, and each zone reflects a greater or lesser susceptibility of effects to objective or subjective processes. Finally, all zones are governed by the "match" principle, that is, that the outcomes of particular leader and follower behavior are affected by the match or fit between behavior and the demands of the surrounding environment.

Zone of Self-Deployment

The first zone depicts the interface of the leader and the environment. The dominant causal process in this zone is the match between the leader's style, (i.e., habitual cognitive, emotional, and behavioral patterns for relating to the social environment) and the demands posed by that environment. The graphic shown at numeral 1 depicts the prediction that when the individual patterns are compatible with or "fit" the demands of the environment, the leader is said to be "in-match." This notion of person–environment fit or match as a predictor of positive individual or group outcomes is central to many organizational theories. As discussed above, a series of studies by Chemers and his colleagues (Chemers et al., 1985, 1986, 1991) showed that in groups led by in-match leaders, leaders and followers reported higher levels of confidence and optimism.

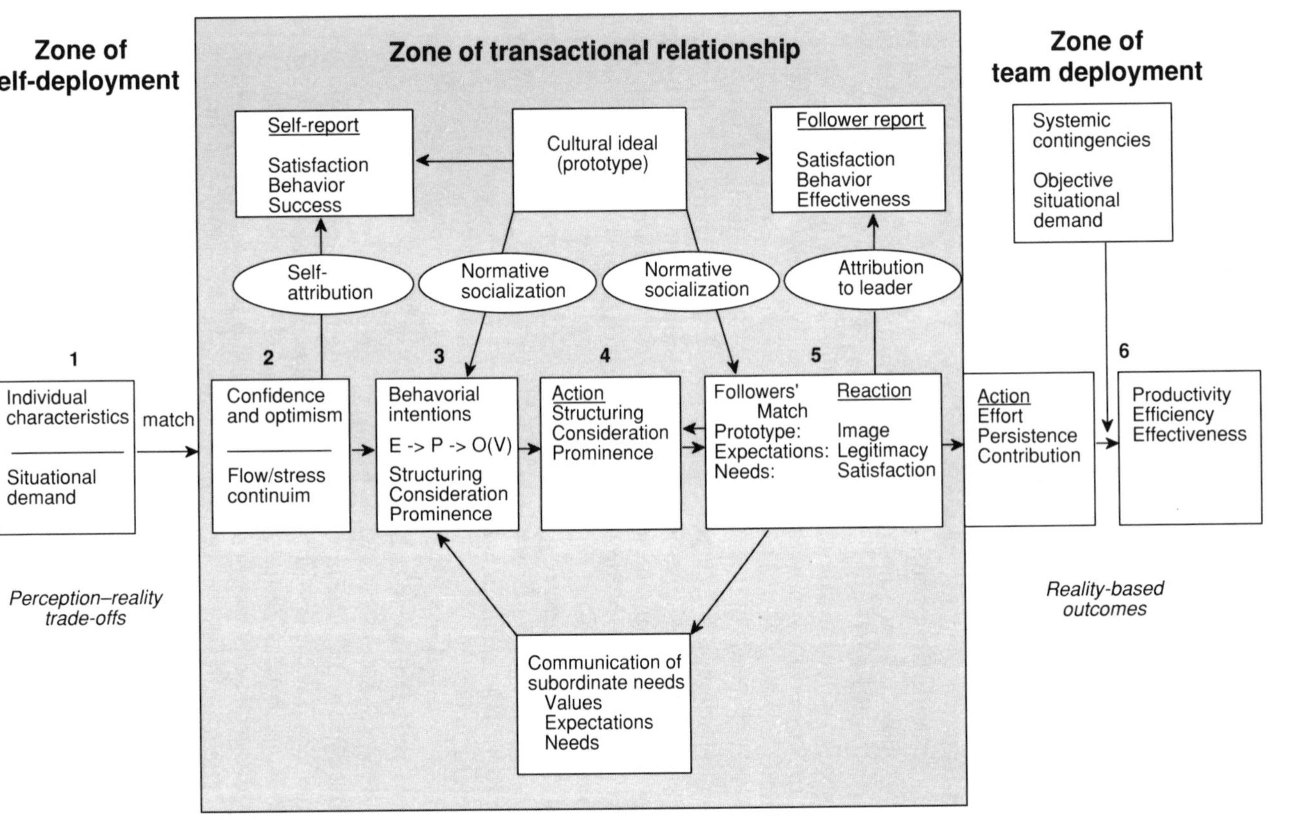

Figure 12.1 An integrative model of leadership.

While the match concept is central to the contingency model, it contributes to other theoretical perspectives in social, organizational, or health psychology. For example, Anderson (1987) has studied the effect of fit between person and environment on the performance and satisfaction of nurses and nursing administrators. Anderson measured the level of self-monitoring of these persons. Self-monitoring (Snyder, 1974) is a construct predictive of a person's sensitivity to social expectations and ability and willingness to comply with those expectations. Anderson found that for people occupying jobs that were nontraditional for their sex (i.e., male nurses and female administrators) the individual's self-monitoring score was positively correlated with satisfaction and performance, but was uncorrelated for those in "gender-congruent" assignments. He concluded that the high self-monitor's ability to read subtle social cues and respond to them helped them to cope with discontinuities between their own inclinations and the expectations of others.

In another chapter in this volume, Ayman extensively discusses the problems occasioned for women managers by the mismatch between their self-perceptions and those of the superiors, coworkers, and subordinates with whom they interact on the job. Any number of individual variables might interact with situational characteristics, including but not limited to leadership style, gender role, values, task-related abilities, culture, and other factors. Exactly which person and situation variables will be most salient is determined by the particular context.

It should be apparent that the positive affective states ascribed to in-match leaders are very similar to the confidence and optimism also referred to as "self-deployment" by Bennis and Nanus (1985) in their interview study of effective leaders. This reflects a point of integration between the popular, universalistic observations and the contingency formulations that are hypothesized to underlie those observations.

The effects described in the zone of self-deployment are neither totally subjective nor totally objective. They reflect a mix: a "perception/reality trade-off." The degree of fit between the individual and the situation is grounded in objective characteristics of the person and the situation, but it is the phenomenological experience of match that has the greatest effects on the thoughts and emotions of the leader. In the laboratory study by Chemers et al. (1985) reported above, leaders' perceptions of the situational parameters were more predictive of match effects than were the objective assessments of those variables. In other words, how structured the leader *perceived* a task to be or how supportive subordinates were *seen* to be was a better predictor of the leader's performance than were the "objective" nature of the task or the actual reports of those subordinates.

Zone of Transactional Relationship

This zone portrays the dynamics of the interaction of leader and followers. The forces active in this zone are rooted in the perceptions of the interacting parties, and are, to a large degree, divorced from roots in objective aspects of the environment. These forces shape the relationship and exchange between leader and follower that help to determine the degree of motivation, commitment, and satisfaction of each party.

Numeral 2 indicates processes that carry the match effects into the social relationship. The sense of confidence in one's self and optimism about the outcomes of one's actions influence perceptions and expectations. Csikszentmihalyi (1982) uses the term "flow" to describe the phenomenological state experienced by individuals whose task-related capabilities are challenged but not exceeded by the demands of the environment. When action opportunities or challenges are perceived by an actor as overwhelming his capabilities the resulting stress is experienced as anxiety. When skills or abilities greatly exceed challenges, the experience is one of boredom. But when a balance exists, as when a leader's particular style and capabilities match the demands of the environment, a state of flow results in a "dynamic state of consciousness" (Csikszentmihalyi, 1982, p. 23), in which a positive mood and a focused attention predominate. The person feels absorbed, confident, and in control.

If leaders are asked to make self-reports about their functioning, such as behavior, performance, or satisfaction, lacking any good comparative context for providing an objective report of these factors, leaders will tell us what they think they are trying to do, or should be doing. These self reports are heavily normative in character and are strongly influenced by prototypical conceptions, ideal types, or implicit leadership theories. This is one of the most important reasons why self-reports of leader behavior appear universal, at least within a defined cultural group, such as American or western European executives. These individuals share common values and a common theory of effective leadership and ascribe to themselves the components of that theory. For example, if a culture's implicit theory of effective leadership includes participative decisionmaking, inmatch leaders will describe themselves as participative.

Numeral 3 directs attention to the place at which a leader's self-perceptions and feelings join with social influences to give rise to a set of behavioral intentions. I have chosen to represent these intentions as a set of expectations about the utility of particular courses of action, borrowing from expectancy theory (Porter and Lawler, 1968; Vroom, 1964). This should not give the impression that these expectations are necessarily entirely conscious or entirely rational. The intentions, whether conscious or not, are based on the answers to three questions:

1. Am I capable of engaging effectively in this behavior? (E->P; i.e., will effort lead to performance?)
2. Will the effective performance of this behavior probably lead to a particular effect? (P->O; will performance cause the outcome?)
3. Is this outcome desirable? (V; valence.)

For example, a leader might ask herself, "How likely is it that I could give my subordinates a rousing speech about the importance of our organizational goals [performance]? Are they likely to respond by seeing me as a powerful and competent leader [outcome]? How much do I want them to regard me in that way [valence]?" Another leader might ponder whether giving a poorly performing subordinate a stern reprimand will increase the overall productivity of his team.

The model hypothesizes that the first probability, the leader's estimates of the ability to engage in particular behaviors, will be determined by the confidence and optimism arising from match in combination with generalized chronic (trait) self-confidence, and past experience with behaviors and situations of this kind. My thinking here is quite compatible with the concept of "self-efficacy," which plays a prominent role in current approaches to work motivation (Bandura, 1977; Locke and Latham, 1990). Confident individuals will have high-probability estimates about their abilities to engage in required leadership behaviors.

Judgments about the instrumentality of a particular behavioral strategy for producing a particular outcome, will be determined by three factors. The first of these is the leader's habitual predispositions toward some courses of action. For example, a manager might be inclined toward autocratic decisionmaking, sharing very little authority with subordinates, and this inclination may play some role in all of this individual's expectations. This contributor might be thought of as the person's "style" and is the result of his or her personal socialization history. While the leader might use an assessment of the situation in arriving at this decision, I assume that each individual has a propensity or style that is seen as appropriate in a wide range of situations.

A second influence on the leader's expectations comes from the leader's reading of the general expectations of the culture: "What would most people do in this situation?" These influences are not part of the leader's personality or habitual pattern, but are reflective of the contemporary normative standards in the group or organization. The individual's interpretation of thes influences may, of course, be affected by personal biases.

The third set of influences arises from the leader's perception of the particular needs, desires and expectations of the followers. The literature on leader attributions for subordinate performance is central to understanding the leader's perceptions of subordinate needs and expectations. Research by Mitchell and his colleagues (Green and Mitchell, 1979; Mitchell and Wood, 1980) has shown how such factors as consistency, outcome severity, and previous work history influence a manager's judgments about the cause of a problem and the most appropriate course of remedial action. Work by Brown (1984) has discussed how attributions might be affected by poor group performance, and Dobbins (1985) has attempted to look at other moderators of judgments such as the gender of a supervisor or the relative centrality of a subordinate to group functioning.

The valence or desirability of one outcome over another is again determined by an individual's needs and values. These needs are, of course, strongly influenced by the leader's cultural socialization, as well as contemporary contextual forces. A growing body of cross-cultural research on leadership indicates that the most effective leader behaviors will vary from one society to another (Ayman and Chemers, 1983; Misumi, 1990; Misumi and Peterson, 1985; Sinha, 1990).

These expectancies and the behavioral decisions to which they give rise need not be conscious. The social cognition literature indicates that many actions occur without careful calculation (Langer et al., 1978), and that attributions are not made unless habitual patterns are disrupted (Wong and Weiner, 1981). It seems probable, as well, that under stress or pressure leaders fall back on habitual, highly ingrained response patterns rather than employing consciously calculated strategies. This supposition is compatible with Fiedler and Garcia's (1987) assertions that effective leaders use experience to guide behavior under stressful conditions.

At numeral 4, the confluence of expectations and intentions engender actions by the leader. These actions are grouped roughly into the primary categories of leader behavior measured by the venerable leader behavior description questionnaire (LBDQ) (Fleischman and Harris, 1962; Halpin and Winer, 1957). These categories are (1) stucturing or goal-oriented behavior, (2) considerate or morale-oriented behavior, and (3) prominence or ego-oriented behavior. Structuring includes leader behaviors that organize, direct, and provide feedback for the task-related activities of subordinates. Consideration encompasses behaviors, such as being friendly, that provide emotional support to help the subordinate maintain positive feelings about the work situation. Prominence behaviors comprise actions that make the leader appear or feel more salient, such as talking a lot or calling attention to one's own achievements.

Numeral 5 shows that the leader's actions have an impact on the followers that is moderated by follower characteristics, expectations, and needs. The followers' expectations are conceptualized in three categories. First, followers hold expectations about the kind of behaviors that leaders should display to be considered as good leaders. This is the image issue that was discussed earlier. What is included in the followers' ideal leader prototype is heavily influenced by cultural values. Second, the follower holds particular goal-related expectations about the tangible benefits that the follower hopes to attain in any exchange with the leader. The leader's competency to move the group toward task completion or goal attainment falls under this category. Finally, the followers have emotional needs, many of which may not be conscious or rational, but which strongly affect the followers' responses to the leader.

The model predicts that when the leader's actions are seen as consistent with the follower's prototype, an attribution is made that the person is indeed a leader: "That's a leader." When the leader is seen as fulfilling expectations about goal-related activities, he or she is seen as an effective leader: "That's a good leader." When the leader satisfies the follower's personal, emotional needs, follower loyalty and commitment are elicited: "That's my leader!" The more intense the needs of the followers, the more intense and deeply felt is the relationship between follower and leader.

A feedback loops flows between the processes outlined at numerals 3, 4, and 5. Followers communicate their needs and expectations to the leader who interprets the communication and responds. The follower reacts to the leader's actions and the process continues. The quality of action and reaction represents the development of what Hollander (1978) labels the transactional exchange and Graen (1974) calls the "rolemaking process." On the basis of thoughts, feeling, and judgments, the leader acts. Those actions affect the thoughts, feelings, and judgments of followers, who, in turn, react. Those reactions have direct effects on the leader's immediate behavior (e.g., calming down an irate follower) and indirect effects on the leader's expectations (e.g., changing the perception of the instrumentality of a behavior). The perceptions and judgments, actions, and reactions of leaders and followers are the basis of the coaching, attribution, and transactional exchange process of relationship development.

The leader's ability to accurately judge the needs of subordinate and the leader's ability and motivation to meet those needs while aligning subordinate motivation to organizational goals will determine the quality of the relationship. Hollander tells us that leaders who are judged to be competent and fair have great influence. Graen tells us that the leader negotiates a relationship with each follower developing a set of exchanges that can range from relatively impoverished to quite excellent and effective. Bass argues that at the highest level, the exchanges between leader and follower transcend the individualistically oriented self-serving transaction and become "transformational." Transformational leaders by meeting follower needs for a visionary goal, a challenging and interesting job, and an authentic relationship with their leader, change the ways that followers think about themselves and their jobs.

Theories of charismatic leadership (House, 1976) argue that there are leaders who completely transcend the petty exchanges of transactional processes. However, the rewards that the leader offers may be enhanced self-esteem, a sense of purpose, or salvation. When the followers' needs are intense enough, such rewards become highly attractive and supremely motivating. Under such circumstances charismatic or transformational leadership may be seen as a special, elevated case of the more mundane transactional exchange processes that are the basis for all, person-to-person, team leadership.

Those theorists who regard leadership as largely the stuff of subjective social construction are most at home in this zone of leadership process. Almost none of the perceptions that fuel the leader–follower relationship are anchored in any reality outside the subjective world of the participants. That the relationship between leader and follower or team is susceptible to subjective forces does not mean it is artificial or unimportant. Rather than saying that "leadership is *just* a perception," it might be more accurate to say that a major part of leadership is the effective management of perceptions of both self and others.

However, leaders who are able to manage perceptions very effectively, who look like very effective leaders from "inside the group," may not look very effective from an external, more objective vantage point. For example, Adolph Hitler still had the loyalty and support of most of the German people while he made the judgments that lost World War II. At a more mundane level, we all know of leaders who are loved by their subordinates, but can't seem to accomplish the goals of the larger organization. How, then are the transactional effects of leadership related to group performance?

Zone of Team Deployment

As depicted in Figure 12.1, the transactional relationship engenders a level of leader and follower commitment that can be translated into focused group action; that is, the team can deploy its psychological and material resources to accomplish its task. These team actions are grouped into three categories, labeled *effort, persistence*, and *contribution*.

Effort refers to how hard the members of the team are willing to work. *Persistence* refers to the team's ability to maintain their commitment and energy in the face of a daunting task or temporary setbacks. *Contribution* encompasses the relative amount and type of input and degree of participation by followers in determining group actions.

The effects of these team output variables (effort, persistence, contribution) on group or organizational outcomes depend on the demands of the situation or system in which the team is functioning. The group outcomes might be characterized as how much task-defined output the team accomplishes (*productivity*), the relative cost of productivity in terms of time or resources (*efficiency*), or more general measures of how well the group achieves its assigned goal (*effectiveness*).

The interaction of team effort and situational demand on group performance (i.e., team resource utilization) is governed by the contingency principle and anchored in objective consequences. At this point in the process, it is not enough that the followers are loyal and committed to a confident and enthusiastic leader. A satisfied team is not necessarily a productive one. A committed and energized team is not necessarily an efficient or effective one. In other words, the subjective forces that were the essence of relationship development do not hold sway in this province. A leader may have a happy, committed, and highly motivated group of subordinates, but unless the actions of the leader and the followers are appropriate to the demands of the task, success will not be attained.

Some general hypotheses are relevant to the zone of team deployment. We can expect that high levels of effort will be associated with effective performance on simple tasks. When goals and procedures are clear and well understood, a hard-working team is usually successful. Persistence is likely to be effective when the group's task is difficult, aversive, or characterized by vacillations in outcome—the ubiquitous "ups and downs" of group performance. If the team can maintain its commitment in the face of these impediments, it can ride out the hard times with a greater likelihood of eventual success. A leader who can maintain high levels of morale should have more persistent teams.

The complexity, clarity, and certainty in the group's task environment will influence the relative efficacy of directive versus participative leadership. A number of theories of leadership and group performance are based on this premise (Vroom and Yetton, 1973). Autocratic decision procedures in which the leader allows little subordinate participation in problem identification or solution, will be most effective when the task is well understood and the support of followers is assured. When the predictability of the situation is reduced by an unclear problem or a potentially recalcitrant team, more participative decision strategies are thought to be more likely to yield effective outcomes.

Fiedler's contingency model (Fiedler, 1967, 1978; Fiedler and Chemers,

1974, 1984), while not as explicit about the processes underlying group effectiveness as that of Vroom and Yetton, makes similar predictions. Task-motivated leadership with an emphasis on order and direction is seen as most effective under conditions of high clarity or control, while the more participative strategies of the relationship-motivated leader are most effective under conditions of greater ambiguity caused by an unstructured task or a less than cooperative group.

Fiedler and Garcia's (1987) cognitive resource theory represents an elegant attempt to deal with the problems of allocation of leader and follower resources to task effectiveness. Briefly, Fiedler and Garcia focus on the cognitive or intellectual resources of the leader applied to the task. They argue that smart leaders will be more successful on intellectually demanding tasks when they take control of group processes through clear directions. Not surprisingly, less intelligent leaders do more poorly under these circumstances. However, what is not so obvious is the finding that when the leader is under stress, that person's intelligence is uncorrelated or even negatively correlated with group performance. Under stressful conditions, it is the leader's experience that is correlated with success. Thus, the effective deployment of a team's resources, in this case the intelligence and experience of leader and followers, depends on the type of task and the environment.

To reiterate the process, a leader whose personality and abilities are in-match with the demands of the group situation feels a sense of self–environment integration, positive mood, and personal control. These positive cognitive and affective states are experienced as confidence and optimism and translate into high expectations for self and teammates. The specific directions that the expectations take is determined by the leader's sense of what is appropriate in the context and what is needed by the followers. If the leader's perceptions of context and follower needs are accurate and the leader's behavioral execution is good, followers respond with perceptions of the leader's competence and legitimacy and with personal satisfaction and commitment to group goals. The enthusiasm and energy of leader and followers is turned into effective team performance if the decision strategies and behavioral tactics chosen mesh well with systemic demands.

CONCLUSION AND FUTURE DIRECTIONS

I began this chapter by posing two questions. The first asked whether leadership was primarily a real effect or a subjective construction. The integrative model argues that both subjective and objective forces are at work in leadership processes. Part of what makes a leader objectively successful, in terms of the accomplishment of tangible organizational goals, depends on subjective influences. The leader's confidence and optimism help to create a positive image and arouse motivation and confidence in followers. Yet, group and organizational performance are also objectively affected by good leadership, and good leadership is more than image, confidence, or charisma.

The second question concerned the extent to which there exists a universal pattern for effective leadership. The model proposes that one of the reasons that all successful leaders within a particular culture look similar is that the reported descriptions of those leaders are strongly influenced by the prototypes shared by leaders and followers. However, the empirical literature also shows us that prototypes differ across cultures, and that the processes that give rise to the perception of successful leadership are rooted in complex contingencies involving situation, personality, and communication.

The next question must be "Where does this model lead us?" Further explication of the hypothesized relationships presented in the integration suggest some productive areas for future research.

- How are leadership prototypes influenced by cultural values?
- What person and situational characteristics are most important in determining match? What contextual features affect the salience of these variables?
- What are the phenomenological features of match, and how are these communicated?
- When and how do expectancies influence behavior? What is the role of individual differences in expectancies?
- What tactics do subordinates use to communicate their needs to superiors, and which strategies are most effective?
- How do the processes of productive leadership develop over time?
- What is the role of decisions made on emotional, nonconscious levels rather than cognitive, rational bases?

On a practical level, an integrative model helps us to see how contemporary theories relate to one another. We can ascertain the points of agreement and the findings with broad empirical support. These points of agreement become the basis for education and training efforts for leadership practitioners. Likewise, the recognition of what we don't know and the aspects of our theories that don't travel well cross-culturally will identify areas for caution and reflection.

Hopefully, the most important benefit of an integrative theory is to help researchers to see that the study of this tremendously complex but important phenomenon is a collective endeavor. Connections between theories and approaches may result in larger blocks of integrated knowledge that can provide platforms for the next generation of theory, research, and application.

References

Anderson, L. R. (1987). Self-monitoring and performance in non-traditional occupations. *Basic and Applied Social Psychology, 8*, 85–96.

Ayman, R., and Chemers, M. M. (1991). The effect of leadership match on subordinate satisfaction in Mexican organizations: Some moderating influences of self-monitoring. *International Review of Applied Psychology, 40*, 299–314.

Bandura, A. (1977). Self-efficacy: Toward a unifying theory of behavioral change. *Psychological Review, 84*, 191–215.

Bass, B. M. (1985). *Leadership and performance beyond expectations*. New York: Free Press.

Beach, L. (1992). Four revolutions in decision theory. In M. M. Chemers and R. Ayman (Eds.), *Leadership theory and research: Perspectives and directions*. San Diego, CA: Academic Press.

Bennis, W., and Nanus, B. (1985). *Leaders: The strategies for taking charge*. New York: Harper & Row.

Brown, K. A. (1984). Explaining poor group performance: An attributional analysis. *Academy of Management Review, 9*, 54–63.

Calder, B. J. (1977). An attribution theory of leadership. In B. M. Shaw and G. R. Salancik (Eds.), *New directions in organizational behavior* (pp. 179–204). Chicago, IL: St. Clair.

Cantor, N., and Mischel, W. (1979). Prototypes in person perception. In L. Berkowitz (Ed.), *Advances in experimental social psychology* (Vol. 12, pp. 3–52). New York: Academic Press.

Chemers, M. M. (1983). Leadership theory and research: A systems-process integration. In P. B. Paulus (Ed.), *Basic group processes* (pp. 9–39). New York: Springer-Verlag.

Chemers, M. M. (1987). Leadership processes: Intrapersonal, interpersonal, and societal influences. In C. Hendrick (Ed.), *Group processes: Review of personality and social psychology* (Vol. 8, pp. 252–277). Newbury Park, CA: Sage.

Chemers, M. M., Hays, R. B., Rhodewalt, F., and Wysocki, J. (1985). A person-environment analysis of job stress: A contingency model explanation. *Journal of Personality and Social Psychology, 49*, 628–635.

Chemers, M. M., Hill, C. A., and Sorod, B. (1986). Personality-environment match and health: Support for the contingency model. Paper presented at the meeting of the American Psychological Association, Chicago, IL.

Chemers, M. M., and Skrzypek, G. J. (1972). An experimental test of the contingency model of leadership effectiveness. *Journal of Personality and Social Psychology, 24*, 172–177.

Chemers, M. M., Sorod, B., and Akimoto, S. A. (1991). [The phenomenology of leadership effectiveness.] Unpublished raw data.

Csikszentmihalyi, M. (1982). Toward a psychology of optimal experience. In L. Wheeler (Ed.), *Review of personality and social psychology* (Vol. 2, pp. 13–36). Beverly Hills, CA: Sage.

Dobbins, G. H. (1985). Effects of gender on leaders' responses to poor performers: An attributional interpretation. *Academy of Management Journal, 28*, 587–598.

Eden, D., and Leviatan, U. (1975). Implicit leadership theory as a determinant of the factor structure underlying supervisory behavior scales. *Journal of Applied Psychology, 60*, 736–741.

Fiedler, F. E. (1967). *A theory of leadership effectiveness*. New York: McGraw-Hill.

Fiedler, F. E. (1978). The contingency model and the dynamics of the leadership process. In L. Berkowitz (Ed.), *Advances in experimental social psychology* (Vol. 11, pp. 59–112). New York: Academic Press.

Fiedler, F. E., and Chemers, M. M. (1974). *Leadership and effective management*. Glenview, IL: Scott-Foresman.

Fiedler, F. E., and Chemers, M. M. (1984). *Improving leadership effectiveness: The leader match concept*, 2nd ed. New York: Wiley.

Fiedler, F. E., and Garcia, J. E. (1987). *New approaches to effective leadership: Cognitive resources and organizational performance*. New York: Wiley.

Fiedler, F. E., and House, R. J. (1988). Leadership theory and research: A report of progress. In C. L. Cooper and I. Robertson (Eds.), *International review of industrial and organizational psychology*. London: Wiley.

Field, R. H. G., and House, R. J. (1990). A test of the Vroom-Yetton model using manager and subordinate reports. *Journal of Applied Psychology, 75*, 362–366.

Fleishman, E. A., and Harris, E. F. (1962). Patterns of leadership related to employee grievances and turnover. *Personnel Psychology, 15*, 43–56.

Graen, G. (1976). Role-making processes with complex organizations. In M. D. Dunnette (Ed.), *Handbook of industrial and organizational psychology* (pp. 1202–1245). Chicago: Rand-McNally.

Graen, G., and Schiemann, W. (1978). Leader-member agreement: A vertical dyad linkage approach. *Journal of Applied Psychology, 63*, 206–212.

Green, S. G., and Mitchell, T. R. (1979). Attributional processes of leaders in leader-member interactions. *Organizational Behavior and Human Performance, 23*, 429–458.

Griffin, R. N. (1981). Relationships among individual, task design, and leader behavior variables. *Academy of Management Journal, 23*, 665–683.

Halpin, A. W., and Winer, B. J. (1957). A factorial study of leader behavior descriptions. In R. M. Stogdill and A. E. Coons (Eds.), *Leader behavior: Its description and measurement* (pp. 39–51). Columbus, OH: Bureau of Business Research.

Hater, J. J., and Bass, B. M. (1988). Superior's evaluations and subordinates' perceptions of transformational and transactional leadership. *Journal of Applied Psychology, 73*, 695–702.

Hershey, P., and Blanchard, K. H. (1977). *Management of organizational behavior*, 3rd ed. Englewood Cliffs, NJ: Prentice-Hall.

Hofstede, G. (1981). *Culture's consequences: International differences in work-related values*. Beverly Hills, CA: Sage.

Hollander, E. P. (1958). Conformity, status, and idiosyncrasy credit. *Psychological Review, 65*, 117–127.
Hollander, E. P. (1978). *Leadership dynamics: A practical guide to effective relationship.* New York: Free Press.
House, R. J. (1976). A 1976 theory of charismatic leadership. In J. G. Hunt and L. L. Larson (Eds.), *Leadership: The cutting edge.* Carbondale, IL: Southern Illinois University Press.
House, R. J., and Dessler, G. (1974). The path-goal theory of leadership: Some post-hoc and a priori tests. In J. G. Hunt and L. L. Larson (Eds.), *Contingency approaches to leadership.* Carbondale, IL: Southern Illinois University Press.
House, R. J., and Mitchell, T. R. (1974). Path-goal theory of leadership. *Journal of Contemporary Business, 3*(4), 81–98.
Hunt, J. G. (1984). Organizational leadership: The contingency paradigm and its challenges. In B. Kellerman (Ed.), *Leadership: Multidsciplinary perspective.* Englewood Cliffs, NJ: Prentice-Hall.
Jones, E. E., and Davis, K. E. (1965). From acts to dispositions: The attribution process in person perception. In L. Berkowitz (Ed.), *Advances in experimental social psychology* (Vol. 2, pp. 219–266). New York: Academic Press.
Kelley, H. H. (1967). Attribution theory in social psychology. In D. Levine (Ed.), *Nebraska symposium on motivation 1967* (pp. 192–238). Lincoln, NE: University of Nebraska Press.
Kerr, S., and Jermier, J. M. (1978). Substitutes for leadership: Their measurement and meaning. *Organizational Behavior and Human Performance, 22*, 375–403.
Kouzes, J. M., and Posner, B. Z. (1987). *The leadership challenge: How to get extra-ordinary things done in organizations.* San Francisco: Jossey-Bass.
Langer, E., Blank, A., and Chanowitz, B. (1978). The mindlessness of ostensibly thoughtful action: The role of "placebic" information in interpersonal interaction. *Journal of Personality and Social Psychology, 36*, 635–642.
Locke, E. A., and Latham, G. P. (1990). Work motivation and satisfaction: Light at the end of the tunnel. *Psychological Science, 1*, 240–246.
Lord, R. G., Binning, J. F., Rush, M. C., and Thomas, J. C. (1978). The effect of performance cues and leader behavior in questionnaire ratings of leadership behavior. *Organizational Behavior and Human Performance, 21*, 27–39.
Lord, R. G., and Mahar, K. J. (1989). Perceptions of leadership and their implications in organizations. In J. Carroll (Ed.), *Applied social psychology in business organizations.* Hillside, NJ: Erlbaum.
Meindl, J. R. (1990). On leadership: An alternative to the conventional wisdom. In B. A. Staw (Ed.), *Research in organizational behavior* (Vol. 12, pp. 160–203). New York: JAI Press.
Meindl, J. R., and Ehrlich, S. B. (1987). The romance of leadership and the evaluation of organizational performance. *Academy of Management Journal, 30*, 91–109.
Misumi, J. (1990). Recent developments in leadership PM theory. In R. Ayman (Chair), *Establishing a global view of leadership: East meets west.* Symposium conducted at the International Congress of Applied Psychology, Kyoto (July).
Misumi, J., and Peterson, M. F. (1985). The performance-maintenance (PM) theo-

ry of leadership: Review of Japanese research program. *Administrative Science Quarterly, 30*, 198–223.

Mitchell, T. R., and Wood, R. E. (1980). Supervisors' responses to subordinate poor performance: A test of an attributional model. *Organizational Behavior and Human Performance, 25*, 123–128.

Peters, L. H., Hartke, D. D., and Pohlmann, J. T. (1985). Fiedler's contingency theory of leadership: An application of the meta-analytic procedures of Schmidt and Huner. *Psychological Bulletin, 97*, 274–285.

Phillips, J. S., and Lord, R. G. (1981). Causal attributions and perceptions of leadership. *Organizational Behavior and Human Performance, 28*, 143–163.

Porter, L. W., and Lawler, E. E., III (1968). *Managerial attitudes and performance.* Homewood, IL: Richard Irwin.

Schein, E. H. (1985). *Organizational culture and leadership.* San Francisco: Jossey-Bass.

Simonton, D. K. (1987). *Why presidents succeed.* New Haven, CT: Yale University Press.

Sinha, J. B. P. (1990). The nurturant task style of leadership. In R. Ayman (Chair), *Establishing a global view of leadership: East meets west.* Symposium conducted at the International Congress of Applied Psychology, Kyoto (July).

Snyder, M. (1974). Self-monitoring of expressive behavior. *Journal of Personality and Social Psychology, 30*, 526–537.

Strube, M. J., and Garcia, J. E. (1981). A meta-analytical investigation of Fiedler's contingency model of leadership effectiveness. *Psychological Bulletin, 90*, 307–321.

Tetlock, P. E. (1981). Pre- to postelection shifts in presidential rhetoric: Impression management or cognitive adjustment? *Journal of Personality and Social Psychology, 41*, 202–212.

Vroom, V. H. (1964). *Work and motivation.* New York: Wiley.

Vroom, V. H., and Yetton, P. W. (1973). *Leadership and decision-making.* Pittsburgh, PA: University of Pittsburgh Press.

Wong, P. T. P., and Weiner, B. (1981). When people ask "why" questions, and the heuristics of attributional research. *Journal of Personality and Social Psychology, 40*, 650–663.

Yukl, G. A. (1981). *Leadership in organizations.* Englewood Cliffs, NJ: Prentice-Hall.

Zullow, H. M., Oettingen, G., Peterson, C., and Seligman, M. E. P. (1988). Pessimistic explanatory style in the historical record. *American Psychologist, 43*, 673–682.

13

Directions for Leadership Research

Martin M. Chemers
Department of Psychology
Claremont McKenna College

Roya Ayman
Department of Psychology
Illinois Institute of Technology

CONCLUSIONS

In an area of study as active and varied as leadership, no single collection of essays can provide a comprehensive perspective. Yet the 12 preceding chapters of this book do offer a relatively broad look at the field. The conclusions about the directions that we draw from these readings, while not meant to be exhaustive, may be reflective of some of the dominant trends in contemporary scholarship. We feel especially confident about our predictions when the indicators of a particular point of view are widespread among our authors. In this final chapter, we will offer our interpretation of the likely future directions revealed in the work in this volume.

We identify some approaches that have been important positions in leadership research for a long time and show no sign of diminishing relevance. Some other theoretical issues have become topical more recently and promise to grow in importance. Finally, we will suggest a few concerns that appear to be new and different directions of significance.

Leadership Theory and Research: Perspectives and Directions

Contingency

The reader may not find it surprising that a book dedicated to Fred Fiedler would conclude that contingency approaches have been important to the advancement of understanding in leadership studies. What is somewhat more surprising is how pervasive contingency theorizing has become. Almost every chapter in this collection recognizes that generalizations about leadership effects must be moderated by particular circumstances.

From the traditional contingency theorists, second and third order models are developing. Fiedler is working toward uniting the contingency model of leadership effectiveness (Fiedler, 1967, 1978) with cognitive resource theory (Fiedler and Garcia, 1987), employing linkages between motivation, behavior, intelligence, task, authority relations, and follower support. Similarly, Chemers bases his integrative approach on principles of "match" or fit between leader, follower, and environment adding cultural values and individual needs as active ingredients in the match process.

In an approach very compatible with Chemers's, House and Shamir have woven together particular and universal elements to describe charismatic leadership effects. The path–goal theory (House, 1971) concept that the effects of particular leader behaviors depend on their fit with follower needs is married to the more universalistic effects of self-concept and self-esteem on intrinsic motivation and commitment. And even here in the discussion of the most psychologically powerful effects of leaders, House and Shamir remind us that motive arousal potential of the leader's message is bounded by the leader's personal nature (e.g., Patton versus Gandhi), the followers' susceptibility to the message, and the appropriateness of the motive to the situation.

Triandis reminds us that cross-cultural psychology as a discipline is rooted in a recognition of the contingency principle. Both the power and subtlety of culture as a moderator of interpersonal relations are apparent in this analysis. The implications of cultural contingencies are also basic to the problems of interaction, perception, and communication discussed by Ayman and Mai-Dalton.

However, in addition to the theories where we might predict that contingency notions would be important, we find them in less anticipated locales. McGrath and Gruenfeld reveal the importance of contingency effects in group development, particularly in their references to Poole's adaptive structuration theory (Poole and Roth, 1988), which recognizes situational influences in the development of group-decision strategies. Ilgen, Major, Hollenbeck, and Sego also attend to the interactive effects of task, technology, rewards, and decision structures as necessary elements in understanding team effectiveness.

Beach informs us that the most viable models of decisionmaking are contingency models. The strategy selection model (Beach and Mitchell, 1978) in which the choice of a decision strategy for approaching a decision is contingent on the nature of the decision, the importance of its consequences, and available time has much in common with leadership models like cognitive resource theory (Fiedler and Garcia, 1987) and Vroom and Yetton's (1973) normative decision theory.

The foregoing doesn't deny that certain elements in leadership processes may be less amenable to contingency explanations. Hollander's process of leader legitimation emphasizing the leader's task-related competence and commitment to group values is a good candidate for universal validity. Bass and Avolio make a good case for broad applicability of at least the general qualities of transformational leaders across culture, organizational levels, and task domains. Nonetheless, contingency formulations appear to have a strong foothold in the thinking of most, if not all, theorists in leadership and organizational effectiveness and promise to endure as useful explanatory vehicles.

Process

Another venerable concern in leadership research is the necessity to address underlying processes. However, the interest in process seems to be more substantial and the nature of the processes under study different from those of earlier examinations. Three characteristics of the processes being proposed bear mentioning: (1) a subtlety and complexity that eschews simplistic explanations, (2) an emphasis on more naturalistic contexts for study, and (3) a recognition of the importance of temporal factors.

Fiedler's essay opens with the admission that contingency models, regardless of empirical support for their predictions, will remain ultimately less satisfying without an explanation of process. He then proceeds to present a way of approaching contingency effects that carries layer upon layer of complex interactions. Rather than apologizing for this complexity, he argues that "pretzel-shaped interactions" are necessary to explain a complex world.

House and Shamir sound much the same note complaining that earlier theories of visionary, charismatic, or transformational leadership describe leader behavior and follower effects, but fail to explain the processes that connect them. They argue that commonalities among these theories can be made clear by uncovering the processes. Arguing from the same stance,

Chemers presents a model with enough boxes and arrows to stock an archery tournament. Complexity seems almost a virtue for these writers.

Overlaid on the complex nature of these analyses is also a tendency to approach our phenomena with greater subtlety. This is especially apparent in the culturally focused treatments. Triandis presents "cultural syndromes" in which interlocking sets of values are seen as influencing not only expectations, behaviors, and reactions of participants but also as providing frames of reference in which the very perception of reality is mediated. Ayman asks us to go beyond regarding perceptual biases in leadership reports as measurement error to recognize that perception is the very basis of leadership. She challenges us, as does Mai-Dalton, to add to our already complex leadership equations, an appreciation for the intricacies of multicultural leadership encounters. We will address the growing importance of perceptual or constructionist concepts later in this chapter.

One of the ways in which leadership researchers have in the past tried to avoid being overwhelmed by the complexity of their subject matter was by giving less than full attention to group phenomena. Theories that are focused on the leader's personality or behavior often treat followers as a backdrop; as relatively undifferentiated aspects of the leader's situation or as reactors to the leader's actions. The chapters that deal directly with group processes (i.e., McGrath and Gruenfeld, Ilgen et al. and Mai-Dalton) make it clear why leadership theorists have not wanted to address group processes, and at the same time, why we must.

McGrath and Gruenfeld flatly propose that relevant theories of group process must recognize the complexity inherent in group activity. They dismiss conventional methods of reducing analytic complexity such as regarding all behavior not concerned with immediate task accomplishment as "off-track" and therefore irrelevant. Instead, they present a set of group process models that attends to multiple, simultaneous modes of group activity that may loop back over each other and are affected by the environmental and temporal context.

This emphasis on context is most apparent in these group models, but will also become or already is becoming important in leadership theory as well. Both McGrath and Gruenfeld and Ilgen et al. warn that at least some of our research must take place in naturalistic contexts in which real groups, with a past, present, and anticipated future, work on real tasks. While organizational psychologists, including leadership researchers, have never avoided the naturalistic contexts of "real-world" organizations, we have tended to regard the disorderly uniqueness of those settings as a problem rather than an opportunity.

Except in a few cases, such as the role of experience in Fiedler's work, we have similarly treated temporal variables as too complex, conceptually or methodologically, to include in our studies. Ilgen et al. argue cogently that the question of whether the members of a group expect to ever see each other again is the single most important boundary condition in the generalizability of group findings. Added to the widely acknowledged importance of continuity in group life, McGrath and Gruenfeld bring other important aspects of time. The role of timing in group members' adjustments to each other and to tasks, even in the ways that time and deadlines define tasks, are excellent candidates for hot research topics now and in the future.

It is worth adding here that trends appearing in the contemporary organizational design literature will call for the inclusion of research on groups and teams in the leadership literature. The emphasis on facilitating innovation in both large and small organizations has increased interest in team management that facilitates creativity and intrinsic motivation, such as in self-managing teams (Hackman, 1986). As Ilgen et al. point out such innovation organizational designs and practices will call for new types of leadership.

Subjectivity

Social constructionist challenges (Gergen, 1985) to the positivist traditions in modern psychology have become more pervasive in recent years. North American social scientists have lagged a bit behind their European counterparts in this regard (Dachler, 1988). We have neither the space nor the expertise to address this debate at the philosophical level. Yet, several of the chapters in this book make it clear that perceptual or subjective constructions play an important role in leadership. We think that this is a theoretical question that is gaining momentum.

Perceptual components in the leadership process can be treated in a number of ways. They can be seen as threats to the validity of our conceptualizations of leader behavior and its effects. For example, Bass and Avolio are sensitive to criticisms of the transformational leadership theory to the effect that the behaviors that are described as characteristic of these highly effective leaders are "just" attributions. In other words, the characteristics of transformational leaders are inferred by observers of high-performing leaders, and the specific behaviors are based on prototypes or implicit leadership theories held in memory. Bass and Avolio try to answer this criticism by pointing out that most of the items in the multifactor leadership questionnaire (MLQ) (Bass, 1985) have specifically behavioral referents and do not ask for attributions. Unfortunately, as Ayman aptly points out, such questionnaires simply shift the focus to perceptions of behavior. Almost any direct measure of leadership is based on the perceptions of the leader, followers, superiors, or observers, all of which are subject to biases.

Bass and Avolio raise some other questions, more difficult to dismiss. If these perceived behaviors have no basis in reality, why are they (1) reliable across various sources of rating (e.g., subordinates, peers, and superiors), (2) strongly associated with objective performance outcomes, and (3) relatively similar across cultures? One constructionist answer to these questions is that since all these sources hold similar implicit theories, they impute the same characteristics to any leader who is associated with high-performance outcomes, real or perceived. However, Bass and Avolio ask another very good follow-up question: "Why do all these sources have the same implicit theories if they are not grounded in real effects?"

Some authors appear to deal with this dilemma by simply regarding observer judgments as being composed of part "true score" and part error. Hollander seems to take this position. For example, in a discussion of followers as the leader's most important strategic audience, he makes the point that followers know their leader on a day-by-day basis and have ample opportunities to observe the leader's behavior and overcome short-term manipulations of image. At another point, he discusses whether simply talking a lot will give the appearance of competency and earn legitimacy for an emergent leader. Addressing the timing of such participation, Hollander argues that such behavior might have a positive effect at the early stages of the group's life when people and tasks are relatively unknown. Later in the group cycle, members will be in a better position to judge the *true* expertise and competency of the individual. Chemers seems to take a similar position, arguing that different aspects of the leader–follower–environment relationship are more or less susceptible to distortion, and that ultimately effective leaders must help move the group toward the accomplishment of the mission.

House and Shamir seem to regard subjectivity as a valid aspect of leadership performance. That the charismatic leader affects the perceptions of followers, that those perceptions are not always veridical, and that charismatic leaders go out of their way to manipulate the image held by followers, is, for House and Shamir, sum and substance of a major part of charisma. Mitchell would probably be inclined to agree that leaders, even highly touted leaders, are not always what they appear to be.

The cross-culturally oriented authors agree that perception plays a major role in leadership, but would like to make perception itself the object of study or manipulation. Ayman and Triandis agree that more data about the content of ideal leader prototypes would be useful to have. Triandis suggests that these data would provide a higher-order contingency variable reflecting what leadership models are appropriate to a particular culture. Ayman clearly recognizes the strong impact of subjectivity on leadership judgments, but sees that impact as a fitting object of study rather than an embarrassing weakness in our theories or measures. Ayman and Mai-Dalton might see data on cultural differences in prototypes as providing a basis for awareness training to reduce intercultural misattribution in the workplace. There seem to be many reasons to expect a growth in attention to the role of perception in leadership.

Culture

In the preceding pages, we have alluded to cultural differences in leadership several times. We don't wish to belabor this point, so further discussion of the role of culture in leadership studies will be relatively brief. Of the 12 contributors to this book, 8 bring some aspect of culture into their analysis. It is the central concern of the chapters by Triandis, by Ayman, and by Mai-Dalton. It is also a central feature of the integration offered by Chemers.

Cultural factors are also important to the analyses offered by the transformational theorists, House and Shamir and Bass and Avolio, for somewhat different reasons in each case. Arguing from the more universalist position, Bass and Avolio are interested in the common features of outstanding leaders across different cultures; while House and Shamir, reflecting contingency concerns, address the differences in cultures that make one audience or another more susceptible to the specific appeal of a particular charismatic.

Although their discussions are not directly concerned with cultural differences, both Mitchell and Ilgen et al. refer to the role of values, particularly individualism versus collectivism, in relation to their subject matter. Mitchell is concerned with the potential for self-serving exploitation of power by leaders whose values emphasize personal, short-term gain over collective responsibility. Ilgen et al. recognize that teamwork-enhancing systems are easier to implement when collectivist values discourage selfish motives in the interest of group identification. Too many organizational theorists have recently argued for the adoption of social systems, such as Japanese management strategies, without sufficient appreciation for the role that culturally mediated work values play in the acceptability of such systems.

It is our observation that interest in cultural aspects of organizational functioning has never been higher. Newspaper and magazine articles, professional conference programs, and reviews and books attest to this interest. As we maintained in the introductory chapter of this volume, some of the interest arises out of the growth of international and multinational business activity. However, there are reasons, besides pragmatic benefits, for regarding cultural variables as important additions to leadership research. Cross-cultural research carries the possibility of disentangling effects of variables that are confounded in unicultural designs. The potential gains of cross-cultural analyses can be theoretical as well as practical.

The reason for choosing the last two topics as possible trends in future research was not that they were so widely prevalent throughout the book. Rather, they are remarkable, because they were mentioned at all.

Ethics

Perhaps it is as Mitchell suggests that the perception of the culpability of leaders has made us more aware of ethical issues. Whatever the cause, the questions of "leadership toward what ends" that Hollander poses near the end of his chapter is showing up in treatments that previously were exclusively concerned with the questions of "what works and why?"

Several of this book's authors reflected on the fact that if strong leadership can have powerful effects, it can have powerfully bad effects. Mitchell's discussion of administrative accountability was the most direct confrontation of these issues, but they are present in other chapters. Hollander talks about the "dark side of charisma." Likewise, House and Shamir point out that just because charismatic leaders couch their appeal in the language of moral commitment doesn't mean the causes that they espouse are always morally valid. Bass and Avolio are also sensitive to questions of values when they argue that transformational leadership does not always have to be autocratic or elitist.

Recognizing the potential for good as well as for harm, the chapters on workplace diversity adopt an ethical perspective. While somewhat muted in Ayman's appeal for understanding of the plight of the nontraditional manager, the ethical tone is loud and clear in Mai-Dalton's entreaty for a humane response to the problems of the members of multicultural organizations.

Some may argue that the responsibilities of scientific research do not include the fostering of ethical conduct, nor is the scientific method well suited to answering moral questions. Nonetheless, we feel that the encouragement of the application of our research to the solution of social problems is well within the tradition of action research (Lewin, 1948), and its stimulation at this moment is both timely and appropriate.

Emotions and Nonconscious Processes

Leadership theories usually portray the leader as rational and logical. The leader has expectancies about the probabilistic outcomes of various courses of action and chooses the one that has the greatest likelihood of accomplishing his objectives. The expectancies are based on rational assessments of the important characteristics of the task or mission to be accomplished and of the subordinates and their needs and interests. This view of the leader represents the underlying assumption in models like Vroom and Yetton's (1973) normative decision theory. According to that model, leaders are instructed to choose a decision strategy ranging from time-efficient, autocratic procedures to follower-motivating, participative choices after the leader has assessed the degree of clarity and information available in the problem and the degree of support likely from subordinates. Similarly, in path–goal theory (House and Mitchell, 1974), the leader chooses to engage in structuring or considerate behaviors based on an assessment of the degree to which the follower needs one or the other. It is not as clearly discussed, but it follows from the logic of these approaches, that the followers will respond to the leader in terms of similarly enlightened self-interest.

These models and others of similar ilk do not usually consider the possibility that the leader's emotions might interfere with the rational assessment of situational demands or impede the leader's ability to act in a manner logically consistent with that assessment. A few models do portray a leader whose actions are influenced by personality characteristics that are not completely under conscious and volitional control. For example, the motivational patterns revealed by the least preferred coworker (LPC) scale (Fiedler, 1967; Fiedler and Chemers, 1984) predispose the leader to respond in ways that are limited and habitual. The task-motivated leader is likely to respond with positive affect to subordinates who work hard and diligently, is likely to focus on task related aspects of group interactions ignoring interpersonal issues, and is likely to become punitive when followers are uncooperative (Fiedler and Chemers, 1984; Rice, 1978). Other models that include chronic orientations to the environment, such McClelland's work on the need structures of managers (McClelland and Boyatzis, 1982), also conceive of a leader who is predisposed to certain constrained perceptions or courses of action.

The neat and tidy views of rational leaders may be another casualty of more realistic and complex views of leadership. Several of our authors present a different picture of leader, followers, or group process; more spontaneous, disorganized, and irrational. For example, Fiedler's new conceptualization of the effects of stress on leaders includes strong emotional effects (e.g., anxiety) that are not prevalent in most theories. Fiedler's new leader is prone to a certain mindlessness under pressure, babbling on while his intellectual machinery spins hopelessly disconnected from rational problem solving. If the hapless leader isn't lucky enough to have a storehouse of responses programmed by experience, the outcomes are likely to be pretty bad. Fiedler's leader, regressing to earlier, more primitive, more deeply ingrained, coping modes is not coolly in control of his or her behavior. The success or failure of the leader's actions is dependent on an almost accidental fit with the demands of the task.

There is a hint of the same sort of leader in Chemers's integrative model. Although the leader is supposedly generating rational expectancies of what is or is not likely to be effective behavior, several nonrational processes intrude. First, the leader's sense of efficacy is dependent on pervasive self-confidence and optimism that arises from personality–situation match that is as much perception as reality. Then the instrumentality of various behaviors is strongly influenced by habitual (read "nonconscious") orientations or motivations. Further, Chemers admits that unless habitual patterns are disturbed the whole expectancy process may occur automatically. Finally, when the leader interprets and responds to follower reactions, strong emotions like the relationship-motivated person's fear of conflict may energize the leader's reactions without careful, rational assessments. The followers in Chemers's model can also be carried away. For example, the most positive response from followers is elicited not by behavior that is prototype consistent or is seen as leading to good group performance, but by behavior that meets the followers' emotional needs.

In this respect, Chemers is reflecting the insights from the transformational models of Bass and Avolio and House and Shamir. These authors agree that the most telling component of charismatic or transformational leadership is that followers have an intensely emotional connection with the leader. This deep attachment to and identification with the leader results in the followers' satisfaction, self-esteem, and well-being becoming dependent on their relationships with the leader. House and Shamir go on to show how once this strong emotional bond is made, the leader may proceed to use symbolic actions designed to arouse follower motives without full conscious awareness on the part of the followers. Can any of us who have seen the films of Hitler's Nuremberg rallies not appreciate the powerful emotions generated by the torchlight parades, giant swastikas, and the cadences and timbre of Hitler's bombastic speeches?

Ayman also discusses automatic processing of perceptual information about leaders and followers integrating processes below conscious awareness. Both Ayman and Mai-Dalton address the anxiety and distress that nontraditional leaders and followers might experience as a result of alienation from their colleagues and the larger organization.

Beach argues that the highly rational, economic models of managerial decision making do not agree with reality. Decisions tend to be made in ways that may involve habitual predispositions, attempts to avoid decision making, or emotions. This view is shared by Ilgen et al. and McGrath and Gruenfeld in discussions at the group level. Ilgen et al. describe the kinds of panic driven cognitive processes that may have been present in recent military disasters involving poor decisions. McGrath and Gruenfeld bring to our attention theories of group dynamics that reveal the disorganized side of groups (e.g., Poole and Roth, 1988) or the ways in which group members may generate their own socially transacted reality (Altman and Rogoff, 1987).

What these various views have in common is the sense that a realistic understanding of group processes will not be served by a depiction of groups in which leaders and followers calmly and rationally analyze problems, identify potential courses of action, weigh the courses for relative utility, decide on the best course, and then engage in the designated behaviors. Our models must capture the strong affective reactions that are part of social life and recognize the interactions of emotion, cognition, and behavior in group activity. The integration of emotion into theories of leadership represents a daunting challenge. Even as our models begin to accommodate these novel concepts, we must face the fact that our methods are not well suited to these questions. Many of our research designs are heavily dependent on self-conscious reports by leaders and followers, who do not have access to emotional reactions or processes below full awareness.

In conclusion, there appears to be no dearth of interesting questions to occupy the leadership and small groups field in the years to come. As we approach the end of a century, many authors seem to be thinking in terms of integration of existing theories. We believe that this will be a positive state of affairs. In a field long characterized as fragmented and contentious, a move toward integration has the potential to coalesce and redirect our efforts in productive venues. The six directions gleaned from this book are some of many possible ways of categorizing and organizing trends. We hope that these ideas and those arising in other collections or journals will help us to move forward.

References

Altman, I., and Rogoff, B. (1987). World views in psychology: Trait, interactionist, organismic, and transactionalist approaches. In D. Stokols and I. Altman (Eds.), *Handbook of environmental psychology*. New York: Wiley.

Bass, B. M. (1985). *Leadership and performance beyond expectations.* New York: Free Press.

Beach, L. R., and Mitchell, T. R. (1978). A contingency model for the selection of decision strategies. *Academy of Management Review, 3*, 439–449.

Dachler, H. P. (1988). Constraints on the emergence of new vistas in leadership and management research: An epistemological overview. In J. G. Hunt, B. R. Baliga, H. P. Dachler, and C. A. Schriesheim (Eds.), *Emerging leadership vistas.* Lexington, MA: Heath.

Fiedler, F. E. (1967). *A theory of leadership effectiveness.* New York: McGraw-Hill.

Fiedler, F. E. (1978). The contingency model and the dynamics of the leadership process. In L. Berkowitz (Ed.), *Advances in experimental social psychology* (Vol. 11). New York: Academic Press.

Fiedler, F. E., and Chemers, M. M. (1984). *Improving leadership effectiveness: The Leader Match concept*, 2nd ed. New York: Wiley.

Fiedler, F. E., and Garcia, J. E. (1987). *New approaches to effective leadership: Cognitive resources and organizational performance.* New York: Wiley.

House, R. J. (1971). A path–goal theory of leadership. *Administrative Science Quarterly, 16*, 321–338.

Gergen, K. J. (1985). The social constructionist movement in modern psychology. *American Psychologist, 50*, 266–275.

Hackman, J. R. (1986). The psychology of self-management in organizations. In M. S. Pallak and R. O. Perloff (Eds.), *Psychology and work: Productivity, change, and employment.* Washington, DC: American Psychological Association.

McClelland, D. C., and Boyatzis, R. E. (1982). Leadership motive pattern and long term success in management. *Journal of Applied Psychology, 67*, 737–743.

Lewin, K. (1948). *Resolving social conflicts.* New York: Harper & Row.

Poole, M. S., and Roth, J. (1988). Decision development in small groups V: Test of a contingency model. *Human Communications Research, 15*, (4), 549–589.

Rice, R. W. (1978). Construct validity of the least preferred co-worker score. *Psychological Bulletin, 85*, 1199–1237.

Vroom, V. H., and Yetton, P. W. (1973). *Leadership and decision-making.* Pittsburgh, PA: University of Pittsburgh Press.

Author Index

Subject Index

ISBN 0-12-170609-5